Ingor Wellcome

The plan of redemption by our Lord Jesus Christ

Carefully examined and argued by inquiring into God's revealed purpose in the creation of man. Fourth Edition

Ingor Wellcome

The plan of redemption by our Lord Jesus Christ
Carefully examined and argued by inquiring into God's revealed purpose in the creation of man. Fourth Edition

ISBN/EAN: 9783337262044

Printed in Europe, USA, Canada, Australia, Japan

Cover: Foto ©Lupo / pixelio.de

More available books at **www.hansebooks.com**

THE
PLAN OF REDEMPTION

BY OUR

LORD JESUS CHRIST:

CAREFULLY EXAMINED AND ARGUED,

BY INQUIRING INTO

GOD'S REVEALED PURPOSE IN THE CREATION OF MAN,
THE ADAMIC LAW, THE OLD AND NEW COVENANTS, ATONEMENT
BY THE DEATH AND BLOOD OF CHRIST,
UNIVERSAL RESURRECTION OF THE DEAD, THE JUDGMENT,
THE ISRAEL OF GOD,
KINGDOM OF GOD, MILLENNIUM, ETC., ETC.

BY

I. C. WELLCOME AND CLARKSON GOUD.

"The redemption of their soul is precious." DAVID.
"Search the Scriptures." JESUS.

FOURTH EDITION.

LONDON:
KELLAWAY & Co., BIBLE AND SCRIPTURAL TRACT REPOSITORY,
10 WARWICK LANE, PATERNOSTER ROW.
—
1874.

PREFACE.

In putting forth this work to the public, we have sought, as much as our studies and abilities would allow, to supply a want which has long been felt and acknowledged by many of the household of faith and others seeking light on the works of God. While much has been written on various subjects taught in the Bible, but few have treated upon, as *special topics*, the leading principles of Revelation, to bring together the passages which embody the FUNDAMENTAL DOCTRINES of the COVENANTS, and the ATONEMENT BY JESUS CHRIST, out of which grow all other parts of the SYSTEM OF REDEMPTION.

We have long desired to see a well-matured work on the chief topics embraced in this book; and not being aware that such a work is before the public, we have for several years contemplated the publication of the results of our investigations on these topics, which we now do.

We have sought to lead the mind of the reader into the Bible, to "search the Scriptures," to grasp the foundation principles, to strengthen the faith of those who believe in God, and confirm the hope of those who waver.

We have followed no man, nor class of men, in doctrine or theory, in arriving at the conclusions found in this book; but, while we have studied the works of others, and found many good things of much value, and many of the ideas, in one form or another, which are embraced in our range of argument, yet the Bible has been our only authority and text-book: by that alone we settle all questions of theology, quoting the ideas of men only to show that others have been in the same school with us, and found the same gems of truth, if not the same SYSTEM.

Our range of argument differs in many points from any others we have seen, and our conclusions will of course provoke criticism: with this we should not complain when honestly done.

Truth shines more clearly when closely tested; and, as error is of no value, it should be pointed out and discarded. This is a part of Christian duty.

We do not claim to have arrived at all the truth on these subjects, nor to have attained to a perfect understanding of the plan of redemption. We give the light we have found in the Scriptures, hoping to awaken a deeper interest in the investigation of the Bible, and to produce greater harmony of views among Christians, and therefore more united action in leading sinners to Christ.

We have noticed two general classes of religious books; one of which leads the mind of the reader into the Bible, to study and think more of its value and importance; the other of which leads the mind out of the Bible, to rest upon other wisdom, and to adopt the doctrines of men. We hope ours is of the best class.

The work was commenced and considerably advanced in 1865; but other duties, with almost constant travel and labor to supply the calls for preaching, have prevented us from issuing it as early as intended. This is our apology to those who have subscribed for and long waited its appearance.

May the Lord bless its perusal to the good of those who read it, and in due time bring them and the writers to the haven of eternal rest.

I. C. WELLCOME,
C. GOUD.

YARMOUTH, ME., March, 186⁻.

CONTENTS.

CHAPTER I.
GOD'S DESIGN IN THE CREATION OF MAN.

1. The Common View examined. 2. All Things and Creatures created to glorify God. 3. Man created to have Dominion. 4. Man created in the Image of God. 5. God's Benediction. 6. His First Command. 7. The First Dominion. . . . . 13—21

CHAPTER II.
MAN'S ORIGINAL CONDITION.

1. Adam's Primeval Condition. 2. His Moral Condition. 3. His Physical Condition. 4. His Duties. 22, 23

CHAPTER III.
MAN'S APOSTASY AND FALL IN VIOLATING GOD'S LAW, OR COVENANT.

1. Eden a Sample. 2. The Tree of Knowledge. 3. First Penal Command. 4. The Reward of Obedience. 5. Adam's Sin. 6. His Knowledge. 7. The Means of Knowledge. 8. Man's Great Apostasy. 9. Refuses Instruction. 10. Moral Corruption of the Race. 11. Man responsible for Ignorance of God. 12. Shadows of Atonement. 13. Abel's Offering. 14. Results of Faith. . . . . 24—33

CHAPTER IV.
MAN'S RELATIONS TO GOD UNDER THE FIRST COVENANT.

1. Call of Abraham. 2. Promises to Faith. 3. Abrahamic Hope. 4. First Covenant. 5. Old Covenant a Mirror and Teacher. 6. The Law added. 7. When added. 8. Where added. 9. For what added. 10. Aaronic Priesthood. 11. First Covenant of Ten Commandments. 12. The First Covenant abolished. . . . . 34—61

CHAPTER V.

UNIVERSAL REDEMPTION BY THE DEATH OF CHRIST.

1. Man is sold under Sin. 2. Adam lost all for himself and Race. 3. Our Race in Adam. 4. Happiness. 5. Immortality. 6. Eternal Life. 7. Loss of Physical Constitution. 8. Right of Probation. 9. Life. 10. All dead. 11. Christ's Death. 12. Christ's Authority. 13. Christ saves all Men. 14. All made Righteous. 15. Two Salvations. 16. The Way opened for Sin to be forgiven. 62–85

CHAPTER VI.

THE NECESSITY FOR AN ATONEMENT.

1. The Race unreconciled to God. 2. All were lost. 3. Under Sentence of Death Man not capable of Contract. 4. The Proverb in Israel. 5. Our Losses summed up. 6. The Tree of Life. 7. Men and all Animals are Souls. 8. Adam not Immortal. 9. The Tree of the Knowledge of Good and Evil. 10. Death. 86–102

CHAPTER VII.

THE UNIVERSAL ATONEMENT BY THE DEATH OF CHRIST.

1. Unconditional Atonement. 2. Nature of Atonement. 3. God gave his Son. 4. Covenant between the Father and Son. 5. Death of Christ. 6. The Types of the Law. 7. The Lord's Passover. 8. Adam and the Race lost. 9. All have sinned. 10. Unconditional Salvation. 11. Christ's Flesh for the Life of the World. 12. Ransomed from Death. 13. Man Reprieved. 14. On Probation. 15. Way to the Tree of Life. 16. Pardon offered to all. 103–122

CHAPTER VIII.

THE CONDITIONAL ATONEMENT BY THE BLOOD OF CHRIST.

1. Special Salvation. 2. Man under New Law. 3. Infant Salvation. 4. Salvation for the Heathen. 5. Our Responsibility. 6. Christ our Prophet. 7. Our High Priest. 8. Blood of Atonement. 9. Remission of Sins. 10. Cleansing from Sin. 123–139

CHAPTER IX.

MAN'S RELATION TO GOD UNDER THE NEW COVENANT.

1. Time of making the First Covenant. 2. The giving of New Law. 3. Its Characteristics. 4. The New Law Identified. 5. Given in Moab. . 140–158

CONTENTS.

CHAPTER X.
THE NEW BIRTH.

1. To be born again. 2. Drs. Adam Clarke, Taylor, Macknight. 3. Terms "begotten," "generate," "born of God." 4. A New Man. 5. Obeying the Spirit. 6. Instruction to Nicodemus. 7. Expectation of the Jews. 8. Blindness concerning the Kingdom of God. 9. Christ the First Fruits of the New Birth. 10. Conversion not a New Birth. 11. Objections considered. 12. The Ransomed Children of Zion. 13. Invitation. . . . . 159—181

CHAPTER XI.
THE EARTH REDEEMED.

1. The Earnest of our Inheritance. 2. The Earth to be restored. 3. Adam's Progeny. 4. The Earth's Curse. 5. Christ the Redeemer. 6. Glorious Promises. 7. The Earth to be burned — Scripture Testimony. 8. Extracts from Dr. Edward Hitchcock, Dr. Knapp, John Wesley, Thomas Chalmers, Tholuck, Pollok, &c. 9. Regeneration of the Earth. The Bible. Cowper.. 182—207

CHAPTER XII.
THE EARTH GLORIFIED.

1. Promised with an Oath. 2. Meaning of Glory. 3. Visible Exhibitions of God's Glory. 4. Scripture Testimony. 5. The Second Adam to bring in Earth's Glory. 6. How and when it shall be. 7. A Miniature of that Glory. 8. Who will share that Glory. . . . . 208—215

CHAPTER XIII.
THE JUDGMENT.

1. A Time for Judgment. 2. Meaning of Terms. 3. Various Opinions. 4. Judgment for Adam's Sin. 5. The Reprieved. 6. All to suffer the Penalty. 7. Exceptions. 8. Christ the Redeemer. 9. Judgment for Personal Sin. 10. Christ a Curse for us. 11. All Power given Him. 12. The Dead to be raised. 13. All shall honor Christ. 14. Will give Life Eternal to those who obey Him. 15. The Gospel a Witness. 16. Two Resurrections. 17. Order of the Judgment. 18. The new Covenant. 19. Objections. 20. Responsibility under the new Covenant. 21. Christ our Passover. 22. Illustrations. 23. Believers sealed for Redemption; Wicked doomed to Condemnation. 24. Our Fate fixed forever. 25. May *now* choose Life or Death. 26. The sad Separation. 27. A Time appointed for this. 28. Christ in the Glory of His Power. 29. Conclusions. . . . . 216—245

CHAPTER XIV.
THE KINGDOM OF GOD.

1. The Kingdom of the first Importance. 2. Desires after Things holy 3. The Kingdom of Israel. 4. Its Overthrow. 5. A better Kingdom. 6. Vision of God's Kingdom. 7. The Place of the Kingdom. 8. The Universal Prayer. 9. Who are Heirs. 246—271

CHAPTER XV.
THE BOOK OF LIFE.

1. Books. 2. Book ordained to Life. 3. The Lamb's Book of Life. 4. Fatality. 5. Names blotted out. 6. The Books opened. 7. The Book of Remembrance. 8. The Wicked blotted out of the Book. . . . . 272—283

CHAPTER XVI.
RESURRECTION OF THE DEAD.

1. Extract from Adam Clarke. 2. Cause of Scepticism. 3. Sad Results of False Premises. 4. The Bible not to be abandoned. 5. Old Testament Promises. 6. New Testament Promises. 7. Two Resurrections. . . . . 284—306

CHAPTER XVII.
THE ETERNAL SALVATION OF GOD'S PEOPLE.

1. The Things of the Spirit. 2. The Author of Salvation. 3. Christ — God and Man. 4. Christ perfected through Sufferings. 5. Materialism. 6. The Subjects of Salvation. 7. The Elect. 8. Predestination. 9. Election made sure. 10. The Triumphal Song. . . . . 307—327

CHAPTERS XVIII AND XIX.
GOD'S PEOPLE ISRAEL.

1. Who are the True Israel. 2. Cain and Abel, heads of Two Classes. 3. Faith the Dividing Line. 4. Genealogy of God's Children. 5. Call of Abram. 6. Hagar and Ishmael a Type. 7. Jewish Nation a Type. 8. Birth of Isaac. 9. Hagar and Ishmael cast out. 10. Jewish Nation divorced. 11. Abraham's Seed. 12. The Name Jew. 13. The Name Israel, its proper Use. 14. Christ's Use of it; Paul's application. 15. Paul's Comments on the True Israel. . . 328—389

CHAPTERS XX AND XXI.
THE MILLENNIUM.

1. The Promise of a Reign with Christ. 2. Christ's Throne. 3. The Thousand Years' Reign of Judgment. 4. Why the Apocalypse was rejected. 5. The Millennium rejected by Rome. 6. Whitbyan Millennium. 7. Prophecy of False Teachers. 8. Did Christ and Popes reign conjointly? 9. Scriptural Millennium. 10. Christ's Advent. 11. The Devil bound. 12. Thrones of Judgment. 13. The First Resurrection. 14. Rest that remaineth. 15. Burning Day. 16. The Wicked raised. 17. Satan loosed; Gog and Magog. 18. The Devil tormented. 19. Lake of Fire. 20. Objections considered. . . 390—452

INTRODUCTION.

A GOOD understanding of the fundamental principles of the purpose and plan of the All-wise God in creating our world, peopling it with a race of intelligent beings subject to his control, and in instituting the great plan of redemption of that race who fell under the sentence of his law by disobedience, will be admitted by all to be of the greatest importance, both in obtaining a correct view of the attributes of the God and Father of our Lord Jesus Christ, and in leading the human mind to obtain the benefits of that redemption which is through the blood of Christ, so as to glorify the Father of mercies and God of all grace.

These principles are revealed in the Scriptures of truth, and when understood or clearly comprehended, the character of our heavenly Father shines forth in such loveliness as to gain the admiration and attract the affections of those who are capable of approving that which is most excellent and most lovely.

A disregard for or want of understanding of these grand principles, which underlie and interlace all that God has revealed to man, has led many to strange and sad conclusions, sometimes followed by the most excessive and disastrous results, by inditing and fostering doctrines derogatory to the character of God, contradictory to his revealed word, subversive of true righteousness, and unhealthful to the human mind.

Religious doctrines or theories, when imbibed and publicly acknowledged, generally become a firm persuasion of the human mind, especially if they have cost their possessors any considerable sacrifice of money or position in society, or met with much opposition from friends. And from that point in his history where the mind fixes upon, or takes a theological position, man does not usually, in his studies, search for the fundamental principles of truth (believing he has them already), but for any and every species of collateral evidence or incidental developments which seem to justify and strengthen his cherished opinions as being correct.

In other words, he does not study his Bible and the book of nature especially to learn what they teach, so much as to learn what *he can find in them* which seems to sustain or favor his own theological ideas. The natural tendency to form opinions, on subjects of great depth and importance prematurely, with the accompanying error of seeking to prop up our early and hasty conclusions with whatever testimony can be made to look in that direction, instead of long, and careful, and thorough examination, clear deductions, and frequent testings of all our conclusions by the application of close criticisms, should lead us to greater caution, and more arduous, patient, and thorough study of the Bible, and of nature, before we settle down with the positive feeling that we have fully learned the true basis of Christian doctrine and faith.

In opposition to the general course above stated we take the position, that no system of doctrine is shown to be correct because certain texts, or portions of testimony from the Bible, or from any other source, seem to teach it: but that system of doctrine is correct which the Scriptures are found to teach in all their testimony united — that system which is the subject matter of revelation.

When one comprehends pretty clearly that system, he finds no cause for the labored and hazardous efforts which many make in seeking to harmonize the great variety of statements of the Scriptures; he sees that harmony already exists, and only needs to be studied to learn the relations of one part to the other.

There exist an affinity of testimony, a blending together of ideas, a cropping out of the same great central truths, in all parts of the Scriptures. Instead of conflicting voices and antagonistic principles, are harmonious strains of love, goodness, mercy, benevolence, and perfection, based upon wisdom and justice, blending mercy and judgment in the government of our Creator, and revealing the perfect plan of a perfect and Almighty God, to bring about a perfect and immortal state for his own glory, and the eternal happiness of all who decide to submit to his government and live in harmony with his purposes.

We do not presume to give a perfect analysis of the plan of redemption in the following work, nor claim to fully comprehend and properly identify all points of Bible doctrine.

A crown of a thousand diamonds, exquisitely set, may not be correctly estimated by any inspector so as to give the true and relative dimensions, value, and importance of each diamond; yet if he has a good acquaintance with its precious materials, and with the nature and use of a crown, he may give a very true and important estimate and decision upon all the most vital points in such a matter.

The Bible embraces a system of principles and truths more exquisitely wrought than any crown; of greater variety and importance, and of more value than all the diamonds and crowns in the world.

The doctrine of ATONEMENT is the grand and central DOCTRINE of the Bible: on it, and out of it, grow all other truths worth our attention: and yet it is a doctrine on which there has been, and still is, much controversy; which proves it a doctrine not well understood, and that many, who, though they claim to believe an atonement has been made for sin, do not know its nature.

One class, who believe that Christ died for all the race of man, claim that this fact secures the eternal salvation of all; while others claim that if Christ died in man's stead, man ought not to die; another class claim that Christ died for only one class of the race, and that class are sure of salvation; each seem to find it difficult to explain their view so as to show it to be in harmony with the Scriptures, and applicable to man's condition.

We have devoted considerable space in this work to the subject of the atonement; and while we do not accept the applications and explanations commonly made by teachers, we think we see its vast importance to the race, and its true application to the condition in which sin has placed us. We ask the reader to carefully examine our position, and the Bible evidences of it. It will be in some respects new, but this does not prove it untrue.

The hope of presenting in a clear and instructive manner the leading principles revealed in the Scriptures, with the chief points of doctrine, and their practical bearing upon men, and which we believe to be of special importance to all, has prompted us to prepare the following pages for the public; not claiming to have learned all, but to have comprehended some, at least, of the most important points by which we may hope to continue to learn the mind and will of God, so long as it shall please him to keep us in the school of Christ.

Advancement in scriptural knowledge induces growth in grace and love for our fellow-men; preparing us for the better discharge of all our duties, and especially for leading sinners to Christ, and the building up of one another on our most holy faith.

THE PLAN OF REDEMPTION

BY

OUR LORD JESUS CHRIST.

CHAPTER I.

GOD'S DESIGN IN THE CREATION OF MAN.

"Thou madest him to have dominion over the works of thy hands."
Psa. 8 : 6.

We are entering upon the investigation of a subject which some regard as speculative and unwarranted by the Scriptures; yet, while we are assured that the Bible gives a revelation of the mind of the Author of our being concerning his creatures, we are convinced that his design in our creation is also to be understood by his record.

It has been stated and argued by many, that the original design in creating man was, "to glorify God and to enjoy him forever." We do not doubt that there is truth in this statement. Yet it does not appear sufficiently specific and broad to develop the subject, for the same statement will as properly apply to the lower and higher orders of creation, as to man. We find it clearly stated in Revelation, "Thou art worthy, O Lord, to receive glory, and honor, and power, for thou hast created all things, and for thy pleasure they are and were created." Rev. 4 : 11. Again, "For by him were all things created that are in heaven, or that are in earth, visible and invisible, whether they be thrones, or dominions, or principalities, or powers, all things were created by him and for him." Col. 1 : 16.

No one can fail to see by this testimony, that all things else were created for God's glory, as well as man. There is much Scripture testimony to this point: we need quote only one or two more texts: "All thy works shall praise thee, O Lord." Psa. 145 : 10. This is full and conclusive, and embraces all of God's works; but we will hear once more: "The heavens declare the glory of God, and the firmament showeth his handy work." Psa. 19 : 1. With such clear and positive testimony that all things were created for God's glory, man included, we prefer to examine revelation more closely to ascertain what the Lord has stated regarding his design in the creation of man as a specific class of intelligences.

The text which stands at the head of this chapter is very explicit. It is spoken of MAN, in distinction from all other beings, and asserts the purpose or design of God in his creation: "Thou madest him to have dominion over the works of thy hands." Language more clear and direct than this cannot be found. Let us now turn our attention to the proof of the Psalmist's assertion, and see if the statement is sustained. We will notice the language of the Lord himself on this point: —

"And God said, Let us make man in our image, after our likeness, and let them have dominion over the fish of the sea, and over the fowl of the air, and over the cattle, and over all the earth, and over every creeping thing that creepeth upon the earth." Gen. 1 : 26.

In this statement of the Lord, most clearly and fully expressed, we have his determination and design in creating man. In the next following verses we have the record of God's action of creating them, his benediction, command, and promise. The account is plain and full of meaning. Let us read it : "So God created man in his own image ; in the image of God created he him ; male and female created he them. And God blessed them, and God said unto them, Be fruitful, and multiply, and replenish the earth, and subdue it, and have dominion over the fish of the sea, and over the fowl of the air, and over every living thing that moveth upon the earth." Gen. 1 : 27, 28.

How grand, how clear and simple, are the words of God on this point ! How broad the command ! How extensive the promise ! Man created in the image, the likeness of God, placed upon this terrestrial globe, covered with its vast varieties of vegetation, and its myriads of classes of living creatures, and commanded to fill it with his own species, and to subdue it, cultivate it, and bring it into use, with the promise of ultimate dominion over it. Such is the sentiment of the words of God which we have quoted, which show that the primary object of God in creating man was, that he should be ruler of the earth, and of all the lower grades of creatures which he hath created upon it. Consequently, man was created in the likeness of God, with capacity to rule or govern. To develop this capacity, he was commanded to subdue the earth and all the lower grades of animal creation, preparatory to entering upon the "dominion." And in doing this, he would represent and glorify God, who by his own almighty power governs all the works of his hands in all worlds.

The command of God to Adam, above quoted, is the first which God gave to man. We will quote it again, to keep its prominent features clearly before us: "Be fruitful, and multiply, and replenish the earth, and subdue it, and have dominion over the fish of the sea, and over the fowl of the air, and over every living thing that moveth upon the earth."

This first command and promise embrace several very important points which underlie all that is afterwards revealed in the Scriptures concerning man's final destiny, and shows the design of God concerning him, as before stated.

By it we learn that man was to multiply his species sufficiently to fill the earth with them to a proper number, or population, for their enjoyment and happiness, to subdue it, cultivate, arrange, and guide its products and creatures to their own convenience, bringing all its appliances and its privileges to a point of perfect adaptation and usefulness for the race which were to inhabit the earth, that they might enter upon the exercise of all that is embraced in the term "have dominion over."

SUBDUE IT.

We are aware that the idea that man was required to subdue, or train and guide, a new-made world, which was declared by its Maker to be "*very good*," seems very objectionable to some minds, because they conclude that this good world was in a state of absolute perfection in degree, as well as in kind. The same objection could be as properly urged against multiplying the species, and replenishing or filling the earth.

But when the facts are carefully examined, it will appear that, although the earth and all it contained were "very good," and were doubtless perfect in kind, yet they were in a crude and incipient state, subject to the arrangement and control of man for his own convenience, as he should multiply and fill the earth; all of which is implied in the term "subdue it."

When the race should have spread over the earth, cultivating and preparing it to their convenience, until it was fully subdued and filled, and man's probation ended, and immortality bestowed, then the promised "dominion" could be properly exercised over a subdued and immortal world.

DOMINION.

It is proper here to consider the nature of the dominion mentioned in the text, and when it was to be exercised. It is generally supposed to embrace the control and government of the new-made world as it came from the hand of its Creator, and that this power was given

Adam to exercise when placed in the garden of Eden. But this idea may need modification.

We readily admit that the term "dominion" embraces all that is claimed for it, and more. But that it was to be exercised in its proper sense in the then existing condition of the world, or began in Eden, we cannot admit.

Before man can "have dominion," or control a world, he is to learn to control himself, and to fill and subdue the earth. We freely grant that *Adam* entered upon an incipient stage of that control or rule, according to his capacity, which man was to exercise over this world and the inferior grades of animals as they increased upon earth. This is implied in the command, "subdue it." The privilege was given to man to cultivate, arrange, and subdue, until the time for real or actual dominion. And for the instruction and encouragement of Adam, the Lord gave him a sample of what the earth would become when subdued. Let us look at this sample: "And the Lord God planted a garden eastward in Eden; and there he put the man whom he had formed. And out of the ground made the Lord God to grow every tree that is pleasant to the sight, and good for food; the tree of life also in the midst of the garden, and the tree of knowledge of good and evil." Gen. 2 : 9.

This was an illustration of what the whole earth would become under the care and cultivation of man, in obedience to his Maker. Adam accepted the trust, and entered upon his duties; but that this incipient stage was the actual dominion referred to, we do not admit, for the following reasons : —

I. Because we do not find the testimony of Scripture to sustain the idea.

II. Because the Scriptures do testify to the fact that this dominion involves the idea of a FILLED, SUBDUED, MATURED WORLD.

Let us examine the testimony of prophecy relating to the final gaining of that dominion by Christ, which Adam failed to obtain, through his disobedience: — "And thou, O tower of the flock, the stronghold of the daughter of Zion, unto thee shall it come, even the FIRST DOMINION; the kingdom shall come to the daughter of Jerusalem." Micah 4: 8. This prophecy can refer to no other than Christ and his church. He is the STRONGHOLD of the daughter of Jerusalem. He is the TOWER of the flock.

"The first dominion" is evidently the one mentioned in Genesis 1: 28, and which Adam would have attained to when he and his posterity had finished their work of filling the earth and subduing it. That this is the true idea the declaration of Christ fully settles. When speaking of the final triumph of his church, he says (Matt. 25: 34), "Then shall the king say unto them on his right hand, Come, ye blessed of my Father, inherit the kingdom prepared for you from the foundation of the world."

What other kingdom or dominion is mentioned in the Scriptures and called the FIRST DOMINION, and said to be prepared FROM THE FOUNDATION of the world, beside the one cited in Genesis 1: 26–28? We find no other. By the Psalmist, the Lord testifies directly to this view again: "Thou hast made him [man] a little lower than the angels [for 'a little while lower'— Hebrew *margin*], and hast crowned him with glory and honor. Thou madest him to have dominion over the works of thy hands; thou hast put all things under his feet." Psa. 8 : 5, 9.

This important passage is quoted by Paul in his argument on the mission and work of Christ, and is then commented on by him thus : "For in that he put all in subjection under him, he left nothing that is not put under him. But now we see not yet all things put under him. But we see Jesus, who was made a little lower than the angels [or a little while inferior], for the suffering of death, crowned with glory and honor, that he, by the grace of God, should taste death for every man." Heb. 2 : 6-9.

The above declarations, which form the basis of many prophecies and discourses in the Scriptures, and which will be treated upon in future chapters of this work, are too explicit to admit of any other application than such as we have shown is made by Micah, David, Christ, and Paul.

They clearly reveal the fact that God designed man to dwell on the earth, to subdue, train, and prepare it for his habitation, and finally to have dominion over it and all it contained, in an immortal and eternal state. But sin has entered, a train of evils has followed, God's design is not yet accomplished. The work is not perfected; but it will be done in due time, and none can hinder. The dark pall which has seemed to cover the glorious end for which all things were created, from the view of short-sighted mortals.

has been rent by the Son of God; the light of revelation shines gloriously through "the vail that is spread over the nations," and it will be finally removed. Sin is not to triumph; it is to be wiped out and its author destroyed. God will do all his pleasure, and produce a perfect work. This determination is indicated in the scriptures we have already cited, and especially declared by the Lord in the following words: "Remember the former things of old; for I am God, and there is none else; I am God, and there is none like me, declaring the end from the beginning, and from ancient times the things that are not yet done, saying, My counsel shall stand, and I will do all my pleasure." Isa. 46: 9, 10. There are many items to make up the whole of the plan of redemption. We purpose in future chapters to bring out some of the chief of them, after taking a look at the woe and wretchedness sin has brought upon this world, which was once so fair and good.

CHAPTER II.

MAN'S ORIGINAL CONDITION.

"Lo, this only have I found, that God hath made man upright, but they have sought out many inventions." — *Eccl.* 7 : 29.

In the preceding chapter we treated upon the creation of man, and God's design in that creation. We will now examine the Scriptures in relation to the original condition of man as he came from the hand of his Creator. Many speculative ideas have been advanced in reference to this point, both as to his moral and his physical condition. Some have asserted that Adam had no moral character, because he knew nothing, and his mind was wholly undeveloped, until he sinned. Others have held that he was an immortal being, *morally* like God. It is not our intention to enter largely upon such topics, but to examine what the word of the Lord reveals concerning him. This is enough for our purpose.

It seems quite certain that the all-wise God would not have given such an important command to an undeveloped infant mind; neither does it appear wise that he should have trusted such a one in his beautiful garden to " dress and keep it ; " nor that he would have committed to such a mind the naming of all the animals he created ; yet all this he did with Adam. And what God did in these matters shows that man's mind was developed ; and that he had extensive wisdom. But it is clearly shown in the Scriptures that man was not all that is sometimes claimed for him. He was not an immortal being, although he was morally good and upright, and, continuing in obedience to God's law in the discharge of the duties assigned him, would, in due time, have received immortality at the hand of his Creator. That he was morally and physically "very good" is explicitly stated by God himself. Gen. 1 : 31. "And God saw every thing that he had made, and, behold, it was very good." That he was made upright is declared in the text at the head of this chapter. Yet his physical condition was such that he was susceptible of dying, as is fully shown in his early history.

First. God had provided for him the tree of life, not to give life, but to sustain him in life.

Second. The penalty of God's law is death, which he incurred by transgression, and which was inflicted.

Third. It is certain that immortality is not subject to death.

Fourth. That man would have attained to immortality "by patient continuance in well doing," Paul declares in Rom. 2 : 6, 7 : "To them who by patient continuence in well doing seek for glory, and honor, and immortality, eternal life" will be rendered. This shows man must seek it to obtain it. But man did not do well. He was created in the image of God, endowed with noble faculties of mind, capable of imitating God and glorifying him, capable of great expansion, mentally and numerically, capable also of disobeying God, of seeking out many inventions, of losing his home, and his life, and of falling short of the dominion placed before him.

CHAPTER III.

MAN'S APOSTASY AND FALL IN VIOLATING GOD'S LAW OR COVENANT.

"They are all gone aside, they are altogether become filthy, there is none that doeth good, no, not one." — *Psa.* 14 : 3.

The text we have quoted is one of many of its class which come directly in our line of argument on the subject of man's fallen condition. It implies that he was once in the way, pure, upright, and good. How changed his condition! how dark the picture! The inquiry at once arises, How came this change? Was man in the fault? Before replying to these questions, we will take a retrospective view of the primeval condition of man, which we have already presented in a former chapter.

He was "made upright," morally and physically good, "very good." Their work was laid out before them, viz., to multiply, and replenish or fill the earth, and subdue it, with the prospect of ultimate dominion over all the earth, with all that God had created upon it. This prospect was presented to Adam as an object of faith and hope, and as an incentive worthy his utmost care and attention.

The first command of God, and, accompanying it, the first prospect of future blessedness ever presented to man, embrace the following ideas: Perform the duties imposed, then "have dominion.' A specimen of its qualities, resources, magnificence, and beauties is placed before him in the garden which God himself planted in Eden, to show him what the whole earth would be, under its subdued and cultivated state. This sample was "the *face of the earth*," from which Cain was afterwards driven into its wilds, or uncultivated parts. But Adam was first "put into it, to dress it and keep it." A beautiful home indeed, with unbounded resources for enjoyment.

Of the fruit of all the trees of this garden of God's own planting, in the midst of which was the tree of life, he might freely eat, with but one exception, viz., "But of the tree of the knowledge of good and evil thou shalt not eat of it, for in the day thou eatest thereof thou shalt surely die." (*Margin*, dying thou shalt die. The Arabic renders it, Thou shalt deserve to die. The Targum has it, Thou shalt be subjected to death.)

In this prohibition we have the first penal commandment of God to man; and man being on probation for dominion and immortality, God placed him under this penal law to prove him by a test of his fidelity to his Creator. It was a position involving momentous consequences. If he obeys this command he has a continual right to the tree of life, to perpetuate life until his work is completed and he receives his dominion.

To bring more clearly before the mind of the reader what was presented to Adam as an object of hope, and which is yet to be obtained by the faithful, we will here quote a few parallel texts: "And God blessed them, and God said unto them, Be fruitful, and multiply, and replenish the earth, and subdue it: and have dominion over the fish of the sea, and over the fowl of the air, and over every living thing that moveth upon the earth." Gen. 1 : 28. "Thou madest him to have dominion over the works of thy hands; thou hast put all things under his feet." Psa. 8 : 6. "For such as be blessed of him shall inherit the earth." Psa. 37 : 22. "For the upright shall dwell in the land, and the perfect shall remain in it." Prov. 2 : 21. "Blessed are the meek, for they shall inherit the earth." Matt. 5 : 5.

Such is the result of being blessed of God when man's duties are finished as a race. Then is the time for obtaining immortality also, as the following scriptures clearly show : "Who will render to every man according to his deeds. To them who, by patient continuance in well doing, seek for glory, and honor, and immortality, eternal life." Rom. 2 : 6, 7. "For this corruptible must put on incorruption, and this mortal must put on immortality. So when this corruptible shall have put on incorruption, and this mortal shall have put on immortality, then shall be brought to pass the saying that is written, Death is swallowed up in victory." 1 Cor. 15 : 53, 54.

As before stated, Adam occupied a position involving momentous consequences. If he disobeyed, he must be excluded from the garden, deprived of the tree of life, and finally receive the wages of sin, which is death. Read Gen. 2 : 17 ; 3 : 17, 24. Rom. 6 : 24. Adam disobeyed, was shut out from the garden of God, cut off from the tree of life; the prospect of dominion was blighted; and he, with all his posterity, was doomed to toil, care, sorrow, and sickness, and to the train of physical and moral evils which have followed, and finally lead to death.

We find man in this situation in consequence of sin. It is a singular position. He had an acquaintance with God; knew his goodness, his law, and his righteousness, enjoyed his associations and counsels; yet, in the light of all this, he stands arrayed against his God, and chooses to walk contrary to him, and risk the consequences that would follow.

When turned from the garden, Adam was acquainted with the following facts: —

I. That God was the Creator of this world.

II. That God was his rightful Sovereign and Lawgiver.

III. That it was his duty to serve and obey him.

IV. That, for his disobedience to that Lawgiver, he was shut out of the garden, under the sentence of death, to till the ground until he should die and return to dust.

And he, with such knowledge of God and his law, of himself, his duty, and destiny, with the heavens spread out over him, and the earth beneath him, with their wonderful varieties, all declaring the glory, wisdom, goodness, and power of God, as the Scriptures represent: "The heavens declare the glory of God, and the firmament showeth his handy work. Day unto day uttereth speech, and night unto night showeth knowledge. There is no speech nor language where their voice is not heard." Psa. 19:1, 3. And could not intelligent man understand such a voice? Yes. Some have understood, and were led to their Creator for further instruction, and were guided in the right way, as the histories of the faithful demonstrate.

But the mass of mankind would not listen to the voice of God, and he suffered them to follow their own ways. Paul, when speaking upon this point, while preaching to the heathen about God, says, "Who in times past suffered all nations to walk in their own ways. Nevertheless he left not himself without a witness, in that he did good, and gave us rain from heaven, and fruitful seasons, filling our hearts with food and gladness." Acts 14 : 16, 17. Let us hear another witness on this point. "Have ye not known? have ye not heard? hath it not been told you from the beginning? have ye not understood from the foundation of the earth? It is he that sitteth upon the circle of the earth, and the inhabitants thereof are as grasshoppers; that stretcheth out the heavens as a curtain, and spreadeth them out as a tent to dwell in; that bringeth the princes to nothing; he maketh the judges of the earth as vanity. . . . Lift up your eyes on high, and behold who hath created these things, that bringeth out their host by number: he calleth them all by names by the greatness of his might, for that he is strong in power; not one faileth. . . . Hast thou not known? hast thou not heard, that the everlasting God, the Lord, the Creator of the ends of the earth, fainteth not, neither is weary?" Isa. 40 : 21–28. Surely God has not kept himself in secret places, that he could not be known. But let us look still further into this matter, ye who excuse yourselves for being ignorant of God and his claims.

"Remember this, and show yourselves men; bring it again to mind, O ye transgressors. Remember the former things of old, for I am God, and there is none else; I am God, and there is none like me." "Declaring the end from the beginning, and from ancient times the things that are not yet done, saying, My counsel shall stand, and I will do all my pleasure." Isa. 46:8, 10.

We will now hear Paul speak of the guilt of men for being ignorant of God: "Because that which may be known of God is manifest in them, for God hath showed it unto them. For the invisible things of him from the creation of the world are clearly seen, being understood by the things that are made, even his eternal power and Godhead. So that they are without excuse." Rom. 1:19, 20.

With these facts and Scripture testimonies, it is clearly proved that by a proper regard for these means of wisdom, with the revelation of God's will and purposes, through patriarchs, prophets, and holy men, man might have retained a good degree of the knowledge of God, and of his own relations and duties to him, to the latest generations of posterity. Yet notwithstanding all these means of knowledge, we find man sunk in moral darkness, ignorant of God and his laws, and regardless of his own relations and duties to him. And this condition and its cause is aptly stated by the apostle Paul in the following: "Because that when they knew God, they glorified him not as God, neither were thankful, but became vain in their imaginations, and their foolish heart was darkened. Professing themselves to be wise, they became fools, and changed the glory of the incorruptible God into an image made like corruptible man, and to birds, and fourfooted beasts, and creeping things. Wherefore God also gave them up to uncleanness through the lusts of their own hearts. . . . Who changed the truth into a lie, and worshipped the creature more than the Creator, who is blessed forever, Amen. . . . And even as they did not like to retain God in their knowledge, God gave them over to a reprobate mind, to do those things that are not convenient. Being filled with all unrighteousness, fornication, wickedness, covetousness, maliciousness, full of envy, murder, debate, deceit, malignity, whisperers, backbiters, haters of God, despiteful, proud, boasters, inventors of evil things, disobedient to parents, without understanding, covenant-breakers, without natural affection, implacable, unmerciful; who, knowing the judgment of God, that they which commit such things are worthy of death, not only do the same, but have pleasure in them that do them." Rom. 1 : 21–33.

This graphic description of man's moral condition, and the cause of it, should be well considered by us all. It is a true account of the heart of all the race, although these fruits are not developed in all to the same extent. Some of our readers may wish to be excepted from being identified in this class. Such should read, "As it is written, There is none righteous, no, not one; there is none that understandeth, there is none that seeketh after God. They are all gone out of the way; they are altogether become unprofitable; there is none that doeth good, no, not one. Their throat is an open sepulchre, with their tongue they have used deceit, the poison of asps is under their lips. Whose mouth is full of cursing and bitterness. Their feet are swift to shed blood. Destruction and misery are in their ways. And the way of peace have they not known. There is no fear of God before their eyes. Now we know that what things soever the law saith, it saith to them who are under the law; that every mouth may be stopped, and all the world become guilty before God." Rom. 3 : 10–19.

If any are still dissatisfied with the picture here given of the human heart in the state of nature, they should listen to Paul again : "Now the works of the flesh are manifest, which are these : adultery, fornication, uncleanness, lasciviousness, idolatry, witchcraft, hatred, variance, emulations, wrath, strife, seditions, heresies, envyings, murders, drunkenness, revellings, and such like." Gal. 5 : 19–21. These are the fruits of the flesh, and being so, Paul exclaims, " For I know that in me (that is, in my flesh) dwelleth no good thing." With such facts before us, together with what we all know of the character of our race, it is not difficult to understand how man became ignorant of God and his laws; and in view of this same testimony, who will deny that the fault rests upon man for his ignorance and degradation? Especially when we take into consideration the scriptural history of a portion of the race, who learned God's purposes and promises, were healed of their moral pollutions, and became obedient to his law; as in the case of Abel (Gen. 4:4), who through faith made an offering to God, which typified both a crucified Saviour of sinners, and the final portion of the wicked. See Lev. 3:2, 11. Psa. 37:20. Or, as in the days of Seth (Gen. 4:6), "Then began men to call on the name of the Lord," (or. *to call themselves* by the name of the Lord. — *Margin.*) Or in the case of Enoch (Gen. 5:22, 24), who "walked with God three hundred years," and prophesied of the future coming Lord who was to destroy the wicked (Jude 14), and was finally translated, having "had this testimony that he pleased God." Heb. 11, 5. And also in the cases of Noah, whom God calls "*righteous;*" Abraham, called "*the father of the faithful;*" Lot, who is called "*just;*" David, the "*man after God's own heart;*" Elijah, who "*went up in a chariot of fire;*" Zechariah and Elisabeth, who "walked in all the commandments and ordinances of the Lord blameless," with others of the faithful in all ages, who, through faith in God, found mercy and forgiveness of sins, and became the servants of the Lord. Heb. 11th chap.

What a contrast is presented in the Bible between the race of man in their fallen, sinful state, and the class who have been reclaimed from their sinfulness by faith in the blood of Christ! The one is estranged from God, unwilling to be taught by him, seeking to forget the knowledge of God, changing the truth into a lie, following their own vain imaginations, full of evil inventions, cursing, and bitterness, corrupting themselves and their posterity, filling the world with violence, cruelty, oppression, war, darkness, and death, while the other class is receiving instruction from God, inquiring to know his will, accepting the developments of his infinite mind and plan of mercy and grace, confessing their dependence and ignorance, acknowledging his goodness and mercies, giving thanks to him for his innumerable blessings, confidently trusting in him for future deliverance from the effects of sin, and for eternal life and happiness; being at peace with him and with man, cultivating the graces of the Spirit, bearing its fruits, and exerting a hallowed influence upon such as are not ripe in iniquity. Thus they represent God among men, and seek to bring the apostate world back to that path of wisdom and virtue which leads to God, to peace, and life eternal.

Between these two points are found all grades of character, being led on from the centre to the depths of moral corruption, or in the other direction to the highest degree of moral purity and Christian virtue, by the two classes of agents engaged in leading the human mind from God or to him.

But it may be asked, "Why was not the sentence of the law speedily executed upon Adam?" We reply, Because God, in his infinite wisdom, was pleased to pursue another course; viz., to accept Christ as a sacrifice, grant a reprieve to man, give him a term of probation for his recovery from rebellion, and for eternal life by a resurrection from death (after he should die) to immortality, of which we shall speak more particularly in another chapter. Let us study God's plan of redemption, and we shall admire the depths of his wisdom and the riches of his goodness.

CHAPTER IV.

MAN'S RELATIONS TO GOD UNDER THE FIRST COVENANT.

"Wherefore then serveth the law? It was added because of transgressions, till the seed should come to whom the promise was made." — *Gal.* 3 : 19.

In the foregoing chapter we have presented man in his fallen and degenerate state, sunken in idolatry and heathen darkness, following the *ignis fatuus* of carnal pleasure, in gratification of his sensual lusts, forgetful of God, living in uncleanness and vile affections, to work out "all uncleanness with greediness" (see Rom. 1 : 24, 26. Eph. 4 : 19), the remembrance of God nearly erased from the mind, "not loving to retain God in their knowledge." Rom. 1 : 24, 28.

In this state of things God was pleased to reveal his plan to rescue his name, his law, and his purposes from forgetfulness and reproach among men.

In pursuance therefore of his promise contained in the sentence against the serpent, in the garden of Eden, "*I will put enmity between thee and the woman, and between thy seed and her seed; it shall bruise* [crush] *thy head, and thou shalt bruise his heel*" (Gen. 3 : 15), he called Abram, and said unto him, "*Get thee out of thy country, and from thy kindred, and from thy father's house, unto a land that I will show thee; and I will make of thee a great nation, and I will bless thee and make thy name great, and thou shalt be a blessing; and I will bless them that bless thee, and curse him that curseth thee; and in thee shall all families of the earth be blessed.*" Gen. 12 : 1-4. Again, "And the Lord said unto Abram after that Lot was separated from him, *Lift up now thine eyes, and look from the place where thou art, northward, and southward, and eastward, and westward, for all the* LAND *which thou seest, to thee will I give it, and to thy seed forever; and I will make thy seed as the dust of the earth, so that, if a man can number the dust of the earth, then shall thy seed also be numbered.*" Gen. 13 : 14-17. See also Gen. 15 : 5-7. "And he brought him forth abroad, and said, Look now toward heaven, and tell the stars, if thou be able to number them; and he said, So shall thy seed be. *And he believed in the Lord, and he counted it to him for righteousness.* And he said unto him, I am the Lord, that *brought thee out of Ur of the Chaldees, to give thee this land to inherit it.*" Also read Gen. 28 : 13, 14.

Reader, pause here for a moment and reflect upon the righteousness attributed to Abram. What righteousness was it that secured to Abram and his seed the land referred to in the foregoing texts? Was it that of the law? Certainly not. Please re-read the sixth verse, quoted above. Was it not the righteousness of faith? How, then, can it be claimed by the natural descendants of Abraham — the Jewish nation — as such? By what rule can any man, Jew or Gentile, claim it on any other principle than that of faith? We will let Jesus testify in this case, in his address to Saul of Tarsus, while meeting him on his way to Damascus (Acts 26: 17): "Delivering thee from the people and from the Gentiles, unto whom now I send thee, to open their eyes, and to turn them from darkness to light, and from the power of Satan unto God, that they may receive forgiveness of sins, and INHERITANCE among them [the seed of Abraham by faith] which are sanctified by FAITH that is in me." That Paul preached the same is seen in Gal. 3:29: "If ye be Christ's, then are ye *Abraham's seed, and heirs according to the promise.*" See also Eph. 1:11, 14.

We will hear Paul again: "But that no man is justified by the law in the sight of God, it is evident, *for the just shall live by faith*, and the law is not of *faith*." Gal. 3:11, 12. Once more: "For if the INHERITANCE be of the LAW, it is no more of promise, but God gave it to Abraham by promise. So then they which be of *faith are blessed* [with the promise of the inheritance] *with faithful Abraham.*" Verses 9 and 18. And yet again: "For the promise that he should be the heir of the world [habitable globe], was not to Abraham or his seed through the law, but through the *righteousness of faith.* For if they which are of the law be heirs, faith is made void, and the promise made of none effect." Rom. 4:13, 14.

Now, if the reader wishes to find the root and germ, or original plan, of this inheritance (kingdom or dominion), turn to Gen. 1:24–28, and as you read remember that this benediction or blessing was concerning *things to come.* "And God said, Let the earth bring forth the living creature after his kind, cattle, and creeping thing, and beast of the earth after his kind, and it was so. And God made the beast of the earth after his kind, and cattle after their kind, and every thing that creepeth upon the earth after his kind, and God saw that it was good. And God said, Let us make man in our image, after our likeness, and let them have dominion over the fish of the sea, and over the fowl of the air, and over the cattle, and over all the earth, and over every creeping thing that creepeth upon the earth. So God created man in his own image, in the image of God created he him, male and female created he them.

"And God blessed them, and God said unto them, Be fruitful, and multiply, and replenish the earth, and subdue it, and have dominion over the fish of the sea, and over the fowl of the air, and over every living thing that moveth upon the earth."

We will now read Psa. 37:22: "For such as be blessed of him shall inherit the earth, and they that be cursed of him shall be cut off." Christ also promises the same (Matt. 5:5): "Blessed are the meek, for they shall inherit the earth." Now, be it remembered that the foregoing promises are those embraced in the New Covenant, and are some of the "better promises" upon which it is established. See Heb. 8:6. This is in contrast with the first, or law covenant, from Sinai, of which we shall speak presently.

These promises, therefore, do not vest in, or belong to, the Jewish nation, nor any other nation as such, but in, or to, those, and only those, "of every nation, kindred, tongue, and people, under heaven, *who walk in the steps of that faith of our father Abraham, which he had yet being uncircumcised.*" Rom. 4 : 12. For in this faith, and this only, is he the heir of the world, and the father of many nations; and in this faith only, dear readers, can you be Christ's disciples, Abraham's seed, and heirs of the promise. Rom. 4 : 12, 13. Gal. 3 : 29.

Yet we do not understand this rule to apply to infants and idiots, as we shall show in another chapter.

Dear reader, are you, who have the light of the gospel, thus allied to these precious promises? If so, "lift up your head and look up, for your redemption draweth nigh;" the time to possess this inheritance is at hand. But if not, O, turn *now* and embrace them; fly for your life; lay hold on the hope set before you. Let not the words "*too late*" sting thy soul when there is no help.

With the foregoing remarks, we pass to speak of the law, or first covenant, and the Jewish nation.

FIRST COVENANT.

Paul, who was perhaps the most prominent of Jewish converts to Christ, as respects education, knowledge, zeal, and love of kindred, becomes so thoroughly imbued with the inspiration of Christ, that he teaches the same gospel. In speaking of the fallen nature of man under the law, he declares that the Jew is no better than the Gentile in the eyes of the law, saying, "What then? are we [Jews] better than they [Gentiles]? No, in no wise; for we have before proved both Jews and Gentiles, that they are all under sin, . . . that every mouth may be stopped, and all the world may become guilty before God; therefore by the deeds of the law there shall no flesh be justified in his sight."

The reason he assigns for this conclusion is, "For by the law is the knowledge of sin." Rom. 3: 9, 19, 20. In view of this fact he anticipates an objection, and meets it on this wise: "What advantage then hath the Jew? or what profit is there of circumcision?" He replies, "Much every way; chiefly because that unto them were committed the oracles of God." Rom. 3: 1, 2. This enabled them to learn the covenants and promises of God, and embrace them if they would. Yet while a few accepted them, the mass rejected them, which leads Paul to argue (verse 3), "Shall their unbelief make the faith [promise] of God without effect? [Answer.] By no means; yea, let God be true, but [though he prove] every man a liar." Verse 4.

His language to the Galatians, in reproof for seeking justification by the law, is the same. He argues that the promised inheritance can only be obtained by *faith*, and asks, "Wherefore then serveth the law? [Answer.] It was added [to the promise] because of [to make known the] transgressions [For how long?] till the seed [Christ] should come, to whom the promise was made." Gal. 3: 19. But we shall speak more fully on this point in another place. We pass now to inquire, —

I. What law was added to the promise?
II. When was the law added?
III. Where was the law added?
IV. For what purposes was the law added?

I. We remark, and intend to show, that this added law was the covenant of ten commandments, with all its ordinances, as stated by Paul: "Then verily the first covenant had also ordinances [or ceremonies] of divine service, and a worldly sanctuary." Heb. 9: 1–5. See also verse 16. "Now this I say, that the covenant [promise to Abraham and his seed] that was confirmed before of God in Christ, the LAW [covenant from Sinai], which was *four hundred and thirty years after*, cannot disannul, that it should make the promise of none effect." Gal. 3: 17. "For if the inheritance be of the law, it is no more by promise. But God gave it to Abraham by promise." Verse 18.

But the objector will say that this *law, which was added four hundred and thirty years after the promise* to Abraham, was *not the ten commandments*. We reply, The fallacy of this objection may be fully exposed by following the apostle in his argument to the Galatians, in which he presents the two covenants (cited above) in plain contrast, until he arrives at the following conclusion in unmistakable language. He exclaims (Gal. 4: 21), "Tell me, ye that desire to be under the law, do ye not hear the law? For it is written, Abraham had two sons, the one by a bondmaid, the other by a free woman. But he who was of the bondwoman was born after the flesh [covenant relating to Abraham's seed after the flesh] (Gen. 15: 13, 18; 16: 9; 17: 20), but he of the free woman was by promise. Which things are an allegory, for these are [represent] THE TWO COVENANTS [testaments], the [first] one from the

Mount Sinai, which gendereth to bondage, which is [represented by] Agar [Hagar]. For this Agar is [represents] Mount Sinai in Arabia, and answereth to [is a type of] Jerusalem, which now is, and is in bondage with her children. But Jerusalem [represented by the free woman] which is above is free, which is the mother of us [Christians] all."

There is no bondage here. Praise the Lord for gospel freedom! There is where Christians go for help, to the heavenly Jerusalem. Please observe the contrast once more: "And it shall come to pass, when ye be multiplied and increased in the land, in those days, saith the Lord, they shall say no more, the ark of the covenant of the Lord, neither shall it come to mind, neither shall they remember it, neither shall they visit it, neither shall that be done any more." Jer. 3 : 16–18. "But ye are come unto Mount Sion, and unto the city of the living God, the heavenly Jerusalem, . . . and to Jesus, the Mediator of the New Covenant." Heb. 12 : 22.

But it is claimed by some, that there was more than one covenant made on Sinai. This is more easily said than proved. The Scriptures speak of TWO COVENANTS, and only two, as being made with Israel and Judah. The one of ten commandments, given on Sinai, with its ordinances, is called "the *first*," and "*old*," because it was the first code given to that people, and in contrast with the *new*, of which we shall speak more particularly hereafter. Let us now look at the nature of a covenant.

COVENANT.

"Covenant, — a mutual consent or agreement of two or more persons to do or forbear some act or thing, a contract, stipulation. A covenant is created by deed in writing, sealed and executed, or it may be implied in the contract. In theology, the covenant of works is implied in the commands of God to man." — *Webster*. The covenant of ten sayings was spoken by God in the hearing of the people, which so terrified them that they withdrew and requested Moses to speak with them, but that God should not speak with them lest they should die; and Moses expressly states why God spoke thus to them (contrary to what some claim, that the ten sayings were so much more holy than that which was yet to be spoken, that God would not suffer Moses to speak or write them). Hear him: "And Moses said unto the people, Fear not, for God is come to prove you, and that his fear may be before your faces, that ye sin not. . . . And Moses drew near unto the thick darkness where God was" (Exod. 20: 20–21), "and God spake unto him the statutes and judgments [ordinances] in pursuance of that covenant, and Moses delivered them to the people, all of which they promised to observe, and to be obedient." Exod. 24: 7. "And Moses wrote all THE WORDS of the Lord [including, therefore, the ten commandments], and rose up early in the morning," and prepared for the confirmation of the covenant, by offering the usual sacrifice of such occasions. See Exod. 24: 4–7. "He [then] took the book of the COVENANT, and read it in the audience of the people, and they said, All that the Lord hath said will we do, and be obedient." Ver. 7. Then Moses "took the blood [of the sacrifice of dedication; see Heb. 9:18], and sprinkled it upon both the book and the people, and said, Behold the blood of the covenant which the Lord hath made with you concerning all these words." Compare Exod. 24:8. Heb. 9:19.

The reader must be convinced, whether he admits it or not, that this covenant of ten commandments, with its judgments and statutes, were all spoken by the Lord on Sinai, recorded in a book, and read by Moses in the audience of the people, accepted by them, ratified by sacrifice, dedicated with the blood of that sacrifice, and proclaimed as God's covenant with Judah and Israel, as above described, before Moses was called into the mount to receive it on the tables of stone.

But the claim has been set up by a class of teachers, that there was more than one covenant made on Mount Sinai, as God gave other laws there besides the covenant of ten commandments, and Exod. 19:5 is cited as proof. But this verse is spoken in reference to the covenant which he was about to introduce with his own voice from Sinai, as we have shown above: "If ye will obey my voice indeed, and keep my covenant [this voice they had never heard, but were about to hear it pronouncing his covenant], then ye shall be a peculiar treasure unto me above all people, for all the earth is mine." Exod. 19:5.

This is a proposition on the part of God that if they would obey his voice and keep his covenant, then they should share the blessings; to which when they had agreed (ver. 8), the Lord directed Moses to prepare the people to witness his descent on the mount, and to hear his voice pronouncing that covenant; all of which was done, and then the voice was heard and the covenant given. This testimony is clear, and shows our II. and also our III. propositions, WHEN and WHERE the law was added. But the above-named class of objectors claim that because the *law of the* Aaronic *priesthood* was given at Sinai, therefore it is the "first covenant," and of which Paul treats in Heb. 8 : 6, 8. We deny that any covenant was made with the Aaronic priesthood at Sinai. The above claim proceeds upon the principle that because a covenant is a law, therefore all laws are covenants.

We further reply, that while we admit that the Sinaic covenant of ten commandments did involve the right on the part of God to make all other laws for the government of Israel, yet these laws were no more covenants than the fact that all guineas are gold proves that all gold coins are guineas. In support of the above singular claim, a text is often quoted from Num. 25 : 12, 13, "Wherefore say, Behold I give unto him [Phinehas the son of Eleazar, the son of Aaron the priest, v. 11], my covenant of peace, and he shall have it, and his seed after him, even the covenant of an everlasting priesthood." We reply to this, that the above covenant made with Phinehas concerning the Aaronic priesthood was not made at Sinai in Arabia, but in the land of Moab. Proof: "And the children of Israel set forward and pitched in the plains of Moab, on this side Jordan by Jericho." Num. 22 : 1. Compare this with

Num. 25: 1, 12, 13, just quoted. It was also forty years after the covenant of ten commandments at Sinai, and when all the fathers with whom it was made were dead, except Caleb and Joshua. Proof: In giving the covenant made with Phinehas and the sum of the congregation of the children of Israel then alive, we read, " But among these there was not a man of them whom Moses and Aaron the priest numbered, when they numbered the children of Israel in the wilderness of Sinai. For the Lord had said of them, They shall surely die in the wilderness; and there was not left a man of them, save Caleb the son of Jephunneh, and Joshua the son of Nun." Num. 26: 64, 65. And further: This covenant was made with Phinehas, of the tribe of Levi; but the *first* covenant was made with the fathers of Judah and Israel, at Sinai, in the day when the Lord took them by the hand to lead them out of Egypt. See Heb. 8: 9. We should not think men who make such blunders as above very safe teachers, to say the least.

Let us now proceed to identify the covenant of ten commandments as the first covenant, of which Paul speaks in Heb. 9: 1: "Then verily the first covenant had also ordinances of divine service, and a worldly sanctuary." We think we have already clearly shown in the foregoing remarks, that there was but one covenant made with the fathers of Israel and Judah at Sinai. To this covenant the definite article "THE" is prefixed by Moses; "the book of THE covenant," "the blood of THE covenant." Exod. 24: 7, 8. "And he wrote upon the tables the words of THE covenant, the ten commandments." Exod. 34: 28.

Here we will digress from our point for a time, to meet an objection often raised against this position by the class of teachers above referred to, viz. : That there were two covenants made on Mount Sinai; one of ten commandments, and another concerning the Levitical priesthood; that they are entirely separate; and that while the latter is disannulled, the former is yet in full force on believers.

The strenuous efforts of seventh-day teachers to make this statement appear true has so confused the minds of many honest persons that they fail to see, or, if they see, do not appreciate, the true relation of the priesthood to the covenant.

The above claim, if admitted, would prove fatal both to the law and the priesthood, and to the hope of the people, so far as they (the people) are concerned. But Paul, in his Epistles to the Hebrews and Galatians, places this subject in such a light that those teachers are fully aware that if the aforesaid idea fails, their seventh-day theory falls to the ground. Hence they claim that the covenant of ten commandments says nothing about priesthood, ordinances, or sacrifices.

But let us examine the relation of the priesthood to the (law) covenant. The word *priest*, then, according to Webster, is "from words that signify *a chief, one that presides, to stand before*, contracted from *presbyter*, elder, or overseer, *originally* and *properly one that officiates at the altar;* hence Cain, Abel, and all the patriarchs were priests." And hence all the idolatrous nations had their priests, because their covenants with their gods required service or sacrifice, consequently God said (Exod. 23 : 32), "Thou shalt make no covenant with them, nor with their gods."

All of God's penal covenants requiring service or sacrifice of life, must of necessity have an officiating priest; and the very fact that such sacrifice is offered, most clearly proves that such covenant or law has in some way been broken, because a sacrifice implies atonement, and the idea of making an atonement where no offence has been committed is preposterous.

In Heb. 7 : 11, we read that the people received the law (whatever law it was) under the Levitical priesthood. Query: Did Paul mean to give us the astounding information, that the people received the covenant of the *Levitical priesthood under the Levitical priesthood?* Clearly not. What law, then, was it? Was it not the covenant of ten commandments, made with that people of whom he was speaking? Certainly it was. But the *Aaronic priesthood* was not organized until after the first covenant was made, accepted, dedicated, and proclaimed. Compare Exod. 24 : 7, 8, with Exod. 40 : 12, 16.

How did the people receive the law (of ten commandments) under the Levitical priesthood? We answer, The Levitical priesthood was in existence before the people left Egypt, though not organized by covenant until the days of Phinehas, a long time after the law was given on Sinai. Moses and Aaron were both Levites (Exod. 2 : 2), and directed the sacrifice of the passover in Egypt. THEY WERE PRIESTS. See Exod. 17 : 15. Again, the Levitical priests were among the people at Mount Sinai, when God came down to deliver the first covenant to Israel. See Exod. 19:22, 24. "And let the PRIESTS also, which come near to the Lord, sanctify themselves, lest the Lord break forth upon them. . . . And the Lord said unto Moses, Away, get thee down, and thou shalt come up, thou, and Aaron with thee; but let not the PRIESTS and the people break through to come up unto the Lord, lest he break forth upon them." But up to this time we have no account of any covenant with the Levitical priesthood further than the fact that God chose leaders and ministers of Israel from that tribe before they left Egypt, and they offered the sacrifice, with whose blood Moses confirmed or dedicated the covenant which God gave at Sinai. Exod. 24:7, 8.

Thus we see that the law was received under the Levitical priesthood; and it was this law, thus spoken, which Moses wrote and read in the audience of the people, and which they accepted, and Moses ratified with blood, and proclaimed to be *the covenant which the Lord had made with them concerning all these words* (Exod. 24:8. Compare with Exod. 34:27, 29), and to which the people could have access, and learn, and teach to their children, and which *was afterwards* inscribed on tables of stone, to be preserved with the golden pot of manna, and Aaron's rod that budded, in the most holy place, where no mortal eye penetrated, nor feet trod, save those of the high priest once a year.

This, therefore, is the only covenant which the Lord made with Israel at Sinai. It was under this covenant, and in pursuance of, and with direct reference to it, that the Aaronic priesthood was afterwards organized, and a covenant made with Phinehas. See Exod. 40 : 12. It is further claimed by these objectors, that the covenant of ten commandments says nothing about priesthood, sacrifices, or ordinances, while Paul, in Hebrews, makes reference to all these in connection with the old or first covenant.

Let us examine this objection. ORDINANCE is defined thus : " A rule established by authority, a permanent rule of action, a law or statute of sovereign power."— *Webster*. This being so, then we prove that every one of the ten commands are ordinances. "Thou shalt have no other gods before me. Thou shalt not bow down thyself to them nor serve them." Exod. 20 : 3, 5. Does not this imply most clearly, that they were to worship and serve him? But what was it to serve God? Jesus said to Satan, "It is written, Thou shalt worship the Lord thy God, and him only shalt thou serve." And Moses understood that to *serve God* was to offer sacrifice to him. " Our cattle," said he to Pharaoh, "also shall go with us ; there shall not a hoof be left behind ; for thereof must we take to *serve the Lord our God*, and we know not with what we must serve the Lord until we come thither." Exod. 10 : 26.

We find that Abel also was serving the Lord when he brought his sacrifice unto the Lord from the firstlings of his flock, and by this kind of service " he obtained witness that he was righteous, God testifying of his gift, and by it he, being dead, yet speaketh." Heb. 11 : 4.

A sacrifice of life of necessity implies a broken law. Abel therefore acted with reference to a violated law, whose penalty was death, in which he was in some way involved, and which required an atonement, of which we shall say more elsewhere in this work.

Whenever a sacrifice is necessary a priest is demanded: thus it is shown not only that the covenant of ten commandments is a code of ordinances, but that it required both sacrifices and a priesthood; and so closely are they allied that the apostle Paul uses them interchangeably, thus: "If perfection were by the Levitical priesthood, — for under it the people received the law, — what need was there that another priest should arise?" Heb. 7: 11. Compare this with verse 19: "For the law [received under, and administered by, the Levitical priesthood] made nothing perfect; but the bringing in of a better hope [the new covenant established upon better promises, under the priesthood of Jesus Christ, Heb. 9: 15] did [make something perfect], by the which [better hope] we draw nigh to God."

This new covenant therefore required sacrifice, first, of the blood of Christ; second, on the part of the people who believe on him, as stated by Paul: "I am now ready to be offered." 2 Tim. ch. 4. Again, "I beseech you therefore, brethren, by the mercies of God, that ye present your bodies a living sacrifice, holy, acceptable unto God, which is your reasonable service." Rom. 12: 1.

Let us illustrate these points by the government of the United States. Its constitution is a covenant of the people, and is the basis of all other laws which are passed by the government in pursuance thereof; and these all fall back upon the constitution for their authority, and like all other civil governments it requires sacrifice in some form, even to the taking of life, and that to a fearful extent, as late experience furnishes sufficient proof. Thus the objection which has been raised, that "the ten commandments say nothing about ordinances, sacrifices, or priesthood," betrays ignorance of God's covenants not very commendable in Christian teachers.

Having shown the fallacy of these several objections, we return to our point, viz., to identify the covenant of ten commandments as the *old* or *first covenant*, of which Paul speaks in Hebrews, chs. 8 and 9. First, then, we have shown that there was but one covenant made at Sinai, and that covenant was the ten commandments.

"And he wrote on the tables of stone the words of the covenant, the ten commandments." Exod. 34: 28. This covenant was made with the fathers at Sinai, and being the only one made at Sinai, it must be the covenant which Paul calls THE FIRST, for he says the first covenant was made with the fathers in the day when the Lord took them by the hand to lead them out of the land of Egypt. Hear him. "For if that *first covenant* had been faultless, then should no place have been sought for the second; for, finding fault with them, he saith, Behold, the days come, saith the Lord, when I will make a new covenant with the house of Israel and with the house of Judah; not according to the covenant I made with their fathers in the day when I took them by the hand to lead them out of Egypt." Heb. 8: 7, 9.

When God spoke the law from Sinai, with its judgments, "Moses wrote ALL THE WORDS of the Lord, and rose up early in the morning, and builded an altar under the hill, and twelve pillars according to the twelve tribes [not the one tribe of Levi only, as has been asserted] of Israel." Exod. 24:4. "And he took the book of THE COVENANT [which God had spoken on Sinai], and read in the audience of the people; and they said, All that the Lord hath said will we do, and be obedient. And Moses took the blood and sprinkled it on the people, and said, Behold the blood of THE COVENANT which the Lord hath made with you concerning all these words." Ver. 7, 8. Compare this with Exod. 34:27, 28: "And the Lord said unto Moses, Write thou these words, for after the tenor of these words have I made a covenant with thee and with Israel. And he wrote upon the tables the words of THE COVENANT, the ten commandments." Remember, no other covenant was made with Israel at Sinai.

Let us now compare the above with the covenant Paul speaks of in Heb. 9:1, and see if they are not the same. Here he introduces the first covenant, and the sanctuary in which it was deposited. He then describes the outer and inner court of that sanctuary, then the inner tabernacle or court, called the Holiest of all. Ver. 2 and 3. Then he proceeds to describe what was in the Holiest of all, viz., the golden censer, the ark of the (first) covenant, in which was the golden pot that had manna, and Aaron's rod that budded, and the tables (of stone) of the (first) covenant.

How plain, then, that the first covenant is that written on the tables, and deposited in the ark for safe keeping. But Paul proceeds to argue it out more clearly still. Verses 18 and 19: he says, "Whereupon neither the first testament [covenant] was dedicated without blood; for when Moses had spoken every precept [of the first covenant] to all the people according to the law, he took the blood of calves and of goats, with water, and scarlet wool, and hyssop, and sprinkled both the book and all the people, saying, This is the blood of the testament [covenant] which God hath enjoined [spoken from Sinai] unto you." See Exod. 24 : 6, 9, quoted above, and then ask yourselves, candid readers, if you would dare to say that the covenant on the tables of stone and Paul's first covenant are not the same?

Having shown *what* law was added to the promise, also *when, how,* and *where* it was added, and the first covenant given, we pass to show,—

IV. For what purpose it was (given) added.

First. We are informed by Paul, who raised the question, that "it was added because of transgressions, till the seed should come to whom the promise was made."

Second. It was given in fulfilment of God's promise to Abraham in answer to the question, "Lord God, whereby shall I know that I shall inherit it?" Gen. 15 : 8.

I. The passage at the head of this chapter informs us that the law "was added [to the promise] because of transgressions"— on account of transgressions.— *Em. Diaglott,* Gal. 3 : 19.

The sense of this passage may be expressed thus: God's law, as given to Adam, involved his sovereignty and right to rule as the one lawgiver, as well as to make promises, as shown in his first benediction; and also the duty of man to obey whatever law he chose to make for the government and discipline of man. It was God's right to promise and command: it was man's duty to trust his word, believe his promise, obey his command, and hope for the reward; this sovereignty, on the one hand, and duty, on the other, having been disregarded in the first transgression, and sin thereby entering the world, infecting the whole race, involving them in all its dreadful evils; our heavenly Father, in choosing a people from among the nations of the earth in whose history he would revive these relations, and make them a pictorial and typical nation, called Abram, gave him a promise through Christ, involving the same promise as the one to Adam in Eden. Gen. 1:28; 15:14, 15.

Four hundred years after this, to put that people, and through them the world, in mind of his right as sovereign Lawgiver, he introduces (as he had told Abraham he would) the law covenant in form, to expose the sin of Adam and his race in transgressing his law, which had brought upon them the miseries they suffer, and also to continually admonish them of their lost condition, and point them to Christ as their only help, their Redeemer and Saviour, who would bruise the serpent's head, and to, and through whom the original promise should be fulfilled.

Thus the law reveals man's fallen, sinful, lost condition, and in its ordinances, as a schoolmaster, points us to Christ.

To the above sentiments agree the declarations of Paul, "Therefore by the deeds of the law shall no flesh be justified in his sight, *for by the law is the knowledge of sin.* But now [since the faith has come] the righteousness of God without the law is manifested, being witnessed by the law and the prophets, even the righteousness which is by faith of Jesus Christ, unto all and upon all them that believe, for there is no difference [under the law], for all have sinned, and come short of the glory of God." Rom. 3 : 20, 23.

Thus, while the law exposes our sinfulness by nature, it affords no relief, but by its types points to Christ, the faith and righteousness of God, as our only hope. It is to us the tree of the knowledge of good and evil, and by that tree in Eden the law was presented in emblem to Adam; the eating of whose interdicted fruit has proved our ruin, and in which there is NO LIFE.

Again, the apostle, in speaking of Adam's offence, says, "Moreover, the law entered [was introduced] that the offence might abound." Rom. 5 : 20. Again he says, "I had not known sin but by the law, for I had not known lust except the law had said, Thou shalt not covet." Rom. 7 : 7. Therefore this law is always against us; "it is contrary to us." But thanks be to God, Jesus has suffered its curse to redeem us from it: to him its shadows point; he has nailed it to his cross, bringing us from under it, to accept and obey the new covenant, sealed with his blood — the royal law — "Whatsoever ye would that men should do unto you, do ye even so unto them."

The (old covenant) law is a standing monument of man's fall and condemnation, not made void through faith, but its authority fully established and its claims fully met by Jesus, in our behalf, while we pass under the law of faith to Christ, which is now our master and teacher. This first law or covenant was given for the government of man in the flesh, and is by Paul sometimes called "a law in the flesh," "the law of sin and death," which is in my members, constantly condemning and killing, but never justifying and giving life.

The promises, therefore, under this law pertain exclusively to this mortal life (since Adam by sin forfeited the right of dominion, which involved the prospect of eternal life), and are referred to by Paul, in contrast with the *better promises* upon which the new covenant is founded (see Hebrews, ch. 8), and are recorded in Exodus, 23 : 22–32 : "But if thou shalt indeed obey his voice, and do all that I speak, then I will be an enemy unto thine enemies, and an adversary unto thine adversaries. For mine angel shall go before thee, and bring thee in unto the Amorites, and the Hittites, and the Perizzites, and the Canaanites, the Hivites, and the Jebusites: and I will cut them off. . . . And ye shall serve the Lord your God, and he shall bless thy bread and thy water; and I will take sickness away from the midst of thee. There shall nothing cast their young, nor be barren, in thy land : the number of thy days shall be fulfilled. I will send my fear before thee, and will destroy all the people to whom thou shalt come, and I will make all thine enemies turn their backs unto thee. And I will send the hornets before thee which shall drive out the Hivite, the Canaanite, and the Hittite from before thee. By little and little will I drive them out from before thee, until thou be increased and fill the land. And I will set thy bounds from the Red Sea even unto the Sea of the Philistines, and from the desert unto the river: for I will deliver the inhabitants of the land into your hand; and thou shalt drive them out before thee. Thou shalt make no covenant with them, nor with their gods."

The above promises, and many others like them, give the limits of all the promises of the old covenant, showing that they do not extend beyond this mortal life.

II. The law was added in fulfilment of God's promise to Abraham in answer to the question, "Lord God, whereby shall I know that I shall inherit it?" Gen. 15 : 8.

In all of God's dealings with his children, he has some wise purpose to accomplish. We have shown how God made promise to Abraham and his seed, that he would give them the land east, west, north, and south, for an everlasting inheritance.

In Gen. 15 : 7, we hear God saying, —

"I am the Lord that brought thee out of Ur of the Chaldees, to give thee this land to inherit it." To this Abraham replied, "Lord God, whereby shall I know that I shall inherit it?" This is a question of great importance, not only to Abraham, but to all believers in all generations. Reader, mark well this question, and its answer. God had made promise to Abraham that he would give him the land for an everlasting possession. He had believed God's promise. Yet we hear him asking confirmation of the promise, not for himself, but for the benefit of future generations. "Lord God, whereby shall I know that I shall inherit it?" Gen. 15 : 8–21.

Before the Lord complies with this request for surety he directs Abraham to prepare a sacrifice for the confirmation of a covenant. When this is done we find Abraham in a waiting position : "And when the sun was gone down a deep sleep fell upon Abraham, and lo, an horror of great darkness fell upon him." This is emblematical of death, as shown in verse fifteen, and teaches an important lesson. Abraham is then told that his seed (in the flesh) should "be a stranger in a land that is not theirs, and shall serve them four hundred years." The promise of their return (out of Egypt) is then given. We next hear God making a covenant concerning his seed *in the flesh*, in which he promises them (NOT ALL the land he had PROMISED HIM, AND HIS SEED) that portion of land lying between the River Nile and the River Euphrates, then inhabited by certain heathen tribes, viz., "the Kenites, and the Kenizzites, and the Kadmonites, and the Hittites, and the Perizzites, and the Rephaims, and the Amorites, and the Canaanites, and the Girgashites, and the Jebusites." Now, let it be remembered that this arrangement concerning his seed in the flesh has no reference to Abraham in person, but is in answer to the question, "Lord, whereby shall I know that I shall inherit it?" (the whole earth. See Rom. 4 : 13), and is therefore a sign and seal for believers, in all after generations (Rom. 4 : 11), that the original promise to Abraham and his seed (Christ) concerning that land shall be fulfilled

In this covenant with Abraham, therefore, God promises to make his seed in the flesh a typical nation, and establish with that people his covenant pertaining to the flesh, or mortal life, the token of which (circumcision) he gave to Abraham. See Gen. 17: 10, 11. "He that is born in thy house and he that is bought with thy money must needs be circumcised, and *my covenant shall be in your flesh* for an everlasting covenant, and the uncircumcised man child whose flesh of his foreskin is not circumcised, that soul shall be cut off from among his people ; he hath broken my covenant." Verses 13, 14. Here the Lord promises Abraham that he will establish his covenant with him and his seed after him in their generations, and that covenant was to be *in their flesh.* In pursuance of this instruction, Abraham received circumcision, a sign or token of the covenant entered into, or, as Paul has it (Rom. 4: 11), "a seal of the righteousness of faith." And when the four hundred years' service of his seed in Egypt was fulfilled, the Lord brought them out according to his promise, "with great substance ;" and then from Mount Sinai God established his covenant with them, as he had promised Abraham he would do, the token of which was circumcision (the same as given to Abraham, Gen. 17: 11), and gave them that fiery law of which Moses spoke when blessing the people before his death. "The Lord came from Sinai, and rose up from Seir unto them ; he shined forth from Mount Paran, and he came with ten thousand of his saints [angels] ; from his right hand went a fiery law for them." Deut. 33: 2. Thus the seed of Abraham in the flesh was established in the most miraculous manner as a nation under that fiery law from Sinai, with all the ordinances of divine service, or symbolic institutions, as a pictorial nation.

And thus in answer to Abraham's question, "Lord God, whereby shall I know that I shall inherit it?" Gen. 15 : 8. He has God's arrangement concerning his seed in the flesh and the token of that arrangement; and all believers in subsequent ages have the history of that typical nation, and God's faithfulness with them, to confirm their faith that the original promise to Abraham and his seed in Christ (Gal. 3 : 29) shall be fulfilled in due time.

Paul, in commenting on these points, says of the descendants of Abraham, "Now all these things happened unto them for ensamples, and they are written for our admonition, upon whom the ends of the world are come." 1 Cor. 10 : 11. As certain therefore as the foregoing arrangement has been fulfilled in the Hebrew nation, just so surely the original promise to Abraham and his seed (Gal. 3 : 16), and all who are Christ's (Gal. 3 : 29), will be fulfilled at the time appointed. Our remarks, then, upon the old covenant, embrace the following points : —

1. It was given to rescue God's name and his law from forgetfulness among the children of men, and to keep the promised dominion before them.

2. In the eyes of this law all men are sinners, condemned to die, and no life or justification is to be obtained from it.

3. This is the law which succeeds, or was added to, the promise, both to Adam in its germ, and to the descendants of Abraham in pursuance of God's promise to him, in its development on Sinai.

4. It is identical with the *first covenant*, mentioned

by Paul in Hebrews, and *the* covenant, and *the only* covenant made with Judah and Israel at Sinai.

5. It was added to the promise four hundred years after the promise made to Abraham, to reveal or give the knowledge of man's sinfulness by nature; and with its types points to Christ as the atoning sacrifice for sins.

6. It was given as a sign and seal to believers, in the then future generations, that the promise to which it was added should be fulfilled in due time. Amen, and amen.

CHAPTER V.

UNIVERSAL REDEMPTION BY THE DEATH OF CHRIST.

"Christ hath redeemed us from the curse of the law, being made a curse for us, for it is written, Cursed is every one that hangeth on a tree." — *Gal.* 3 : 13.

"But God commendeth his love toward us, in that, while we were yet sinners Christ died for us." — *Rom.* 5 : 8.

The subject involved in the proposition at the head of this chapter, and contained in the above texts, and a mass of other scripture of like import, is of vast importance, deserving our most careful consideration, lying, as we think, at the very base of the entire plan of salvation by Jesus Christ. A misunderstanding and wrong application of these scriptures lead not only to false conclusions, but pave the way to a misunderstanding of many other scriptures, resulting in the idea that all men would finally be saved and enjoy eternal life, while other scriptures plainly contradict such an idea. On the other hand, a correct view and proper application of this subject enlightens the mind to see the grand harmony which exists in the Scriptures of truth on the great plan of redemption.

We claim that our texts plainly teach unconditional and universal redemption by the death of Jesus Christ. This we shall attempt to show by the current testimony of the Scriptures, as prerequisite, or absolutely necessary as a preparatory measure for the eternal salvation of any of the race of Adam. But let us keep constantly in mind the fact that Christ, the anointed of God, is presented in this scripture as the great benefactor of our race. He is the "Alpha and Omega, the beginning and the ending, saith the Lord, which is, and which was, and which is to come, the Almighty." Such is the active agent in our text, the personage who has accomplished the mighty work for our race, declared to be "redemption from the curse of the law."

To properly appreciate the work Christ has done for us, that we may give him our affections and obedience, it is very important to understand the real meaning of the words used to express that work, — "REDEEMED US FROM THE CURSE OF THE LAW." The words "*redeemed,*" "*redemption,*" and "*purchased,*" are of frequent use in the Scriptures, and refer to our race as a whole, to parties, to persons, and to things. The text quoted at the head of this chapter, and others we shall quote, clearly refer to the whole race of man, and teach a universal and unconditional redemption of the race from all the effects of Adam's transgression, from under the law which he violated, and whose penalty rested on him and all his posterity.

Let us here state the definition of these terms: —

REDEEMED, "ransomed, delivered from bondage, distress, penalty, liability, or from the possession of another, by paying an equivalent."

REDEMPTION, "to purchase back, to ransom, to liberate or rescue from captivity or bondage, or from any obligation or liability to suffer, or to be forfeited, by paying an equivalent, as, to redeem prisoners or captured goods, to redeem a pledge, to rescue, to recover, to deliver from."— *Webster*.

We are now prepared to consider the question, Was man — the race of man — ever placed in a condition which called for such redemption? To this the Scriptures furnish a full reply. "Wherefore as by one man sin entered into the world, and death by sin, and so death passed upon all men, for [or in whom — *margin*] all have sinned." Rom. 5:12. "By the offence of one, judgment came upon all men to condemnation." Rom. 5:18. "In Adam all die." 1 Cor. 15:21. Adam is our representative head. In these scriptures we are clearly shown that by the transgression of Adam all his posterity became involved in the consequences which befell him. He becomes a sinner; we are in him, and are involved in the corruption of his nature, and are called sinners in the passive sense, not in the active sense, for we had no will or action in his transgression; yet the results of his fallen nature rest upon us; the elements of sin are in us, his posterity, because they were in him who begat us. Therefore we are recognized as sinners, though we are not to be blamed for his act. Death being the penalty for his sin, it was executed upon him by depriving him of "the tree of life;" and through weakening, wearing, and consuming processes for nine hundred and thirty years, he returned to dust.

We sprang from that degenerate, diseased, consumptive, dying stock, and therefore have his physical nature, and also die, under the sentence pronounced against

Adam. The law he violated resting upon him and all who were in him, is the reason why his posterity die. This was "the curse of the law." Death is a curse from God. It is the penalty of God's law. Adam and his posterity fell under that curse. In order for man to be placed on probation, or trial, to obtain life, he must be redeemed first from the law that holds him in death. He cannot be a party to a covenant or contract for his own salvation unless he is redeemed from the curse of Adamic law.

We shall find, in the investigation of this subject, that Adam placed himself and posterity in a very sad and helpless condition by his transgression; but that we, his posterity, place ourselves, by our rejection of Christ as our Lawgiver and our Sacrifice, in quite another and much worse condition. These two conditions resulting from two causes, one from the voluntary action of Adam, affecting all his race, the other from the voluntary action of that portion of his posterity which finally reject salvation by faith in the blood of Christ, — these two conditions of our race, properly understood, explain why the doctrine of the atonement is stated in the Scriptures under two heads, or in two branches. In this chapter we shall argue only the first condition of man, as caused by the transgression of Adam, together with the unconditional and universal redemption of our race from that condition by the death of Christ, as the first part of the atonement. This will lead us to consider our loss by the transgression of Adam; and it is quite important to understand this, that we may know how much is attributed to Adam, and how much to Christ, in the unconditional redemption.

It will be well here to mention some things we did not *absolutely* lose in Adam, that our readers may not anticipate too much in unconditional redemption.

I. We did not lose perfect happiness in Adam. This he never attained to. He was on probation, or trial, for an inheritance and "dominion," which would have been given him had he obeyed his Maker, and matured to that degree of perfection contemplated in the command, " Replenish the earth, and subdue it." As, therefore, we did not lose this in Adam, we cannot expect it as among the things Christ is to purchase back for us, unconditionally.

II. Adam did not lose *immortality* for us. This he never possessed. Had he been immortal he could not have died. This is impossible from the nature of the thing. He must have been alive now, and all his posterity also.

We will examine the primary definition of IMMORTALITY : "The quality of never ceasing to live or exist, exemption from death."

IMMORTAL : "Having no principle of alteration or corruption, exempt from death, having life or being that shall never end." — *Webster*.

Was this quality in Adam's nature? Let us read: "But of the tree of the knowledge of good and evil, thou shalt not eat of it; for in the day thou eatest thereof thou shalt surely die;" or, as the Hebrew is rendered in the margin, "dying thou shalt die." The Arabic renders it, "Thou shalt deserve to die." The Targum has it, "Thou shalt be subject to death."

Adam did eat "of the tree of the knowledge of good and evil," and we are shown in the record that his condition was wonderfully changed. "In the sweat of thy face shalt thou eat bread, till thou return unto the ground, for dust thou art, and unto dust shalt thou return." Gen. 2 : 17; 3 : 6, 19. Again we read, "And all the days that Adam lived were nine hundred and thirty years, and he died." Gen. 5 : 5.

With these facts before us, it would be a great abuse of scriptural reasoning and language to claim that Adam ever possessed immortality. Therefore, as we did not lose immortality in Adam, we cannot expect it to be given to the race as one of the restored blessings by the death of Christ. By Christ's sufferings and death he restores what was really lost by Adam, and not what was not lost. If he ever bestows immortality on any of Adam's race, it will be a gift, and not a restoration of a lost possession. It is true that immortality is to be gained by the children of God, and gained by virtue of the blood of Christ, through "the washing of regeneration and the renewing of the Holy Spirit." It will be given "to those who by patient continuance in well doing seek for" it (Rom. 2 : 7), which is very much more than being "redeemed from the curse of the law."

We are redeemed from the curse of the law, or from the death we die under the law, that we may become probationers, and seek the pardon of our own transgressions, by the blood and intercessions of Christ, and through faith accept him as our *Lawgiver*, *Sacrifice*, and *Life-giver*, as we have argued in its appropriate place. The above two points not being carefully kept in view as distinct from each other, has produced much confusion in religious theology.

III. We did not lose eternal life in Adam. The fact that Adam died, fully refutes the idea that Adam ever possessed eternal life. Eternal life is unending life; the life of Adam ended in *nine hundred and thirty years*, if the record of his death is true (Gen. 5:5); otherwise we might believe that Satan spoke the truth to Eve when he said, "Ye shall not surely die." Gen. 3:4. Some do believe it true. Were Adam yet alive, some naturalist or historian would have given some account of him to at least a portion of his numerous posterity; but such is not the fact. Adam died.

We see, then, that *perfect happiness*, *immortality*, and *eternal life* are qualities which Adam did not possess, consequently could not lose, absolutely; these were in prospect for him and his posterity, had he and they lived in obedience to the Lord. It does not follow, therefore, that because Christ redeems *all* unconditionally from what we lost in Adam, he will bring us *all* unconditionally into the possession of what we never possessed in Adam. We lost very much in Adam without our will or action, and this much Christ has purchased back, and will bestow upon us unconditionally, without our will or action, that we may seek for the better things in Christ which were set before Adam. Let us, therefore, now consider what we did lose in Adam by his transgression.

OUR LOSS IN ADAM.

I. We lost a *good, healthful, physical constitution.* This Adam did possess; thus it is written, "And God said, Let us make man in our image, after our likeness, . . . So God created man in his own image, in the image of God created he him." Gen. 1: 26, 27. "And the Lord God formed man of the dust of the ground, and breathed into his nostrils the breath of life; and man became a living soul." Gen. 2: 7. "And God saw every thing that he had made, and, behold, it was very good." Gen. 1: 31. Adam, thus created and pronounced by his Creator to be very good, was settled in the garden which God had planted, "to dress it and keep it;" but his duties were more extensive than this, for we read that after Adam and his companion were created, "And God blessed them, and God said unto them, Be fruitful, and multiply, and replenish the earth, and subdue it." Gen. 1: 28. This vast work could not be expected of a diseased, sickly, dying man, and posterity. "And the Lord God commanded the man, saying, Of every tree of the garden thou mayest freely eat; but of the tree of the knowledge of good and evil, thou shalt not eat of it; for in the day thou eatest thereof thou shalt surely die" (or, as the Hebrew is rendered, "dying thou shalt die"—*margin*). Adam disobeyed this command. His physical condition was changed, his privileges were abridged. "And unto Adam he said, Because thou hast hearkened unto the voice of thy wife, and hast eaten of the tree of which I commanded thee, saying, Thou shalt not eat of it, cursed is the ground for thy sake; IN SORROW shalt thou eat of it ALL THE DAYS OF THY LIFE, . . . And now, lest he put forth his hand, and take also of the tree of life, and eat, and live forever; therefore the Lord God sent him forth from the garden of Eden, to till the ground from whence he was taken." Gen. 3 : 17, 22, 23.

His life was limited by days. From this time onward Adam was a dying being, deprived of the tree of life that he might not repair the wasting energies of his physical nature: various processes of sapping, wasting, wearing and consuming him were working disease and death.

In this weakened, diseased, and dying condition of Adam and Eve, we, their posterity, were begotten. The stream has not cleansed itself, or the race regenerated themselves. The stream has not risen above the fountain, nor the bad tree yielded good fruit. The question and answer of Job (14 : 4) upon this subject meet the point: " Who can bring a clean thing out of an unclean? Not one." We do not find it difficult to understand that the feeble, sickly physical condition of man originated in our first parents, and has been transmitted to us without abatement: in fact, it has been greatly augmented. The sickness, pains, groans, and languishing of the race of man testify to this fact. The want of sight, of hearing, of speech, with other deformities, also declares this loss, and the death of infants and of youths tells of the physical weakness of man. All this came upon us by Adam, and all these evils will be unconditionally removed from the entire race of Adam ty the death of Christ; yet this redemption does not secure eternal life to any except those incapable of actual sin: all others have incurred a debt themselves by their own sins.

If I find a family upon an estate which has been mortgaged, and the right of redemption forfeited by their ancestors' imprudence and extravagance involving them in debt, and I have the means and the will to pay off the old debt and free the estate from encumbrance, this does not prevent the family from imprudence and excess which would involve them in debt on their own account, and which they must pay, or find other means of release from the debt.

II. We lost in Adam the right of probation and hope of eternal inheritance by any desire or effort we may make. His sin ended his probation and his hope of eternal inheritance by any future act of obedience to the law: the curse of that law, thus broken, blighted all future prospects; its penalty was, "Dust thou art, and unto dust shalt thou return." Gen. 3: 19.

From this helpless and hopeless condition we are redeemed by the sufferings and death of Christ, as stated in the text at the head of this chapter. "Christ hath redeemed us from the curse of the law, being made a curse for us."

III. The third item we will notice, which we lost in Adam, is life. This we have already anticipated in our remarks and quotations on other points, but we will now give it special attention. Paul tells us that "Adam was made a living soul," which agrees with the original account of his creation. "And the Lord God formed man of the dust of the ground, and breathed into his nostrils the breath of life, and man became a living soul" (Gen. 2 : 7), as also all other animals are said in scripture to be living souls. Gen. 1 : 20, 21, 24, 30; 7 : 22 — Heb. *nephesh*, living soul. As we have before remarked, this life was not eternal life. It is stated in the record to be LIFE — no more, no less. We shall use the terms *life* and *death* according to BIBLE THEOLOGY, and not according to the theology of Plato, Zoroaster, Pythagoras, Socrates, Aristotle, or other theologians of modern times, who adopt their philosophy on these points.

The term *soul*, in Gen. 2 : 7, is in the Hebrew *nephesh*, and found in the *Hebrew text* of the Old Testament seven hundred and fifty-two times, and is said to be the only word (with two unimportant exceptions — Isa. 57 : 16. Job 30 : 15) there rendered *soul*.

The word *nephesh* is first found in Gen. 1 : 20 — "And God said, Let the waters bring forth abundantly the moving creature that hath life;" *margin*, "soul;" Heb. *nephesh chaiyah* — soul living.

In Gen. 1 : 21, it occurs again, thus: "And God created great whales, and every living creature [*nephesh chaiyah*, living soul] that moveth, which the waters brought forth abundantly, after their kind, and every winged fowl after his kind." The third instance is in Gen. 1 : 24: "And God said, Let the earth bring forth the living creature (*nephesh chaiyah* — living soul) after his kind, cattle and creeping thing, and beast of the earth after his kind." The same occurs again in Gen. 1 : 30, where life (Heb. *margin*, a living soul —

nephesh chaiyah) is applied to every beast, fowl, and creeping thing. Here we have the *first* uses of the term *living soul* in the book of inspiration, and applied to all living creatures prior to the creation of man. This, therefore, must be the primary use of the term, it being first used by God himself. We find in Dr. Clarke's comment on the *Hebrew* term *nephesh chaiyah* this remark : "a general term to express all creatures endued with animal life, in any of its infinitely varied gradations."

We next find *nephesh chaiyah* applied to Adam. Gen. 2 : 7 : "And the Lord God formed man of the dust of the ground, and breathed into his nostrils the breath of life, and man became a living soul"— *nephesh chaiyah*. Such was Adam — a living soul. The tree of life was furnished, having the quality to continue his life, as is clearly shown in the Lord's statement (Gen. 3 : 22) : "And now, lest he put forth his hand, and take also of the tree of life, and eat, and live forever." The life of Adam, therefore, was a trial life, the continuance of which depended on his having access to the *tree of life*, while this privilege depended on his obedience to God. Had Adam continued in obedience during his term of probation, it appears, from the nature of the case, he would have received immortality as a gift from God. Not having done so, that blessing was not bestowed; therefore the penalty of the law could be executed, and Adam's life end. Such the record shows to have been done, as we have frequently quoted.

We have shown above, that the term *nephesh* in the Hebrew, and rendered soul in Gen. 2 : 7, is applied to beasts, birds, fishes, creeping things, &c., as properly as to man. It represents the being, the animal, or the man. The word is variously rendered in the Bible, as, man, men, him, himself, he, me, myself, we, her, herself, thee, thyself, they, themselves, yourselves, any, one, lust, ghost, thing, his own, she, mortally, will, tablets, the dead, fellows, greedy, breath, discontented, deadly, hearty, appetite, pleasure, fish, desire, mind, heart, creature, beast, body, life, reason, soul, — in all, forty-four different ways. In Gen. 2 : 7, as in most other cases, it refers to the whole being — man; and this is shown to be the primary use of the term.

The distinguished Hebrew lexicographer Parkhurst says, "As a noun, *nephesh* hath been supposed to signify the spiritual part of man, or what we commonly call his soul. I must for myself confess that I can find *no passage* where it hath undoubtedly this meaning."

Here we have good authority for rejecting the idea of any who claim that the soul — *nephesh* — is a spiritual part of man. We will now apply the principle as we find it defined in the Bible, and develop the subject. Adam was a living man; he disobeyed God, and lost his life; and when the law was executed upon him, he became a dead man — a dead *nephesh* — soul. In death all that constituted *man* returned to dust: " Dust thou art, and unto dust shalt THOU return." He being our progenitor, we are doomed to share the same penalty. We are "sold under sin," and the law asserts the claim on us because we were in him and are of him. The Lord states this very plainly. In giving the history of some of Adam's posterity, the record concerning Seth reads, "and he *died;*" of Enos, "and he *died;*" of Enoch, that he was "translated, that he should not see *death.*" This last, as also the case of Elijah, are exceptions from the condition of the race, and are recorded as such. The law as really held the posterity as it held Adam; all were equally involved until the claim of the law was met. This being so, MAN as a race was disposed of, and in prospect of the execution of the law, none are left alive. "Death passed upon all." And all were dead, prospectively; they had no rights, except to toil, suffer, and die; they cannot be put under discipline to amend and regain their lost estate. Should they be able to live strictly right from any given point, yet they are under sentence of death, and they must die; or, could they pay a ransom for their personal sins, still they are mortal, and must die. No promise of life beyond the penalty of the law could be made, no terms of mercy proposed; all were "sold under sin." Rom. 7: 14 The law took life, but could not give it back; consequently, Paul argues, "For if there had been a law given which could have given life, verily righteousness [justification to life] should have been by the law;" or, as the Emphatic Diaglott has it, "*able to make alive.*" Such being the condition of man by Adam's sin, we can see that there is a deep meaning in the scriptures which treat of Christ as man's Redeemer. The plan of universal redemption meets his necessity, releases man from the claim of that broken law, and puts him under new law ("the law of faith"), which we shall show in its proper place.

This raises the race from the condition of prisoners sentenced to destruction, to the condition of subjects, with rights and privileges, subject to discipline, with reward and punishment — life and death — set before them, in a state of probation or trial for eternal life.

THE DEATH OF CHRIST.

To effect this redemption the Son of God proposed to take on him Adam's original nature, and meet the claim of that violated law in his own person, as we shall show by the following testimony: " Who, being in the form of God, thought it not robbery to be equal with God, but made himself of no reputation, and took upon him the form of a servant, and was made in the likeness of men. And being found in fashion as a man, he humbled himself, and became obedient unto death, even the death of the cross. Wherefore God also hath highly exalted him, and given him a name which is above every name, that at the name of Jesus every knee should bow, of things in heaven, and things in earth, and things under the earth. And that every tongue should confess that Jesus Christ is Lord, to the glory of God the Father." Phil. 2 : 6–11. This passage conclusively shows that Christ not only becomes a sacrifice for man, but that this act places man "under law to Christ." Thus Paul continues to argue in his Epistles to the church : " For to this end Christ both died and rose, and revived, that he might be Lord both of the dead and living, . . . for we shall all stand before the judgment seat of Christ. For it is written, As I live, saith the

Lord, every knee shall bow to me, and every tongue shall confess to God. So then every one of us shall give account of himself to God." Rom. 14: 9-12.

In the face of such palpable facts, we are surprised that Christian men will teach that a large portion of our race will never come forth from death to give account of themselves.

The fact is clearly shown that the Son of God became our Mediator as soon as Adam sinned; as it is written, he is the "Lamb slain from the foundation of the world." Rev. 13: 8. On this principle we can understand the declaration of God to the serpent in Eden, "And I will put enmity between thee and the woman, and between thy seed and her seed; it shall bruise thy head, and thou shalt bruise his heel." Gen. 3: 15. Here is the bud of redemption in this promise. Christ himself had entered into covenant with the Father, to undo for man what sin had done, by "redeeming him from the curse of the law." From this time man passes into the hands of the purchaser, and becomes amenable to his law [of faith] or new covenant. Therefore the names of the race are recorded in the Lamb's book of life, to be retained or blotted out as their case may terminate at the close of their probation, of which we have spoken more fully in another chapter.

Let us hear the testimony of Christ on this point: "The Father loveth the Son, and hath given all things into his hands." John 3: 35. "For as the Father hath life in himself, so hath he given to the Son to have life in himself; and hath given him authority to execute judgment also, because he is the Son of man.'

John 5 : 26, 27. We will hear him again on this subject: "For the Son of man is come to save that which was lost." Matt. 18 : 11. It is true that something besides man was lost; but man is fully included in that loss. In another statement Jesus very clearly tells the price he gives for the redemption of the race of Adam: "And the bread that I will give is my flesh, which I will give for the life of the world." John 6 : 51. Again, when Jesus is speaking of the death he should die, he gives the idea in forcible language. "And I, if I be lifted up from the earth, will draw all men unto me." John 12 : 32.

These statements are of universal application, and clearly refer to the recovery of ALL the race from the bondage of death under Adamic law, to open the way for them to accept him as their eternal Saviour. While these scriptures may be dark sayings to those who do not "*study* to show themselves approved unto God, workmen that needeth not to be ashamed, rightly dividing the word of truth," and also to those who do not "search the Scriptures" with the key of faith, still "it is plain to him that understandeth;" and David says, "The entrance of thy word giveth light." Let us *enter* and *walk* in it.

We will now examine a prophecy of Isaiah on the subject of universal redemption. It will instruct us. "Yet it pleased the Lord [the Father] to bruise him [the Son]; he [the Father] hath put him [the Son] to grief: when thou [Father] shalt make his [Son's] soul an offering for sin, he [the Father] shall see his [Son's] seed, he [the Father] shall prolong [raise him to life] his days, and the pleasure of the Lord [the Father] shall prosper in his [Son's] hand. He [the Father] shall see of the travail of his [Son's] soul, and be satisfied: by his knowledge shall my righteous servant justify many." Isa. 53:10, 11. In the above language we are shown that the claim of the law was met by the travail of Christ's soul, or the making his soul an offering for sin, which satisfies justice, and redeems the race from the curse of the law. It should be particularly observed that we have here the prediction of a sacrifice for the sin of Adam (and the race in him) equal to the demand of the law against him. Adam — that living soul (*nephesh chaiyah*) — must return to dust, from whence he was taken. In the above prediction of Christ's sufferings, his SOUL (Heb. *nephesh chaiyah*) is made an offering for sin; consequently we hear him say, "My soul is exceeding sorrowful, even unto death." Matt. 26:38. "Reproach hath broken my heart, and I am full of heaviness; and I looked for some to take pity, but there was none; and for comforters, but I found none. They gave me also gall for my meat; and in my thirst they gave me vinegar to drink." Psa. 69:20, 21.

Christ is the only being in the universe who could redeem man from the curse of the law. Angels could not do it, for they did not possess man's nature, therefore had not an equivalent to pay. There was not one of Adam's race who could do this; all were "sold under sin." "None of them can by any means redeem his brother, nor give to God a ransom for him, that he should still live forever, and not see corruption." Psa.

49 : 7–9. Therefore Paul argues that Christ "took not on him the nature of angels, but he took on him the seed of Abraham." Heb. 2 : 16. He was of the seed of Abraham and of David, as pertaining to the flesh. for a special purpose, as Paul declares, as follows : " Bu when the fulness of the time was come, God sent fort! his Son, made of a woman, made under the law, to redeem them that were under the law." He then explains the primary object of this redemption from the Adamic law, viz., "that we might receive the adoption of sons." Gal. 4 : 4, 5. The Son of God had " life in himself ; " it was not a forfeited life. He obeyed the law, and had the right to life unlimited. The word declares, "Thou lovest righteousness and hatest wickedness; therefore God, thy God, hath anointed thee with the oil of gladness above thy fellows." Psa. 45 : 7. The apostle Peter, in speaking of him, says, " who did no sin, neither was guile found in his mouth." Therefore the law could not claim his life. He gave it for man ; and we hear Christ declaring it in the following language : " As the Father knoweth me, even so know I the Father. . . . Therefore doth my Father love me, because I lay down my life, that I might take it again. No man taketh it from me, but I lay it down of myself. I have power to lay it down, and I have power to take it again. This commandment have I received of my Father." John 10 : 15–18. "I have authority to lay it down, and I have authority to take it again." *American Bible Union Version.* — "This commission I have received from my Father." *Campbell's Version.* — Here we find one with a heart to redeem, an equivalent

to pay, and an opportunity to purchase man from the bonds of the law which held him in death. Christ is the one; and he says that he has the "power," "authority," "commission," "right," or privilege to lay down his life, and also to take it again, and that he received this from his Father; and again he tells us, "No man taketh it from me, but I lay it down of myself."

Dear reader, let this subject receive your careful attention. Christ voluntarily gave up life on which there was no claim by any other, and paid the claim of the law against man. He took it again, voluntarily, from the Father, who raised him from death to live forevermore, and to bestow eternal life on all who obey him. This is the foundation on which Paul builds while declaring the gospel of Christ: "Therefore as by the offence of one [Adam] judgment came upon all men to condemnation, even so by the righteousness of one [Christ] the free gift came upon all men unto justification of life. For as by one man's disobedience many were made sinners, so by the obedience of one shall many be made righteous." Rom. 5 : 18, 19.

We are fully aware that some make use of this class of texts to sustain an erroneous idea of religious theology by claiming from them more than they teach; but because of this we should not seek to overlook them, nor so interpret them as to make them teach less than their true import; neither should we fear to examine them closely, to learn what they do teach. Let us fairly examine the terms in *this* last passage, which deter many from giving it a proper place in theology with its true value: "*The free gift came upon all men unto justification of life."* Again: *"So by the obedience of one shall many* [all] *be made righteous."*

In the above passage the fact stands out too plainly to be denied, that the free gift to justification of life came upon all men. It is equally true that the *many made righteous* by the obedience of Christ comprehend the *same number that were made sinners* by the disobedience of Adam, while that number is expressly declared by Paul, in the 12th verse, to include ALL THE RACE. Such a conclusion is thought to be positive proof of universal salvation. This we shall not attempt to deny; but we claim that while it does teach universal salvation, it is only a salvation or redemption from Adamic bondage in death — redemption from the claim of that law which held the race in its possession. No more, no less.

Both these terms are used to express the relation persons hold to the claims of law, by having met those claims, or by having been released from charges brought against persons. Adam violated the law of God: its penalty was death; he became indebted to the law to that amount; this forfeited his right to live, also the right of his posterity, for they were in him, and follow his condition; it demanded himself and all of his; he could not free himself from the claim. But to meet this claim Christ "gave himself a ransom for all, to be testified in due time;" *not to save man from dying*, but to release him from that condition in which death placed him, and to *bring him back from death;* consequently Adam and his posterity have a reprieve from immediate death, and a right to be resurrected from death, when they do die. He is also justified in living again, for the *free gift to live again* after death came upon all men by virtue of the ransom which Christ gave. Man is made righteous in the eyes of that law, having met its claim and been purchased out from its dominion by Christ's death. Christ did not die to save Adam and his race from dying, but to purchase them out from the condition in which they were held by virtue of the law. This having been accomplished for man, the law has no further claim, and man is *made righteous* by a full release from it. Man now owes his life to his Benefactor who loosed the bonds of death from him that he might live again. Consequently man is under law to Christ, and not under Adamic law, or the law Adam violated. See 1 Cor. 9, 21. This being so, we have the fact freely stated in what are often considered universalists' texts, such as we have already noticed; and others we will now quote on this point: "For there is one God, and one Mediator between God and man, the man Christ Jesus, who gave himself a ransom for ALL, to be testified in due time." 1 Tim. 2 : 5, 6. And yet another like it: "For therefore we both labor and suffer reproach, because we trust in the living God, who is the Saviour of ALL MEN, specially of those that believe." 1 Tim. 4 : 10.

In this last passage there is mention made of two salvations — one of *all men;* a second and *special* one, *of those that believe.* The first is salvation from death by Adam, through the death of Christ. The second is salvation from the second death for our own sins, through the atoning blood of Christ. Jude calls the first "the common salvation," in distinction from "the [new covenant] faith once delivered to the saints." Jude 3.

All this class of scriptures, of which we have quoted only a few passages, clearly shows the rescue, redemption, and salvation of the race of man out from the dominion of death, and out from all disabilities which came upon them by Adam's sin, freeing them from that wherein they were bound. This redemption was provided at the fall of Adam; it was prospective, and embraced in the early promises; it gave a reprieve from immediate execution of the law; gave man a new law, bringing the race under responsibility to their Redeemer, to be henceforth accountable to him, for the *life given them by him*, to believe in him and obey his law while living in the day of probation granted, as they are to be judged by him for their conduct under his law, which is called the "new covenant," "royal law," "law of faith," "perfect law of liberty," "law of the spirit of life," &c., in distinction from that law called the "old covenant," "law of condemnation," "law of sin and death," "law of works," &c. Therefore Paul states, "For to this end Christ died and rose, and revived, that he might be Lord both of the dead and living: . . for we shall all stand before the judgment seat of Christ." Rom. 14: 9, 11.

In conclusion, we remark, the foregoing argument and proof show, —

I. That Adam, by transgression, brought *weakness, sickness, sorrow, and death* upon himself and his race.

II. That the race were thereby excluded from all rights of existence and probation for immortality and eternal life.

III. That Christ, by the suffering of death in the flesh, has purchased the race from that condition, and PROSPECTIVELY REDEEMED them from all the evils Adam brought upon them, as a preparatory measure for giving them probation and pardon for their own sins, through faith in his shed blood, which is argued in our chapter on the atonement.

CHAPTER VI.

THE NECESSITY FOR AN ATONEMENT.

Atonement presupposes two parties at variance, or one party opposed to another, as in our subject — God, the offended, and man the offender in unreconciliation to God. We propose to examine this subject under three heads.

First. The necessity for an atonement.

Second. The universal atonement by the death of Christ.

Third. The conditional atonement by the blood of Christ.

I. The necessity for an atonement.

In entering upon this subject, we shall consider man, first, in his alienated and lost condition, together with the effect of his transgression upon his forfeited inheritance and upon all the animal creation.

The Scriptures abundantly show that the condition of Adam in his fallen state is the condition of the race. "When we were enemies, we were reconciled to God by the death of his Son. . . . Wherefore, as by one man sin entered into the world, and death by sin, and so death passed upon all men, for that [in whom — *margin*] all have sinned." Rom. 5 : 10, 12. Our race was a unit in Adam: we shall therefore use Adam in this chapter as the representative of the race, and will apply to them equally as to him.

The word ATONE, or reconcile, is compounded of *at* and *one*, and signifies "to unite or agree."

ATONE. To agree, to be in concordance, to accord.

ATONEMENT. Agreement, concord, reconciliation after enmity or controversy. — *Webster*.

The texts at the head of this article plainly show that the condition of Adam under the first transgression was the condition of all the race in their relation to God and his law. All were sinners, and "death passed upon all, for all had sinned." All were unreconciled, and enemies to God; and Rom. 5 : 10 shows the remedy God had provided, viz. : " When we were enemies, we were reconciled to God by the death [not the blood] of his Son." Also, in Rev. 13 : 8, Christ is stated to be the "Lamb slain from the foundation of the world." Thus fallen under sin, unreconciled to God, and an enemy of God, Adam was under sentence of death: " Dust thou art, and unto dust shalt thou return." This is not eternal death, nor the death of an immortal soul, as some vainly imagine, but the death of the man whom God had formed of the dust of the ground; and in this condition Adam had no rights but to die, and in him the race must perish without the mediation of a third party. The violated law offers no remedy. It could not give life; it knows no mercy. Thus the apostle argues : " He that despised Moses' law died without mercy under two or three witnesses." Heb. 10 : 28. And again : " No flesh shall be justified in his sight [by the law], for by the law is the knowledge of sin." Rom. 3 : 20. Also, in further proof of this position, we hear Paul saying, " For if righteousness come by the law, then Christ is dead in vain." Gal. 2 : 21. Consequently all were lost.

In this condition, without a mediator and atonement, man had no rights; God could not treat with him as a free agent; he was disposed of; sold under sin, he must die; and no progeny or descendants could follow, else the proverb, "The fathers have eaten sour grapes, and the children's teeth are set on edge" (Ezek. 18: 2), would be most true and just; for God would have suffered a poor, fallen, degenerate, sinful, dying race to issue from a vile and corrupt stock, who had become thus vile and corrupt by his own voluntary act, and for which issue (who could have had no voluntary part in bringing upon themselves this wretched condition) he had provided no help, and to whom no possible hope could be held out by any effort which could be made, either on their own part or on the part of those who were the authors of their existence.

The injustice of such a conclusion, and of this proverb in Israel, is fully shown in that God hath provided a remedy, and declared to the author of this evil, "The seed of the woman shall bruise [Heb. *crush*] the serpent's head." And in view of this provided remedy, he inquires, "*What mean ye, that ye use this proverb concerning the land of Israel*, saying, The fathers have eaten sour grapes, and the children's teeth are set on edge? As I live, saith the Lord God, ye shall not have occasion any more to use this proverb in Israel. Behold, all souls are mine: as the soul of the father, so also the soul of the son, is mine: the soul that sinneth, it shall die." Ezek. 18: 2, 4. We find the same fact stated by Jeremiah also: " In those days they shall say no more, The fathers have eaten a sour grape, and the children's teeth are set on edge; but every one shall die for his own iniquity; every man that eateth the sour grape, his teeth shall be set on edge." Jer. 31: 29, 30. He then speaks of the remedy, thus: "Behold, the days come, saith the Lord, that I will make a new covenant with the house of Israel and with the house of Judah." Verse 31. And not only so, but, had God found no ransom, and Adam died without issue, the whole plan in creating him would have failed, and the devil would have triumphed. Let us read the purpose of God: "And God said, Let us make man in our image, after our likeness, and let them have dominion over the fish of the sea, and over the fowl of the air, and over the cattle, and over all the earth, and over every creeping thing that creepeth upon the earth. . . . And God blessed them, and God said unto them, Be fruitful, and multiply, and replenish the earth, and subdue it, and have dominion," &c. Gen. 1: 26–28. Nor would it avail to reason that God could have created another man in the place of Adam: his purpose in regard to Adam would still have been a failure. And not only this, but Satan would have pursued the same device with the new-made man. But this would not do: Satan must be foiled; his head must be crushed. Amen.

Having shown the hopeless state of man by Adam's transgression so far as any effort which he could make to reclaim himself, or anything the law could do for him, we now pass to consider the effects of Adam's transgression upon the earth and the animal creation.

This is presented to us first in Gen. 3: 17: "Because thou hast . . . eaten of the tree of which I commanded thee, saying, Thou shalt not eat of it, CURSED is the GROUND for thy sake; in sorrow shalt thou eat of it all the days of thy life. Thorns also and thistles shall it bring forth unto thee, and thou shalt eat the herb of the field . . . till thou return unto the ground." Paul gives us a grand comment on this: "For the creature was made subject to vanity, not willingly, but by reason of him who hath subjected the same in hope. . . . For we know that the whole creation [every creature — *margin*] groaneth and travaileth in pain together until now." Rom. 8: 20, 22. "For the creature was subjected to suffering." *Whiting.* — "For the creation was made subject to vanity." *Union Version.*

These scriptures and many others show clearly that the evil results of Adam's sin fell not only on him, but upon all the creation which God had pronounced *good*, "VERY GOOD." But this point we have argued more fully in another chapter of this work. In view of these facts our loss in Adam may be summed up as follows: —

1. We lost in Adam our right to live. This right was involved in the command (Gen. 1: 28), "Be fruitful, multiply, and replenish the earth, and subdue it." Also in Gen. 2: 16: "And the Lord God commanded the man, saying, Of all the trees of the garden thou mayest freely eat." This includes the tree of life, whose fruit was not to give life, but to preserve life. We do not argue that Adam's life was eternal life. No term of time was given by which to measure it. Its perpetuity depended on his obedience to the command of God. Thus it is written: "But of the tree of the knowledge of good and evil, thou shalt not eat of it, for in the day thou eatest thereof, thou shalt surely die." Gen. 2: 17.

2. We lost in Adam the *prospect of eternal life*, and dominion over the earth (Gen. 1 : 28), which was based on the condition of obedience to the law of God. Adam had right to the tree of life, which would have preserved his life forever. See Gen. 3 : 22. "Lest he put forth his hand, and take also of the tree of life, and eat, and live forever." He had this prospect laid before him in the *benediction*, "And God blessed them, and God said unto them, Be fruitful, and multiply, and replenish the earth, and subdue it, and have dominion," &c. Gen. 1 : 28. This dominion is referred to by the Psalmist: "Thou madest him [man] to have dominion over the works of thy hands." Psa. 8 : 6. We find Paul also arguing upon it as a matter of much importance. He quotes Psa. 8 : 6, and refers it to " the world to come." Heb. 2 : 5, 9. Again, we find a graphic statement of this matter by the prophet : " And thou, O tower of the flock, the stronghold of the daughter of Zion, unto thee shall it come [what come?], even the *first dominion; the* KINGDOM shall come to the daughter of [new] Jerusalem." To this add the statements of Christ, " Blessed are the meek, for they shall inherit the earth" (Matt. 5 : 5), and again, " Come, ye blessed of my Father, inherit the *kingdom prepared for you from the* FOUNDATION *of the* WORLD." Matt. 25 : 34.

In the above texts Jesus refers to the same dominion presented to Adam ; and that it was an eternal dominion is settled by Christ's words in the 46th verse of Matt. 25th : "And these [the wicked] shall go away into everlasting punishment, but the righteous into life eternal." All this was in prospect for Adam on condition of obedience to God, and was lost by his transgression.

3. We lost in Adam a state of probation or trial preparatory to eternal life, and the dominion. Gen. 1: 28. Psa. 8: 6. If Adam had obeyed the law of God, which he might and ought to have done, no death would have entered nor curse blighted the fair creation of God, which he had pronounced "very good." Then we, his posterity, in pursuance of that law would have gained the promised dominion. But alas! in the hour of temptation, by a single act of disobedience, his prospects were blighted in a moment, and all was lost. "By one man sin entered into the world, and death by sin; and so death passed upon all men, for that [being in him] all have sinned." Rom. 5: 12.

4. We lost in Adam a good, sound, and healthful organism, both physical and mental; for thus it is written: "And God saw everything that he had made, and behold, it was very good." Gen. 1: 31. In this respect man was holy, else God created and gave breath of life to an unholy being. We do not use the term *holy* as a moral attribute in reference to character or action, but in reference to his physical, mental, and moral organism; for, though thus created, Adam formed a very unholy moral character. We find the word defined thus: "Holy — whole, entire, complete, sound, unimpaired." *Webster*. The term *holy* was once applied to a spot of ground: "The ground whereon thou standest is holy ground." It is also used in reference to other things, as, the holy Sabbath, holy temple, holy city, holy vessels, holy oil, &c.

Let no one therefore conclude that, because Adam lost for himself and his race a good physical, mental, and moral organism, and that because Christ by his death will effect a restitution of all things, the wicked are entitled to a good moral character. This does not follow: a good moral character in God's sight is gained by faith in the atoning blood of Christ. Much theological speculation has obtained in our world as to what was man's original nature; the nature and effect of the tree of life; the character and object of the tree of the knowledge of good and evil; and of the nature of the penalty of the law of God which Adam incurred by his sin, and which now holds his race. Although we have discussed these points in other parts of this work, yet a few remarks may be in place here.

We are told (Gen. 2:7) that man was formed of the "dust of the ground;" that the Lord breathed [*blew*] into his nostrils the breath of life, and man [formed of dust] became "a living soul." That this living soul was formed of dust is so plainly stated that we think no unbiassed mind can fail to see it. This man was made in the image of God, both male and female. Gen. 1:27. Here, again, theologians have gone to the end of their wits to ascertain what this *image* consisted in, as pertaining to man. Some have claimed that it was immortality; but we find the term *image* defined thus: "A representation or similitude of any person or thing formed of a material substance, as an image wrought out of stone, wood, or wax." *Webster.* "God formed man in his own IMAGE." Jesus asks concerning the penny (Matt. 22:20), "Whose is this *image* and superscription? They say unto him, Cæsar's." We point to man, and ask, "Whose image is he?" The Scripture answers, "God's." Gen. 1 : 2, 7 ; 5 : 1 ; 9 : 6. "Adam begat a son in his own likeness, after his own *image*, and called his name Seth." But Adam was in the likeness and *image* of God; hence his son Seth must have been in the same likeness and image. Will any one claim that Adam begat an immortal soul?

Man is a living soul : the beasts are also living souls (Gen. 1 : 30, *margin*, Heb., *a living soul*). Man received from God the breath of life, or spirit of life. So also have the beasts (Gen. 7 : 21, 22, *margin*, Heb., the breath of the spirit of life). "For that which befalleth the sons of men befalleth beasts, even one thing befalleth them : as the one dieth, so dieth the other ; yea, they have *all one breath;* so that a man hath no preeminence above a beast; for all are vanity, all go to one place, all are of the dust (Gen. 2 : 19 ; 3 : 19), and all return to dust again." Eccl. 3 : 19, 21.

The same Scripture terms which are claimed to prove the natural immortality of Adam, or his consciousness in death, may be claimed with equal propriety to prove the immortality of the beasts, and their consciousness in death. Take the atonement by the death of Jesus Christ out of the Bible, and the future of man after death would be an eternal blank; hence Paul argues, "If the dead rise not, then is not Christ risen" (1 Cor. 15 : 16, 18, 19) ; "then they also which are fallen *asleep* in Christ are PERISHED. If in THIS LIFE only we have hope in Christ, we are of all men most miserable ;" and closes this point by saying, "If after the manner of men

I have fought with beasts at Ephesus, what advantageth it me *if the dead rise not:* let us eat and drink, for to-morrow we die." Verse 32.

If Adam was made immortal he could not have died; but Adam did die; therefore he was not immortal. Immortality is an innate principle of undying nature, not to be lost by a change of circumstances. We are now prepared to inquire, What were the nature and object of the tree of life in its relation to man?

It is certain that its properties were not to give life, for Adam had received that from his Maker before he saw the tree of life. Nor was it to make him immortal, for, as we have shown, Adam was made mortal (like other animals), to generate his species, with the prospect of immortality and dominion before him; and it would seem absurd to suppose that God would give him free access to the tree whose fruit would change that nature from mortal to immortality, before he had fairly entered upon the work assigned him (Gen. 1: 28), for it is a fair and reasonable conclusion that the two trees in the midst of the garden, viz., the tree of life, and the tree of the knowledge of good and evil, would first attract his attention; and being forbidden to eat of the latter, he would first partake of the former.

Eternal life would be the inevitable product or result of immortality, while free access to, and partaking of, the tree of life, would preserve the life of a mortal man forever (Gen. 3: 22), as well as nine hundred or one hundred years, and yet not make him immortal, as immortality is not the result of life, but eternal life is the legitimate result of immortality. Again, Paul informs us that immortality is an object or condition to be sought "by patient continuance in well doing" (Rom. 2 : 7), and is recompensed with eternal life. Neither of these did Adam possess, nor did they grow in nature's garden, but were placed in the distance as an object of pursuit, and to be given to the victors when the race was ended.

> Onward, then; let wisdom speed thy flight,
> The victor's crown to wear.

What, then, was the object of the tree of life? We think Adam (as all other animals) was constituted to generate his own species and supply the earth with man (Gen. 1 : 28), subject to change, decay, and loss of life, by a change of circumstances. If he eat of the forbidden fruit he must "surely die;" being in this condition, the tree of life was provided (not to give, but) to perpetuate his life until his work of replenishing the earth and subduing it (preparatory to his having dominion over it, provided he did not forfeit it by sin) is done. This is clearly proved from Gen. 3 : 22 : "And now, lest he put forth his hand and take also of the tree of life, and eat and live forever." Adam had free access to the tree of life while in the garden (Gen. 2 : 16) : if left there after he sinned, with free access still to that fruit, such was its nutritious power to counteract the waste of his nature (not to change that nature to immortality, but to preserve his life), he would never die, and God's denunciation against sin would never be fulfilled; hence the Lord "drove out the man, and placed cherubims and a flaming sword to keep the way of the tree of life." Gen. 3 : 24.

With these remarks upon the tree of life we will now consider the tree of the knowledge of good and evil, the eating of whose fruit has brought so much suffering and death into the world. Various opinions have been put forth on this subject. Some have taught that God intended that man should eat of its fruit, notwithstanding he forbade him to eat thereof, because they can see no other way in which man could obtain the knowledge of *good* and *evil*, and they cannot admit that God would keep man an ignoramus all his days, not knowing that he was naked, &c.

Without stopping to examine these opinions, we will give our readers what we think the true light on this subject. Although the Scripture account of this tree is very brief, yet enough is revealed to give a just clew to the true idea.

First, then, we remark that the name of this tree, like that of the tree of life, and many other Scripture names, is expressive of its peculiar characteristic in its relation to man, as Abraham is a name expressive of his relation to all nations —"For a father of many nations have I made thee." Gen. 17 : 5. The name Ishmael is expressive of God's care for him ; that is, " God shall hear." Gen. 16 : 11. Israel is a name expressive of his relation to God; i. e., "a prince of God." Gen. 32 : 28 ; see *margin*. So the tree of life is expressive of its effect on man if permitted free access to its fruits. Gen. 3 : 22. Thus the tree of the knowledge of good and evil also is expressive of its design to give man the knowledge of good and evil. Gen. 3 : 22. But here comes the grand secret, says the objector. How could man obtain the knowledge embodied in the tree without eating its fruit? And if it was designed to give man that knowledge, why was he forbidden to partake of it?

These are fair questions, and we will endeavor to give them a candid answer, in the light of truth, premising first that there are two ways of obtaining property or knowledge; as when a friend exhibits to my view a purse of gold, with the proposition that I should serve him a term of years for its possession. He hangs it up on his premises, and forbids my touching it on pain of forfeiting my claim. Now, I may obtain the purse by an honest, faithful performance of the duties imposed, enduring the trial and labor to the end of the term; and this would be the legitimate influence of the sight of the purse and the prospect of obtaining it; or, refusing to endure the toil in prospect of the good, I may break the contract, steal the purse, and suffer the consequences.

Again, my friend may have an amount of useful knowledge, and commit it to paper, with the intention of giving it to the public in a legal manner; but I, in my covetousness, may steal his manuscript and put myself in possession of the knowledge it contained, at the risk of the consequences; or I may wait and receive it lawfully upon the terms he has the right to prescribe.

All just law is designed to give the knowledge of good and evil, and it is our duty to obtain that knowledge by a careful study, observation, and conformity to that law, and not by transgressing and suffering its penalty. In the first case it justifies, in the latter it condemns us. "A prudent man [by study and right reason] foreseeth the evil and hideth himself, but the simple pass on and are punished." Prov. 22: 3.

Adam, before he was placed in the garden, had no means of knowing good and evil, like the children who came out of Egypt having no knowledge (Deut. 1 : 39) between good and evil; but when placed in the garden, under law and restriction, to discipline and test his fidelity to his rightful Sovereign and Lawgiver, the way was open for him to obtain the knowledge of good and evil, gradually and lawfully, by bringing his intellectual and moral faculties into requisition and trial. See Heb. 5 : 14. "But strong meat belongeth to them that are of full age, even those who by reason of use [exercise] have their *senses* [reasoning faculties] *exercised* to *discern* both *good* and *evil*." This text fully confirms the position we have taken. The child cannot know good and evil until he is brought in contact with, or placed under law (see Deut. 1 : 39; Isa. 7 : 15, 16; also 2 Sam. 19 : 35), nor can an old man in his second childhood.

We think that no well-enlightened mind will ever claim that one MUST disobey a just law and suffer its penalty in order to learn the difference between good and evil. This he should learn by a careful study of the nature and intention of just law. Adam was subjected to the government of law, with its penalty before him, to test his fidelity to his only rightful Lawgiver: he was tempted; he transgressed that law, and fell. Gen. 3 : 17. Jesus was placed in similar circumstances when on earth in the commencement of his work. "God sent forth *his Son*, made of a woman, made *under the law*." Gal. 4 : 4. "He was tempted of the devil." Matt. 4 : 1. "He was in all points tempted like as we are, yet *without sin*." Heb. 4 : 15. He passed the ordeal in triumph, and therefore " he is able to redeem them that were under the law" (Gal. 4 : 5), and hence to restore that which was lost by the fall. Amen.

Having shown, as we think, that the tree whose fruit Adam was forbidden to eat, was designed to give the knowledge of *good* and *evil* in a lawful manner, we now inquire, What was the penalty of that law which Adam transgressed in eating its fruit?

The Lord declared that penalty to be death. Adam was formed of the dust of the ground; he did not live until he received the breath of life from God; but when he did receive it, he became literally a living soul (Gen. 2 : 7), as all other animals were. Gen. 1 : 30, *margin*. It was this living soul that God placed in the garden, and to whom he said, "Thou shalt surely die." Gen. 2 : 17. This is the first time the word was ever used in this world, so far as the record shows; and if it ever has its literal and primary signification in the Bible, we think it must be here. Adam's life was literal, and death is its opposite; God so defines it. Gen. 3 : 19. " In the sweat of thy face shalt thou eat bread till thou RETURN UNTO THE GROUND, FOR OUT OF IT WAST THOU TAKEN, FOR DUST THOU [living soul, Adam] ART, AND UNTO DUST SHALT THOU RETURN."

If this is not death in its most literal sense, we fail to see what language can express it. This is the whole penalty of the law —"The wages of sin is death" (Rom. 6 : 23), the living soul being deprived of that life which he received from God when he breathed or blew into his nostrils the breath of life, which gave him life literally; and to this agrees the whole tenor of Scripture.

"Thou takest away their BREATH; they DIE and return to THEIR DUST." Psa. 104: 29. This text is spoken not only of man, but of all flesh; this is the definition given by inspiration; we know of no lexicon which gives any other as the primary definition of the term *death*. "If he [God] gather unto himself his spirit and his breath, all flesh shall perish together, and man shall *return again unto dust*." Job 34: 14, 15. "When lust hath conceived, it bringeth forth sin [as in Eve when tempted to eat the forbidden fruit], and sin, when it is finished, bringeth forth death." James 1: 15. This is the fruit, the finality, the entire fulfilment of the penalty of the broken law; this death penalty fell alike on Adam and all his posterity, they being a unit in him; this is fully shown by Paul in his triumphant argument in defence of the literal resurrection of the dead. 1 Cor. ch. 15. After showing that Christ literally died, and as literally rose from the grave and lived again, he says, "For since by man [Adam] came death, by man [Jesus Christ] came also the resurrection of the dead [living again]; "for as in Adam all [men] die [the race being a unit in him], even so in CHRIST [he assuming their position in death for their redemption, Gal. 3: 13] shall all [men] be made alive [raised from the dead], but every man in his own order."

Compare the above with Paul to the Romans: "By one man [Adam] sin entered into the world, and death by sin, and so death passed upon all men." Rom. 5: 12.

If these scriptures do not prove the penalty of the law which Adam incurred for himself and his race to be literal death, the extinction of literal life, the returning of the living soul to the dust from whence he was taken (Gen. 3 : 23), then we conclude there is no force in the doctrine of the death of Christ as an atonement for our race.

We have thus summed up our losses in Adam under these four general heads, which we think involve the whole consequence of the first transgression; this brings us to consider their recovery by the death (not by the blood) of Christ, in the first branch of the atonement, which we will do in the following chapter.

CHAPTER VII.

THE UNIVERSAL ATONEMENT BY THE DEATH OF CHRIST.

PART FIRST.

The subject of atonement is revealed to us, in the Scriptures, in two parts, or branches; the first being accomplished by the DEATH of Christ under the FIRST, or OLD COVENANT, or LAW OF WORKS (to redeem man from the curse of that law, Christ being made a curse for man), and is *unconditional* and *universal* in its application to, and its effects upon, all our race.

The second is accomplished by the BLOOD of Christ in the NEW COVENANT, or LAW OF FAITH, and is CONDITIONAL (1 John 1 : 7, 9), being limited in its application to adults, and in its final blessings to believers. We will now examine the *first branch*.

THE ATONEMENT BY THE DEATH OF CHRIST.

In the former chapter we have defined the terms ATONE and ATONEMENT, but it will be in place here also. ATONE is compounded of *at* and *one*, and signifies to unite or agree, to be in concordance, to accord. ATONEMENT, agreement, concord, reconciliation after enmity or controversy. — *Webster.*

Let us now examine the following scriptures: "For since by man [Adam] came death, by man [Jesus] came also the resurrection of the dead; for as in Adam all [men] die, even so in Christ shall all [men] be made alive" (1 Cor. 15 : 21, 22) ; or, "As by Adam all die, so by the anointed also will all be restored to life."—*Em. Diaglott.*

In this scripture it is fully demonstrated that as Adam's sin brought literal death upon all his race, so Christ removes that literal death from all that race. But it may be asked, By virtue of what act of Jesus Christ is this penalty removed? The Scripture answers, By his death.

We have before stated that the atonement is revealed to us in the Scriptures in two parts or branches, relating to two covenants. The first branch, being effected by the death of Christ, relates to the first or old covenant, and results in the removal of the consequences of the first or Adamic transgression, and is therefore universal in its application to, and its effects upon, the race and the lost inheritance. The second branch is by the blood of Christ, and relates to the second or new covenant. We have also stated that our race was a unit in Adam; the sentence of the law against him was therefore equally against the race. "By one man sin entered into the world, and death by sin, and so death passed upon all men, for that all have sinned." Rom. 5 : 12.

Thus death rested upon the unit and involved the race in him: all are dead. *Death passed upon all.* All being prospectively dead, no covenant, contract, or agreement could be made with him, he having no rights but to die; hence the race must become extinct by the execution of the unit. Therefore, so far as anything he could do to rescue himself, all was lost. In this state of the case, the Son of God interposes in man's behalf, covenants with the Father to assume man's original nature and responsibilities, magnify and honor the law which had been broken, redeem him from death, and give him another day of probation, under another law or covenant. This great fact is plainly set forth in the following texts: "Who, being in the form of God, thought it not robbery to be equal with God, but made himself of no reputation, and took upon him the form of a servant, and was made in the likeness of men; and being found in fashion as a man, he humbled himself, and became obedient unto death, even the death of the cross. Wherefore God also hath highly exalted him, and given him a name which is above every name, that at the name of Jesus every knee shall bow, of things in heaven, and things in earth, and things under the earth; and that every tongue should confess that Jesus Christ is Lord, to the glory of God the Father." Phil. 2 : 6, 11. And again: "For God so loved the *world* that he gave his only begotten Son [to redeem the world and lay a foundation for hope], that whosoever believeth in him should not perish, but have everlasting life." John 3 : 15. "Surely he hath borne our griefs, and carried our sorrows [shared them with us]." Isa. 53 : 4. "He took part of the same." Heb. 2 : 14. "We did esteem him stricken, smitten of God [not of man, but in man's behalf], and afflicted [we esteemed him thus treated on his own account]. But he was wounded for our transgressions, he was bruised for our iniquities, . . . with his stripes we are healed [redeemed from the curse of the law — death]." "As the Father knoweth me, even so know I the Father [showing a perfect agreement between them]. . . . Therefore doth the Father love me, because I lay down my life that I might take it again. *No man taketh it from me, but I lay it down of myself* [his own voluntary act to redeem Adam, that from his race he might procure a people under the new covenant, washed in his own blood, to inherit the redeemed earth]. I have power to lay it down, and I have power to take it again. This commandment have I received from my Father." — "I have *authority*," &c. "This *commission* have I received from my Father." "This *right* or *privilege*." See *Campbell's Version*, also *Emphatic Diaglott, American Bible Union*, and other versions on this text. John 10 : 15, 18.

The above scriptures, and many more which might be quoted, clearly establish the fact that an agreement or covenant was made between the Father and the Son from the foundation of the world, that Christ should come in the flesh (see 2 John 7), fulfil the law (Matt. 5 : 18), suffer, the just for the unjust (1 Pet. 3 : 18), and thereby redeem Adam, and in him the race, from death, and the earth from the curse, and place him on a second probation, under a law (of faith in Christ). Gal. 3 : 13. 1 Cor. 9 : 21), which, when broken, could only give life on repentance towards God, and faith towards our Lord Jesus Christ, and whose penalty is the second death. Rev. 21 : 8.

In pursuance of this agreement, when it was time, or

"when the fulness of the time was come, God sent forth his Son, made of a woman, made under the law, to redeem them that were under the law, that we might [under the new covenant, or law of faith] receive the adoption of sons." Gal. 4:4, 5.

Thus Adam, and in him the race who had by the first transgression been prospectively stricken from a state of life and probation, and over whom the dark pall of death was cast, were, by virtue of the above-named covenant, reprieved from the immediate execution of the sentence of the violated law, and their names *placed in the* LAMB'S BOOK OF LIFE, of which we shall say more in another place. And this redemption forms the first branch of the atonement, and is accomplished by the DEATH (not the blood) of Christ, as we shall now proceed to show.

DEATH OF CHRIST.

We remark, then, that this atonement is effected by the sacrifice of Christ in his death.

"Christ our passover is sacrificed for us." 1 Cor. 5:7. "But now once in the end of the world hath he appeared to put away sin by the sacrifice of himself." Heb. 9:26. When Paul is speaking of the atoning sacrifices of the law, he says (Heb. 10:1, 4) they were shadows of good things to come; yet they could never remove the sins brought to view by them year by year; they only shadow forth the sufferings of Christ and the effect of his blood on believers. All sacrifices requiring the slaying of the victim show that the law under which they are offered has been broken, and that its penalty is death; and as the law of works could not give life (Gal. 3:21), it knew no mercy. Heb. 2:2, and 10:28. Therefore it did not require, of necessity, the shedding of blood, but the death of the victim, which might have been accomplished without the shedding of blood. But the atonement of Christ contemplated not only the redemption of our race from death, but also the forgiveness of the sins of the people against the new covenant, which would be an act of mercy through his intercession as high priest by his own blood. "For without the shedding of blood there is no remission." Heb. 9:22.

The types of the law which shadow forth this atonement are deeply instructive to Bible students. The first one we shall present is

THE LORD'S PASSOVER,

Instituted in Egypt; yet other sacrifices had been offered by all the ancient patriarchs, from Abel down to Abraham, all teaching the same grand truths; yea, we suggest that the first sacrifice ever offered was in Eden, where the law was first broken, and the curse pronounced, where the sentence of the violated law was declared, and the first promise of redemption was made. The seed of the woman shall bruise the serpent's head. For we are informed (Gen. 3:21) that the Lord God made coats of skins, and clothed Adam and his wife, after they had sinned, and saw their nakedness, and were ashamed.

These skins may have been obtained from animals

offered under the direction of the Lord, as a sacrifice, and shadow *of the atonement.* Covering their nakedness and hiding their shame may have been suggestive of the protection provided *in the atonement.*

But in the institution of the Lord's passover in Egypt, the subject of sacrifices is clearly emblematical. The passover lamb was slain on the night of the exode from Egypt; the body of the lamb constituted a feast; all the people ate of it. "And thus shall ye eat it, with your loins girded, your shoes on your feet, your staff in your hand; and ye shall eat it in haste; it is the Lord's passover." Exod. 12: 11. Nothing of this consecrated lamb was to remain until the morning; or, if any part did remain, it must be burned with fire. See verse 10. Thus all the congregation of Israel were physically nourished by the flesh of the lamb. Yet only Caleb and Joshua, of all that vast multitude over twenty years old (Num. 14: 29, 31), entered the promised land. Deut. 1: 35.

The body of this lamb is a type of the body of Jesus that was broken for sin; it became food for the whole nation; but not so with the blood: that was used for a very different purpose, for thus it is written: "And ye shall take a bunch of hyssop and dip it in the blood of the lamb that is in the basin, and strike the lintel and the two side-posts with the blood that is in the basin, and none of you shall go out at the door of his house until the morning." Exod. 12: 7, 22.

This blood thus sprinkled upon the door of the houses of Israel was to protect (not the whole congregation, for they were not all in danger) the first born in every family from the power of the destroying angel which passed through the land of Egypt to slay the first born of every house in Egypt, both man and beast. Exod. 12 : 12. Only a remnant, therefore, of Israel were saved by the blood (see Heb. 11 : 28), while all of the people ate of the flesh. And this type brings to our mind the Lamb slain from the foundation of the world. In this paschal institution we have the following ideas presented : —

I. The paschal lamb is a symbol of Christ.

II. Its death is a type of Christ's death.

III. Its blood is a type of the blood of Jesus.

It commemorates Israel's exode or departure from Egypt; it anticipates the atonement of Christ and the marriage supper of the Lamb in the kingdom of God (see Rev. 19 : 8, 9), for thus it is written : "Jesus said unto them, With desire I have desired to eat this passover with you before I suffer; for I say unto you, I will not any more eat thereof until it be fulfilled in the kingdom of God." Luke 22 : 15, 16. He is brought as a lamb to the slaughter. Isa. 53 : 7.

These types have their antitypes thus : As the typical lamb sacrificed at the passover was food for ALL the congregation, so the flesh or body of the Lamb of God in his death, pledged from the foundation of the world (Rev. 13 : 8), became a sacrifice to redeem Adam and all his race from the curse of the violated law. Gal. 3 : 13. Not that he forgave the crime and saved him from dying, or from suffering the penalty of that law, for then none would die; but to raise the flesh — the body — from the dark grave to life again. "For to this end Christ both *died* and rose and revived, that he might be Lord both of the dead and living." Rom. 14: 9. This is in proof that Christ must die to obtain authority over the dead, and the reason is obvious when we consider that the law knew no mercy. Gal. 3 : 21. The law demanded full satisfaction, but it could not restore life; hence no righteousness, justification, or release could be obtained from it; otherwise "Christ is dead in vain." Gal. 2 : 21.

If no other object had been in view but redemption from the grave, no blood need have been shed, for the shedding of blood implies remission of sins (Lev. 17 : 11. Heb. 9 : 22), and no remission was admitted by that law; if therefore Jesus had died without shedding one drop of his blood, the law would have been satisfied. We find in the case of Adam's sin and condemnation, the execution of the sentence of the law was suspended under the mediation of Christ, at the time, as illustrated in the typical mediation of Moses. Exod. 32 : 9, 14. While Moses was in Mount Sinai, receiving the law on tables, the people made the golden calf. "And the Lord said unto Moses, I have seen this people, and behold, it is a stiff-necked people; now, therefore, let me alone, that my wrath may wax hot against them, and that I may consume them." But Moses pleads in their behalf, and says, "Turn from thy fierce wrath, and repent of this evil against thy people;" and it is recorded that "the Lord repented of the evil which he thought to do unto his people."

This was not forgiveness, but a reprieve, as we shall see; for Moses went down from the mount, and when he saw the people worshipping the calf, he threw down the tables of stone and broke them, called the Levites to him, commanded them to slay every man his brother, companion, and neighbor; and three thousand fell in one day, as an exhibition of God's wrath. Moses then returns to the Lord to make an atonement, confesses their crime, asks that they may be forgiven, or, if not, that he may be blotted out of God's book. The Lord replies, "*Whosoever hath sinned against me, him will I blot out of my book.* Therefore, now go, lead the people unto the place of which I have spoken unto thee: behold, mine angel shall go before thee; nevertheless, in the day when I visit I will visit their sin upon them." Exod. 32 : 26, 34.

This shows their sin was not forgiven, but the execution of the sentence deferred, by reprieve, for a time. In view of this principle, Solomon says, "Because sentence against an evil work is not executed speedily, therefore the heart of the sons of men is fully set in them to do evil." Eccl. 8 : 11. The atonement and intercession of Christ, with reference to the Adamic law [of works], does not procure the forgiveness of that offence of Adam, but a reprieve or suspension of execution, to give a second probation, while he offers mercy, salvation, and eternal life, under the law of faith or new covenant, by virtue of his blood.

Thus "God is long-suffering to us-ward, not willing that any should perish, but that all should come to repentance." 2 Pet. 3 : 9.

In further proof of the correctness of the view of the atonement and intercession of Christ as set forth by the law, please read Num. 14th chapter. The Lord inquires how long the people will provoke him after all he had done for them, and says, "I will smite them with pestilence and DISINHERIT them;" but Moses pleads for them, and the Lord says, "I have pardoned according to thy word." That this pardon is not a forgiveness of their sin, but a reprieve, a delay of the execution of the sentence, is established by verse 29, where the Lord says, "Your carcasses shall fall in this wilderness, and all that were numbered of you according to your whole number, from twenty years old and upward. . . . Ye shall not come into the land concerning which I sware to make you dwell therein." Num. 14: 11, 30.

To this view all the law types of the atonement agree: the body — the flesh — serves as food for the physical system, or to burn upon the altar; it was never carried into the holy of holies; they pointed only to the resurrection of the physical body, the resuscitation of the race, and the lost inheritance. But not so with the blood, as we shall show in its proper place.

Having shown the bearing of the law of types on this point, we shall now present the direct testimony from the Old and New Testaments. Thus saith the prophet: "Surely he hath borne our griefs and carried our sorrows; yet we did esteem him *stricken*, smitten of God, and afflicted. But he was *wounded* for our transgressions, he was bruised for our *iniquities*, and the chastisement of our peace was upon *him*, and with *his* stripes we are healed." Isa. 53: 4, 5. This scripture clearly teaches that Christ's sufferings and death were to remove our griefs and sorrows, and to heal us from the effects of the fall, by raising all the race from death. "All we like sheep have gone astray [no exception to this rule]; we have turned every one to his own way, and *the Lord hath laid on him* the iniquity of us all" (Heb. *margin*, "hath made the iniquity of us all to meet on him)."

That the sin of Adam and his race was laid on Christ is generally admitted by believers in the Bible; but to what extent the sin of Adam affected his race, and which was laid on Christ, is not so generally understood. We will quote a few texts on this point, which will help the understanding. "Behold, I was shapen in iniquity, and in sin did my mother conceive me." Psa. 51 : 5. "The wicked are estranged from the womb, they go astray as soon as they be born, speaking lies." Psa. 58 : 3. Job asks, "Who can bring a clean thing out of an unclean? Not one." Job 14 : 4. All this is the effect of the first transgression; and this is met and removed by the death of Christ. Paul, in referring to this point, says of Christ, "Who was delivered [to death] for our offences, and was raised again for [to raise us] our justification." Rom. 4 : 25.

If Jesus died for our offences, then the debt was paid, and not forgiven; and the law is satisfied, for Jesus died; and the race are free, for Jesus rose. "The free gift came upon all men unto justification of life." Rom. 5 : 18. "He rose for our justification." Peter, in speaking on the same point, says, "Who his own self bare [not forgave] our sins in his own body on the tree, . . . by whose STRIPES [not blood] ye were healed [not forgiven]." 1 Pet. 2 : 24.

It may be claimed that these scriptures apply only to believers. We will let the scriptures settle this question; let us hear Paul: "We trust in the living God, who is the *Saviour of all men;* specially [the Saviour] of those that believe. *These things command and teach.*" 1 Tim. 4: 10, 11. If Paul means what he says, then *all men* are, or will be, saved, and this doctrine he tells us to "*command and teach.*" We will do so. YET, beside and above this, there is a *special salvation* to believers. That believers are included in the first salvation mentioned is too plain to be denied. But believers are saved from *their sins,* by the blood of Christ, through repentance and faith. Their sins are *remitted, forgiven;* consequently the penalty of that law by which we are bound to Christ — the law of faith, not of works, — is never executed on them.

Through what means, then, and from what, does " the living God" save all men? Do you claim that it is by the blood of Christ, and from the penalty of the new covenant, *the law of life?* If so, then all men are forgiven, for Christ says expressly, "This is my blood of the new testament [law] which is shed for many for the remission of sins." Matt. 26: 28. Thus, if your answer be correct, all men are entitled to eternal life, and there is *no special* salvation. This cannot be true; we will let the Bible answer the question. Jesus says, "And I, if I be *lifted up from the earth,* will draw all men unto me; this he said signifying what *death* he should die." John 12: 32, 33.

The obvious meaning of this passage is, if he *died* he would save all men from the power and effects of the first transgression, restoring them to life from the dead (see Rom. 5 : 19), sinless in the eyes of the Adamic law — the law of works; not by his blood, but by his *death*, not by the forgiveness of sins, but by *dying* and paying the claim, satisfying the law by purchasing them out from death. Paul says, " We thus judge, that if one [Christ] died for all, then were all [sentenced to die] dead; and that he died for all, that they which live should not henceforth live unto themselves, but unto him which DIED for them, and rose again." 2 Cor. 5 : 14, 15.

In this passage, the apostle, constrained by the manifestation of Christ's love, judges two things: 1st. If Christ DIED FOR ALL [men], *then all were* [doomed to die] *dead;* and 2d. That he did die for all in order that the living might no longer live for themselves, but for " him who *died* and *rose* again on their behalf." *Em. Diaglott.*

The plain meaning of the apostle's first point is, that the fact of Christ's *dying for all*, proves that the sentence of the first law (law of death) had passed upon *all*, because " in Adam all have sinned." Rom. 5 : 12. And in his second point he declares that he *did die for all;* that the living (being thereby brought into a probationary state under the new covenant, or " law of life," and made accountable to Christ) should not live to themselves, in sin, but should believe on, and live for Christ, who died for them and rose again, and thus they would gain the *special salvation.*

Once more, the apostle affirms, "For there is one God, and one Mediator between God and men, the man

Christ Jesus, who gave himself a ransom for all, to be testified in due time." 1 Tim. 2 : 5, 6. But from whence will he ransom them? The Lord answers, "*I will* RANSOM *them from the* POWER *of the* GRAVE; I will REDEEM *them from* DEATH. O DEATH, I will be thy plagues; O GRAVE, I will be thy DESTRUCTION. Repentance shall be hid from mine eyes." Hosea 13 : 14.

This is one of the things God has proposed of which he declares he will not repent. This ransom must include all of the race, for the following reasons : 1st. Paul says, that Jesus " gave HIMSELF a ransom for ALL." 2d. It is from the power of the grave, which covers the race. 3d. It is a redemption from death; therefore it is a resurrection. 4th. It is the plagues of death; it is the destruction of the grave, which would not be the fact if it was limited to the righteous. It cannot refer to " the second death," for then it would not be a ransom of all, for " the second death has no power over the righteous " (Rev. 20 : 5), neither is there any redemption provided for those who suffer the second death.

That this redemption does not turn upon the human volition or will, but is the unalterable purpose of the living God, is proved by the declaration at the close of the promise — "*Repentance* shall be hid from mine eyes." We will examine a few more passages on this point. " For as in [by] Adam all die, even so in [by] Christ shall all be made alive; but every man in his own order." 1 Cor. 15 : 22. This can never be accomplished until all who die shall be raised from death, both the righteous and the wicked. This only can effect the destruction of death, and is the third point in making all men alive by Christ's death.

Paul further explains by what means this is done. "Forasmuch, then, as the children are partakers of flesh and blood, he also himself likewise took part of the same; that through death he might destroy him that had the power of death, that is, the devil; and deliver them who through fear of death were all their lifetime subject to bondage." Heb. 2 : 14, 15. Again : "For when we were yet without strength [helpless under sentence of death], in due time Christ died for the *ungodly*." Rom. 5 : 6.

We are also informed of the same fact further, thus : "God commendeth his love toward us in that while we were yet sinners [made so by the disobedience of Adam, verses 12, 19], Christ DIED for us. . . . When we were enemies we were reconciled to God [the atonement was made] by the DEATH of his Son. . . . Therefore, as by the offence of one [Adam] sentence [judgment] came upon ALL men, so also through one righteous act [of Jesus Christ in being obedient unto death, even the death of the cross, Phil. 2 : 8], sentence came on ALL men to JUSTIFICATION OF LIFE." Rom. 5 : 7, 10, 18. — *Em. Diaglott.* "For as through the disobedience of one man, the many [the race] were constituted *sinners* [in the eyes of the Adamic law], so even through the *obedience* [unto death] of the one, the many [the race] will be constituted righteous [in the eyes of the Adamic law."] — *Emp. Diaglott*, ver. 19.

But we will not multiply quotations further on this point : enough has been presented to show the correctness of the position we have advocated above. We will, however, remark, that there are a few passages where the atonement is treated upon with reference to believers, in which its two branches are not so distinctly marked. Examples: in John 6: 50, 51, where Jesus says, the bread which cometh down from heaven, which a man may eat and live forever, is his flesh, which he will give for the *life* of the *world*. In these two verses there is an ellipsis, which is filled in verses 53, 54, by adding "*my blood*." "Then Jesus said unto them, Verily, verily, I say unto you, Except ye eat the flesh of the Son of man, and drink his blood, ye have *no life in you*. Whoso eateth my flesh, and drinketh my blood, hath eternal life. He that eateth my flesh and drinketh my blood, dwelleth in me, and I in him."

Thus it will be seen, if the flesh of Christ purchases the *life of the world* — the race — from death, the blood must cleanse, or "purge the conscience from [sin] dead works to serve the living God," by faith in the virtues of that blood, in order to secure eternal life; all of which clearly implies the voluntary acceptance of the atonement by an act of faith. May this be the happy condition both of the readers and writers.

Our argument then, on this point, sums up thus: —

I. As all men were lost in death by the sin of Adam, all being in him, so all men are saved by the DEATH of Christ, out from death and from all the consequences of the first transgression, without any voluntary action on the part of the race. Being passive in the Fall, they are passive also in the Redemption, and must be made alive by a resurrection from the grave; and thus our right to live is gained in Christ.

II. By Christ's intercession with the Father, the sentence of the law was not speedily executed upon Adam, but reprieve was granted (and not forgiveness), and he placed on a second probation, under a law which could give life (Rom. 8:2), by which the race are placed on trial for eternal life, on condition of repentance and faith, before the sentence of God's violated law is executed upon us. Let us improve the hour of God's mercy and long forbearance, and gain the glorious prize.

III. Thus our state of probation, with the prospect of eternal life and dominion, which was lost, involuntarily on our part, in Adam, is involuntarily restored to us by the intercession of Christ, and his offering himself, "from the foundation of the world," to die for our redemption.

We will here remark, it should be remembered that Jesus is not now interceding at the right hand of the Father for the redemption of the world, for that redemption is a fixed fact, secured by his DEATH. But he is there interceding: for he "entered heaven with his own BLOOD, there to appear in the presence of God for us." "Wherefore he is able to save them also to the uttermost that come unto God by him, seeing he ever liveth to make intercession for them." Heb. 7:25.

IV. As we lost involuntarily in Adam a good, sound physical and mental organism, so, by the *death* and *resurrection* of Christ, we involuntarily have them restored.

Let us examine the prophecy of Isaiah on this point. "Surely he hath borne our griefs and carried our sorrows; yet we did esteem him stricken, smitten of God, and afflicted." Isa. 53 : 4. The evangelist applies this prediction to the healing of our physical infirmities, a pledge of which Christ gave while here. "He has himself carried off our infirmities, and borne our distresses." *Emp. Diaglott*, Matt. 8 : 17. This he said in reference to Christ's healing the sick, and casting the devils out of those who were brought unto him.

Christ's death is ample satisfaction for the claim of the violated law, and removes the curse from the earth and all its inhabitants; this is involved in the terms saved, redeemed, restored, reconciled, made righteous, justified, all which terms are used to show the effect of his death and resurrection on the race and the earth, for it also is to be restored. See Rom. 8 : 19, 23. But this does not secure immortality and eternal life unconditionally to the race. That is obtained through the superabounding grace of God, by "repentance toward God, and faith toward our Lord Jesus Christ"—a being cleansed by his blood. Christians have the Holy Spirit, "which is the earnest of the inheritance until the redemption of the purchased inheritance." Eph. 1 : 14. Thus, through repentance and faith, the way to the tree of life is open to all. "Jesus saith, I am the way, the truth, and the life; no man cometh unto the Father but by me." John 14 : 6. And in view of the foregoing scriptural facts, it must be a fearfully perverted use of the word of God, and one which is subversive of the whole plan of redemption as revealed in the Scriptures of truth, to teach the idea of the non-resurrection of any one of Adam's race who dies.

In concluding our remarks on this part of the most

vital and important of all subjects ever made known to the sons of men, we would urge upon our readers the duty of making a wise improvement of this door which Christ has opened before us, by removing from us all the difficulties entailed upon us, in prospect of giving us eternal life through his blood, by the forgiveness of our sins, if we will believe in and obey him. We entreat of you who have not done so to accept of this grace, open your hearts, and receive this gospel of mercy, pardon, and salvation. You are enjoying a life of reprieve, granted by the offering of the body of Christ, that in it you may seek and obtain the forgiveness of your sins, and live to glorify him in this world, that when you are raised up from the dead, you may come up immortal, to die no more.

CHAPTER VIII.

THE ATONEMENT, CONTINUED.

PART SECOND.

THE CONDITIONAL ATONEMENT BY THE BLOOD OF CHRIST.

"For this is my blood of the new testament, which is shed for many for the remission of sins." — *Matt.* 26: 28.

Having stated that the atonement is presented in the Scriptures in two branches, and shown that the first part is accomplished by the death and resurrection of Christ, that it is universal in its application to, and effects upon, our race, the earth, and the whole creation (Rom. 8: 19–23), in their redemption from the effects of the first transgression, we now proceed to show that all the adult portion of our race are brought under a *new law*, which has since been denominated "the new covenant," "law of faith," "law of the spirit of life," "the royal law," &c. (Jer. 31: 31. Rom. 3: 27; 8: 2. James 2: 8), in distinction from the "old covenant," "law of works," "law of sin and death," &c., of which we shall speak presently.

Under this law there is a special salvation to be obtained, — not by paying its penalty or suffering to death, as in the case of the first covenant, or *letter* which *killeth*, whose ministration was death, but by virtue of the blood of Christ, to cleanse away our sins against the new covenant (not the old), through "repentance toward God, and faith toward our Lord Jesus Christ," thus saving us *from* suffering to death — *the second death;* while the unrepenting, unbelieving, *will* fall under its power.

"Behold, the days come, saith the Lord, when I will make a new covenant with the house of Israel and with the house of Judah." Heb. 8 : 8. Of this covenant we shall speak more at length in another chapter. We will remark here, however, that this covenant is founded upon and sealed by the blood of Jesus, and can give life.

The propriety — perhaps it would be proper to say the necessity — of such a law will appear when we consider that Adam was made a living soul, in a condition to multiply, and replenish the earth, and subdue it, preparatory to immortality and dominion over it, and all things it contained; with a perfect physical, mental, and moral organism; with the tree of life to perpetuate his life (until his work was done); all of which were pronounced by our Creator VERY GOOD. Gen. 1 : 31.

With all these advantages at hand, with the law of God for his instruction, government, and discipline, making no provision for his disobedience, as there was no necessity for nor propriety in it, Adam transgressed and fell, involving his race in the curse and the evils in which we now find ourselves. Therefore, had reprieve and repentance been granted us to make a second trial for obedience to that violated law, it could not have benefited us, as it could not give us life from the penalty already resting upon us, — which was *death*. That law could not give life; therefore no righteousness could come by it (Rom. 8 : 3), it "being weak through the flesh;" its penalty must be executed upon us, and all perish at last, or, if we had been redeemed from death and placed under that law, there was no assurance that we should keep it better than Adam did.

But infinite wisdom, mercy, and goodness has provided a more excellent way, for "Christ hath redeemed us from the *curse of the law, being made a curse for us;* for it is written, *Cursed is every one that hangeth on a tree.*" Gal. 3 : 13. "For the *law of the spirit of life in Christ Jesus* hath made me free from the *law of sin and death;* for what the law could not do in that it was weak through the flesh, God sending his own Son in the likeness of sinful flesh, and for [*even by an offering for sin, Emp. Diag.*] sin, condemned sin in the flesh, that the righteousness of the law might be fulfilled in us who walk not after the flesh [the law of sin and death], but after the Spirit." Rom. 8 : 2, 4. How clearly the fact is here stated, that Christ, being made a curse for us, redeems us from the curse of the first law, which was powerless for our help, placing us under a *new law*, called by Paul "the law of the spirit of life," because it is a law which has power to give life. The letter [first law, on tables] killeth, but cannot make alive; but the [law of the] Spirit giveth life. O, how much better adapted to our condition is the latter than the former *law!*

What excuse will the unbeliever have when arraigned to receive reward under this *life-giving* law? "How shall we escape if we neglect so great salvation? Heb. 2 : 3. Again, the Word declares, "For him who knew no sin, he made a sin offering on our behalf, that we might become God's righteousness in him." 2 Cor. 5 : 21, *Emp. Diag.* Here, again, we are informed that the SPOTLESS ONE, the LAMB OF GOD, " once suffered for sins, being put to death in the flesh " (1 Pet. 3 : 18) ; the Father " bruised him," " put him to grief," " made his soul an offering for sin " (Isa. 53 : 10), that we might be brought under the law of life, the law of faith, which could give righteousness, and through faith could justify us, in the sight of God, from all things from which we could not be justified by the law of Moses." Acts 13 : 39. This is " the righteousness of faith " (Rom. 10 : 3, 6), " the righteousness of God without the law [of works] " (Rom. 3 : 21), " the righteousness of God which is by faith of Jesus Christ, unto all and upon all them that *believe*, for there is no difference [between Jew and Greek]. For all have sinned and come short of the glory of God " (Rom. 3 : 22, 23) — God's righteousness, of which the unbelieving world are ignorant, as were the unbelieving Jews. Rom. 10 : 3.

This law is by Paul called " the gospel of Christ, the power of God unto salvation [not to all men, but] to every one that believeth, both Jews and Greeks ; " the gospel [law] in which the righteousness of God *by faith* is revealed *in order to faith*, as it is written, But the righteous by faith shall *live*. Rom. 1 : 16, 17 ; Heb. 10 : 38, *Emphatic Diaglott*. Reader, if you are out of Christ, permit us to remind you that although you have the righteousness of the old law imputed to you by the death of Christ, yet without the righteousness of God, which is by faith in the blood of Christ under the new law, you must suffer its penalty in the second death. "Except ye eat the flesh of the Son of man, and drink his blood, ye have no [eternal] life in you." John 6: 53. 1 Cor. 9: 21. Gal. 6: 2. That all adults are under this new law, and are to be judged by it, is clearly revealed: "For God so loved the world that he gave his only begotten Son, that whosoever believeth in him should not perish, but have everlasting life." John 3: 16. "He that believeth on him is not condemned, but he that believeth not is condemned already, because he hath not believed in the name of the only begotten Son of God."

Therefore justification of life from the grave by the death of Christ secures eternal life to no one, but restores them to the same sinless state from which Adam by transgression fell, involving his race in sin; so that the infant and imbecile will receive eternal life as the gift of God, and be raised immortal with all the saints, because no sin of unbelief or action attaches to them, they having never voluntarily transgressed any law. Hence the prophet says, "Lo, children are an heritage of the Lord: and the fruit of the womb is his reward." Psa. 127: 3. Yea, he hath ransomed them from death, and will suffer them to come to him; he will pronounce his blessing upon them, and "give unto them eternal life, and they shall never perish." But the adult portion are under the law of faith, as before shown; and these two laws are presented in contrast in the New Testament by Paul, thus: "The *law of the spirit of life;*" "the *law of sin and death*" (Rom. 8 : 2); "the *letter killeth,* but the *Spirit giveth life.*" (2 Cor. 3 : 6, 8); *ministration of death written in stones; ministration of the Spirit* rather glorious; *law of works, law of faith.* Rom. 3 : 28.

This law of faith had its germ in Eden, the scene of the transgression and our fall. Thus, it seems, inasmuch as God had determined to sacrifice his only begotten Son, and make his soul an offering for sin, he would offer the first typical sacrifice ever offered on earth by the slaying of beasts, — to impress upon our first parents a sense of their guilt, and to signify to them his purpose to provide a remedy for their fall, and thus teach them the means through which the *seed* of the *woman* should *bruise* or crush *the serpent's head*, and he, the serpent, should *bruise his heel* (a promise upon which our faith still clings, as did Paul's when he said, "The God of peace shall bruise Satan under your feet shortly") — and thereby also to procure skins to cover them and hide their shame. Indeed, we may well suppose all this would arise from that love which gave his only Son to redeem and save us.

Again: the offering of Abel was a development of the working of this law of faith, and so on down through to the watery deluge: so perfectly did Enoch walk by it, that God translated him, because he pleased God. We find the law of faith working and developing itself in the patriarchal age also. Paul says, "Without faith it is impossible to please God; and in the 11th chapter of the Epistle to the Hebrews, he traces the workings and power of this law, which should make our hearts thrill with joy and thanksgiving to God that it was ever given. Yea, and even in the dark shades of heathenism, as we are shown in the Scriptures, specimens of its power are manifested where tradition and the book of nature are the only theological rules through which it could be studied. The apostle says, —

"When the Gentiles, which have not the law [written] do by [studying the righteousness of God] nature the things contained in the [written] law, these, having not the law, are a law unto themselves, which show the works of the *law written in their heart, their conscience* also bearing them witness, and their thoughts the mean while accusing or else excusing one another." Rom. 2 : 15, 16.

That this law is embodied in the new covenant, the law of faith, is evident from its being written in the heart, and therefore by the Spirit, and not the old covenant or letter on stones. They are, therefore, to be judged by the law of the new covenant. This view is sustained by the following verse : "But he is a Jew which is one inwardly, and circumcision is that of the *heart in the Spirit*, and not in the letter." Rom. 2 : 29.

Again it is written (concerning the heathen), "Who in time past suffered all nations to walk in their own ways; nevertheless he left not himself without a witness, in that he did good, and gave rain from heaven and fruitful seasons, filling our hearts with food and gladness." Acts 14 : 17 ; 17 : 22, 30. To this also agrees the testimony of the Psalmist : "The heavens declare the glory of God, and the firmament showeth his handywork: day unto day uttereth speech, and night unto night showeth knowledge." "There is no speech nor language where their voice is not heard. And in view of this the prophet exclaims, "The law of the Lord [thus written in the volume of nature] is perfect, converting the soul; the testimony of the Lord is sure, making wise the simple." Psa. 19 : 1–7. Please read the whole psalm. Paul refers to it thus: "But, I say, Have they not all heard? Yes, verily, their sound went into all the earth, and their words unto the ends of the world." Rom. 10 : 18. From these scriptures it is shown that the working of this "royal law" of faith is not confined to those who have the written word, but is preached through the works of nature by the Spirit, and finds disciples in heathen lands, in whose hearts it is written by the Spirit.

But it may be asked, Why, then, would you preach the gospel to the heathen? We will let Paul answer this question. When he went into the idolatrous city of Athens, planting his feet on Mars' hill, he exclaimed: "Ye men of Athens, I perceive that in all things ye are too superstitious; for, as I passed by, and beheld your devotions, I found an altar with this inscription: TO THE UNKNOWN GOD. Whom, therefore, ye *ignorantly worship*, him declare I unto you." Acts 17 : 22, 23.

Here, in a heathen city, where the true God was acknowledged and worshipped, though ignorantly, Paul thought proper to preach the gospel; nor did he preach in vain; for he found many converts, among whom were "Dionysius the Areopagite, and a woman named Damaris, and others with them."

Why preach the gospel in Jerusalem? They were in a similar condition, with the Scriptures in their hands, as the Greeks with the volume of nature for their study. Paul says of them, "For I bear them record, that they have a *zeal* of God, but *not according to* KNOWLEDGE. For they, being IGNORANT *of God's righteousness*, and going about to establish their own righteousness, have not submitted themselves unto the righteousness of God." Rom. 10 : 2, 3.

The object of preaching should be to expound and urge the truths of God home upon every man's conscience in the sight of God, whether from the book of nature or revelation, and whether upon civilized or heathen nations.

> The fields are white, and faithful laborers few.
> Then send, O Lord, thy heralds forth,
> From east to west, from south to north,
>   Thy gospel to proclaim,
>   That all the heathen, far or near,
>   May seek thy truth in filial fear,
>   And glorify thy name.

It may be well to inquire here, What is the transgression of this law? The Scripture answers, Unbelief. "He that believeth not is condemned already, because he hath not believed in the name of the only begotten Son of God." John 3 : 18. The natural man is a sinner by nature; nor can he be anything else by nature: as well might the "Ethiopian change his skin, or the leopard his spots." The corrupt branch of a corrupt tree cannot bring forth good fruit, neither a bitter fountain send forth sweet water. "Men do not gather grapes of thorns, nor figs of thistles." Therefore there is no man by nature good; "no, not one." "All have gone out of the way; they have altogether become unprofitable." This condition is the result of the fall, and death is the inevitable consequence of this condition; "for sin, when it is finished, bringeth forth death," as we have before shown. "For the wages of sin is death," and from this sin and death Jesus died to redeem us, and from it we shall be delivered as passive as we were passive in the fall. "For since by man came death, by man came also the resurrection of the dead; for as in Adam all [men] die, even so in Christ shall all [men] be made alive." Thus death shall be destroyed. The responsibility, therefore, of our natural condition does not rest on us, but on Adam.

It may then be asked, How is the sinner made responsible for his sins in this world? We reply, By disbelieving the word of God, and thereby rejecting the offers of mercy and grace as presented in the gospel. "Light has come into the world, and men love darkness rather than light, because their deeds are evil." God extends forgiveness under the new covenant, on conditions of repentance and faith, but the sinner refuses to accept it. Yet the Holy Spirit reproves; the word of God is preached and published; the people of God invite and admonish: thus men are kept under *restraint*, and though the wrath of man is often manifested, yet it shall praise God, "and the remainder of wrath shalt thou [Lord] restrain," says David; while the *grace of God* enables the believer to "keep his body in subjection," and to "yield his members as instruments of righteousness" unto God, and to "present his body a living sacrifice, holy, acceptable unto God, which is our reasonable service." Thus they are saved from sin in this life, and in the end the second death will have no power over them.

Let us illustrate this point. We will suppose two men to have fallen involuntarily into a loathsome pit, from which they have no power to extricate themselves, and in which, without assistance, they must perish. In this condition a friend approaches, and offers to rescue them, and cleanse their filth, on condition that they confess their helplessness, accept his hand, and own him as their benefactor and deliverer. Reader, at what point would the responsibility of remaining in the pit be thrown upon those men? Would you not say, At the very point where help was offered and refused? For certainly it was not before. But suppose one of those men accepts the proffered hand, is delivered, cleansed, saved, and, by the side of his deliverer, entreats his fellow sufferer to accept the same kind hand that saved him, but he still refuses: would not his blood be upon his own head?

Sinner, Jesus finds you in your native state of sin and death. He died to redeem you, and thereby brings you under the law of faith and obedience to himself. In the gospel he submits to you the whole plan of redemption; he offers you present salvation from personal sin and guilt, to enable you by his grace to break off from sin, to overcome the world, the flesh, and the devil, and to give you eternal life in the end — all on condition of repentance and faith. "For with the heart man believeth unto righteousness, and with the mouth confession is made unto salvation." Rom. 10: 10.

But what is the result of unbelief? The penalty of the law, which requires faith, on which salvation, immortality, and eternal life are offered, is the second death; for we are informed that "he that overcometh shall not be hurt of the SECOND DEATH." Rev. 2:11. "Blessed and holy is he that hath part in the first resurrection: on such the second death hath no power." Rev. 20:6. But the fearful, and UNBELIEVING, and the *abominable*, and *murderers*, and *whoremongers*, and *sorcerers*, and *idolaters*, and *all liars*, shall have their part in the lake which burneth with fire and brimstone, which [*part*] is the second death." Rev. 21:8. This death must succeed the resurrection from the first death; this is the DEATH which is everywhere in the gospel set over against LIFE, EVERLASTING LIFE, ETERNAL LIFE. "If ye live after the flesh [according to the flesh]; ye shall DIE; but if ye, through the spirit, do mortify [crucify] the deeds of the body [unbelief, pride, lust, envy, murder, theft, lying, and all other evil propensities], ye shall LIVE." Rom. 8:13.

We come now to inquire in what part of the work of Christ, in his official capacity, is this *law of life* based; for the Son of God is presented in the Scriptures, in three successive official capacities.

First, in his PROPHETIC or ministerial office.

Second, in his PRIESTLY office.

Third, in his KINGLY office.

1. Moses says, "The Lord thy God will raise up unto thee a PROPHET from the midst of thee, of thy brethren, like unto me: unto him shall ye hearken." Deut. 18:15, 18. Acts 3:22 7:37. And in this

capacity he was typified by the PASCHAL LAMB, selected from the flock on the tenth day of the month, and slain on the fourteenth day of the month.

Jesus was introduced by John, from among his brethren, as "the LAMB OF GOD that taketh away the sin of the world." John 1 : 29. Also by the Father at his baptism: "This is my beloved Son, in whom I am well pleased." Matt. 3 : 17.

This was in the fourth year before his death for the redemption of the world.

II. In his PRIESTLY office, in which he is now acting at the right hand of the Father; for of him Paul says, "The Apostle and HIGH PRIEST of our profession, Christ Jesus." Heb. 3 : 1. Under him, therefore, we receive our law and profession. Again, the apostle says of him, "He became the author of eternal salvation unto all them that obey him; called of God an *high priest* after the order of Melchisedec." Heb. 5 : 9, 10.

Again, the apostle, while speaking of the inefficiency of the typical sacrifices to cleanse, says, —

"But Christ being come an *high priest* of good things to come, by a greater and more perfect tabernacle, not made with hands, that is to say, not of this building, neither by the blood of goats and calves, but by *his own blood*, he entered in once into the holy place, having obtained eternal redemption for us [believers]." "For if the blood of bulls and goats, and the ashes of an heifer sprinkling the unclean, sanctifieth to the purifying of the flesh, how much more shall the BLOOD of Christ, who through the eternal Spirit offered himself [gave himself up a sacrifice] without spot to God, purge your conscience from dead works [works of death, *Em. Diaglott*], to serve the living God." Heb. 9: 11, 14. "And for this cause he is the mediator of a new covenant, so that HIS DEATH having taken place for a *redemption* of the transgressions against the *first covenant* [which held the race involuntarily in death], those having been invited [through the new covenant] might receive the promise of aionian [eternal — *Common Version*] inheritance." Heb. 9: 15. — *Em. Diaglott.*

In all the above passages of Scripture, the Saviour is presented in his official character as high priest, in heaven itself (the antitype of the holiest of all on earth), officiating with his own blood; for it is said, "If he were on earth he should not be a priest;" and here we repeat, that priests never carried the body of the victim sacrificed into "the holy of holies;" it was left in the outer court, to be used as food, or burned on the altar, while the blood was offered by the high priest in the holiest of all, to obtain forgiveness.

Therefore the blood of Jesus affects no one but those who have transgressed the law of faith voluntarily, and who repent, believe, and obtain mercy through the blood of the Lamb. (Infants and imbeciles, having never violated this law of faith, have no conscious guilt or sin to be forgiven; they "are the heritage of the Lord, and his reward," by virtue of universal redemption by the *death and resurrection* of our Saviour, and not by his blood; while all voluntary rejecters of offered mercy and grace perish in the second death.)

This official work of Christ is shadowed forth in the law types of the atonement, especially in the Lord's

Passover. Exod. ch. 12. The blood of this lamb was not to save the *congregation* of Israel from the plague of the destroying angel, but the FIRST BORN *in every house*, a small portion of the people. They typify God's elect, chosen people, washed from sin in the blood of the Lamb. Rev. 1 : 5.

We would here press upon the attention of the reader, that while the flesh of the lamb served as food to nourish the body, and was eaten by all the people, yet *only two* of that vast multitude (children excepted) entered the typical land of rest; even so the flesh of Jesus, which he gave for the life of the world, to bring the physical man from the dark grave, will not secure eternal life to any responsible person of the human race. On the other hand, as the *blood* (which was never to be eaten, on pain of death; see Gen. 9 : 3. Ex. 17 : 10, 12) of the paschal lamb saved none of the Israelites except the FIRST BORN in every house; so the BLOOD of the Lamb of God will save none except the repenting, believing, God-loving company who have washed their robes and made them white in the BLOOD of the Lamb (Rev. 7 : 14), under the new covenant; for thus it is written of Jesus by the evangelist (when instituting the Lord's supper, which is the gospel or new covenant *passover*, to continue to signify the same great truths contained in the passover of which he was then eating, and which was then and there to *pass away*), "And he took the cup and gave thanks, and gave it to them, saying, Drink ye all of it, for *this is my blood of the* NEW TESTAMENT, which is shed for many for the REMISSION of sins." Matt. 26 : 27, 28. "This cup is the new testament in my blood, which is shed for you." Luke 22 : 20. Two facts are here especially stated : —

1. This blood is shed for REMISSION.

2. That it is of and in the new testament, showing that it does not belong to the old, or law covenant, as that admitted of no forgiveness, for it required the death of the offender; while the law of faith was established in mercy for the forgiveness of sins, and therefore required BLOOD to cleanse from guilt.

Consequently the Scriptures declare, "Without the shedding of BLOOD there is no remission." "How much more shall the BLOOD of Christ . . . purge your conscience from dead works." Heb. 9 : 14, 22. "Now the God of peace, . . . through the BLOOD of the everlasting covenant, make you perfect in every good work to do his will." Heb. 13 : 20. "Redeemed from your vain conversation with the precious BLOOD of Christ, as of a lamb without blemish and without spot." 1 Pet. 1 : 18, 19. "But if we walk in the light, as he is in the light, . . . the BLOOD of Jesus Christ his Son cleanseth us from all sin." 1 John 1 : 7.

These passages, and many more which we might quote, show conclusively that the second branch of the atonement, or law of faith (which, by many readers, is too often blended with the first branch, and which was accomplished by the death of Christ), is accomplished by the BLOOD of Christ in the *new testament*, and is limited to believers exclusively, resulting in eternal redemption, even the forgiveness of sins here, and the resurrection to immortality and eternal life when Jesus comes. Our subject then sums up thus : —

1. The adult portion of our race are brought under a new covenant and law of faith, called also the law of the spirit of life.

2. This law has no claim on infants and imbeciles.

3. It requires repentance and faith on the part of all accountable persons.

4. It is the only law under and through which we can obtain God's righteousness, justification from our sins, and eternal life.

5. The transgression of this law is wilful unbelief.

6. This law condemns all accountable unbelievers to eternal punishment (which is shown to be the second death), as they reject the atonement.

7. That this law is established in or by the BLOOD of Christ, for the forgiveness of personal sins against this covenant, of and in which Christ is the High Priest, who ever liveth to make intercession for us.

8. That the application of this BLOOD is limited to believers, and is the second branch of the atonement.

9. This branch of the atonement will be accomplished when Jesus shall have finished the work of his mediatorial office, and will result in the final redemption to immortality and eternal life of all who have "washed their robes and made them white in the BLOOD of the Lamb," at the second advent and revelation of our Lord Jesus Christ, "to be admired by all them that believe in that day." Amen.

CHAPTER IX.

MAN'S RELATION TO GOD UNDER THE NEW COVENANT.

"For if the first covenant had been faultless, then should no place have been sought for the second. For finding fault with them, he saith, Behold, the days come, saith the Lord, when I will make a new covenant with the house of Israel and with the house of Judah." — *Heb.* 8 : 7, 8.

In the above scripture the existence of two covenants is plainly stated, one called the *first*, the other the *second* — the new covenant. The first of these was made with the *fathers* of Judah and Israel; the second with the *house* of *Israel* and the *house* of *Judah themselves.* The time of making the first covenant was in the day when the Lord took the fathers of Judah and Israel by the hand to lead them out of the land of Egypt, and is the covenant of ten commandments, as we have shown in our chapter on the Old Covenant. This covenant was the code which in its germ was given to Adam, and, in an elementary sense, may be called the Adamic covenant, for the government of the Adamic race while multiplying, replenishing, and subduing the earth: it was contained in "the tree of the knowledge of good and evil," and, had the rules of this covenant been kept, no sin or death would have entered our world, and no other covenant would have been required. So says the text at the head of this chapter. The fathers of Israel being a representative people, this covenant is given to them for the benefit of the world, to give the knowledge of man's relation to God under a broken law, together with symbols, types, and ordinances, setting forth God's plan of redemption, as shadows of good things to come, which plan was, — "Christ, given for a covenant of the people, for a light of the Gentiles, to open the blind eyes, to bring out the prisoners from the prison, and them that sit in darkness out of the prison-house." Isa. 42 : 6,. 7. "For God so loved the world, that he gave his only begotten Son, that whosoever believeth in him might not perish, but have everlasting life." John 3 : 16.

This plan, which also had its germ in Eden (as before shown, in the promise that the seed of the woman should bruise the serpent's head), was afterwards embodied in the second, or new covenant with the house of Israel, and which, when sealed with the blood of the testator, was to entirely supersede and take the place of the first covenant, which had become faulty and weak through the default of one of the parties; man had broken it, and under it "the Lord regarded them not."

This covenant is presented in a code of laws, and is called "the law of works:" the new covenant is also a code of laws, and called "the law of faith" (Rom. 3 : 27), of which we design mainly to treat in this chapter.

I. First, then, we shall speak of the necessity of a new covenant. The apostle informs us in our text that if the first covenant had been faultless, there should no place have been sought for the second.

What, then, was the fault with this covenant? A

few passages of Scripture will show. It was a *broken* covenant — " which my covenant they brake, although I was an husband unto them, saith the Lord." Jer. 31: 32. "Because they continued not in my covenant, and I regarded them not, saith the Lord." Heb. 8: 9. The penalty of this covenant brought death; and not being susceptible of amendment after being broken, and knowing no mercy, and being in man's flesh, it is powerless for man's help: under it man had no right but to die. Therefore Paul says it was weak through the flesh. Rom. 8: 3. And again he says, " The letter [law] killeth, but the Spirit [the law of the Spirit] giveth life. But if the ministration of death, written and graven in stones, was glorious, . . . which glory was to be done away, how shall not the ministration of the Spirit be rather glorious! For if the ministration of condemnation be glory, much more doth the ministration of righteousness exceed in glory." 2 Cor. 3: 6–8.

The foregoing testimony shows us that the covenant on stones — the decalogue law — *killeth;* its *ministration* is *death;* it is condemnation; thus its power, and its only power, is to convince of sin, and lay us in death, whither we all tend. Therefore the apostle says, " There is verily a disannulling of the commandment going before, for the weakness and unprofitableness thereof; for the law made nothing perfect, but the bringing in of a better hope did, by the which we draw nigh to God." Heb. 7: 18, 19.

The above scripture, and many more which might be cited, show very clearly the necessity of a new covenant, which, thanks to a merciful God, has been furnished in the law of faith, which supersedes the law of works.

II. The marks which characterize the new covenant

The token of the old covenant was circumcision in the flesh, signifying the end of generation, and consequently the death and extermination of the race. The token of the new covenant is "circumcision of the heart, in the spirit, and not in the letter" (Rom. 2:29), causing the person to "love the Lord with all the heart, and with all the soul." Deut. 30:6. Again: the first covenant was written on tables of stone. The new covenant is written in the heart. Thus it is written:—

"For this is the covenant that I will make with the house of Israel after those days, saith the Lord: I will put my laws into their mind, and write them in their hearts; and I will be to them a God, and they shall be to me a people; and they shall not teach every man his neighbor [brother], saying, Know the Lord: for all shall know me [who have this law written in their hearts], from the least to the greatest." Heb. 8:10, 11. While it is true that the real Christian teaches sinners to know the Lord, he does not teach other real Christians to know the Lord, for they know him already, and can only have that knowledge increased by instruction which we can give in "teaching one another," and "building one another up on our most holy faith." None can claim the promises of this covenant except those who have it thus written, "not with ink, but with the Spirit of the living God, not in tables of stone, but in fleshly tables of the heart." 2 Cor. 3:3.

Paul, in the eleventh chapter of Hebrews, gives us

a catalogue of saints who had this law of faith thus written, beginning with Abel and running down through to his own time, and saying, "Without faith it is impossible to please God." In another place he declares that "the law [old covenant] is not of faith." Gal. 3:12. Having shown some of the marks of this new covenant, we come now to identify it in the Scriptures, which is our third proposition.

III. We have before remarked that there are but two covenants mentioned in the Scriptures as being made with the descendants of Abraham. The first was made with the FATHERS of *Israel* and *Judah* when the Lord took them by the hand to lead them out of the land of Egypt; and was made at Sinai (Horeb). Now, if we can find a covenant made with ISRAEL and JUDAH, beside the one made with their *fathers at Sinai*, we shall have found the new covenant; especially if it bears the aforesaid marks of that covenant. We will turn our attention, then, to Deuteronomy (which name signifies *second law*); and we find Moses, forty years after the exode from Egypt (during which they had wandered in the wilderness, and received the first covenant from Sinai), lodging by the springs of Pisgah, in the valley over against Beth-peor, in Moab. Here he recapitulates to the people their history in the wilderness, and the giving of the *first covenant* at Horeb (Sinai), together with its statutes and judgments; the fathers to whom that covenant was made being all dead, except Caleb and Joshua, because of their breaking that covenant: their carcasses had fallen in the wilderness, as God had said they should.

All these things Moses rehearses in their ears, and urges them to obedience in view of God's dealings with their fathers and with them in the past; he begins in the fourth chapter to introduce another covenant, — the covenant of mercy, in the first two verses; urging them, in view of the past, to take diligent heed to *the law which he lays before them this day*, to the ninth verse; then holding before them, in the past tense, the scenes at Sinai (Horeb), he rehearses the first covenant again, as given there; he reminds them, in verse 24, that "God is a consuming fire," even "a jealous God." In verses 25 to 28, he warns them against idolatry and image worship, solemnly protesting, if they violated this covenant, as their fathers had the first one, that they should utterly perish as a nation, and be scattered among the nations of the earth; which denunciation Jesus repeated when he wept over Jerusalem, and which has been fully accomplished by their rejection of the Messiah, the Mediator of this covenant, which facts are this day before our eyes. And though now scattered among the nations, as Moses said they should be, yet in this condition he presents to them the doctrine of mercy (Deut. 4 : 29–31 — a doctrine unknown in the first covenant, as facts had shown). "But if from thence thou shalt seek the Lord thy God, thou shalt find him, if thou seek him with all thy heart and with all thy soul. When thou art in tribulation, and all these things are come upon thee, even in the LATTER DAYS [in the gospel dispensation] if thou turn to the Lord thy God, and shalt be obedient unto his voice (for the Lord thy God is a merciful God), he will not forsake thee, nor destroy thee, nor forget the covenant of thy fathers" [Abraham, Isaac, and Jacob]." See Exod. 6:8. Gen. 15:18; 26:3; 28:13. We then find him encouraging them to repentance, faith, and obedience, in view of God's forbearance and long-suffering with their fathers in Egypt and in the wilderness; reminding them, at the same time, that this forbearance was not on their account, but because of his love to their fathers, Abraham, Isaac, and Jacob. Verses 32-39. In all these encouraging words of Moses, we find no promise of a return to Jerusalem nor Palestine, yet he makes *this* promise: "Thou shalt keep, therefore, his statutes and his commandments, which I command thee this day, that it may go well with thee, and with thy children after thee, and that thou mayest prolong thy days upon the earth, which the Lord thy God giveth thee, forever [the new earth]. Verse 40. Moses next refers to the new law, statutes, and judgments, which he set before Israel this day, forty years after they left Egypt, on the east side of Jordan, in the land of Moab; and in chapter 5:1-3, he presents the two covenants in contrast, thus: "And Moses called all Israel, and said unto them, *Hear, O Israel, the statutes and judgments which I speak in your ears this day*, that ye may learn them, and keep and do them. The Lord our God made a covenant [the first one] with us in Horeb (Sinai). THE LORD MADE NOT THIS COVENANT [this second one, which I speak in your ears this day] with our fathers [in the wilderness], but with us, even us, who are all of us here alive this day."

In these verses we have the two covenants in contrast; the *first* given in Horeb, with their fathers and themselves; the *second*, forty years later, in Moab, by the springs of Pisgah, with those yet alive and present, and *not with their fathers*. This second covenant, made with Israel after the days of *their fathers*, who were all then dead excepting Caleb and Joshua, must therefore be the new covenant. But we have other and clearer testimony in Deuteronomy, 29th chapter: let us examine it. "These are the words OF THE COVENANT WHICH THE LORD COMMANDED MOSES TO MAKE WITH THE CHILDREN OF ISRAEL IN THE LAND OF MOAB, BESIDE THE *covenant which he made with them in Horeb*." This demonstrates our point.

"And Moses called unto all Israel, and said unto them, Ye have seen all that the Lord did before your eyes in the land of Egypt unto Pharaoh, and unto all his servants, and unto all his land; the great temptations which thine eyes have seen, the signs, and those great miracles; yet the Lord hath not given you an heart to perceive, and eyes to see, and ears to hear, unto this day." Deut. 29: 1, 4.

This darkness of heart and blindness of eyes represent their condition under the old covenant, as expounded by Paul. "But their minds were blinded; for until this day remaineth the same vail untaken away in the reading of the old [covenant] testament, which vail is done away in [the new covenant] Christ." 2 Cor. 3: 14. Moses, after speaking of their state of darkness under the old covenant, charges them to keep the words of the new covenant, which the Lord commanded him to make with them, and then says, "Ye stand this day all of you before the Lord your God, your captains of your tribes, your elders and your officers, with all the men of Israel, your little ones, your wives, and thy stranger that is in thy camp, from the hewer of thy wood unto the drawer of thy water, that thou shouldest enter into covenant with the Lord thy God, and into his oath, which the Lord thy God maketh with thee this day, that he may establish thee to-day for a people unto himself, and that he may be unto thee a God, as he hath said unto thee, and as he hath sworn unto THY FATHERS, TO ABRAHAM, TO ISAAC, AND TO JACOB. Neither with you only do I make this covenant and this oath, but with him that standeth here with us this day before the Lord our God, and also with him that is not here with us this day [Gentile converts]." Deut. 29 : 10–15.

No stronger testimony can be required to prove that the above covenant which Moses was called to make in Moab with the children of Israel is the same as mentioned in Jer. 31 : 31, 32, and by Paul, Heb. 8 : 8. This covenant can be readily traced by the Bible student through the book of Deuteronomy in distinction from the old one. In ch. 31 : 9, we learn what Moses did with it : " And Moses wrote this law, and delivered it unto the priests, the sons of Levi, which bare the ark of the [old] covenant of the Lord, and unto all the elders of Israel," directing them to teach it to the people. Verses 10–13. " When Moses had made an end of writing the words of this law in a book, until they were finished, that Moses commanded the Levites, which bare the ark of the [old] covenant of the Lord, saying, Take this book of the [new] law and put it in the SIDE of the ark of the [old] covenant of the Lord your God, that it may be there for a witness against thee [when violated]." Verses 24, 25.

We wish to call the attention of the reader to the fact that Moses did not seal this new covenant with blood, as he did the first; this must be done by Christ, the testator. This second and new covenant, thus arranged and taught the people, was the book of hope revealing Christ, to which the old schoolmaster was continually pointing, and admonishing them of this law of faith as their only refuge from sin, and from final destruction.

With these remarks upon this covenant, as revealed in Deuteronomy, we will inquire whether it bears the marks of the new covenant, and the acknowledgments of the Saviour and his apostles. The token of the new covenant is "CIRCUMCISION OF THE HEART IN THE SPIRIT, and not in the letter, whose praise is not of men, but of God" (Rom. 2 : 29), which signifies the "crucifying of the flesh with the affections and lusts." Gal. 5 : 24.

"CIRCUMCISE, therefore, the foreskin of your heart, and be no longer stiff-necked." Deut. 10 : 16. In Deuteronomy, chap. 30, we find Moses exhorting the people to repentance, though scattered among the heathen, saying, "And the Lord thy God will CIRCUMCISE THINE HEART, and the heart of thy seed [those who repent], to love the Lord thy God with all thine *heart*, and with all thy soul." Thus Paul and Moses agree on this point. Again: the *new covenant* is written IN THE HEART, and we think that none are circumcised in the heart to love God with all their hearts, and with all their souls, without having the law of faith written in their hearts, nor without the assurance that the Lord is their God, and they are his people.

We will hear Paul and Moses once more on this covenant. Moses says concerning this [second] covenant which he commands them *this day*, " It is not hid from thee, neither is it far off. It is not in heaven, that thou shouldest say, Who shall go up for us to heaven, and bring it unto us, that we may hear it and do it. Neither is it beyond the sea, that thou shouldest say, Who shall go over the sea for us, and bring it unto us, that we may hear it and do it. But the WORD is very nigh unto thee, in *thy mouth and in thy* heart, that thou mayest do it." Deut. 30: 11–13. And Paul quotes this language of Moses on the new covenant in contrast with what he says on the old, and paraphrases and explains it. " Christ is the end of the law [old covenant] for righteousness to every one that believeth. For Moses describeth the righteousness which is of the law [old covenant], that the man which doeth those things shall live by them. But the righteousness which is of faith [the new covenant] speaketh [readeth] on this wise: Say not in thine heart, Who shall ascend into heaven? that is, to bring Christ down from above, or, Who shall descend into the deep? that is, to bring up Christ again from the dead. But what saith it? The word is nigh thee, even in thy mouth, and in thy heart: that is the word of faith, which we preach; that if thou shalt confess with thy mouth the Lord Jesus, and shalt believe in thine heart that God raised him from the dead, thou shalt be saved."

This comment of Paul on the [second or] new covenant by Moses demonstrates that this "*covenant beside the one in Horeb*" (Deut. 29 : 1), and Paul's *law of faith* (Rom. 10 : 6), are identical; otherwise we have no rule by which to prove that any New Testament text is a quotation of one from the Old. It might easily be shown that the New Testament writers, in quoting for gospel instruction, generally quote from Deuteronomy. As sure, therefore, as the *nationality* of that typical people was utterly destroyed by rejecting that covenant in rejecting Christ, its administrator, so surely all *individuals* who reject it will finally perish. Let us " take heed lest any of us fall after the same example of unbelief."

We will here remark that when this covenant was fully "brought to light in the gospel" by the mission of Christ, **RATIFIED** and **SEALED BY HIS BLOOD**, as the testator and its ministers appointed, it entirely superseded the old "schoolmaster," **or** law of works, as a rule of action; and Paul says it *is abolished*. Having identified the new covenant, we pass to notice some of its advantages.

IV. The advantages of this covenant over the first are these: The old covenant could give the knowledge of sin (Rom. 3 : 20; 7 : 7), but could not justify the offender. Its demand was vengeance.

The new law can forgive and justify the offender by repentance and faith. Heb. 8 : 12.

The old kills; the new gives life (2 Cor. 3 : 6); the old could not give righteousness.

" If righteousness come by the law, then Christ is dead in vain." Gal. 2 : 21. The new can give righteousness.

"If we confess our sins, he is faithful and just to forgive us our sins, and to cleanse us from all unrighteousness." 1 John 1 : 9.

The ministration of the old IS DEATH. 2 Cor 3 : 7.

The new, by the Spirit, being written in the heart giveth life from the dead. Rom. 8 : 11. These are a few of the many advantages of the new covenant over the old.

V. The commandments of this covenant are for our life and good. Some of these are, "Hear, O Israel: The Lord our God is one Lord: and thou shalt love the Lord thy God with all thine heart, and with all thy soul, and with all thy might." Deut. 6 : 4, 5. "Thou shalt not avenge, nor bear any grudge against the children of thy people, but thou shalt love thy neighbor as thyself. I am the Lord." Lev. 19 : 18. That these commandments belong to the new law — the law of faith — is proved by the instructions of Christ to the scribe who asked him, " Which is the first commandment of all? And Jesus answered him, The first of all the commandments is, Hear, O Israel: The Lord our God is one Lord: and thou shalt love the Lord thy God with all thy heart, and with all thy soul, and with all thy mind, and with all thy strength: this is the first commandment. And the second is like, namely, this: Thou shalt love thy neighbor as thyself. On these two commandments hang all the law and the prophets." Mark 12 : 29. Matt. 22 : 37, 40. The reader should observe that these two commandments are not found in the decalogue of ten commandments of the old covenant, but in Deut. 6 : 4, and Lev. 19 : 18, and are of the new covenant.

In Christ's Sermon on the Mount, recorded in Matt. ch. 5, 6, and 7, we hear him contrasting his commandments of the new law with those of the old, and sums them up as follows : " Therefore all things whatsoever ye would that men should do to you, do ye even so to them : for this is the law and the prophets." Matt. 7 : 12. Paul also gives us something on the new law. " Owe no man anything, but to love one another : for he that loveth another hath fulfilled the law. For this, Thou shalt not commit adultery, Thou shalt not kill, Thou shalt not steal, Thou shalt not bear false witness, Thou shalt not covet ; and if there be any other commandment, it is briefly comprehended in this saying, namely, Thou shalt love thy neighbor as thyself." Rom. 13 : 8, 9. See also Deut. 4 : 2, 10–12, 17. In the above quotation of Paul, it is very evident that he refers to the commandments of the new covenant, by Moses in Deuteronomy, and by Christ in Matthew, from the fact that he does not quote from the decalogue, nor give all of the commandments of it, but remarks, " *If there be any other commandment*, it is briefly comprehended in this saying, namely, Thou shalt love thy neighbor as thyself." We conclude, therefore, with James the aged, " If ye fulfil the *royal law* according to the scripture, Thou shalt love thy neighbor as thyself, ye do well." James 2 : 8.

VI. Having presented some of the leading commandments of the new covenant, we pass to speak of the means by which men are enabled to keep them.

We have shown this covenant to be one of mercy: all men who come to the years of accountability, and neglect to believe in and confess Christ, are transgressors of this "law of faith," and must have forgiveness, or perish; and the word declares that "Without the shedding of blood there is no remission." Heb. 9 : 22. But God alone, in Jesus Christ, can forgive sins, and no *blood*, except Christ's, *can cleanse from sin.* Therefore we hear Jesus saying, at the last supper with his disciples, when he took the cup and gave it to them to drink it, "For this [represents] is my blood of the new testament, which is shed for many for the remission of sins." Matt. 26 : 28. Luke 22 : 20. The apostle gives us the argument on this subject in the Epistle to the Hebrews, and explains how it is brought about: "For if the blood of bulls and of goats, and the ashes of an heifer, sprinkling the unclean, sanctifieth to the purifying of the flesh, how much more shall the BLOOD of Christ, who through the eternal Spirit offered himself without spot to God, purge your conscience from dead works to serve the living God." Heb. 9 : 13, 14. Paul informs us of the relation the church sustains to this covenant: "Take heed, therefore, to yourselves, and to all the flock of God, over the which the Holy Ghost hath made you overseers, to feed the church of God, which he hath purchased with his own BLOOD." Acts 20 : 28.

These are but specimens of the scriptural argument, showing the fact that this covenant, with its blessings, is based upon, and made sure by, the BLOOD of Christ. "He that eateth my flesh [which redeems the race from the grave] and drinketh my blood [which cleanses the conscience from sin], hath eternal life." The Scriptures abound in such facts and arguments on this point.

VII. The promises of this covenant are very numerous, and of all importance. We shall quote a few of them, to set the reader on the line. "And the Lord said unto Abram, after that Lot was separated from him, Lift up now thine eyes, and look from the place where thou art, northward, and southward, and eastward, and westward : for all the land which thou seest, to thee will I give it, and to thy seed forever." Gen. 13 : 14, 15.

Jesus said to those who believed on him, " If ye continue in my word, then are ye my disciples indeed ; and ye shall know the truth, and the truth shall make you free." John 8 : 31, 32. And Paul tells us the benefits of being Christ's : "And if ye be Christ's, then are ye Abraham's seed, and heirs according to the promise." Gal. 3 : 29. Once more from Moses' new covenant : "Thou shalt keep therefore his statutes, and his commandments, which I command thee this day, that it may go well with thee, and with thy children after thee, and that thou mayest prolong thy days upon the earth, which the Lord thy God giveth thee, forever." Deut. 4 : 40.

This prolonging of our days in the earth must refer to the everlasting inheritance promised Abraham and his seed ; consequently, we hear Jesus saying, "Blessed are the meek, for they shall inherit the earth. Blessed are they which hunger and thirst after righteousness, for they shall be filled. Blessed are the pure in heart, for they shall see God. Blessed are the peacemakers, for they shall be called the children of God." Matt. 5: 5–9. Precious promises indeed are these. "And this is the will of him that sent me, that every one which seeth the Son, and believeth on him, may have everlasting life: and I will raise him up at the last day." John 6: 40. "My sheep hear my voice, and I know them, and they follow me: and I give unto them eternal life, and they shall never perish, neither shall any man pluck them out of my Father's hand." John 10: 27, 28. "But godliness is profitable unto all things, having promise of the life that now is, and of that which is to come." 1 Tim. 4: 8. "If we have been planted together in the likeness of his death, we shall be also in the likeness of his resurrection." Rom. 6: 5. "But if the spirit of him that raised up Jesus from the dead dwell in you, he that raised up Christ from the dead shall also quicken your mortal bodies by his spirit that dwelleth in you." Rom. 8: 11. "When Christ, who is our life, shall appear, then shall ye also appear with him in glory." Col. 3: 4.

What a prospect is before the children of God! Surely the Lord seeks to allure us away from the trifling toys of the earth in its present condition. Again we hear Jesus saying, as he comes in glory to execute judgment and bestow rewards, "Come, ye blessed of my Father, inherit the kingdom prepared for you from the foundation of the world." Matt. 25: 34. "He that overcometh shall inherit all things; and I will be his God, and he shall be my son." Rev. 21: 7. We do not wonder that Peter declared that God had "given unto us exceeding great and precious promises, that by these we might be partakers of the divine nature."

> " Lift your glad voices ! He conquered the grave —
> Jesus Immanuel, almighty to save.
> Shout to the tyrant, ' Thy chains are all broken ; '
> Sing, for the voice of Jehovah hath spoken.
>   Open the portal,
>   Ransomed immortal ;
> Life shall endure with eternity's wave." — *D. T. Taylor.*

VIII. Let us now take a short look at the curses of this covenant on those who despise it, or disregard and forsake it.

"See, I have set before thee, this day, life and good, and death and evil. But if thine heart turn away, so that thou wilt not hear, but shalt be drawn away, and worship other gods, and serve them, I denounce unto you this day, that ye shall surely perish." Deut. 30 : 15–18. Jesus says, in speaking of the doom of the wicked, " These shall go away into everlasting punishment." Matt. 25 : 46. Paul and John give us the nature of that punishment which shows it to be most fearful. " The Lord Jesus shall be revealed from heaven, with his mighty angels, in flaming fire, taking vengeance on them that know not God, and that obey not the gospel of our Lord Jesus Christ ; who shall be punished with everlasting destruction from the presence of the Lord, and from the glory of his power." 2 Thess. 1 : 7–9. " But the fearful, and unbelieving, and the abominable, and murderers, and whoremongers, and sorcerers, and idolaters, and all liars, shall have their part in the lake which burneth with fire and brimstone ; which [part] is the second death." Rev. 21 : 8.

Fearful indeed is the end of the wicked. How terrible the thought, that while the Lord has made such ample provision for the rescue of the lost, at such a price as the blood of his Son, yet multitudes will perish, because, as Jesus remarks, "they will not come unto me that they may have life." Life and death are set before us, and we are urged to choose life, that we may live.

> "Come at the Saviour's call! hark! hear the cry;
> Turn, sinners, one and all: why will ye die?
> Why will you mercy spurn — heed not my call?
> Sinners, turn, sinners, turn, my blood's for all.
>
> "Come at the Spirit's call! hasten away!
> Lest vengeance on you fall, no more delay.
> Come to the gospel stream, drink and rejoice;
> Sinners, turn, sinners, turn; make Christ your choice."

Dear reader, what a contrast between the blessings and the curses of this covenant! Let us well consider the consequences of rejecting or neglecting to accept the offers of this great salvation. That both the readers and the writers of this work may escape its denunciations, and obtain its blessings, is our humble prayer. Amen.

CHAPTER X.

THE NEW BIRTH.

"Verily, verily, I say unto thee, Except a man be born again, he cannot see the kingdom of God" (John 3:3) — " he cannot discern the reign of God." — *Campbell.*

The doctrine of the new birth is seen by the careful Bible student to be of great importance, for all who do not attain to it must be shut out of the kingdom of God, and deprived of "eternal salvation." We cannot too closely examine its foundation principles, nor be too anxious to attain unto its privileges.

In entering upon the examination of this subject we feel that its vast importance demands a more thorough investigation and statement than it has usually received, and will bring us to conclusions not generally considered; for this reason we beg the candid scrutiny and prayerful attention of our readers. It may be in place here to introduce a few extracts from able Bible scholars, touching this subject, before we proceed with our investigations.

Dr. Adam Clarke, in his comment on 1 John 2:29, remarks, "The *titles* bestowed on Christians in the New Testament have been misunderstood by many. *What belongs, strictly speaking, to the* PURE *and* HOLY, *is often applied to those who, though bound by their* PROFESSION *to be such, were very far from it.* This has been strongly denied by writers who should have known better. Dr. Taylor has handled this point well in his "Key to the Apostolic Writings," from which I have given copious extracts in my Preface to the Epistle to the Romans, from the conviction that the subject had been most dangerously misapprehended, and that several of the worst heresies which disgrace religion had sprung from this misapprehension. With some, Dr. Taylor's being an *Arian* was sufficient to invalidate any testimony he might offer; but it is no discovery of Dr. Taylor; it is what every attentive, *unprejudiced* reader finds on reading the Old Testament in connection with the New. Perhaps those who have too little grace, sense, and candor to search for themselves may be pleased that Dr. Macknight saves them the trouble."

"Dr. Macknight, after having remarked that the words *born of him* (1 John 2: 29) should have been translated *hath been begotten of him*, which is the literal signification of the word γενναω (gennaō), *gigno, I beget* ["born of God" being nowhere found in the Scripture], goes on to say, 'To understand the import of the high titles which in the New Testament are given to the disciples of Christ, viz., *the begotten of God*, as here, — *children of God*, as in the next chapter — *heirs of God* (Rom. 8: 17) — *elect of God* — *adopted of God* — *saints* — *a royal priesthood* — *a holy nation* — *a peculiar people* (1 Pet. 2: 9), the following observations may be of use.

"'1. These high titles were anciently given to the Israelites as a nation, because they were separated from mankind to be God's visible church, for the purpose of preserving the knowledge and worship of Him in the world, as the only true God.

"'This appears from God's own words. Ex. 29 : 3, &c. : "*Tell the children of Israel, ye have seen what I did to the Egyptians; and how I bare you on eagles' wings, and brought you unto myself: now, therefore, if ye will obey my voice indeed, and keep my covenant, then ye shall be a peculiar treasure unto me above all people, and ye shall be unto me a kingdom of priests, and a holy nation.*" Deut. 14 : 1 — "*Ye are the children of the Lord your God, for thou art a holy people to the Lord thy God.*" In particular the title of *God's Son, even his first born,* was given to the *whole Israelitish nation,* by God himself (Ex. 4 : 24), chiefly because they were the descendants of Isaac, who was supernaturally begotten by Abraham, through the power which accompanied the promise. Gen. 18 : 10 — "*Lo, Sarah shall have a son.*" So Paul informs us (Rom. 9 : 7), "*Neither because they are the seed of Abraham, are they all children* [of God]; *but in Isaac shall a seed be to thee — the children of the flesh, these are not the children of God, but the children of promise are counted for a seed.*" Isaac and his descendants, whom Abraham procreated through the strength which accompanied the promise, being more properly procreated by God than by Abraham, were *the children of God:* they were a fitting image to represent the invisible church of God, consisting of believers of all ages and nations, who, being regenerated by the Spirit of God, are the true children of God, and heirs of the heavenly country of which Canaan was a type.

"'2. As the promise, *Lo, Sarah shall have a son,* which was given to Abraham when he was a hundred years old, and Sarah was *ninety,* implied that that son was to be supernaturally procreated, so the promise given to Abraham (Gen. 17 : 5), "*A father of many nations have I constituted thee,*" implied that the many nations of believers, who by this promise were given to Abraham for a seed, were to be *generated by the operation of the Spirit of God;* producing in them faith and obedience.

"'This higher generation, by which believers have the moral image of God communicated to them, is well described, John 1 : 12 — *As many as received him, to them gave he power to be called the sons of God, even to them who believe on his name, who were* BEGOTTEN, *not of blood, nor of the will of the flesh, nor of the will of man, but of God.*'"

The above, from Dr. Macknight, we think, gives some correct ideas in the direction of our inquiries. The terms and titles used in Scripture to illustrate the grace of God, and the conversion and salvation of man, are largely drawn from natural law and titles familiar among men. And the terms *begotten, generate, born, children,* are understood in nature. Let us define the terms used in this subject.

BEGET. To procreate, as a father, a sire, to generate, as to beget a son.

GENERATE. To beget, to procreate, to produce a being similar to the parent, to cause to be, to bring into life.

BORN. Brought forth as an animal. To be born is to be produced, or brought into life. — *Webster.*

Before there can be a birth, there must, of necessity, be a begetting; and even then a birth is not certain, as thousands of cases in nature fully attest. These facts in nature should be well considered, as our subject is closely allied to them. "A master in Israel" seemed not to have understood them, or rather knew not that these principles in nature were applied by Christ to the work of grace to illustrate God's method of reproducing from the old stock, or fallen, sinful race of dying mortals, a new, obedient, and immortal family of children. Man begets children in his own likeness, of his own blood and own nature, corruptible, mortal, and dying; but, as we have argued in other chapters of this work, God reproduces, regenerates man by his own chosen agencies, in his own image, and his own undying nature, to enjoy eternal life. Let us study the record of it.

Man is a sinner, an alien from God by wicked works, doomed to die "the second death" for his own sins, and worthy to die, "for the wages of sin is death, but the gift of God is eternal life through Jesus Christ our Lord." Rom. 6 : 23. But before mercy and eternal life can be proposed to man, he must be redeemed from the penalty of Adamic law : this Christ has done for him, and he is to be brought out from under the Adamic law by a resurrection from death. Yet this does not make him a *new man*, nor give him a *new nature*, but restores him to the nature Adam had before he sinned — dependent on the tree of life, or some other source of life, to perpetuate life in him. Then he stands sentenced to die again under another law for his own guilt. In this condition the Lord comes to man with "*the gospel of Christ, which is the power of God unto salvation to every one that believeth; to the Jew first, and also to the Greek."* Rom. 1:16.

The apostle James recognizes the effect of the gospel in believers thus: "Of his own will BEGAT he us with the word of truth." James 1:18. These, then, who had accepted Christ as their lifegiver, were begotten of God by his own will, through the agency of the word of truth. Paul also testifies to the same point: "For though ye have ten thousand instructors, yet have ye not many fathers; for in Christ Jesus I have BEGOTTEN you through the gospel." 1 Cor. 4:15. Again: "My son Onesimus, whom I have BEGOTTEN in my bonds." Phil. 10. "My little children, of whom I travail in birth again until Christ be formed in you." Gal. 4:19. Once more: "Not by works of righteousness which we have done, but according to his mercy he saved us, by the *washing* [BATHING—*Bible Union;* BATH—*Em. Diaglott*] of REGENERATION, and the renewing of the Holy Ghost." Titus 3, 5.

Thus far the truth on this subject looks very plain, and shows the work to be one of all importance to every sinner. We will now examine other passages of the same class, where the word *born* occurs in our common version, but is said to be improperly so rendered. We shall quote them in other versions. "No one who has been BEGOTTEN by God practises sin; because his seed abides in him, and he cannot sin, because he has been BEGOTTEN by God." 1 John 3:9.—*Em. Diaglott.* " Whosoever hath been BEGOTTEN of God doth not work sin, because his seed abideth in him; and he cannot sin, because he hath been BEGOTTEN of God."—*Macknight*, and *Bible Union*. Several other versions render it *begotten*. "Beloved, we should love each other, because love is from God, and EVERY ONE WHO LOVES has been BEGOTTEN by GOD, and knows God." 1 John 4 : 7.— *Em. Diaglott, Bible Union*, and *Macknight's versions*. "EVERY ONE WHO BELIEVES that Jesus is the ANOINTED one, has been BEGOTTEN by God, and every one who loves the begetter loves the one BEGOTTEN by him. . . . We know that EVERY ONE who has been BEGOTTEN by God does not sin; but the one BEGOTTEN by God guards himself, and the EVIL one does not lay hold of him." 1 John 5 : 1, 18. — *Em. Diaglott.*

We have thought best to quote these several passages in connection, to show the one grand idea in them all, which is, that the hearts of all true believers have been changed and renewed, manifesting the principles of the divine nature, loving God, ceasing to practise sin, guarding against it, and are said to be *begotten* by God through his *truth* and *Spirit*. We wished also to place these scriptures in array before the minds of those who, on account of the strong language used in our common version of 1 John 3 : 9 — *does not commit sin, cannot sin* — have been much perplexed about applying it to believers in this life, and have applied it beyond the resurrection, in the perfect world, especially because the term *born of God*, as rendered in our version, gives some sanction to such an application.

With these better renderings, added to the current sentiment of the other passages of the same class, which we have quoted, and which, most certainly, apply to believers in this state of probation, we must admit that 1 John 3:9, applies here also, and that Christianity has a deeper meaning than many suppose, and the work of regeneration is a more thorough change of heart and life than many professedly converted persons exhibit. 1 John 5:18, conclusively proves that the same principles of the third chapter, ninth verse, do apply to this mortal state of believers. But we will add one more on this point. "And now, dear children, abide in him, so that when he shall appear we may have confidence, and not be put to shame by him, in his PRESENCE. If you know that he is righteous, you know that every one PRACTISING RIGHTEOUSNESS has been BEGOTTEN by him." 1 John 2:29. — *Em. Diaglott.*

The gospel accepted, and its power applied to the heart by the Spirit of God subduing the moral nature of the believer, lays the foundation for a new man, or generates a new life, which, if properly appreciated, will produce an immortal, physical nature in "the resurrection of the just." For there must be care exercised by the believer, or he will not retain the new life commenced in his soul. The Scriptures fully caution us on this point. "That ye put off concerning the former conversation the old man, which is corrupt according to the deceitful lusts, and be renewed in the spirit of your mind; and that ye put on the new man, which, after God, is created in righteousness and true holiness." Eph. 4:22–24.

This is not in man to perform of himself. He is not able to do this. The apostle had before stated the principle on which it is done. "For we are his workmanship, created in Christ Jesus unto good works, which God hath before ordained that we should walk in them." Eph. 2 : 10. "For it is God that worketh in you both to will and to do of his good pleasure." Phil. 2 : 13. The apostle prays for us on this wise : " that he would grant you, according to the riches of his glory, to be strengthened with might by his Spirit in the inner man." Eph. 3 : 16. And to teach us the importance of having the Spirit of God, he gives us a statement of its fruits. Gal. 5 : 22. We are also told that, "After ye believed, ye were sealed with that Holy Spirit of promise, which is the earnest of our inheritance until the redemption of the purchased possession." Eph. 1 : 13. Then we are exhorted, "Grieve not the Holy Spirit of God, whereby ye are sealed unto the day of redemption." Eph. 4 : 30. We are also taught, "Walk in the Spirit, and ye shall not fulfil the lusts of the flesh." The language of Peter is very clear and forcible on the duty of care and attention after we have been *begotten* by the truth, in order that we may attain to the new birth, and enter into the kingdom of God. In referring to those "elect according to the foreknowledge of God the Father, through sanctification of the Spirit, unto obedience and sprinkling of the blood of Jesus Christ," he says, "Blessed be the God and Father of our Lord Jesus Christ, which according to his abundant mercy hath BEGOTTEN us again unto a lively [*living*] hope by the resurrection of Jesus Christ from the dead, to an inheritance incorruptible, and undefiled, and that fadeth not away, reserved in heaven for you, who are kept by the power of God through faith unto salvation, ready to be revealed in the last time. . . . Seeing ye have purified your souls in obeying the truth through the Spirit unto unfeigned love of the brethren, see that ye love one another with a pure heart fervently; being born [BEGOTTEN] again, not of corruptible seed, but of incorruptible, by the word of God, which liveth and abideth forever." 1 Pet. 1 : 2, 3, 4, 5, 22, 23. "According as his divine power hath given unto us all things that pertain unto life and godliness, through the knowledge of him that hath called us to glory and virtue: whereby are given unto us exceeding great and precious promises; that by these ye might be partakers of the divine nature, having escaped the corruption that is in the world through lust. And beside this, giving all diligence, add to your faith virtue, and to virtue knowledge, and to knowledge temperance, and to temperance patience, and to patience godliness, and to godliness brotherly kindness, and to brotherly kindness charity. For if these things be in you, and abound, they make you that ye shall neither be barren nor unfruitful in the knowledge of our Lord Jesus Christ. But he that lacketh these things is blind, and cannot see afar off, and hath forgotten that he was purged from his old sins. Wherefore the rather, brethren, give diligence to make your calling and election sure: for if ye do these things, ye shall never fall; for so an entrance shall be ministered unto you abundantly into the everlasting kingdom of our Lord and Saviour Jesus Christ." 2 Pet. 1 : 3–11.

The reader cannot fail to see that being converted by accepting of Christ through the gospel does not insure us a part in the kingdom of God, unless 'we hold fast the confidence and the rejoicing of the hope firm unto the end." Heb. 3:6.

Those who do not thus continue never come to the new birth, consequently never enter into the kingdom of God; while those who do "walk in the Spirit," and "continue in the word," will be brought forth into life eternal by "the resurrection of life" (John 5:29), be "*born again*," born from the dead to the fulness of life and immortality.

It will be seen, by careful attention, that this doctrine is involved in much that is said in the Bible on the subjects of conversion, obedience to the end, and a resurrection to eternal life, and an introduction into the kingdom of God. We find it incorporated into Paul's sublime argument in Rom. ch. 8, on the final restitution, on this wise: "But ye are not in the flesh, but in the Spirit, if so be that the Spirit of God dwell in you. Now if any man have not the Spirit of Christ, he is none of his. And if [the Spirit of] Christ be in you, the body is [doomed to death — corruptible] dead because of sin, but the Spirit [produces] is life because of righteousness. But if the Spirit of him that raised up Jesus from the dead dwell in you, he that raised up Christ from the dead shall also [give life] quicken your mortal bodies by his Spirit that dwelleth in you." Rom. 8: 9–11. "And God hath both raised up the Lord, and will also raise up us by his own power." 1 Cor. 6:14. "For ye are [under sentence of death] dead, and your life is hid with Christ in God. When Christ, who is our life [giver], shall appear, then shall ye also appear with him in glory." Col. 3:3, 4.

When Christ was instructing Nicodemus on the *new birth*, he remarks, "That which is born of the flesh is flesh, and that which is born of the Spirit is spirit." We hear Paul discussing this point on this wise, while arguing the resurrection of the people of God: "The first Adam was made a living soul; the last Adam was made a quickening spirit. The first man is of the earth, earthy; the second man is the Lord from heaven. As is the earthy, such are they also that are earthy; and as is the heavenly [the Lord from heaven], such are they also that are heavenly. And as we have borne the image of the earthy [first Adam], we shall also bear the image of the heavenly. Now this I say, brethren, that flesh and blood [the natural descendants of Adam or of Abraham] cannot inherit [have no claim to] the kingdom of God." 1 Cor. 15 : 45, 50.

Peter also gives the same idea on the same subject. "For Christ also hath once suffered for sins, the just for the unjust, that he might bring us to God, being put to death in the flesh, but quickened [raised to life] by the Spirit." 1 Pet. 3 : 18. This was the method by which Christ "was made a quickening spirit," and which led Paul to argue, "But now is Christ risen from the dead and become the FIRST FRUITS of them that slept." 1 Cor. 15 : 20. The resurrection of Christ is elsewhere shown to be a *birth*, and as it certainly was not his first, it must be his second birth, a pattern for his followers. Let us read. "Who hath delivered us from the power of darkness and hath translated us into [*changed us for* — EM. DIAGLOTT] the kingdom of his dear Son, in whom we have redemption through his blood, even the forgiveness of sin. . . . And he is the head of the body, the church, who is the beginning, the FIRST BORN from the dead; that in all things he might have the preëminence." Col. 1 : 13, 14, 18. All this testimony, and this class of scriptures, shed light on the doctrine of the *new birth*, and aid us in understanding the meaning of Christ's saying to Nicodemus, "Except a man be *born again*, he cannot see [enter into] the kingdom of God;" because the kingdom is an immortal one, and belongs to the heirs of God through Christ and the resurrection from the dead, as we have clearly shown elsewhere. While Nicodemus came to Jesus by night for instruction, he was not free from the error of Judaism, that blinding notion, that, by virtue of being the real descendants of Abraham according to the flesh, and sign of circumcision, the Pharisees inherited and held title to the kingdom of God, and would enter into and enjoy it, when established, by virtue of a natural birth.

This fallacious notion was the great source of the nation's apostasy and blindness, which prevented them from accepting Christ and his gospel; and we find the discourses and parables of Christ constantly directed against it. This accounts for the apparent abruptness of his language to Nicodemus on the introduction of conversation. "Verily, verily, I say unto thee, Except a man be born again, he cannot see the kingdom of God." Your *birth* from the stock of Abraham does not entitle you and your nation to the kingdom of God.

The term "*verily*," twice repeated, was considered by the Jews to have all the solemnity and strength of an oath, and when used by our Lord on this occasion, must have awakened the interest of this "ruler of the Jews" to learn the nature of the second birth, and also of the kingdom of God; for it showed him that he was ignorant of both.

Let us remember the fact that the Jews had so far wandered from the path of light and truth, that they. "made void the law by their traditions," and were "teaching the fear of the Lord by the precepts of men;" that they claimed all the promises of God as being especially to them, because they descended from Abraham, and we can understand something of the blindness of Nicodemus. They had a belief, it is true, that God was to establish his kingdom and fulfil his promises to "Abraham and his seed," and that they were "his seed," and the rightful heirs. They looked for a Messiah, to grow up among them, of the seed of Abraham and of David, to introduce himself in some mysterious way, assume the title and royalty of king, acknowledge their nation as the people of God and subjects of his kingdom, entitled to all its privileges; who should put down all their oppressors, and fulfil the grand predictions of the prophets of his glorious reign; but they expected it to be in this mortal state.

Consequently, from the time the heavenly messenger announced to the shepherds on the plains of Judea the glad news, "For unto you is born, this day, in the city of David, a Saviour, which is Christ the Lord," until Jesus was introduced, by "a voice from heaven," to the multitude who witnessed his baptism in Jordan, "the people were in expectation, and all men mused in their hearts" concerning him. When he began to call on them to *repent*, to "be converted and become as little children," or "ye shall not enter into the kingdom of heaven," and openly told his hearers, "Except your righteousness exceed the righteousness of the Scribes and Pharisees, ye shall in no case enter the kingdom of heaven," — we have no reason to wonder that "they were astonished at his doctrine." Even his disciples, who accepted him as their divine teacher, were slow to learn that his "kingdom was not of this world."

There were other Jews besides this "*ruler*" who believed Jesus was from God, but did not feel willing to give up their national standing. "And Jesus said to those Jews which believed on him, If ye continue in my word, then are ye my disciples indeed, and ye shall know the truth, and the truth shall make you free. They answered him, We be Abraham's seed, and were never in bondage to any man; how sayest thou, Ye shall be made free? Abraham is our father." John 8: 31. With this feeling of national righteousness and royal blood, Nicodemus was bewildered, and could not understand the nature of God's kingdom, nor who were the true heirs to it, neither that a change to immortality must be obtained before they could see it, or enter and enjoy it.

With this blindness, produced by an erroneous theory, he came to Christ, and listened with surprise to the solemn and mysterious saying which embodied both a symbol and a literal statement of fact — "Verily, verily, I say unto thee, Except a man be born again, he cannot see the kingdom of God;" or, as more fully stated afterwards, "Except a man be born again, he cannot enter into the kingdom of God." Some have supposed the expression *cannot see,* in the third verse, embraces a different idea from *cannot enter into,* in the fifth verse, the first referring to an *ocular view,* which would require a new birth for the wicked, as certain passages indicate that they *will yet see* God's children "in the kingdom, and they themselves thrust out." We understand each expression to contain the same idea, the term *see* being used here, as in Deut. 1 : 36, Job 7 : 7 and 17 : 15, and many other places, to signify *enjoy,* to *participate,* and includes only the regenerate — the true heirs of the kingdom of God.

The fact that Nicodemus thought of the kingdom of God and its blessings as belonging to this mortal state, is seen in his desire, to know how a man could "be born when he is old," and shows his entire ignorance of Christ's meaning. He comprehended a birth only into this mortal, corruptible world. "Jesus answered, Verily, verily, I say unto thee, Except a man be born of water and of the Spirit, he cannot enter into the kingdom of God."

This reply comprehends two births, and explains each to differ in nature from the other: the first, *of water,* — as every living child is born *of the flesh,* and "is flesh," bringing us to bear the image of the first Adam, who was "of the earth, earthy;" the second, *of the Spirit,* brings those who gain such a birth into the immortal state, in "the image of the heavenly," the immortal Son of God (see 1 Cor. 15 : 45–50), and, consequently, into the kingdom of God.

To explain more fully the difference in the nature of these two births, and the superiority of the latter, Jesus adds, "That which is born of the flesh is flesh, and that which is born of the Spirit is spirit [is spiritual — *Whiting*]. Marvel not that I said unto thee, Ye must be born again [*margin* — from above]."

Having clearly stated the point of difference in the two, he brings a figure from nature to illustrate the latter: "The wind bloweth where it listeth, and thou hearest the sound thereof, but canst not tell whence it cometh, nor whither it goeth; so is every one that is born of the Spirit." John 3 : 8. This illustration increased the astonishment of Nicodemus; he had never seen a person in this condition, with power to come and go as the wind, unobserved, and with swiftness; he knew full well that no mortal body could travel in that manner, unseen. Who could be so changed as to transport himself as the wind? "How can these things be?" he asked. "Jesus answered, Art thou a master in Israel, and knowest not these things?" Israel had the oracles of God — the Old Testament Scriptures, in which were found all *these things*. A master in Israel ignorant of the promises and covenant of God to the fathers, to Abraham, Isaac, and Jacob, which were to be fulfilled in an immortal world by a resurrection to eternal life (see Heb. 11 : 13, 16, 35]; ignorant of the "hope of the twelve tribes of Israel" (Acts 25 : 6. 8); ignorant of the nature of the kingdom of God, which was clearly stated to be eternal, and enjoyed by all the children of God, which must involve their resurrection to an immortal state

(Dan. 2 : 44 ; 7 : 27) ; ignorant of the promises of the resurrection of the Lord's people to eternal life (Isa. 26 : 19–21. Ezek. 37 : 12–14. Dan. 12 : 2) ; ignorant of the fact that Enoch and Elijah were quickened to immortality by the Spirit, and were so changed, electrified, or rather spiritized (which is equal to the resurrection), that they could ascend up to heaven as the wind can come and go (Gen. 5 : 24. 2 Kings 2 : 11) ; ignorant, too, of the promise that "they that wait upon the Lord shall renew [change] their strength ; they shall mount up with wings as eagles ; they shall run, and not be weary ; and they shall walk, and not faint." Isa. 40 : 31.

But he was not the only master in Israel who knoweth not these things ; there are some yet living. "Art thou a master in Israel, and knowest not these things? Verily, verily, I say unto thee, We speak that we do know, and testify that we have seen ; and ye receive not our witness. If I have told you earthly things, and ye believe not, how shall ye believe if I tell you of heavenly things?" Jesus had seen the change — the translation of Enoch and Elijah, therefore could properly say, *We testify that we have seen.* He had spoken to Nicodemus of the natural, flesh birth, by water, and earthly existence, in contrast with the Spirit birth ; he had illustrated the latter by a natural figure, — the wind, air in motion, which is connected with this temporary state ; thus he could say, *I have told you earthly things,* and ye believe not.

As further proof that we have presented the true and scriptural doctrine of the new birth, we call attention again to the fact that Christ is expressly declared to be "*the beginning, the first born from the dead*" (Col. 1: 18), and "the first fruits of them that slept" (1 Cor. 15: 20), by rising from the dead.

With these facts we add the historical account of Christ after his resurrection: his manifestation to Mary at the sepulchre was supernatural; again, when he made himself known to two of his disciples at Emmaus, "he vanished out of their sight." Luke 24: 31. Also when he suddenly appeared among his disciples as they were assembled with closed doors for fear of the Jews, he terrified them by that strange manner of conveyance, *as the wind*. John 20: 19. Luke 24: 35, 40. Here were exhibitions of one *born of the Spirit*, who could come and go as the wind — a *spiritual body;* and afterwards "he was taken up, and a cloud received him out of their sight;" just as Paul declares the resurrected and changed saints will "be caught up to meet the Lord in the air" when he returns. 1 Thess. 4: 15, 17.

Objections to this view of the subject will arise in the minds of those who do not have clear ideas of the kingdom of God, and of the resurrection of the dead, and who have been taught that conversion constitutes the new birth, and that the kingdom of God is the church. We will notice several insurmountable difficulties attending this application.

It would follow that without *conversion* one cannot enter into the *church*. Are there no unconverted persons in the church? Again: "Except your righteousness exceed the righteousness of the Scribes and Pharisees, ye shall in no case enter into the" — church. Do all church members exceed the Scribes and Pharisees in righteousness? "It is easier for a camel to go through the eye of a needle, than for a rich man to enter into the " — church. Are there no " rich men " in the church? no " covetous," no " unrighteous " ones in the church? none but those " greater than John the Baptist "?

The error of this position is seen at a glance; but others apply the new birth to conversion, and locate the kingdom in heaven, or on the new earth. Let us notice this view.

Do we know of any converted persons? All will claim they believe they do. "The wind bloweth where it listeth, and thou hearest the sound thereof, but canst not tell whence it cometh and whither it goeth; *so is every one that is born of the Spirit.*" Are any of us so? Do we know of any who are? Have we read of any of the holy ones of old who could *come and go as the wind?* We know of only Enoch, Elijah, and Christ. Are none converted? We think many have been and are being converted, begotten of God, by his Spirit and word.

But some take yet another position — that it is the Spirit by which we are converted, born, that *comes and goes as the wind.* And do we not know from whence the Spirit of God cometh? Are we not told that it comes from God? And does not the Spirit which converts enter and dwell in the hearts of believers? We think all real Christians will admit this.

With all deference to the opinions of good men, we feel obliged to adopt the position we have advocated above, as a grand and glorious doctrine of regeneration, which chimes with all other parts of the plan of grace.

But there is another objection sometimes urged — that believers are often called "the sons of God," "children of God," "heirs of God," and the "family of God." How can these be true titles if we have not arrived at the new birth? We reply, that these terms, like many others, are applied to believers in prospect of what they are to be in a future time, if they "continue in the faith," "continue in his goodness," and "be not moved away from the hope of the gospel." Here we "stand by faith," "walk by faith." Paul says, "For ye are all the children of God by faith in Christ Jesus." Gal. 3: 26. Children are recognized in the natural sense before they are born (Rom. 9: 11), and millions of them are never brought forth in birth: this many know. In the language of another, "The very instant conception has taken place, there lies the vital germ of a man. True, it is hidden, and it is helpless; . . . it is from the first moment, potentially and *in radice*, a man, with a body and soul, destined most surely, by the will of the Creator and by his law, to be developed into the fulness of human existence. No one can prevent that development without resisting and annulling one of the most sacred and important laws established by the Divine Author of the Universe; and he is a *criminal*, a *murderer*, who deals an exterminating blow to the incipient man."

This is a true statement of fact, and it is known that there are many murderers of this class. Let the above illustrate the moral condition of believers in Christ. The moment the truth has taken possession of the heart, it begins to form a new character, a *new man;* the element of new life is there, destined by the will of the Creator, and by his divine law, to change and renew the whole man, soul and body, and be developed into the fulness of an immortal being by the *new birth*, the resurrection from the dead to immortality. Sin alone can prevent such a development, and strike the fatal blow to exterminate this incipient child of God. Can such an extermination take place? We believe it can, and often does. Not all who are begotten of God continue in his grace and attain to the new birth, as is clearly shown by the scriptures already quoted in this chapter. If the new birth is conversion, then, as no one who is born can be unborn, it would follow that no converted person could become an apostate from God. As some converted ones do depart from God and become great apostates, it therefore follows that conversion is not the new birth. Several grievous errors have been promulgated in the Christian church, growing out of the error that conversion is the new birth.

When we gain the new birth — are born of the Spirit — we shall be the children of God *in facto;* then will be everlasting deliverance from mortality and evil — "Neither can they die any more, for they are equal unto the angels, and are the children of God, being [because they are] the children of the resurrection." John 20: 36. The plan of grace will yet produce a "holy nation" of immortal subjects like their glorious King. The prophet has well described their birth: "Who hath heard such a thing? who hath seen such a thing? Shall the earth be made to bring forth in one day? or shall a nation be born at once? for as soon as Zion travailed, she brought forth her children. Shall I bring to the birth, and not cause to bring forth? saith the Lord." Isa. 66 : 8, 9.

Zion will bring forth her children; she has been promised a family of immortal ones, even the redeemed of the Lord. The birth of Isaac by the promise of God was not a meaningless circumstance; it was an important type. Sarah brought forth the promised son, although from a dead body. Jerusalem, which is above, will bring forth her promised children from the dead. "Refrain thy voice from weeping, and thine eyes from tears, for thy work shall be rewarded, saith the Lord; and they shall come again from the land of the enemy; and there is hope in thine end, saith the Lord, that thy children shall come again to their own border." Jer. 31 : 16, 17.

Though they are now in the sleep of death, the promise of God is sure — " The ransomed of the Lord shall return and come to Zion with songs and everlasting joy upon their heads; they shall obtain joy and gladness, and sorrow and sighing shall flee away." Isa. 35 : 10.

Shall we be among them, dear reader? Shall we so trust the grace of Christ, and walk in his ways, abiding in his love, that when the royal family, *the holy nation, shall be born from the dead at once, in one day,* we may "enter into the kingdom of God"? If so, we must love and obey Christ.

CHAPTER XI.

THE EARTH REDEEMED.

"Which is the earnest of our inheritance until the redemption of the purchased possession." — *Eph.* 1:14.

In procuring the redemption of the lost race, provision has been made for the recovery of the lost residence also. The originally designed dominion and homestead is to be rescued from the usurper, and cleansed from all the evils and corruptions brought upon it by sin and the curse; then the earth will be made all it was originally intended to become under the obedient care of man, when commanded to "replenish and subdue it."

As we have shown in former chapters, man lost all by sin: he was turned from the garden, deprived of the tree of life, doomed to wander in toil and pain over the earth, cursed, for his sake, with thorns and thistles, and numerous other sources of pain and trouble. In this condition Adam's posterity have been a progeny of perverted, puny, trafficking, changing, dying mortals; and, instead of filling the earth with a pure, upright, holy, industrious race of living ones, to cultivate and make it like the garden of God, and then unitedly be constituted immortal, and "have dominion" over it, and all it contained, they have been filling it with violence and misery, saturating the ground with the life-blood of their fellows, in selfishness and revenge, to determine which should rule over the others, and who should own and occupy such portions of it as each might covet for himself.

As intimated above, in connection with the fall of Adam, we hear the Lord saying, "Cursed is the ground for thy sake; in sorrow shalt thou eat of it all the days of thy life. Thorns also and thistles shall it bring forth unto thee, and thou shalt eat the herb of the field. In the sweat of thy face shalt thou eat bread, till thou return unto the ground, for out of it wast thou taken, for dust thou art, and unto dust shalt thou return." Gen. 3:17, 19.

By this we learn that the Lord cursed not man only, but the lower orders of the animal creation, and the earth also. So it is explained by Paul: "For the creature was made subject to vanity, not willingly, but by reason of him who hath subjected the same in hope. . . . For we know that the whole creation groaneth and travaileth in pain together until now." Rom. 8:20, 22. This brought all down upon one common plane, that the relations of each might be equal. Had the inferior animals been permitted to escape the infection of the fall and curse, man would have lost all control over them; nor would he have long found a habitation among them.

Had the earth been left free from the curse, it would not have constantly spoken to our race, in admonition of sin and folly, by the convincing arguments of "labor and sweat," deserts and earthquakes, storms and hurricanes, droughts and simooms, floods and inundations; spontaneous productions of thorns, thistles, briers, noxious plants; poisonous marshes, restless oceans, raging seas, deathly climates, destructive lightnings, and terrific thunders. All these are the effects of sin, and intended to teach man that rebellion against God is an offence of great magnitude.

On the other hand, it would have been constantly tempting man, in his fallen state, to place his supreme affections upon it for its beauty and goodness, instead of looking up to its Author for wisdom, mercy, and help. But, with the curse upon it, the evils it produces, sin is constantly condemned, the justice of God is manifested, and man is admonished that this present world is only a temporary abode, yet exhibiting enough of its original beauty, sources of pleasure and happiness, riches and goodness, to awaken the desires of the human soul to see and enjoy it in all its former excellence, free from the curse, and, with the revelation which God has given us, to inspire the joyous hope of its final restoration, and the completion of its originally designed fulness and perfection, the habitation of perfected man in the enjoyment of the dominion offered to Adam, and procured for us by our Lord Jesus Christ.

Since the fall and curse, many and great efforts have been made by the better portions of our race to invent plans for the removal of evil from our world. Gigantic measures have occupied the minds of many to seek to bring back the hearts of the alienated race to virtue and righteousness. Governments and institutions of various grades and kinds have been projected, instituted, and maintained, with the fond hope of bringing universal peace and happiness to man, and of making the earth a Paradise. But in vain. Added to these, perverted reason and philosophy have invented schemes and religious doctrines to feed the imagination, and lead the mind to fasten upon some foreign region of bliss, in undefined space, and even "beyond space," to inspire the hope of emigrating "one by one"— at death — to the Elysian Fields of an imaginary world, and thus overcome, or get free from, evil.

But all these efforts have failed to bring harmony and peace to this world of wars and tumults, failed to generate virtue and holiness, or to give any good evidence of *a future* triumph, and failed to present any sound basis or argument to produce an unwavering and well-defined confidence of emigrating to some foreign world of bliss for security and happiness.

The wisdom and power of man, combined, can never remove the curse of God, repair the breach sin has made, nor effect a retreat from the field of conflict — the results of sin — to some other world as a substitute for the originally designed habitation of man.

While the well-disposed have been making efforts to rescue and restore, or preparing to move to some foreign world, the more vicious of the race have exhibited abundant fruits of depravity in seeking to oppress and rule their fellows in tyranny and cruelty, that they might control the world in their own way.

In this work, "the devil," "the god of this world," "the prince of the power of the air," leads them on to seek its entire destruction. But while he cannot accomplish this enterprise, he has succeeded in leading man good men to believe the Lord will annihilate it, in order to overcome sin and triumph over the usurper.

But He who "declared the end from the beginning" overrules all, and will "cause the wrath of man to praise him," and destroy the devil and his works, while RESTORING the works of his own hands. God will suffer the better portions of misguided men to use up all their wisdom and power in seeking to renovate and restore the world. He will suffer the devil and his faithful servants to do their worst to make it a perfect wreck. But their day and work are limited. God hath "appointed his bounds, that he cannot pass." Job 14 · 5, 6.

When the Lord said to the serpent, "The seed of the woman shall bruise [crush] thy head," it conveyed the determination to undo by the Lord Jesus Christ all the evil produced by the devil, as was afterwards fully stated in God's revelation. "For this purpose the Son of God was manifested, that he might destroy the works of the devil." 1 John 3 : 8.

If Christ crushes the *head* of the serpent, he destroys *him*. If he destroys the *works* of the devil, he *brings back* or delivers the earth from all moral and physical evils caused by sin. And that the mission and work of Christ contemplate all this is certain from his own clear statements. Let us hear him.

"For the Son of man is come to save that which was lost." Matt. 11 : 18. Man, his home, his treasure, the prospect of future dominion, — all were lost. If Christ saves all these, he saves only what was lost. We should also remember that the world was made for Christ.

Paul, in preaching Christ, says, "All things were created by him and for him." Col. 1:16. And again: "For of him, and through him, and to him, are all things; to whom be glory forever, Amen." Rom. 11:36. Once more: "For it became him for whom are all things, and by whom are all things, in bringing many sons unto glory, to make the Captain of their salvation perfect through suffering." Heb. 2:10.

Although the world was made for Christ, yet Adam was put in possession of it to people and subdue it: instead of doing this, he brought an encumbrance upon it — bartered it away to the devil by sinning: it fell under God's curse. Messiah, God's "only begotten Son," is the rightful heir to it. The Father has decreed that his Son shall have it. This decree is declared in the second Psalm, and the promise repeated; but it must "be redeemed from the bondage of corruption" together with man. This grand truth is beautifully illustrated by Christ in one of his parables. It should be always remembered that parables are never given to teach doctrine, but to illustrate it. Let us read: —

"Again, the kingdom of heaven is like unto treasure hid in a field: the which, when a man hath found, he hideth, and for joy thereof goeth and selleth all that he hath, and buyeth that field." Matt. 13:44. In the same chapter, 38th verse, Christ explains that "the field is the world; the good seed are the children of the kingdom." By purchasing the world Christ purchases the treasure it contained. The greater always contains the less; the world contains the children of the kingdom; they were made in the image of God, and represented in Scripture as God's "jewels"— Heb. "special treasure." See Mal. 3:17. Paul has illustrated them by "gold, silver, precious stones." They have been forfeited, and their possession also, by sin; but they have been redeemed by "Jesus, the author and finisher of our faith, who, for the JOY THAT WAS SET BEFORE HIM, endured the cross, despising the shame." Heb. 12:2.

He sold all he had — his life was given as a ransom. Says Paul, "For ye know the grace of our Lord Jesus Christ, that though he was rich, yet for your sakes he became poor, that ye through his poverty might be rich." 2 Cor. 9. Our riches will consist in being joint heirs with Christ to all he will possess in the world to come. The pledge of these riches is the gift of the Holy Spirit, which, Paul says, "is the earnest of our inheritance until the redemption of the PURCHASED possession, unto the praise of his glory." Eph. 1:14. Paul also gives us a still more conclusive and grand statement of earth's redemption, in language which cannot well be misunderstood or evaded:—

"For the creature was made subject to vanity, not willingly, but by reason of him who hath subjected the same in hope. Because the creature itself also shall be delivered from the bondage of corruption into the glorious liberty of the children of God." Rom. 8: 20, 21. Another version: "For the creation was made subject to vanity, not willingly (but by reason of him who made it subject), in hope that the creation itself also shall be delivered from the bondage of corruption into the glorious liberty of the children of God." — *Bible*

THE EARTH'S REDEMPTION. 189

Union. "For the CREATION was made subject to frailty (not voluntarily, but by HIM who PLACED it UNDER), in hope that even the CREATION itself will be emancipated from the SLAVERY of CORRUPTION into the FREEDOM of the GLORY of the CHILDREN of GOD."— *Em. Diaglott.*

The above statements of the apostle have been dark sayings indeed to those who have not discovered the doctrine of the Lord concerning the REDEMPTION OF THE EARTH. They have labored and toiled, supposed and guessed, and *admitted* what it seemed to teach, but found no place for the doctrine here contained in *their* theory; for they had so interpreted other scriptures as to transport the saints to a *foreign clime* for their eternal home, while the earth was to be annihilated on account of Satan and sin. But the great class of commentators, and eminent Christian writers of all generations who have stood in the front rank as gospel instructors, recognize this glorious doctrine of "RESTITUTION."

Although the earth has suffered much violence, and is to undergo still greater violence to cleanse it from sin and its effects, yet it will endure the purging, and come out of the fire cleansed and suited to the condition of an immortal race and the majesty of an immortal king, who shall sway his sceptre over the redeemed earth, filled with a redeemed and immortal church.

The idea that so important a part of the works of the all-wise God is to be annihilated because sin has entered the world, is not at all in keeping with the character and testimony of our Creator. "Forever,

O Lord, thy word is settled in heaven. Thy faithfulness is unto all generations; thou hast established the earth, and it abideth." Ps. 119 : 89, 90. "The Lord reigneth; he is clothed with majesty; the Lord is clothed with strength, wherewith he hath girded himself: the world also is established, that it cannot be moved. Thy throne is established of old: thou art from everlasting." Ps. 93 : 1, 2. "Bless the Lord, O my soul. O Lord my God, thou art very great; thou art clothed with honor and majesty; who coverest thyself with light as with a garment; who stretchest out the heavens like a curtain; who layeth the beams of his chambers in the waters; who maketh the clouds his chariot; who walketh upon the wings of the wind; who maketh his angels spirits, his ministers a flaming fire; who laid the FOUNDATIONS OF THE EARTH, THAT IT SHOULD NOT BE REMOVED FOREVER." Ps. 104 : 1–5. "For thus saith the Lord that created the heavens; God himself that formed the earth and made it; he hath established it, he created it not in vain, he formed it to be inhabited: I am the Lord, and there is none else." Isa. 45 : 18.

While the Lord is God, he will perform his purpose, and do all his pleasure; and although sin has defiled the earth, filled it with violence and death, brought upon it God's curse, producing innumerable evils, for which it has suffered the mighty revolutions of the flood, changing and deforming its surface, changing its position to the many other planets, causing hot and cold climates, suffering the violence of volcanic eruptions, disclosing the element which God has stored in its bosom for its renovation, it will yet be brought to its final destiny — a perfected, glorified earth.

For thus it is written: "But as truly as I live [saith the Lord], all the earth shall be filled with the glory of the Lord." Num. 14:21. When this *fails* of being fulfilled, the Lord fails to live. The one depends on the other. NEITHER CAN FAIL. But for this to be accomplished, the earth must pass through a baptism of fire, which will remove the curse, consuming the dross, cleansing it of its evils, and changing its form and position to what it originally held among the many planets of the universe.

Let us examine some of the sublime statements of the Lord on this fiery ordeal, by which the earth is to be restored.

"For a fire is kindled in mine anger, and shall burn into the lowest hell, and shall consume the earth with her increase, and set on fire the foundations of the mountains." Deut. 32:22.

"Behold, the Lord maketh the earth empty, and maketh it waste, and turneth it upside down, and scattereth abroad the inhabitants thereof. . . . The earth also is defiled under the inhabitants thereof, because they have transgressed the laws, changed the ordinance, broken the everlasting covenant. Therefore hath the curse devoured the earth, and they that dwell therein are desolate; therefore the inhabitants of the earth are burned, and few men left. . . . The earth is utterly broken down, the earth is clean dissolved, the earth is moved exceedingly." Isa. 24:1, 5, 6, 19.

"For, behold, the day cometh that shall burn as an oven." Mal. 3:1. Once more:—

"But the heavens and the earth, which are now, by the same word are kept in store, reserved unto fire against the day of judgment and perdition of ungodly men. . . . But the day of the Lord will come as a thief in the night; in the which the heavens shall pass away with a great noise, and the elements shall melt with fervent heat, the earth also, and the works that are therein, shall be burned up. . . . Nevertheless we, according to his promise, look for new heavens and a new earth, wherein dwelleth righteousness." 2 Pet. 3 : 7, 10, 13.

Such is to be the change wrought in the earth to bring it back from the curse and cleanse it from defilement for the eternal abode of the righteous.

> " Of Him, the woman's seed,
> Last in the clouds from heaven to be revealed
> In glory of the Father, to dissolve
> Satan with his perverted world, then raise
> From the conflagrant mass, purged and refined,
> New heavens, new earth, ages of endless date,
> Founded in righteousness, and peace, and love,
> To bring forth fruits, joy, and eternal bliss." — *Milton.*

Many persons, who read these scriptures in a disconnected manner and without due reflection, think the earth is to be utterly blotted out. But this reading is not a careful study of the word of God. While Peter is describing this change, he tells us that the heavens and the earth, which were before the flood, "being overflowed with water, perished." 1 Pet. 3 : 6. Yet all believe the present heavens and earth are *of the old* ones before the flood, only changed in form. When we read of the present heavens (firmament) and earth "passing away," being "dissolved," "perishing," "fleeing away, and no place found for them," &c., we are to remember that it is stated of their *present form and structure*, but their elements are to enter a new structure, of new form and beauty, consequently called "new heavens and a new earth."

As we have before stated, this is the doctrine which the great mass of our best Christian writers have always taught and maintained. A book of ten thousand pages of persons and their writings on this subject might be published. How strange that *any* who believe the Bible should not see it! We will here quote a few passages from a lecture by

EDWARD HITCHCOCK, D. D., LL. D.

In speaking of the passage (in 2 Peter, 3d chap.) quoted, he remarks, —

"In the first place, this passage is to be understood literally. It would seem as if it could hardly be necessary to present any formal proof of this position to any person of common sense who had read the passage. But the fact is, that men of no mean reputation as commentators have maintained that the whole of it is only a vivid figurative prophecy of the destruction of Jerusalem. Others suppose the new heavens and new earth here described to exist before the conflagration of the world. But these new heavens and earth are represented as the residence of the righteous, after the burning and melting of the earth, which, according to other parts of Scripture, is to take place at the end of the world, or at the general judgment. How strange that, in order to sustain a favorite theory, able men should thus invert the obvious order of these great events, so clearly described in the Bible! Still more absurd is it to attempt to fasten a figurative character upon this most simple statement of inspiration. It is, indeed, true that the prophets have sometimes set forth great political and moral changes [in such terms]. But in all these cases the figurative character of the description is most obvious; while in the passage from Peter its literal character is equally obvious.

"Take, for example, this statement: '*By the word of God the heavens were of old, and the earth standing out of the water and in the water; whereby the world that then was, being overflowed with water, perished: but the heavens and the earth, which are now, by the same word are kept in store, reserved unto fire against the day of judgment and perdition of ungodly men.*'

"I believe no one has ever doubted that the destruction of the world by water, here described, refers to Noah's deluge. Now, how absurd to admit that this is a literal description of that event, and then to maintain the remainder of the sentence, which declares the future destruction of that same world by fire, to be figurative in the highest degree! Who, that knows anything of the laws of language, does not see the supreme absurdity of thus coupling in the same sentence the most simple and certain literality with the strongest of all figures? What mark is given us by which we may know where the boundary is between the literal and the metaphorical sense? From what part of the Bible, or from what uninspired author, can a parallel example be adduced? What but the strongest necessity, the most decided *exigentia loci*, would justify such an anomalous interpretation of any author? Nay, I do not believe any necessity could justify it. It would be more reasonable to infer that the passage had no meaning, or an absurd one. But surely no such necessity exists in the present case.

"Understood literally, the passage teaches only what is often expressed, though less fully, in many other parts of Scripture; and, even though some of these other passages should be involved in a degree of obscurity, it would be no good reason for transforming so plain a description into a highly-wrought figurative representation, especially when by no ingenuity can we thus alter more than one part of the sentence. I conclude, therefore, that, if any part of the Bible is literal, we are thus to consider this chapter of Peter.

"In the second place, this passage does not teach that the earth will be annihilated.

"The prevailing opinion in this country, probably, has been, and still is, that the destruction of the world described by Peter will amount to annihilation, — that the matter of the globe will cease to be. But in all ages there have been many who believe that the destruction will be only the ruin of the present economy of the world, but not its utter extinction. And surely Peter's description does not imply annihilation of the matter of the globe. He makes fire the agent of the destruction, and, in order to ascertain the extent of the ruin that will follow, we have only to inquire what effect combustion will have upon matter. The common opinion is, that intense combustion actually destroys or annihilates matter, because it is thereby dissipated. But the chemist knows that not one particle of matter has ever been deprived of existence; the fire only changes the form of matter, but never annihilates it. When solid matter is changed into gas, as in most cases of combustion, it seems to be annihilated, because it disappears; but it has only assumed a new form, and exists as really as before.

"Since, therefore, biblical and scientific truth must agree, we may be sure that the apostle never meant to teach that the matter of the globe would ever cease to be, through the action of fire upon it; nor is there anything in his language that implies such a result, but most obviously the reverse.

"If these things be so, then, in the third place, we may infer that Peter did not mean to teach that the matter of the globe would be in the least diminished by the final conflagration. . . .

"In the fourth place, the passage under consideration teaches us that whatever upon or within the earth is capable of combustion will undergo that change, and that the entire globe will be melted.

"The language of Peter has always seemed to me extremely interesting. . . .

"In the fifth place, the passage under consideration teaches that this earth will be renovated by the final conflagration, and become the abode of the righteous.

"After describing the day of God, *wherein the heavens, being on fire, shall be dissolved, and the elements shall melt with fervent heat,* Peter adds, 'Nevertheless, we, according to his promise, look for new *heavens and a new earth, wherein dwelleth righteousness.'*

"The natural and most obvious meaning of the passage surely is, that the *future residence of the righteous will be this present terraqueous globe,* after its entire organic and combustible matter shall have been destroyed, and its whole mass reduced by heat to a liquid state, and then a new economy reared upon its surface, not adapted to sinful, but to sinless beings, and, therefore, quite different from its present condition, — probably more perfect, but still the earth and surrounding heavens. . . . The idea of a future destruction of the world by fire is recognized in various places, both in the Old and New Testaments. Christ speaks more than once of heaven and earth as passing away. And the Psalmist describes the destruction of the heavens and the earth as a renovation. '*They shall perish,*' says he, '*but thou* [God] *shalt endure. Yea, all of them shall wax old like a garment, and as a vesture shalt thou change them, and they shall be changed.*' Psa. 102 : 25, 26.

"As to the promise referred to by Peter, if he really describes the heavenly state, surely it may be found in a multitude of places; wherever, indeed, immortal life and blessedness are offered to faith and obedience. . . .

"I shall quote only one other passage of the Bible on this subject. I refer to that difficult text in Romans which represents *the whole creation as groaning and travailing together in pain until now,* and that *it shall be delivered from the bondage of corruption into the glorious liberty of the children of God.* Rom. 8 : 21, 22.

"I have stated, in a former lecture, that Tholuck, the distinguished German theologian, considers this a description of the present bound and fettered condition of all nature, and that the deliverance refers to the future renovation of the earth.

"Such an exposition chimes in perfectly with the views on this subject which have long and extensively prevailed in Germany. And it certainly does give a consistent meaning to a passage which has been to commentators a perfect labyrinth of difficulties. If this is not its meaning, then I may safely say that its meaning has not yet been found out.

"In view, then, of all the important passages of Scripture concerning the future destruction and renovation of the earth, I think we may fairly conclude that none of them require us to modify the natural and obvious meaning of Peter which has been given. In general, they all coincide with the view presented by that apostle; or if, in any case, there is a slight apparent difference, the figurative character of all other statements besides his require us to receive his views as the true standard, and to modify the meaning of the others.

"We may, therefore, conclude that the Bible does plainly and distinctly teach us that this earth will hereafter be burned up; in other words, that all upon or within it, capable of combustion, will be consumed, and the entire mass, the elements, without the loss of one particle of the matter now existing, will be melted; and then, that *the world, thus purified from the contamination of sin, and surrounded by a new atmosphere, or heavens, and adapted in all respects to the nature and wants of spiritual and sinless beings, will become the residence of the righteous.*

"The wide-spread opinion that heaven will be a sort of airy Elysium, where the present laws of nature will be unknown, and where matter, if it exist, can exist only in its most attenuated form, is a notion to which the Bible is a stranger.

"The resurrection of the body, as well as the language of Peter, most clearly shows us that the future world will be a solid, material world, purified, indeed, and beautified, but retaining its materialism.

"Let us now see whether, in coming to these conclusions from Scripture language, we are influenced by scientific considerations, or whether many discerning minds have not, in all ages, attached a similar meaning to the inspired record.

"Among all nations, the histories of those opinions have come down to us, and especially among the Greeks.

"The belief in the future conflagration of the world also prevailed among the ancient Jews. Philo says that 'the earth, after this purification, shall appear new again, even as it was after its creation.'

"That distinguished Christian writers, in all ages since the advent of Christ, have understood the language of Peter as we have explained it, would be easy to show." — *Lecture on the Future Condition and Destiny of the Earth.*

DR. KNAPP.

Dr. Knapp, one of the most scientific and judicious of theologians, thus remarks upon the passage of Peter already examined: "It cannot be thought that what is here said respecting the burning of the world is to be understood figuratively, as Wettstein supposes; because the fire is here too directly opposed to the literal water of the flood to be so understood. It is the object of Peter to refute the boast of scoffers, that all things had remained unchanged from the beginning, and that, therefore, no day of judgment and no end of the world could be expected. And so he says that originally, at the time of the creation, the whole earth was covered and overflowed with water (Gen. ch. 1), and that from hence the dry land appeared; and the same was true of Noah's flood. But there is yet to come a great fire revolution.

"*The heavens and the earth* [the earth with its atmosphere] *are reserved or kept in store, for the fire*, until the day of judgment. Ver. 10. At that time *the heavens will pass away with a great noise, and the elements will be dissolved by fervent heat, and everything upon the earth will be burnt up.* The same thing is taught in verse 12. But in verse 13 Peter gives the design of this revolution.

"It will not be annihilation: but we expect a *new heavens and a new earth, wherein dwelleth righteousness*, i. e., an entirely new, altered, and beautiful *abode for man, to be built from the ruins of his former dwelling-place, as the future habitation of the pious.* Rev. 21:1. This will be very much the same way as a more perfect and immortal body will be reared from the body which we now possess."—*Theology*, vol. ii. p. 649.

FROM JOHN WESLEY.

"Thus saith the Creator and Governor of the universe: 'Behold, I make all things new,'—all of which are included in that expression of the apostle, 'A new heaven and a new earth.' . . . This is the introduction to a far nobler state of things — the universal restoration which is to succeed the universal destruction. For '*we look*,' says the apostle, '*for new heavens and a new earth, wherein dwelleth righteousness.*' . . . All the elements will be new indeed; entirely changed as to their qualities, although not as to their nature. Let us next take a view of those changes which we may reasonably suppose will then take place in the earth. It will no more be bound up with intense cold, nor parched up with extreme heat, but will have such a temperature as will be most conducive to its fruitfulness. . . . It will no more be shaken or torn asunder by the impetuous force of earthquakes, and will, therefore, need neither Vesuvius nor Etna, nor any burning mountains, to prevent them.

"There will be no more horrid rocks, or frightful precipices; no wild deserts, or barren sands; no impassable morasses, or unfruitful bogs, to swallow up the unwary traveller. . . . Not thorns, briers, or thistles; not any useless or fetid weed; not any poisonous, hurtful, or unpleasant plant; but every one that can be conducive, in any wise, either to our use or pleasure. How far beyond all that the most lively imagination is now able to conceive! We shall no more regret the loss of the terrestrial paradise. For all the *earth* shall be a more beautiful paradise than Adam ever saw." — No. 69, *Wesley's Sermons.*

FROM THOMAS CHALMERS, D. D., LL. D.

In the sermon of the eminent Scotch divine on 2 Pet. 3 : 13, we find the foregoing views so clearly stated, that we extract a few sentences for those to reflect upon who may not have seen it. He says, "This may serve to rectify an imagination of which we think that all must be conscious — as if the grossness of materialism was only for those who had degenerated into the grossness of sin, and that, when a spiritualizing process had purged away all our corruption, then, by the stepping-stones of death and a resurrection, we should be borne away to some ethereal region, where sense, and body, and all in the shape either of audible sound or of tangible substance, were unknown.

"And hence that strangeness of impression which is felt by you, should the supposition be offered, that in the place of eternal blessedness there will be ground to walk upon; or scenes of luxuriance to delight the corporeal senses; or the kindly intercourse of friends talking familiarly, and by articulate converse together; or, in short, anything that has the least resemblance to a local territory, filled with various accommodations, and peopled over its whole extent by creatures formed like ourselves, — having bodies such as we now wear, and faculties of perception, and thought, and mutual communication, such as we now exercise.

"The common imagination that we have of paradise on the other side of death is that of a lofty aerial region, where the inmates float in ether, or are mysteriously suspended upon nothing, where all the warm and sensible accompaniments which give such an expression of strength, and life, and coloring to our present habitation, are attenuated into a sort of spiritual element that is meagre, and imperceptible, and utterly uninviting to the eye of mortals here below; where every vestige of materialism is done away, and nothing left but certain unearthly scenes that have no power of allurement, and certain unearthly ecstasies, with which it is felt impossible to sympathize.

"The holders of this imagination forget, all the while, that really there is no essential connection between materialism and sin; that the world which we now inhabit had all the amplitude and solidity of its present materialism before sin entered into it; that God, so far, on that account, from looking slightly upon it, after it had received the last touch of his creating hand, reviewed the earth and the waters, and the firmament, and all the green herbage, . . . and behold it was very good. They forget that on the birth of materialism, when it stood out in the freshness of those glories which the great Architect of Nature had impressed upon it, that then 'the morning stars sang together, and all the sons of God shouted for joy.' They forget the appeals that are made everywhere in the Bible to this material workmanship; and how, from the face of these visible heavens, and the garniture of this earth that we tread upon, the greatness and goodness of God are reflected on the view of his worshippers. No, my brethren, the object of the administration we sit under is to extirpate sin, but it is not to sweep away materialism.

"By the convulsions of the last day it may be shaken, and broken down from its present arrangements, and thrown into such fitful agitations as that the whole of its existing framework shall fall to pieces, and by a heat so fervent as to melt its most solid elements may it be utterly dissolved. And thus may the earth again become without form and void, but without one particle of its substance going into annihilation. Out of the ruins of this second chaos may another heaven and another earth be made to arise, and a new materialism, the wreck of this mighty transformation, and the world be peopled, as before, with the varieties of material loveliness, and space be again lighted up into a firmament of material splendor." — *Chalmers's Sermon.*

THOLUCK,

the distinguished German divine, remarks, —

"The glorification of the visible creation is more definitely declared in Rev. 21 : 1, although it must be borne in mind that a prophetic vision is here described. Still more definitely do we find the belief of a transformation of a material world declared in 2 Pet. 3 : 7, 12. The idea that the perfected kingdom of Christ is to be transferred to heaven is properly a modern notion. According to Paul and the Revelation of John, the kingdom of God is placed upon the earth, in so far as this itself has part in the universal transformation.

This exposition has been adopted and defended by most of the oldest commentators; for example, Chrysostom, Theodoret, Hieronymus, Augustine, Luther, Koppe, and others. Luther says, in his lively way, 'God will make, not the earth only, but the heavens also, much more beautiful than they are at present. At present we see the world in its working clothes, but hereafter it will be arranged in its Easter and Whitsuntide robes." — *Lectures on Geology and Revelation*, p. 161.

> " So burned the world upon that dreadful day,
> Yet not to full annihilation burned:
> Th' essential particles of dust remained,
> Purged, by the final, sanctifying fires,
> From all corruption; from all stain of sin,
> Done there by man or devil, purified.
> Th' essential particles remained, of which
> God built the world again, renewed, improved,
> With fertile vale, and wood of fertile bough,
> And streams of milk and honey, flowing song,
> And mountains tinctured with perpetual green;
> In clime and season fruitful, as at first,
> When Adam woke, unfallen, in paradise." — *Pollok.*

By the above extracts the reader will see that the view we here advocate is not a novel one, but is the old path, the standard doctrine of Bible believers in the Jewish and Gentile ages. We might cite a thousand names of the most sound, accomplished, and useful teachers and writers the church has always honored as her best expounders, who held and taught the Renovation and Restoration of the earth for the final abode of the righteous.

For a more extended reading on this subject from some four hundred authors of note, please see "*Voice of the Church,*" by D. T. Taylor.

There is not a topic treated upon in the Bible more extensively, or more clearly and forcibly taught, than that of the regeneration of the earth. Jesus often treats upon it in his teachings as a subject of great importance, and as forming one of the leading features of the hope of his church, and objects of attraction. Let us hear him. "Blessed are the meek, for they shall inherit the earth." Matt. 5:5. "But seek ye first the kingdom of God." Matt. 6:33. "Fear not, little flock: for it is your Father's good pleasure to give you the kingdom." Luke 12:32. "Verily I say unto you, that ye which have followed me, in the REGENERATION, when the Son of man shall sit in the throne of his glory, ye also shall sit upon twelve thrones, judging the twelve tribes of Israel." Matt. 19:28. "Verily I say unto you, that at the renovation, when the Son of man shall be seated on his glorious throne, ye, my followers, sitting also upon twelve thrones, shall judge the twelve tribes of Israel." — *Campbell's Version.*

"Indeed, I say to you, that in the RENOVATION, when the SON of MAN shall sit on the throne of his GLORY, YOU, my FOLLOWERS, shall also sit on Twelve Thrones, judging the TWELVE tribes of ISRAEL." — *Em. Diag. and Bible Union Versions.*

So full and thorough had this doctrine been stated in the Old Testament, that Peter, in his remarkable sermon to the Jews on repentance, refers to it on this wise: —

"Repent ye therefore, and be converted, that your sins may be blotted out, when the times of refreshing shall come from the presence of the Lord. And he shall send Jesus Christ, which before was preached unto you; whom the heaven must receive (*retain—Bible Union Version*) until the times of RESTITUTION OF ALL THINGS; which God hath spoken by the mouth of *all his holy prophets since the world began.*" Acts 3 : 19–21.

Such is the glorious prospect before the faithful servants of God. A home is to be provided for them worthy of the Son of God, who has given his blood to redeem them, of which we shall speak more fully in another chapter.

"God
Shall visit earth in mercy; shall descend
Propitious in his chariot paved with love,
And what his storms have blasted and defaced
For man's revolt, shall with a smile repair."

* * * *

"Thus heaven-ward all things tend. For all were once
Perfect, and all must be at length restored." — *Cowper.*

CHAPTER XII.

THE EARTH GLORIFIED.

"But as surely as I live, all the earth shall be filled with the glory of the Lord."— *Num.* 14 : 21.

In the above passage we hear the Lord pledging himself by his *life* to *fill all the earth with his glory.* We may be confident, then, that the promise will be fulfilled. God lives and will live. Much, very much, is said in the Bible about the glory of the Lord, the bright manifestation of his visible glory, as also of the visible glory of Christ, of his saints, and of the heavens and earth. From what is revealed in the Scriptures, it is fully evident that it all originates in the Father, is imparted to his Son, and to his church, and is yet to fill not heaven only, but also the earth.

We often hear men talk, or read what they write, on the subject of God's glory filling the earth, being visibly manifested, &c., when we are led to think they have only read, but never STUDIED, the Bible on this subject. Some, indeed, look for, and teach, that the glory of God is to fill the earth, while our race occupy it in this mortal state. If this is to be so, the Bible will guide us in understanding it on this wise. Let us examine it and see.

From what we have learned in our examination of

the fall of Adam, the effects of sin, the curse, the redemption of the race by the death of Christ, the doctrine of atonement, the gospel and its effects, the destiny of the earth, as presented in other chapters of this work, we arrive at a very different conclusion on this subject. The Lord has visibly manifested a degree of his glory to several of his servants on various occasions, by which we may learn its nature and contemplate the grandeur of the scene when all the earth shall be filled with it. Mortal eyes and strength have been able as yet to bear but a small manifestation of the divine glory; nor do we find reason to expect they ever will.

We will notice a few examples of these visible exhibitions to certain of our race, after noticing the primary meaning of the word GLORY. "It coincides with *clear*, and the primary sense seems to be to open, to expand, to enlarge; glory, then, is brightness, lustre, splendor." — *Webster*.

When the Lord had brought the children of Israel out from Egyptian bondage, and into the wilderness, he several times manifested his visible glory to the murmurers who doubted that he was among them, and to the idolaters who turned from the worship of the true God, to their terror and dismay, and sometimes to their destruction.

When the Lord directed a tabernacle to be made, and sacrifices to be offered, he says, "This shall be a continual burnt offering throughout your generations, at the door of the tabernacle of the congregation before the Lord, where I will meet you, to speak there unto thee. And there I will meet with the children of Israel, and the tabernacle shall be sanctified by my glory." Exod. 29 : 42, 43. When this promise was fulfilled, it was on this wise : "Then a cloud covered the tent of the congregation, and the *glory* of the Lord filled the tabernacle of the congregation." Exod. 40 : 34, 38. When the Lord called Moses up into Mount Sinai, and gave him the "*fiery law*" for the children of Israel, he manifested such a degree of his visible glory to Moses that the children of Israel saw it upon "his face, and they were afraid to come nigh him," and Moses was obliged to "put a veil over his face" to talk with them. See Ex. 19 : 18 ; 34 : 28–35, and 2 Cor. chap. 3. The cloud of God's visible glory was seen by the priests, over the altar and mercy seat in the most holy place in the tabernacle and in the temple. It was seen in the pillar of cloud which went with the children of Israel in their journey through the wilderness. It was seen in vision by Isaiah, in greater magnitude, representing what it will be when "the whole earth is full of his *glory*." Isa. 6 : 1, 3. Ezekiel also was favored with a vision of the *glory* of the Lord as it will be when the words of the promise at the head of this chapter shall be fulfilled.

Such vivid illustrations of God's glory have been given, and such a promise made, that it shall fill all the earth. It has been a subject of much concern and strong hope with the Lord's people. David cries out, "O God, thou art my God; early will I seek thee; . . . my flesh longeth for thee in a dry and thirsty land, where no water is; to see thy power and thy *glory*, so as I have seen thee in the sanctuary." Psa. 63 : 1, 2. "Blessed be the Lord God, the God of Israel, who only doeth wondrous things, and blessed be his glorious name forever, and let the whole earth be filled with his glory: amen, and amen. The prayers of David, the son of Jesse, are ended." Psa. 72 : 18–20.

When this prayer of David is fulfilled, it will be the *end* or accomplishment *of all* for which he has prayed. "When the Lord shall build up Zion, he shall appear in his *glory*. He will regard the prayer of the destitute, and not despise their prayer." Psa. 102 : 16, 17. These passages clearly indicate the time, or manner of time, when the glory of the Lord shall fill the earth.

In Habakkuk we find another prediction on this subject. The prophet says, "For the earth shall be filled with the knowledge of the *glory* of the Lord, as the waters cover the sea." Hab. 2 : 14. This passage states not only that the earth shall be filled with glory, but filled with the *knowledge* of the glory of the Lord. Another passage in Isaiah gives us light on this. In giving a prediction of the coming of the Messiah, and the work he is to accomplish, he says, "Every valley shall be exalted, and every mountain and hill shall be made low, and the crooked shall be made straight, and the rough places plain. And the *glory* of the Lord shall be revealed, and all flesh shall see it together, for the mouth of the Lord hath spoken it." Isa. 40 : 4, 5.

Such prophecies raised a general expectation among the faithful, and an earnest inquiry among the prophets, as is shown by the comments of an inspired apostle while discoursing on this subject : "Of which salvation the prophets have inquired and searched diligently, who prophesied of the grace that should come unto you:

searching what, or what manner of time the Spirit of Christ which was in them did signify, when it testified beforehand the sufferings of Christ, and the *glory* that should follow." 1 Pet. 1 : 10, 11.

From such testimony it is shown that the work of Christ is to be accomplished before the earth is filled with the glory of the Lord. This is made certain by scriptures we shall yet examine on this subject.

Had Adam obeyed the Lord, and filled and subdued the earth, bringing it to a state of the fullest development, then the promised dominion would have been enjoyed by him, as we have argued in other parts of this work. He and his posterity would have then received immortality at the end of their probation, as the gift of God, and the earth been filled with God's visible glory. As Adam came short of all this, our Lord Jesus Christ, the second Adam, will bring it about step by step.

I. Man is redeemed from under the law, brought out from its dominion, and the earth from the curse, by the sufferings and death of Christ.

II. Man is put upon probation, and his sins forgiven, and he cleansed from his unrighteousness, through faith in the blood of Christ; thus saved morally, then saved physically by the resurrection of the just to immortality and eternal life, and glorified by having "our vile body changed, that it may be fashioned like unto the GLORIOUS body of Christ." Phil. 3 : 21.

III. The earth is then to be regenerated or renovated by fire, cleansed from all the defilement of sin and the curse by fire, as shown in our chapter on "the earth renewed;" then "all the earth will be filled with the glory of the Lord"— *his visible glory;* and the people, being immortal, are adapted to enjoy such glory. Then, indeed, the prophecy of Habakkuk can and will be fulfilled: "For the earth shall be filled with the knowledge of the glory of the Lord, as the waters cover the sea." Hab. 2 : 14.

But let us examine the testimony of Christ and his apostles. When our Lord Jesus Christ was here instructing the people and preaching the gospel of the kingdom of God, his disciples were "slow of heart to believe all that the prophets had spoken"— slow to understand the nature of his kingdom. He therefore gave them a vision, which was a *miniature* of his *kingdom* and *glory* that was yet to fill all the earth. Let us reflect on the *appearance* of that GLORY. "Jesus taketh Peter, James, and John his brother, and bringeth them up into an high mountain apart, and was transfigured before them; and his face did shine as the sun, and his raiment was white as the light, shining exceeding white as snow, so as no fuller on earth can white them; and, behold, there talked with him two men, which were Moses and Elias [Elijah], who appeared in glory." Matt. 17 : 2. Mark 9 : 3. Luke 9 : 30. There stood the king who is yet to be seen "seated on the throne of his *glory.*" Here was Moses, who died in the faith, and was buried by the Lord; brought to represent the resurrection and glorification of the sleeping saints; and here was Elijah, who was faithful to God, and was translated a representative of the believers who will be "alive and remain" when Christ shall come and give the kingdom to his redeemed church. Such was the nature of the glory of God, of his kingdom, and of his subjects. That glory will cover all the earth when redemption is completed.

No wonder that the prophets, who, in prophetic visions, saw in the future the abundant glory filling all the earth, shouted for joy and prayed for it to come. We hear Christ saying again, " When the Son of man shall come in his *glory*, then shall he sit upon the throne of his *glory*, and before him shall be gathered all nations; and he shall separate them one from another, as a shepherd divideth his sheep from the goats." Matt. 25: 31, 32. "As surely as I live, all the earth shall be filled with the glory of the Lord."

With such a hope of being redeemed ourselves by " the Lord Jesus Christ, who shall change our vile body, that it may be fashioned like unto his *glorious* body," and be associated with him in his kingdom when he reigns on the throne of his *glory*, on the earth made new and filled with the Father's *glory*, Paul could well say for himself and us, " Therefore, being justified by faith, we have peace with God through our Lord Jesus Christ; by whom also we have access by faith into this grace wherein we stand, and rejoice in hope of the *glory* of God." Rom. 5 : 1, 2.

What multitudes of disciples who have found justification by faith in Christ have seen the promises of the coming glory of God, and rejoiced in the prospect! Yes, and this prospect enables the real Christian to suffer with Christ, and to " rejoice, inasmuch as ye are partakers of Christ's sufferings, that when his *glory* is revealed, ye may be glad also with exceeding joy."

1 Pet. 4 : 13. The prayer which Christ offered to the Father concerning his followers will be answered, " Father, I will that they also, whom thou hast given me, be with me where I am ; that they may behold my *glory,* which thou hast given me, for thou lovedst me before the foundation of the world." John 17 : 24.

But to enjoy and share that glory men must be immortal, like their Lord. Christ was not glorified until after his resurrection, except in the vision on the mount. Christians sometimes pray for God's glory to be revealed without any true idea of what it is. That " glory *will be revealed,* and all flesh shall see it together." It must be after the resurrection of the unjust, at the close of the millennium, of which we may speak more fully in our chapter on the millennium.

> " Come, divine, effectual power,
>   Fallen nature to restore ;
> Wait we for thy presence here,
>   Long to see thy throne appear ;
> Bid the new creation rise,
> Bring us back our paradise.
>
> " Now our universe create
>   Fair beyond its first estate,
> When thine eyes with pleasure viewed,
>   When thy lips pronounced it good ;
> Ruined, now, by sin and curse,
> **Speak it fairer than at first."** — *Charles Wesley.*

CHAPTER XIII.

THE JUDGMENT.

"To every thing there is a season, and a time to every purpose under the heaven." — *Eccl.* 3:11.

NOTWITHSTANDING the fact so plainly stated in the above passage, many forget that there is a time for *judgment* — for reward of the race of man. The terms *judge* and *judgment* being applied to the race, to individuals, to tribes, to cities, and to nations, it is necessary for the Bible reader to carefully examine the use of the words, and the application the Spirit makes of them to the different classes to whom and concerning whom the statements are made: by neglecting to do so, many have become entirely confused in relation to this theological point of doctrine, and consequently failed to see the harmony and force of truth in other important Bible subjects. Therefore many erroneous and strange conclusions are arrived at by such; leading them to talk of the dead saints being in heaven, with crowns of life and harps of gold; of the dead sinners as being in hell torment, undergoing punishment for their sins, or as having been judged, and *executed* by dying: others talk of the *last judgment*, the *general judgment*, the *final judgment*, &c. Some hold that it will be a short space of time when all the race of Adam will be called out of heaven and hell, and undergo an examination of character, a verdict rendered, and the various classes reconsigned to heaven or hell, to enjoy or suffer gradations of reward or punishment according to their grades of goodness or of vice.

Others have taught that the judgment of mankind is going on constantly, and at death all have received reward for their sins, and go, free of guilt, to heaven. Yet others teach that all go to heaven, or to a place of torment, as their cases may be, at death, each to their final reward; therefore they will have no future judgment, as death is the executioner which sends each party to their final places and states; therefore no return of Christ to earth, no calling of the race from their enjoyments or sufferings to give account for their lives in probation, no resurrection from the graves is to be expected, and *no life for the dead.*

It has also been taught that, as death is the penalty for sin, the wicked who die in sin have had their reward, and will never be raised to receive judgment from Christ, &c.

With such a variety of views in the church on so important a subject, who can be surprised at the general jargon of religious theology about the future of man. We do not propose to criticise all these views and notions, but to enter upon a careful examination of the scriptural doctrine of God's judgment on mankind for sin.

THE JUDGMENT FOR ADAM'S SIN.

"For the Father judgeth no man, but hath committed all judgment unto the Son, that all men should honor the Son, even as they honor the Father." — *John* 5 : 22.

The fact that a code of law, ordained to direct and govern men in their conduct, of necessity involves a penalty for its violation, as fully involves a time for the execution of that penalty — a time for judgment of the offender. Penalties may be of various degrees — either moderate and disciplinary in their effects on the offender, or arbitrary and determinate, in vindication of proper authority and honor of law, to deter others from crime. These elements are in all wholesome and good law. When man was placed under law to his Creator, a penal command was given : "But of the tree of the knowledge of good and evil, thou shalt not eat of it; for in the day thou eatest thereof thou shalt surely die." Gen. 2 : 17. This command was violated, and its penalty incurred. Was it due to God as the Author of that law, and to Adam as the willing violator of it, that he should be called to account for his crime and receive its penalty? This question, scripturally settled, opens the way for an understanding of the subject of judgment in the text at the head of this chapter, and all others of its class.

Adam was placed in Eden, under law, with a trial or probationary life, to fulfil the requirements stated in the law, which his Creator gave to control his conduct. The penal command given would test his fidelity to and confidence in God, and thereby form a moral character.

Adam transgressed this penal law: its penalty was DEATH. Gen. 1:28; 2:7, 8, 17; 3:6. He became a criminal, was arrested for his crime, and confessed his guilt in answer to the question of the Judge. Gen. 3:6, 10. The evidence is sufficient; the case is clear; the law is unyielding, and knows no mercy: it must be executed and honored. No further examination is needed in the case: both parties are informed of it. But the execution of judgment is arrested by covenant between the Father and the Son to effect an atonement by the offering of Christ as a RANSOM, to open the way for posterity from Adam, and a second state of probation for the race; not by preventing the execution of the law on Adam and his posterity, but by a *reprieve*. Rev. 13:8. Gal. 4:4, 5. Phil. 2:6, 11. Heb. 2:14. Rom. 5:18, &c. This point is clearly shown in our article on the atonement in another part of this book. But the sentence is declared as follows: "And unto Adam he said, Because thou hast hearkened unto the voice of thy wife, and hast eaten of the tree, of which I commanded thee, saying, Thou shalt not eat of it: cursed is the ground for thy sake; *in sorrow shalt thou eat of it all the days of thy life;* thorns also and thistles shall it bring forth to thee; and thou shalt eat the herb of the field; in the sweat of thy face shalt thou eat bread, till thou return unto the ground; for out of it wast thou taken: for dust thou art, and unto dust shalt thou return." Gen. 3:17–19.

In the above language the sentence is clearly explained by the Judge, and the penalty pronounced in presence of the criminal. The REPRIEVE is also stated with the sentence that Adam might know that time was allowed him *in sweat and sorrow*. "All the days of thy life," is the reprieve. The number of those days depended on the will of the *Lawgiver, Judge,* and *Executioner*—the Lord. We will define the term *reprieve* for those who need it. "Reprieve, to respite after sentence of death, to suspend or delay the execution for a time; as, the *reprieve* of a criminal for thirty days.

"Reprieved, respited, allowed a longer time to live than the sentence of death permits."—*Webster*.

Adam was *judicially* and *virtually* dead, in the day that he sinned, as we have shown above. He was under sentence of death — a subject, an heir, of death. If he lived another day, it was a respite, under condemnation, to die at some time, at the will of his Judge; and the time in his case is given: "And all the days that Adam lived were nine hundred and thirty years, and he died." Gen. 5 : 5.

It is seen in these facts that *judicial* judgment was passed as soon as Adam became a criminal, for then his probation ended; while the *executive* judgment — the execution of the sentence pronounced — was not until many years after. We will define the word in its judicial use.

"Judgment, in law, the sentence or doom pronounced in any cause, civil or criminal, by the judge or court by which it is tried. *Judgment,* though pronounced by the judge or court, is properly the determination or sentence of the law."— *Webster*.

In the case under consideration, the Lord is dealing

with man according to law. The judgment is a law case. When sentence was pronounced against Adam, it was pronounced against all the race that should proceed from him: "By the offence of one, *judgment* came upon all men to condemnation;" all were condemned to die: "In Adam all die." Again: "Wherefore, as by one man sin entered into the world, and death by sin; and so death passed upon all men, for that all have sinned." Rom. 5: 12, 18. 1 Cor. 15: 22.

Thus the whole race were equally under sentence of death, to be continued in life as long as the Judge might suffer it, or executed when the honor of God and the good of the people should demand the removal of those whose cup of iniquity had become full under God's *long forbearance*. Hence the execution of the race (excepting Noah and his family) "by the flood;" of the "*Sodomites by fire and brimstone;*" of the "*three thousand*" in the camp of Israel; of the "*seven nations*" of Canaan; of *Nineveh, Babylon,* and *Jerusalem,* by the sword, by earthquake, and other calamities; as also many other tribes, companies, and individuals, who have been suddenly executed by the will of God, as *ensamples* of his executions of "*judgment and justice*" in the earth. See 1 Cor. 10: 5–11. Jude 5, 7.

But it may be asked, Were not these classes cut off thus for their own personal sins? and if so, will they be raised to be judged and punished again?

We reply, they are clearly shown in the Scriptures to have been *thus* cut off for their superabounding audacity and crimes, and for the maintenance of authority and the public good. But they would have been cut off from life by other processes, as all men are. This was only closing the respite, and executing the Adamic sentence. That they were cut off by execution of the law of faith, for their rejection of the atonement of Christ and proffered mercy (which some of their contemporaries accepted), as shadowed forth in the promises of God and his typical institutions; that they suffered the penalty of the law of their Redeemer, their Purchaser, to whom they owed their reprieve, and probation, and prospective recovery from death, — has not a shade of evidence to support it. Nay, it would be a perversion of judgment to teach such an idea; and God denounces those "who *pervert judgment.*" The evidence is against it.

In civil codes of law the death penalty is found, and in cases where men are convicted of crimes which incur that penalty, they are executed; but *they* were under sentence of death by another and higher law. Does it follow that such die because they are convicted of murder? Is it not rather that they die the sooner for this overt act, as pests of society, than in common habits of life? The man who is hanged, murdered, or otherwise killed by violence, disease, or the exhausting of nature, only pays the debt of Adamic law, falls under the execution of judgment for Adam's sin, though he at the same time may pay the claim of a lesser law.

But God is Judge himself. Psa. 75:7, 8; 94:1, 2. He alone can properly decide when to withhold life, and when to execute the culprits. And should he please to exempt any, as *types,* or allow that, *as death is abolished,* the last generation of them who honor his Son may "*not all sleep*," but be *changed to immortality*, it would be only a divine gratuity, an exception to his law. As we have elsewhere shown, the Lamb of God undertook our case when Adam had brought *judgment upon all men to condemnation* (Rom. 5: 18), obtained a reprieve, became our Redemption, our Lawgiver, and Instructor. Even from the time the promise was made in Eden, that the seed of the woman should bruise (crush) the head of the serpent, the plan of grace has been *the subject* of revelation; and the administration of the civil code of law under Moses (called *the old covenant*), or other typical institutions directed by the Lord, have been introduced to develop Christ's law, — *the law of faith*, — by giving us the knowledge of sin, and by *types and shadows* teaching us a law connected with a *sacrifice of blood for the remission of sins*, called a *New Covenant, the royal law, the perfect law of liberty*, law of faith.

JUDGMENT FOR PERSONAL SIN.

Being bought out from the Adamic law by the Son of God, we are under law to him, and are accountable to him for our present lives, and our conduct in receiving or rejecting the plan of mercy which proposes to make us joint heirs with him, and bestow upon us the gift of eternal life. "The Father loveth the Son, and hath given all things into his hands. He that believeth on the Son hath everlasting life; and he that believeth not the Son shall not see [everlasting] life, but the wrath of God abideth on him." John 3: 35, 36. "All things are delivered unto me of my Father." Matt. 11: 28.

By the above passages, and others of the same class, it is shown that Christ was destined to control this world and to dispose of the people according to the *plan of grace* ordained in him; yet he had not attained to the position to judge the world. Before he takes this office, HE IS TO BE JUDGED. "For God sent not his Son into the world to condemn the world; . . . but he that believeth not is condemned already, because he hath not believed in the name of the only begotten Son of God." "I judge no man." "I came not to judge the world, but to save the world." John 3:17; 8:15; 12:47. This testimony is conclusive on this point; yet we hear Jesus saying on another occasion, "Now is the judgment of this world; now shall the prince of this world be cast out. And I, if I be lifted up from the earth, will draw all men unto me." John 12:31.

To see the force of this passage, we should remember that Christ came to SUFFER JUDGMENT for the race of man. "The chastisement of our peace was upon HIM, . . . and the Lord hath laid on HIM the iniquity of us all" (Isa. 53:5, 6), "hath made the iniquity of us all to meet on him." Heb. *margin.* "That through death he might destroy him that had the power of death [*the prince of this world*], that is, the devil, and deliver them [out of death] who through fear of death were all their lifetime subject to bondage" [of death by Adam]. Heb. 2:14, 15. The race being condemned to die in Adam, by a law which *could not give life* back (Gal. 3:21), leads Paul to argue it on this wise:—

"For what the law could not do, in that it was weak through the flesh, God sending his own Son in the likeness of sinful flesh, and [by an offering] for sin, condemned sin in the flesh." Rom. 8 : 3.

Thus it is seen that when Christ "*was made a curse for us*" by being *lifted up* on the cross, and "bare our sins in his own body on the tree," the *execution of judgment* of this world (of Adam's race) rested upon him, and by it he *conquered death* (entered the strong man's house, bound him, and despoiled him of all his goods) through a resurrection, conquered the devil, paid the purchase price for the race, obtained "the keys of death and of hell"—*hades*. He then met his disciples in Galilee, as he had previously appointed, to commission them anew for the work of "the ministry of reconciliation;" to declare his authority and restate the conditions of his law.

"And Jesus came and spake unto them, saying, ALL POWER IS GIVEN UNTO ME IN HEAVEN AND IN EARTH. Go ye, THEREFORE, and teach all nations [my law—new covenant—the gospel], baptizing them in the name of the Father, and of the Son, and of the Holy Ghost; teaching them to observe all things whatsoever I have commanded you; and, lo, I am with you always, even unto the end of the world." Matt. 28 : 18–20.

This shows the foundation which had been laid to bring all men under Christ, to accept his sacrifice of blood as an atonement for their own sins, and "the gift of righteousness by faith," securing eternal life, or be judged by him for rejecting the Lord that bought them. And, in contemplation of this fact, Jesus said, "And I, if I be lifted up from the earth, will draw all men unto me"—bring all the race out of their graves to stand before my judgment seat, or, as in our introductory text (the Father having once judged — condemned sin in him, as we have shown), "The Father judgeth no man, but hath committed all judgment unto the Son; that all men should honor the Son, even as they honor the Father. . . . For as the Father hath life in himself [existing by himself], so hath he given to the Son to have life in himself [by an agreement to raise him to eternal life], and hath given him authority to execute judgment also, because he is the Son of man." John 5 : 22, 27.

This language is very explicit; and in order to show that this authority would be used in disposing of the entire race, in executing the determination or decision of the law under which they had enjoyed probation, and by which they were justified or condemned, he adds, "For the hour is coming in the which all that are in the graves shall hear his voice, and shall come forth; they that have done good unto the resurrection of life, and they that have done evil unto the resurrection of damnation. I can of mine own self do nothing: as I hear, I judge; and my judgment is just, because I seek not mine own will, but the will of the Father which hath sent me." John 5 : 28-30.

The above passage from the twenty-first to the thirtieth verses sets forth, in a forcible manner, the following facts: —

I. That the Father raises the dead, and causes them to live, all of them, — *the dead*, — free from Adamic law.

II. That the Father has determined that all men

should honor his Son by obeying him, or submit to the sentence of his law — the new covenant; even as all have been obliged to submit to the penalty of the violated law of the Father.

III. That the Father has committed all men into the hands of his Son, to be instructed in the new covenant; and appointed him the teacher and *judge*, to instruct, and to execute his will; and give *eternal life* to all those who believe in the Father, and accept the law of Christ.

IV. That to carry out this determination, and make all men accountable to Christ, the gospel is published in all the world, for a witness to all nations, that all may be without excuse.

V. That all who have died in Adam shall hear the voice of Christ summoning them from the grave, to appear before him, to receive reward according to his law — his covenant; that they shall obey *that* call, and *come forth*, one class unto the resurrection of life eternal — *the gift of God* in Christ · the other class *unto the resurrection of condemnation* — condemned to the second death; these "shall not see life eternal," but a life which Christ purchased for the race when he bought them out from under the Adamic law by his death, and which would have been perpetuated had they accepted his shed blood as a sacrifice for their own sins when in probation; but having rejected it they must die "the *second death*," at the command of Christ the executioner.

The above points are palpable, and are sustained by the current testimony of the Scriptures. They are stubborn facts, which have stood in the way of those theorists who had other systems to advocate, and sceptics whose misunderstanding of the plan of atonement, or whose unwillingness to accept God's "statutes and judgments," has led them to use all their wits and words to evade, or to explain away, the obvious sense and open, plain statements of this passage. It has cost such persons much valuable time, many sermons, books, tracts, and arguments, in seeking to overcome, or bring this passage to yield its position, but in vain; whoever carefully reads it, is made to *feel* the force of its testimony, if he do not acknowledge it, and every effort to criticise it makes its testimony the more clear.

When Christ announces, in connection with his statement of authority to execute judgment, that "I can of mine own self do nothing: as I hear I judge; and my judgment is just, because I seek not mine own will, but the will of the Father which hath sent me," he shows that he has been appointed executor of his Father's will; and he had just stated that his Father's will was, *that all men should honor the Son*, — believe in and obey him, — and if not, that they should PERISH.

This brings us to consider the order of the judgment which is to be prosecuted by our Lord Jesus Christ: this we deem to be of importance, because strange and erroneous views are advocated by men on this subject, which lead some into other fatal errors, or make the whole subject obnoxious to sound reason, and thereby drive others from entertaining the subject at all.

We remark, then, that as judgment presupposes law, with promised blessings and penal commands, also a decision of the character of those made responsible by that law, and a time for the execution of its promises and its sentence on those justified or condemned, therefore, in the subject under consideration, we find, —

I. The law of faith, the new covenant, given as the rule of human conduct towards God and men, - - embraced in two commandments which Christ declares includes ALL OTHERS, viz., " Hear, O Israel : The Lord our God is one Lord ; and thou shalt love the Lord thy God with all thine heart, and with all thy soul, and with all thy might. And these words, which I command thee this day, shall be in thine heart ; and thou shalt teach them diligently unto thy children, and shalt talk of them when thou sittest in thine house, and when thou walkest by the way, and when thou liest down, and when thou risest up. Thou shalt not avenge, nor bear any grudge against the children of thy people, but thou shalt love thy neighbor as thyself : I am the Lord." Deut. 6 : 4-7. Lev. 19 : 18. Matt. 22 : 37.

That these are the fundamental principles of the new covenant, needs only to be examined to be admitted, and that they were embraced in the requirements or duties enjoined on Adam when placed in Eden, — " Be fruitful, and multiply, and replenish the earth, and subdue it," with the promise of having " dominion over it," and the implied prospect of falling short of it if he failed to accomplish those duties, — is well indicated.

That this law was also indicated in the promise that the seed of the woman should bruise (crush) the head of the serpent, and in the statement of reprieve, to Adam, is shown in the comments given in the New Testament on this subject.

Although this law is not brought out on tables of

stone (but on the heart), in the Old Testament (as was the old covenant), yet we find it running through the whole, being witnessed by the law and the prophets, and observed by those who are called the faithful, — the believing children of God in former ages; and in the New Testament, constant allusions are made to the gospel, the faith, the promises, and the hope of the Old Testament, showing that the gospel was the primary rule and light of all time since the fall. Jesus refers to it thus: "Search the Scriptures; for in them ye think ye have eternal life: and they are they which testify of me." John 5: 39. "Do ye think that I will accuse you to the Father? There is one that accuseth you, even Moses, in whom ye trust. For had ye believed Moses, ye would have believed me; for he wrote of me. But if ye believe not his writings, how shall ye believe my words?" John 5: 45–47.

This class of references to the Old Testament shows that the people were responsible for the light of the new covenant before Christ came, and that the Mosaic institution was to shadow it forth, and was a schoolmaster to lead both Jews and Gentiles to Christ.

But some may object to this view, from another saying of Christ, as follows: "If I had not come and spoken unto them, they had not had sin; but now they have no cloak for their sin. He that hateth me, hateth my Father also. If I had not done among them the works which none other man did, they had not had sin: but now they have both seen and hated both me and my Father."

We reply, that this saying confirms the view we have

been stating, for we find the Old Testament scriptures and institutions constantly recognizing Christ and his covenant of mercy yet to be developed and ratified, as the only means of salvation, and foreshadowing the time when Christ would show the purposes of the Father.

Had Christ not come and published these sublime truths, and done these mighty acts which the law and the prophets had said should be fulfilled by him, they would not have been accountable to him, nor to the law or prophets, as they would have testified falsely, leaving the people without a standard or guide to test good and evil.

Peter, while preaching repentance, refers to one of the promises of God through Moses on this wise: "And he shall send Jesus Christ, which before was preached unto you; . . . for Moses truly said unto the fathers, A prophet shall the Lord your God raise up unto you of your brethren, like unto me; him shall ye hear in all things whatsoever he shall say unto you.

"And it shall come to pass that every soul which will not hear that prophet shall be destroyed from among the people.

"Yea, and all the prophets, from Samuel and those that follow after, as many as have spoken, have likewise foretold of these days." Acts 3 : 20–24.

Paul also states the same fact in various forms: "And the Scripture, foreseeing that God would justify the heathen through faith, preached before the gospel unto Abraham, saying, In thee shall all nations be blessed." Gal. 3 : 8. And again, touching universal responsibility to the law of Christ, he says, "For it is written,

As I live, saith the Lord, every knee shall bow to me, and every tongue shall confess to God; for we shall all stand before the judgment seat of Christ: so then every one of us shall give account of himself to God." Rom. 14: 10–12. "That at the name of Jesus every knee shall bow, of things in heaven, and things in earth, and things under the earth; and that every tongue should confess that Jesus Christ is Lord, to the glory of God the Father." Phil. 2: 10, 11.

II. All men are to be judged by the new covenant. But how do the heathen become responsible? Let the word reply: "For the wrath of God is revealed from heaven against all ungodliness and unrighteousness of men, who hold the truth in unrighteousness; because that which may be known of God is manifest in them, for God hath showed it unto them. For the invisible things of him from the creation of the world are clearly seen, being understood by the things that are made, even his eternal power and Godhead; so that they are without excuse." Rom. 1: 18, 19.

These facts being the rule by which God has made those accountable who have not the written law, or "lively oracles of God," led Paul to say further, "But unto them that are contentious, and do not obey the truth, but obey unrighteousness, indignation and wrath, tribulation and anguish, upon every soul of man that doeth evil, to the Jew first, and also to the Gentile; but glory, honor, and peace to every man that worketh good, to the Jew first, and also to the Gentile; for there is no respect of persons with God. For as many as have sinned without [the written] law shall also perish without law; and as many as have sinned in the [written] law shall be judged by the law (for not the hearers of the law are just before God, but the doers of the law shall be justified. For when the Gentiles, who have not the [written] law, do by nature the things contained in the law, these, having not the law, are a law unto themselves, WHICH SHOW THE WORK OF THE LAW WRITTEN IN THEIR HEARTS, their conscience also bearing witness, and their thoughts the mean while accusing, or else excusing one another), in the day when God shall judge the secrets of men according to my gospel." Rom. 2: 8–16.

The careful reader of the scripture above quoted, with its context, will not fail to see that the *law* which Paul alludes to as the rule for *those who sin in the law,* and the law which he says *is written in their hearts* who have it not otherwise, and who work good, is the same which he declares in chap. 1 : 16, to be "*the gospel of Christ,*" and in chap. 2 : 16, "*my gospel.*" The same law is alluded to by the Psalmist when he says, "The law of the Lord is perfect, converting the soul." Psa. 19 : 1–7. Please read all the psalm, also Isa. 40 : 25–30. Rom. 10 : 18.

That all men have personally sinned against the law of Moses,— the old covenant,— and for that will be brought before the judgment seat of Christ, no well-informed person will pretend to claim. But that all persons of sufficient mind to be accountable to law, have sinned against law, is proved clearly enough by the scriptures above quoted, to satisfy all who are properly called *Bible believers.*

The conclusion is therefore unavoidable, that all are under law to Christ, from the time of the reprieve of Adam, and that all probationers have fallen under condemnation by the law of faith for their own sins, being in unbelief, and consequently must gain justification by that law in some way through faith in God as a Saviour of sinners, and through such faith be reformed so as to " WORK GOOD," or receive its penalty — " THE SECOND DEATH."

The plan of grace has been constantly shining from the days of Adam, and will to the end of mortality, and in one form or another has been presented to our race to lead them to God for help and pardon. Solomon calls it "*the path of the just*," which, he says, "is as the shining light, that shineth more and more unto the perfect day;" and by it all have been made responsible to God for the light communicated. "And this is the condemnation, that light is come into the world, and men loved darkness rather than light, because their deeds were evil." John 3 : 19. "For I am not come to call the righteous, but sinners, to repentance." Matt. 9 : 13. "For God sent not his Son into the world to condemn the world" (they being condemned already). " He that believeth on him is not condemned, but he that believeth not is condemned already." John 3 : 18.

That this condemnation is by the *new covenant*, and its penalty "*the second death*," must be admitted, from the fact that all the race were once condemned in Adam before they had light, and do die the first death whether they believe in Christ or not.

III. All men being under condemnation for rejecting

or neglecting the light and truth of God, Christ has become our Passover, having given "his own blood for the remission of sins," and, being raised from death, has "entered into heaven itself, now to appear in the presence of God for us," who comply with the conditions stated in the covenant, viz., "repentance toward God, and faith toward our Lord Jesus Christ." Heb. 9 : 12, 24. Acts 20 : 21.

The apostle Paul, in describing this grace, says, —

"How much more shall the blood of Christ, who through the eternal Spirit offered himself without spot to God, purge your conscience from dead works to serve the living God." And for this cause he is the Mediator of the New Testament, that by means of death, for the redemption of the transgressions that were under the first testament, they which are called might receive the promise of eternal inheritance. For where a covenant exists, the death of that which has ratified it is necessary to be procured (*Em. Diaglott*); for a testament is of force after men are dead, otherwise it is of no force at all while the testator liveth." Heb. 9 : 14–17.

This new covenant, which was first published in Eden, — the seed of the woman shall bruise the serpent's head, — and afterwards manifested as the "law of the Spirit of life," would yet, unless Christ, the author and testator, had ratified it by his own blood, have been of no force as a law, and the people would "not had sin."

But as the covenant is ratified by the death of the testator, it has the authority of law — the law of God.

The fact that a Mediator is provided for man proves that man is condemned by that law which he is Mediator of, and is to be judged by it. If he fails to become reconciled to it, he must meet its penalty. That he may become reconciled to, and be justified by it, Christ has opened a door of hope, by becoming an Advocate for all who come to him in faith, committing their cause into his hands; thus man may enter the court of heaven (where he is condemned as a criminal), by his Advocate, and plead for mercy and pardon through the blood of Christ.

An advocate pleads the cause of those who apply to him to appear in court for them, where they are recorded as criminals, and if in a judicial court, to examine their cause and present evidence why they should not be held accountable, or, if the cause has been decided and the sentence rendered, to seek a reconciliation of the offending party to the law, by a ransom, or a petition, or both.

If, therefore, men who have violated law, where judgment is to be had, and the law executed, do not appear in court personally, or by an advocate to confess, pay a ransom, or obtain pardon, they must suffer the extreme penalty of the law.

In the case under consideration, man is a criminal, Christ is the lawgiver and executioner; yet he has provided a ransom for the sins of the people, for all who place confidence in him, and come to him for assistance, confessing their sins, asking pardon, and pledging themselves to become his servants.

The sinner is in the condition of the man who owes ten thousand talents and has nothing to pay. He has nothing to give as an atonement for his sins; but Christ has, and stands ready to become the advocate and offer his blood for every repenting, confessing one who has faith in him, and resigns all to him as entirely helpless.

"Wherefore he is able also to save them to the uttermost that come unto God by him, seeing he ever liveth to make intercession for them." Heb. 7 : 25.

O, how great is the love of God in the gift of his Son for the salvation of lost men! Come, dear perishing ones, give yourselves to Christ, confess your sins, accept of pardon through his atoning blood, and receive "the gift of God, which is eternal life through Jesus Christ our Lord;" otherwise you must receive "the wages of sin [which] is death." Rom. 6 : 23.

IV. The believing portion of our race have their case settled in this probationary life, and a verdict rendered in their favor; consequently they are "sealed with that Holy Spirit of promise unto the day of redemption." Eph. 1 : 14; 4 : 30. Of such the apostle states again,—

"Nevertheless the foundation of God standeth sure, having this seal: The Lord knoweth them that are his. And let every one that nameth the name of Christ depart from iniquity." 2 Tim. 2 : 19. Such die in the Lord, and the promise is that they "shall come forth to the resurrection of life," or, if "remaining alive, shall be changed in a moment, in the twinkling of an eye, at the last trump."

But the other class of mankind, who are also on trial, on probation, with all the means of securing forgiveness of their sins and justification through the blood of Christ, neglected God's favor, refused to confess their sins, closed their eyes against the light, spurned the invitations of Christ, disbelieved the gospel, resisted the calls of the Holy Spirit, until their day of trial and probation closed, and they have become "vessels of wrath, fitted for destruction:" consequently their doom is sealed at the close of their probation. But they must die the Adamic death, *before* they can die the death due for their own sins; therefore they are reserved in death, unto the day of judgment to be punished (2 Pet. 2:9), and come forth "unto the resurrection of condemnation," to die "the second death."

V. When the probation of our race ends, the *judicial* trial or judgment closes, and the cases of all will be unalterably fixed. Then, "He that is unjust, let him be unjust still; and he which is filthy, let him be filthy still; and he that is righteous, let him be righteous still; and he that is holy, let him be holy still. And, behold, I come quickly; and my reward is with me, to give every man according as his work shall be." Rev. 22:11, 12. He comes to execute judgment.

Dear reader, consider well the subject under consideration. Can you look upon this great, this all-important event with interest? And are you confiding in the merits of the blood of the Lamb of God, as your justification? and do you feel to say, "Come, Lord Jesus, come quickly"?

If you cannot, then turn to him at once, for his pardoning mercy and saving grace.

VI. The judgment of the future will be a judgment of execution.

Each class of mankind having lived under law, and on trial (for eternal life by repenting of their sinfulness, and receiving pardon through faith) form a final character according to the decisions of the law; and thus the entire race come up to the time of execution of the promises and the sentence written in that law. Although they may not, and will not, all understand their own cases, yet there is One who does "understand the heart and try the reins of the children of men." The Lord keeps a record. He has books. We are recorded in them, and the pardon or the sentence there written must stand. "Thou tellest my wanderings: put thou my tears into thy bottle: are they not IN THY BOOK." Psa. 56:8. "Then they that feared the Lord spake often one to another: and the Lord hearkened, and heard it: and a BOOK of remembrance was written before him for them that feared the Lord, and that thought upon his name." Mal. 3:16. "And I saw the dead, small and great, stand before God; and the BOOKS were opened: and another book was opened, which is the BOOK of life: and the dead were judged [rewarded] out of those things which were written in books, according to their works." Rev. 20:12.

This is the final issue, the reward of a lifetime spent in mortality; and the rewards will be just what was written in the books — "*life*," or "*death.*" The Lord has set life and death before us, and asked us to *choose life that we may live;* yea, he has remonstrated, urged, entreated us to do so. If we have accepted it on the terms written in the books, it will be known, and the Judge will raise us up in "the resurrection of life;" for "the foundation of God standeth sure, having this seal: The Lord knoweth them that are his." But if we have misspent this life of probation, and slighted the offers of eternal life, choosing the " ways of death," the Judge will bring us forth in "the resurrection of condemnation,". "condemned already," according to the *things written* in the books. "And whosoever was not found written in the book of life was cast into the lake of fire." Rev. 20:15.

How terrible the consequences of our neglect if we do neglect the grace of God! Jesus gives an account of the rewards of the two classes of mankind, in Matt. ch. 25, in a prophetic declaration. Although he does not there give the order of the transactions, yet they are given in other scriptures. We will quote him:—

"When the Son of man shall come in his glory, and all the holy angels with him, then shall he sit upon the throne of his glory; and before him shall be gathered all nations: and he shall separate them one from another, as a shepherd divideth his sheep from the goats: and he shall set the sheep on his right hand, but the goats on the left. Then shall the King say unto them on his right hand, Come, ye blessed of my Father, inherit the kingdom prepared for you from the foundation of the world."

He then describes the works they had done, which proved that they were the children of God. "Then shall he say also unto them on the left hand, Depart from me, ye cursed, into everlasting fire, prepared for the devil and his angels." He then shows that they had not produced the fruits of righteousness, and declares the final reward of each class for the instruction of those who hear. "And these shall go away into everlasting [eternal] punishment, but the righteous into life eternal." Matt. 25 : 31, 46.

Such are the final issues of probationary life. Those who do not become righteous through Christ, but "obey unrighteousness," meet with eternal punishment; and that punishment is explained by the Lord to be death, — "the second death,"— and by Paul to be "everlasting destruction," in opposition to "eternal life." "But the fearful, and unbelieving, and the abominable, and murderers, and whoremongers, and sorcerers, and idolaters, and all liars, shall have their PART in the lake which burneth with fire and brimstone; which [PART] is the second death." Rev. 21 : 8. "In flaming fire taking vengeance on them that know not God, and that obey not the gospel of our Lord Jesus Christ; who shall be PUNISHED with everlasting DESTRUCTION from the presence of the Lord, and from the glory of his power." 2 Thess. 1 : 8, 9. Thus the Lord "will thoroughly purge his floor [the earth], and gather his wheat into the garner; but he will burn up the chaff with unquenchable fire." Matt. 3 : 12. In doing this, the wicked, — "them which do iniquity" — will be "cast into a furnace of fire, where there shall be wailing and gnashing of teeth." Matt. 13 : 41, 42. There will be "tribulation and anguish" when a host from all nations and tribes, who rejected the light shining from the book of nature, — the works of God; who closed the ear to the "still small voice" of the Spirit of God; who refused the warnings and examples of the good ones among them; who spurned the wisdom of God as "she cried daily in the gates" to the sons of men; who made game and ridicule of God's typical nation and law; who rejected, derided, and crucified the Son of God, saying, "We will not have this man to reign over us;" who have despised his gospel, which offered pardon through the blood they shed in crucifying him; who have "done despite to the Spirit of grace," have set at nought the counsels of the Lord, scoffed at, mocked, and abused his children;—when this class, of all grades of rebels against God's government, shall be called up from the grave to "receive according to that they have done," then there will "be wailing and gnashing of teeth." And who of us shall be among them? All who will not love and obey the Lord, by the assisting grace which he has provided.

VII. There is an appointed time for this judgment: "But now commandeth he all men everywhere to repent; because he hath appointed a day in the which he will judge the world in righteousness by that man whom he hath ordained; whereof he hath given assurance unto all men, in that he hath raised him from the dead." Acts 17:30, 31. As sure, therefore, as God raised up Christ from the dead, so sure is it that an appointment is made for the execution of the law of God, and that by him whom he raised from the dead. This doctrine of the Bible on rewards and punishments differs from the superstitions of men not only as to their nature, but as to TIME also. It is everywhere shown in the Scriptures to be at an appointed time, the close of probationary *time*, the end of human strife and governments, for the destruction of all evil. The apostle states that there shall be "tribulation and anguish upon every soul of man that doeth evil, but glory, honor, and peace to every man that worketh good, IN THE DAY when God shall judge the secrets of men by Jesus Christ according to my gospel." Rom. 2: 9, 10, 16.

This shows an *appointed time* in which every man will receive reward for what he hath done. We do not claim that it is a day of twenty-four hours. It is a time ordained of God in which to do the work, and is not in this mortal life, as men die. Christ does not execute judgment on the people when they die. He himself declares, "When the Son of man shall come in his glory," he will judge or execute judgment. The Son of man does not come at one's death, but at the close of Gentile time, when his "enemies are made his footstool." Daniel describes it thus: "I beheld till the thrones were cast down, and the Ancient of Days did sit, whose garment was white as snow, and the hair of his head like the pure wool; his throne was like the fiery flame, and his wheels as burning fire. A fiery stream issued and came forth from before him; thousand thousands ministered unto him, and ten thousand times ten thousand stood before him: the judgment was set, and the BOOKS were opened . . . and judgment was given [the kingdom was awarded] to the saints of the Most High, and the time came that the saints possessed the kingdom." Dan. 7: 9, 10, 22.

This day, which shall be so terrible to the enemies of God, is to be a joyous day to the people of God; they have been a by-word and reproach among the wicked; they have suffered for righteousness' sake, been set at nought and oppressed; but deliverance is to come. They have been judged by the wicked as their Master was — *unrighteously;* they have expostulated with, prayed for, and wept over their enemies, seeking their salvation, and have met with abuse, scoffing, and derision in return.

But the scene is to change, and a righteous disposition be made of each class of mankind. "Say among the heathen that the Lord reigneth: the world also shall be established that it shall not be moved: he shall judge the people righteously . . . for he cometh, for he cometh to judge the earth: he shall judge the world with righteousness, and the people with his truth." Psa. 96:13. The Lord has an appointment to fill in this work, and he will enter upon his kingly office, and execute the judgments written. "He hath prepared his throne for judgment. And he shall judge the world in righteousness; he shall minister judgment in uprightness." Psa. 9:7, 8. This is what the people fear. If justice is done, the wicked perish. The law they have violated, when executed, causes all "the enemies of the Lord to *perish*. They shall be as the fat of lambs: they shall consume, into smoke shall they consume away." Psa. 37:20. "When mine enemies are turned back, they shall fall and perish at thy presence . . . thou satest in the throne judging right. Thou hast rebuked the heathen, thou hast destroyed the wicked, thou hast put out their name forever and ever." "O thou enemy, destructions are come to a perpetual end, and thou hast destroyed cities; their memorial is perished with them." Psa. 9:3, 6. "Thou didst cause judgment to be heard from heaven; the earth feared and was still, when God arose to judgment, to save all the meek of the earth."

We conclude from the testimony of the Scriptures that Christ shared the penalty of the Adamic law with Adam and his race, that judgment was borne by him, and the judgment of the world fell on him for their recovery. We also conclude that the race are on trial under the law of faith, and are either justified or condemned by it according as they believe or disbelieve it, and that they die under sentence of *second death,* or in promise of eternal life; that when Christ returns to earth, he will execute the sentence and bestow the blessings promised. Reader, which will you choose?

CHAPTER XIV.

THE KINGDOM OF GOD.

"But rather seek ye the kingdom of God; and all these things shall be added unto you." — Luke 12: 31.

The sons of Adam, though depraved and engaged in sin, have constantly manifested their desires for better things than they find in this mortal world. The tide of emigration which has constantly flowed from one continent to another, from one government to another, the revolutions, reconstructions, and efforts to improve human governments, — all speak of anxious desires for better climate, better soil, better society, better government. This is of God. Our all-wise Creator has constituted man with these desires, intending to gratify them to the full, in a legitimate and righteous way, by obedience to himself, in bringing him to a state far better than has been, or can be, attained to in this mortal world. This was implanted in Adam when created and settled in Eden while the world was in an incipient state, with the prospect spread out before him of seeing it filled and matured; his ambition was enhanced by the prospect of attaining to it and enjoying *dominion* over it.

And although sin entered, and man became depraved, rebellious, and dying, still his desires continued, but in a perverted state. Convinced that sin has blighted all prospect of gaining perfection in this world, his desires are intensified by any prospect of progress towards it. Thus he strives and toils to gratify this unsatisfied desire. He plans, invents, prosecutes designs, denies himself, or gratifies his passions in their cravings, hoping to find permanent satisfaction and rest. He emigrates to some country where he hopes to find a government more satisfactory, something nearer perfection; but alas! perfection in its fulness — righteous government — is not here. Therefore God has called our attention to a world of perfection, to be enjoyed by all who comply with the rules necessary to qualify them for citizenship under the government he is yet to establish. To induce man to leave all sinful pursuits and obey him, to give up all false hopes and visions of perfection, and be guided in the right direction to gain the end for which he was created, God has revealed in a very clear manner several of the leading characteristics or features of the world to come, which he has ordained to be the final abode of his people. One of the most prominent of these is the promise and description of

THE KINGDOM OF GOD.

In treating upon either of these several subjects, the scribe well instructed in the Scriptures finds it necessary to make frequent reference to the others, because they are interlaced, or closely related to each other. In our other chapters, therefore, frequent reference is made to the kingdom of God; but as it has not been discussed as a special subject, we enter upon it here because it is one so extensively promised and described in the Bible as of the greatest importance. In fact, it was presented to Adam as the ultimatum of his probation and obedience, and is so presented to the church and to all who will accept Christ and the plan of grace as a reward of faith, endurance, and obedience.

So fully has the human heart been occupied with desire for government, order, and dominion, that the apostate race has made many and strange efforts among all its tribes to organize and sustain kingdoms, though in rebellion against the laws and discipline of God, often making confusion more conspicuous. Very early in the history of man we find them forming kingdoms, which so captivated the hearts of God's select family, who were being trained for a better government, that they cast off his restraint in impatience for a kingdom, and said, "Nay, but we will have a king over us, that we also may be like all the nations; and that our king may judge us, and go out before us, and fight our battles." 1 Sam. 8: 19, 20. This thing displeased the Lord; yet "he gave them a king in his anger, and took him away in his wrath." Hos. 13: 11. This kingdom given to Israel, and organized under Saul, was established under David, and was made in some respects a type of the final kingdom which the Lord has purposed to establish under "David's greater Son," the Lord Jesus Christ, and which we are called upon to *seek* in preference to all things temporal. God has promised a kingdom to his people; and as he is true, it will not fail to come. "I have made a covenant with my chosen. I have sworn unto David my servant: Thy seed will I establish forever, and build up thy throne to all generations." Psa. 89 : 3, 4. In this covenant with David a throne is promised, which implies a kingdom : it is also to be a kingdom *for all generations;* and yet many generations were already dead. Consequently it was not a kingdom in this mortal state, but in the immortal world, made up of resurrected saints of all the generations of Adam. Please read all of this Psalm. In speaking of the king who shall reign, and his seed, the Lord says, "I also will make him my firstborn, higher than the kings of the earth; my mercy will I keep for him forevermore, and my covenant shall stand fast with him. . . . My covenant will I not break, nor alter the thing that is gone out of my lips : once have I sworn by my holiness that I will not lie unto David: his seed shall endure forever, and his throne as the sun before me." Psa. 89 : 27, 28, 34, 36. This covenant, throne, and seed must refer to Christ [the root and offspring of David] and his followers when they are brought to enjoy the everlasting reign. See Psa. 72 : 5, 8.

When speaking of the overthrow of the temporary kingdom established with Israel, God says, " Remove the diadem, and take off the crown: this shall not be the same : exalt him that is low, and abase him that is high. I will overturn, overturn, overturn it; and it shall be no more, until he come whose right it is ; and I will give it him." Ezek. 21 : 26, 27. It belongs to the seed of Abraham, the seed of David, the Son of God, and therefore it is his right to reign when the appointed time arrives and he comes for that purpose.

The crown of Israel was profaned for their wickedness; the Gentiles were exalted from their low condition to universal sway over the kindreds of earth, their time of dominion appointed, their final end declared, in the close of which we are informed, "In the days of these kings shall the God of heaven set up a kingdom, which shall never be destroyed: and the kingdom shall not be left to other people, but it shall break in pieces and consume all these kingdoms, and it shall stand forever." Dan. 2 : 36, 44.

The revelation which the Lord made to Daniel in answer to prayer in regard to Nebuchadnezzar's dream, and the explanation made to the king, show the certainty that God is to establish an eternal kingdom, give its chronological connection with Gentile dominion, the manner of its establishment, and the nature of its subjects. The time of *setting it up* is stated to be at the close of all Gentile rule, all human government. It expressly declares their overthrow and end, to give place to God's kingdom, and locates it where the former dominions — the Babylonian, Medo-Persian, Grecian, and Roman — occupied. It is also stated that "it shall not be left to other people;" those who obtain it will not die and leave it to others; "it shall stand forever."

Such is the kingdom we are called upon to seek, one which God has provided expressly for his children. Is it not worth our utmost care to seek for membership of such a kingdom, that we may share its privileges?

Probably there is not another passage on this subject that has received as much attention, or had as much labor bestowed to overcome or change the special meaning, as the text found in Dan. 2:44. Having other kingdoms in view, men seldom find the keys of the kingdom of God. Let us read the text: "And in the days of these kings shall the God of heaven set up a kingdom which shall never be destroyed; and the kingdom shall not be left to other people, but it shall break in pieces and consume all these kingdoms, and it shall stand forever." But we have the subject more fully stated by God's explaining angel, Gabriel, as Daniel testifies: "I saw in the night visions, and behold, one like the Son of man came with the clouds of heaven, and came to the Ancient of Days, and they brought him near before him; and there was given him dominion, and glory, and a kingdom, that all people, nations, and languages, should serve him: his dominion is an everlasting dominion, which shall not pass away, and his kingdom that which shall not be destroyed." Dan. 7:13, 14.

This language of Daniel presents some of the most sublime ideas of the extent and eternity of the kingdom of God, and is often quoted by teachers to show these grand features, when they entirely neglect, and even reject, the connections with which it is surrounded, because they cannot reconcile them with their ideas of a spiritual reign of Christ. This vision embraced also a view of four great beasts, the last of which had a very peculiar appearance, and had ten horns on his head, among which "came up another little horn." These visions troubled Daniel, therefore he asked an explanation, and was informed, "These great beasts, which are four, are [that is, represent] four kings [kingdoms. See verse 23], which shall arise out of the earth: *but the saints of the Most High shall take the kingdom, and possess the kingdom forever, even forever and ever.*" Verses 17, 18. The angel is careful to explain that although there were to be four human kingdoms, yet the saints shall ultimately take possession of the kingdom occupied by them.

He then goes on to explain the meaning of the fourth beast, his ten horns, or the divisions of that kingdom, then of the *little horn*, which represented a blasphemous civil power, which would *wear out*, destroy, and persecute the people of God, "and prevailed against them until the Ancient of Days came, and judgment was given to [in favor of] the saints of the Most High, and the time came that the saints possessed the kingdom. And the kingdom and dominion, and the greatness of the kingdom under the whole heaven, shall be given to the people of the saints of the Most High, whose kingdom is an everlasting kingdom, and all dominions shall serve and obey him." Dan. 7:21, 22, 27.

The above interpretation of the vision so clearly identifies the four universal empires before stated (Dan. 2:36—43) with the divisions of the last, the Roman, and the blasphemous power which warred against the saints, as the civil character of that ecclesiastical apostate body called the Roman Catholic hierarchy, as to be fully recognized by nearly all expounders of prophecy, worthy of notice, outside the Roman church and its sympathizers. It is a lucid and grand prophetic history of the leading powers of this world, especially so of that most corrupt, blasphemous, and cruelly tyrannical of all governments ever organized among men — the civil power of the Roman church, which for more than thirteen hundred years has worn out, killed, and persecuted the saints of God, under assumptions and titles of the most blasphemous character, whose end is not yet, but soon to come.

This application of the prophecy admitted, the conclusion is positive that the kingdom of God is not yet "set up," and the time not arrived for the saints to possess the kingdom, for it is to occupy all the space which the preceding kingdoms did, all the territory "UNDER THE WHOLE HEAVENS." It is to be set up and possessed at the close of all the others. We say, this application admitted brings the above conclusion, and it is almost universally admitted, while those who have sought to make any other application have made the most fruitless attempts, and shown their arguments to be wanting in scriptural proof and historical facts, and open to the criticisms of all careful readers.

These prophetic statements and explanations give us an account of the king and his subjects, the circumstances and events which introduce his reign, the unending nature of it, also its locality when established.

Let us now examine the testimony of the New Testament, and see whether it confirms the position we have stated: if so, its light will be an increase of that we have already walked in.

It is well known to all careful readers of the Bible, that when Jesus was born in Bethlehem, the Jewish nation were in anxious expectation of the kingdom of God, to be established by the Messiah for whom they looked. They so interpreted the Scriptures we have quoted, but in their great interest to gain deliverance from their bondage, and share the reign and the glory predicted, they entirely overlooked those prophetic predictions, which as clearly state Messiah's humiliation, betrayal, sufferings, and death, and those which describe his intercessions and the promulgation of his gospel to all the nations of the Gentiles.

Therefore, during Christ's ministry, we find them alternating between hope and doubt as to whether he was the promised Messiah; at times they thronged him, charmed with his words, and overwhelmed by his wisdom and his miracles; they were ready to crown him king; then, by his burning truths touching their moral condition, and stating the qualifications requisite for the kingdom of God, and that his kingdom was not of this world, that "the Son of man must be lifted up,"— crucified, — their trembling hope would give way, and, dejected and enraged, they would seek his destruction. Their sinful neglect of the prophetic Scriptures had led them into a sad state of moral blindness concerning the work of the Messiah and his kingdom; therefore he instructed them in parables : —

"And his disciples came, and said unto him, Why speakest unto them in parables? He answered and said unto them, Because it is given unto you to know the mysteries of the kingdom of heaven, but to them it is not given; for whosoever hath [improved], to him shall be given, . . . but whosoever hath not [improved], from him shall be taken away even that he hath." Matt. 13:

10-16. Luke and Mark call it the kingdom of God. See Mark 4:11. Luke 8:9, 10. "Therefore I speak unto them in parables, because they seeing see not, and hearing they hear not, neither do they understand."

This explains the reason why so many of the teachings of Christ concerning the *kingdom of Heaven* and *kingdom of God*, are so dark to those who do not study the prophecies, and why we hear them saying the kingdom was set up when Christ was on earth, or set up at Pentecost, is set up in heaven, is set up in the hearts of believers, &c., &c. It would seem that such persons never heard anything except parables on this subject. But we will examine some PLAIN statements, and not parables.

The time had arrived to raise up the Prince of the house of David, and "the angel Gabriel was sent from God unto a city of Galilee, named Nazareth," to salute Mary, and tell her of the Lord's favor, and of the birth of a son, whose *name should be called* JESUS, adding, "He shall be great, and shall be called the Son of the Highest; and the Lord God shall give unto him the throne of his father David, and he shall reign over the house of Jacob forever, and of his kingdom there shall be no end." Luke 1: 32, 33.

This Gabriel is the same messenger which gave Daniel the interpretation of his visions, and explained to him the time and character of the kingdom of God and its duration. Here we find him again in attendance, announcing the birth of the king, and re-stating the eternal duration of the kingdom; we do not doubt his testimony, for he understood the facts.

Jesus is finally born in a stable, is worshipped by the wise men of the East; his life, sought by the enemies of God, is preserved by God's miraculous interposition; he comes to manhood, is baptized in Jordan, and is publicly introduced to the nation of Israel by the miraculous descent of the Holy Spirit upon him, and by an audible voice from God, saying, "This is my beloved Son, in whom I am well pleased." Matt. 3 : 16, 17.

How insignificant in the estimation of men must all this look as the foundation of an eternal kingdom! yet these are the ways of God, and his purposes will be all fulfilled, whether we comprehend them or not.

We find the anointed Son of God commencing his public labors as a minister for reformation. "From this time Jesus began to preach, and to say, Repent, for the kingdom of heaven is at hand." The command to repent they understood; but what is the meaning of the declaration connected with it? This they did not understand. "And Jesus went about all Galilee, teaching in their synagogues, and preaching the gospel of the kingdom, and healing all manner of sickness and all manner of disease among the people." Matt. 4 : 17, 23.

The gospel of *the kingdom* was the theme, and repentance of sin, a *moral change of the heart*, and a *physical change of the man*, was to be effected to prepare them for a part in that kingdom. Jesus becomes the great Physician; not that he turned his attention to heal *all the sick* in the land, for then none would have died; but mark, it says, healing *all manner of sickness* and *disease*, showing that he had power to cure men of sickness, and bring them into a state of immortality, that they might share the eternal kingdom he was to establish. For this reason he raised some of the dead also, to exhibit his power and purpose. Again we hear him saying, "Many shall come from the east and west, and shall sit down with Abraham, and Isaac, and Jacob, in the kingdom of heaven. But the children of the kingdom [natural descendants of Abraham] shall be cast into outer darkness; there shall be weeping and gnashing of teeth." Matt. 8: 11, 12.

Here is a clear statement that the kingdom about which he was preaching was not to be established in this mortal world, for Abraham, Isaac, and Jacob were dead. He did not teach that the kingdom would be *in* heaven, for he would then have said, they shall *go* from the east and the west, while he says, "they shall *come from the east and west*," to a central point of course, when and where the kingdom shall be organized. We should remember that Jesus is not teaching the Jews *plainly* the nature of his kingdom; they were not in a condition to be taught; yet he was constantly exciting their interest to inquire and learn that it was not what they were expecting.

Therefore we hear him saying, "Blessed are the poor in spirit, for theirs is the kingdom of heaven." Matt. 5: 3. "But seek ye first the kingdom of God." Matt. 6: 33. "But if I cast out devils by the Spirit of God, then the kingdom of God is come unto you." Matt. 12: 28. Then we hear him on shipboard, giving that discourse of parables concerning the kingdom of God, "to great multitudes that were gathered together unto him." They did not understand them; it is expressly stated that they would not. "All these things spake Jesus unto the multitude in parables, and without a parable spake he not unto them, that it might be fulfilled which was spoken by the prophet, saying, I will open my mouth in parables; I will utter things which have been kept secret from the foundation of the world." "Then Jesus sent the multitude away, and went into the house: and his disciples came unto him, saying, Declare [explain] unto us the parable of the tares of the field." This parable comprehended more than any of the others, and attracted especially their attention; they saw there was danger "when any one heareth the word of the kingdom, and understandeth it not," and they ask an explanation. He answered and said unto them, "He that soweth the good seed is the Son of man: the field is the world; the good seed are the children of the kingdom; but the tares are the children of the wicked one; the enemy that sowed them is the devil; the harvest is the end of the world; and the reapers are the angels. As therefore the tares are gathered and burned in the fire, so shall it be in the end of this world. The Son of man shall send forth his angels, and they shall gather out of his kingdom all things that offend, and them which do iniquity, and shall cast them into a furnace of fire; there shall be wailing and gnashing of teeth." Then shall the righteous shine forth as the sun in the kingdom of their Father. Who hath ears to hear, let him hear." Matt. 13: 1–43.

In the above explanation of Christ, we have a foundation which cannot be removed by all the theorists and spiritual-ethereal, sky-kingdom teachers which infest the church of God. The kingdom is here shown to eventually occupy the place of the field. The field is declared to be the (*cosmos-habitable*) world. The wicked — "them which do iniquity" — are to be removed from the earth by the cleansing process of fire; then shall the righteous shine forth as the sun, in the kingdom of their Father, on the field cleansed and made a new earth: And this will be after the harvest, which is the end of the (*age*) world.

Mark! This is not the gradual and progressive growth of a moral institution, or the universal conversion of mankind by the preaching of the gospel and the effusion of the Holy Spirit, but contrariwise. It is done by *the Son of man sending forth his angels to gather those who do iniquity out of his kingdom,* to consume in a furnace of fire.

To do this Christ is to take actual possession of the kingdoms of this world, and exercise *dominion*. And this he is to do as we read in the following texts: "The Lord said unto my Lord, Sit thou at my right hand, until I make thine enemies thy footstool. The Lord shall send the rod of thy strength out of Zion; rule thou in the midst of thine enemies. . . . The Lord at thy right hand shall strike through kings in the day of his wrath. He shall judge among the heathen, he shall fill the places with the dead bodies." Psa. 110: 1-6.

The above is an important passage indeed, one which records the Father's determination that his Son shall judge and dispose of his enemies who will not accept of his mercy and become obedient to his law. This determination was expressed to Abraham also, the father of the faithful, in the following language: —

"And thy seed shall possess the gate of his enemies," (Gen. 22:17), which signifies, to possess the territory and exercise the dominion of his enemies. The same idea is more fully declared in the decree, "I will declare the decree: the Lord hath said unto me, Thou art my Son; this day have I begotten thee. Ask of me, and I shall give thee the [dominion of the] heathen for thine inheritance, and the uttermost parts of the earth for thy possession. Thou shalt break them [the heathen] with a rod of iron: thou shalt dash them in pieces like a potter's vessel." Psa. 2:7–9. The Lord has here declared his DECREE: it will surely be accomplished. All the while he is working to this end. The nations of the earth "have hated both the Father and the Son;" they have despised his law. He has "sent them an Ambassador with conditions for peace;" yet "the kings of the earth set themselves, and the rulers take counsel together, against the Lord, and against his Anointed, saying, Let us break their bands asunder, and cast away their cords from us."

The Lord has sent them a wise Counsellor, an unerring Teacher; but they have despised his counsels and scorned his instruction. He has offered a great Sacrifice, by which they may be forgiven their sins; but they refuse to repent. He has appointed a merciful Mediator, "who is touched with the feeling of our infirmities;" but they have refused the terms of pardon. He has provided a "righteous Judge," who knows the hearts of all, and "will reward every man according as his work shall be." He has provided a glorious King, who has first given his own life to redeem a race of miserable sinners.

whom he invites to accept his offers of pardon, and to receive his divine Spirit, and be governed by his heavenly law, and share in the riches and glories of his immortal kingdom. He has given the gospel (good news) of his kingdom, his plan of government, the nature of his kingdom, the character of his subjects, and the laws and advantages of his reign; but the nations have acted out what the Jews said — "We will not have this man to reign over us."

But the gospel mission of reconciliation must close up, the day of reckoning must come, the time of reward must arrive, the kingdom of God must be set up. Christ must yet occupy the throne of David. The PRAYER of the church, which Christ taught them to pray, "Thy kingdom come, thy will be done on earth as it is done in heaven," must be answered.

> "So when thou shalt on earth appear,
> To fix thy heavenly kingdom here,
> I shall with my Redeemer join,
> Partake the victory divine,
> And, clothed with thy resistless power,
> The conqueror of the world adore." — *Wesley.*

The *promise* of Christ must also be fulfilled. "To him that overcometh will I grant to sit with me in my throne, even as I also overcame, and am set down with my Father in his throne." Rev. 3 : 21. Therefore we find the TIME introduced. "And the seventh angel sounded, and there were great voices in heaven, saying, The kingdoms of this world are become the kingdoms of our Lord and of his Christ, and he shall reign forever and ever. . . . And the nations were angry, and thy wrath is come, and the TIME of the dead, that they should be judged, and that thou shouldest give reward unto thy servants the prophets, and to the saints, and to them that fear thy name, small and great, and shouldest destroy them which destroy [corrupt] the earth." Rev. 11 : 15–18.

In the above passage we are shown that when Christ's enemies become his footstool, he takes possession of the dominion they have exercised, and leaves the throne of his Father, to exercise his authority to reign and execute judgment. John 5 : 27. For this reign the church of God has long waited, and prayed, and sung, and when the blast of the seventh angel's trumpet shall salute the ears of the heavenly host, a song of thanks, such as was never heard before, shall reverberate through the arches of heaven, "Saying, We give thee thanks, O Lord God Almighty, which art, and wast, and art to come, because thou hast taken to thee thy great power, and hast reigned." Rev. 11 : 16, 17. This discovers to us that although it had been decreed that Christ should reign, and "all power in heaven and earth was given him," yet there was an appointed time for him to enter upon the exercise of it, on his own throne, and not on his Father's. At this time the kingdom is in his possession, and it being the time of harvest, he gathers the wheat — the sheep, the children of God — to himself, and also *gathers out of his kingdom*, the dominion which had just passed into his actual possession, all "them which do iniquity," and consumes them in a furnace of fire, and fulfils the decree.

This is clearly described in the following scriptures : " For the Lord himself shall descend from heaven with a shout, with the voice of the archangel, and with the trump of God, and the dead in Christ shall rise first: then we which are alive and remain shall be caught up together with them in the clouds, to meet the Lord in the air; and so shall we ever be with the Lord." 1 Thess. 4 : 16, 17. "And he shall send his angels with a great sound of a trumpet, and they shall gather together his elect from the four winds, from one end of heaven to the other" (Matt. 24 : 31 — "from one extremity of the world to the other" — *Campbell*). Thus the Lord will deliver his "people, every one who shall be found written in the book," at the "time of trouble, such as never was since there was a nation even to that same time." Dan. 12 : 1, 2. Rev. 6 : 15–17; 14 : 14–20. Matt. 13 : 41, 42.

It will be seen in this class of scriptures that the angels of God, who have been messengers of mercy in watching over and ministering to the faithful, and who have "earnestly desired to look into" the plan of redemption, and have rejoiced over repenting sinners, are to be engaged in escorting the Lord's redeemed to the immediate presence of their King; they are also to engage in executing judgment and in cleansing Christ's dominion of his enemies. They have been employed in former times for the defence of the servants of God, and for destroying God's enemies. They are to be in attendance at the inauguration of the Son of God to his kingly office, and engaged in the destruction of his foes.

We will now notice the description which Christ himself gave to his disciples, who were yet entertaining wrong ideas of his work and of his kingdom, having heard it mostly in parables given to the Jews, which they did not understand: "He added, and spake a parable, because he was nigh to Jerusalem, and because they thought the kingdom of God should immediately appear. He said, therefore, A certain nobleman went into a far country to receive for himself a kingdom and to return. And he called his ten servants, and delivered them ten pounds, and said unto them, Occupy till I come. But his citizens hated him, and sent a message after him, saying, We will not have this man to reign over us.

"And it came to pass, that when he was returned, having received the kingdom, then he commanded these servants to be called unto him, to whom he had given the money, that he might know how much every man had gained by trading," &c. Luke 19 : 11, 27. It is not difficult for one well instructed in the things of the kingdom of God to see the meaning of this parable. After it was spoken, Jesus ascended up to Jerusalem, in fulfilment of Zechariah 9 : 9, escorted by "the whole multitude of his disciples, rejoicing and praising God with a loud voice for all the mighty works that they had seen; saying, Blessed be the king that cometh in the name of the Lord;" while Jesus wept over the city and pronounced *its doom*, entered the temple, reproved and ordered out the exchangers and thieves who occupied it. He met and replied to the cavils and inquiries of the chief priests and scribes and elders, who were disturbed by the gospel he preached. Luke ch. 20. His disciples desire to know more about the "sign when all these things shall come to pass. He cautions them against being deceived, and then tells them the leading or great events which will take place after he leaves them; and in describing the fate of the Jewish nation, he says, "And they shall fall by the edge of the sword, and shall be led away captive into all nations; and Jerusalem shall be trodden down of the Gentiles, until the times of the Gentiles be fulfilled. And there shall be signs in the sun, and in the moon, and in the stars; and upon the earth distress of nations, with perplexity: men's hearts failing them for fear, and for looking after those things which are coming on the earth; for the powers of heaven shall be shaken. . . . When ye see these things come to pass, know ye that the kingdom of God is nigh at hand." Luke 21 : 24–31.

This is testimony enough to forever settle the point that the *kingdom of God* is not the church, nor the gospel preached to the church and world. But we will look at one more passage on this point, as it explains the parable of the nobleman who went into a far country to receive for himself a kingdom, and to return, and reckoned with his servants : —

"When the Son of man shall come in his glory, and all the holy angels with him, then shall he sit upon the throne of his glory, and before him shall be gathered all nations; and he shall separate them one from another, as a shepherd divideth his sheep from the goats. . . . Then shall the king say to them on his right hand, Come, ye blessed of my Father, inherit the kingdom prepared for you from the foundation of the world." Matt. 25 : 31–34.

This is the kingdom and dominion set before Adam to possess if faithful, but lost by disobedience, recovered by Christ, and given to the flock of God as their glorious and everlasting home.

Who does not wish to be a subject of such a kingdom, and to enjoy the privilege of entering in to share its unending glories? It will be a kingdom whose "king shall reign in righteousness." Isa. 32 : 1. Its subjects " shall be all righteous : they shall inherit the land forever " (Isa. 60 : 21) ; they are those who became followers of Christ, believed and obeyed his teachings, renounced all the riches, glories, honors, and pleasures of this world, to suffer scorn, and derision, and persecutions for his sake. They are the " poor of this world," the " rich in faith," and the " heirs of that kingdom which God hath promised to them that love him ; " and when Christ comes the second time, to exercise " his dominion from sea to sea, and from the river to the ends of the earth " (Psa. 72 : 8), then they will take the kingdom under the whole heavens, and possess it forever, even forever and ever." Dan. 7 : 22, 27.

Who would not be glad to dwell in that kingdom, where everything, beyond comparison, surpasses the richest, fairest, and best things ever known here? whose King is the Lord Jesus Christ, and whose capital shall exceed in capacity, workmanship, glory, durability, magnificence, resources, and treasures, all the chief cities combined which this world ever built! Put all their best qualities into one, and its grandeur will fade into rottenness when compared with the city of our God, the NEW JERUSALEM — the metropolis of the kingdom of God.

> "Thy walls are all of precious stones,
>   Most glorious to behold:
> Thy gates are richly set with pearl,
>   Thy streets are paved with gold.
>
> "Thy gardens and thy pleasant walks
>   My study long have been;
> Such dazzling views by human sight
>   Have never yet been seen."

There will be no sin, no funeral services, no sick-beds, no diseased or shattered forms, no dilapidated and miserable hovels, no marks of misery or want, no streets of mire and filth, no wasting and wearing and decay, no pestilential air, nothing to pain the heart or disgust the senses. There will be no watchmen there, no bolts nor bars, no policemen nor prisons, no gloom of night, no lamps nor gas lights to chase away the darkness, no irregular walks nor broken pavements. No evil thing shall be there.

But in that city everything will be found that is good; its walls of the most precious stones, its gates of pearl, its streets of pure gold. The glory of God and of the Lamb is the light of it, and there is no night there. And best of all, the Lord will dwell there. "And there shall in no wise enter into it anything that defileth, neither whatsoever worketh abomination, or maketh a lie; but they which are written in the Lamb's book of life." Rev. 21:10, 27.

But for us to obtain a residence in the kingdom of which this city is the capital, we must respect the God who has prepared it for his people; we must respect the Prince who is to occupy the throne, and accept his offers to cleanse us from our sins and make us joint-heirs with himself, that we may share his glory; we must obey his law here, and endure the training required under his discipline to subdue our evil, wayward, stubborn passions, and receive and cherish his Spirit, and be partakers of his nature who has laid down his own life to open the way for us to be made the heirs of such a kingdom.

His requirements are just, and the qualifications are obtained at the cost of his own blood.

"Except ye be converted, and become as little children, ye shall not enter into the kingdom of heaven." Matt. 18 : 3. "It is easier for a camel to go through the eye of a needle, than for a rich man to enter into the kingdom of God." Mark 10 : 25.

True riches are in the kingdom of God; and in order for men to gain them, they must not trust in the uncertain riches of this sinful, perishing world. In order to give the church a clear and tangible idea of the nature and glory of his kingdom, he told several of his disciples they should not taste of death till they see the kingdom of God. A few days after this "he took Peter and John and James, and went up into a mountain to pray. And as he prayed, the fashion of his countenance was altered, and his raiment was white and glistering. And behold, there talked with him two men, which were Moses and Elias; who appeared in glory." Luke 9 : 27, 30.

Here was a miniature of his kingdom, with representatives from the dead and from the changed. It was a vision, and Peter, in his Epistle to the church, comments upon it as representing "the power and coming of our Lord Jesus Christ." 2 Pet. 1:16. The apostle had just described to believers that they should add to their faith "virtue, knowledge, temperance, patience, godliness, brotherly kindness, charity . . . for if ye do these things, ye shall never fall; for so an entrance shall be ministered unto you into the everlasting kingdom of our Lord and Saviour Jesus Christ." 2 Pet. 1:5–11.

To keep the mind of the church constantly directed to this object in preference to all worldly objects, Jesus taught his disciples to pray, "Thy kingdom come, thy will be done in earth as it is done in heaven." This prayer has been ascending to "our Father who art in heaven," for more than eighteen hundred years, from the loving, longing hearts of way-worn pilgrims, who wait for the kingdom of God. They have studied and thought of the time when this glorious day should come; they have sung it in animated strains. Their hope will not be disappointed. The kingdom will come; the day is at hand. Let us be ready to hail the coming King, and be welcomed into his glorious kingdom.

It will be seen by the many scriptures we have quoted on this subject, and also by many others not quoted, that Christ's actual reign on earth begins where all mortal dominions end; that his subjects will enter that kingdom immortal; and that it includes all the children of God of all generations. It will also be manifest to the careful thinker that the establishment of the kingdom of God on earth marks the commencement of the millennium and the spoliation of all the combinations of God's enemies, and the utter destruction of every wicked being on earth from the universe of God. This fact is thoroughly established by the Scriptures of truth, and enters largely into the inaugural song of the redeemed as they unite in the glorious reign with their Redeemer.

"And they sung a new song, saying, Thou art worthy to take the book, and to open the seals thereof: for thou wast slain, and hast redeemed us to God by thy blood out of every kindred, and tongue, and people, and nation, and hast made us unto our God kings and priests; and we shall reign on the earth. And I beheld, and I heard the voice of many angels round about the throne, and the beasts, and the elders: and the number of them was ten thousand times ten thousand, and thousands of thousands; saying with a loud voice, Worthy is the Lamb that was slain to receive power, and riches, and wisdom, and strength, and honor, and glory, and blessing; and every creature which is in heaven, and on the earth, and under the earth, and such as are in the sea, and all that are in them, heard I saying, Blessing, and honor, and glory, and power be unto him that sitteth upon the throne, and unto the Lamb forever and ever." Rev. 5: 9–13.

This shows the Lord to be triumphant over all his foes. It proves to be a contest worthy of God, the Almighty. All who will not obey a righteous rule must perish, and the world be cleansed of rebels, and God's universal government established.

Such a kingdom, dear reader, Jesus has taught us

to seek, while he has opened the way, and assured us
that we may by his grace have "an abundant entrance
into it."

> "Quick as the darted lightnings fly,
> Flashing at once throughout the sky,
> Saviour, thou wilt on earth appear,
> To 'stablish thy dominion here.
> Before the final, general doom,
> We know thou wilt to judgment come,
> Thy foes destroy, thy friends maintain,
> **And** glorious with thine ancients reign." — *Wesley.*

CHAPTER XV.

THE BOOK OF LIFE.

"And the commandment which was ordained to life, I found to be unto death."— *Rom.* 7:10.

THE term *book* may be properly applied to any record of facts, past, present, or to come, and to any system or code of laws, rules, or regulations for any purpose whatsoever; and such books receive their qualifying terms according to their object, or the subjects upon which they treat. Consequently in the Scriptures we read of the book of the WARS of the Lord (Num. 21:14; the book of the ACTS of SOLOMON (1 Kings 11:41); the book of the PROPHETS (Acts 7:42); the book of the LAW, &c.

A code of law, therefore, embracing rules and regulations of life, addressed to the living man Adam, the unit of the race, when he knew no death because he knew no sin, may properly be called a book of life, as it contained the rules of life for a living race, who must have been all included in this code of law, as all were alive in Adam. This original record or statute book of the living is called "The BOOK of the Lord" (Isa. 34:16); and the Psalmist refers to it on this wise: "Thine eyes did see my substance, yet being imperfect; and in thy BOOK all my members were written, which in continuance were fashioned, when as yet there was none of them." Psa. 139 : 16. To the law contained in this book the apostle refers in the text at the head of this chapter, when he says, "And the commandment which was ordained to life."

This law, in its rudiments given to Adam, was set apart for the regulation of the life of the living, as death was then unknown to the race; but Paul says of this book or law, "which was ordained to life, I found to be unto death."

Here the question may be properly raised, If God ordained this book of law for life, how came it to be unto death? The answer to this question is very plain: Man, to regulate whose life it was given, had violated it; he sinned against its Author by transgressing that law, thereby forfeiting his life and the life of his race. For *sin is the transgression of the law*, and the penalty of that law being death, it passed upon all men.

"Wherefore, as by one man sin entered into the world, and death by sin; and so death passed upon all men, for that all have sinned." Rom. 5 : 12. From that day to the present time that law has been found to be unto death; sin was in the world, and death reigned from Adam to Moses, and the giving of the law at Sinai in form to the children of Israel, was to give man the knowledge of sin and of his real condition under its sentence. "The law entered, that the offence [of Adam] might abound"— be developed in the fallen race; therefore, as death fell upon the race in the unit, man had no right to life in view of that law.

This point has been argued and sustained by Scripture authority in other parts of this work.

Thus God's law or statute book, "which was ordained to life ['for life'—*Bible Union Version*]," has ever been "found to be unto death" by Adam's race. It provided no remedy, nor has any remedy been found until it was found in the death of our Lord Jesus Christ as an atonement for the transgressions that were under the first testament, or book of law; and this atonement, be it remembered, was not to save men from dying, but to purchase them from the power of that law of sin and death.

The Scriptures show that the race of man, in their progenitor, had by sin been lost and erased prospectively from God's original statute book, which was ordained to life, *and death had passed upon all, for " in Adam all die."* Under that law all was extinct, blotted out.

In this state of the case, infinite mercy, wisdom, and goodness develop a new plan — that of atonement and redemption by the death of Christ, as is shown in our chapter on universal redemption, and the first branch of the atonement.

As man had been prospectively stricken from the original record or "book of the Lord," being judicially dead, and being prospectively redeemed from death to life, another record or book of life is introduced, called "The Lamb's book of life" (Rev. 21:27), based on the atonement by the slain Lamb, in distinction from the one found to be unto death, under which the race had perished by Adam's sin.

In this atonement the entire race of man is purchased

back to life in their unit head, — Adam, — with their inheritance, by Jesus Christ; for "as in Adam all die, even so in Christ shall all be made alive." 1 Cor. 15 : 22. "As by the offence of one [Adam], judgment came upon all men to condemnation, even so by the righteousness of one [Jesus Christ], the free gift came upon all men unto justification of life." Rom 5 : 18. The price paid for this justification, Jesus says, "*is my flesh, which I will give for the life of the world.*" John 6 : 51. See also Heb. 9 : 15.

Thus the entire race of man in their unit head is embraced in the New Covenant, registered and acknowledged in the Lamb's book of life, or law, which can give or save life, as we shall presently show.

This new book is what Paul calls "the law of the spirit of life in Christ Jesus" (Rom. 8 : 2–5), in distinction "from the law of sin and death," and the law on tables of stone, "who hath made us able ministers of the new testament; not of the letter, but of the spirit; for the letter killeth, but the spirit giveth life." 2 Cor. 3 : 6. The transgression of this new law of life is wilful unbelief; it offers mercy through faith in the atoning blood of Jesus Christ. Matt. 26 : 28. It is this blood that preserves man's life from the power of the second death, as shown in our chapters on the second branch of the atonement and on the new covenant.

The penalty of the new covenant, or law "of the Lamb's book of life," like that of the old covenant, or law "ordained to life," is DEATH; but unlike the old in duration, for it is eternal death, an eternal blotting out of the names from the covenant, or book of life, of those who end their probation in transgression.

When Moses introduced this covenant in Deut. 29th. and 30th chapters (from which Paul quotes in Rom. 10 : 6–10, as the righteousness of faith), he says, "See, I have set before thee, this day, life and good, death and evil, in that I command thee this day to love the Lord thy God, to walk in his ways, and to keep his commandments, and his statutes, and his judgments."

It is certain that Adam's life, and in him the life of the race, depended on his obedience to the Father's rule, law, or book, which was ordained to life, and that his offence against it was fatal to his life; and it is equally certain that the gospel covenant is our rule of life to govern us in this state of probation, and is better than the old, because it provides a remedy for sin, while the former provided none. The sinner may repent and find mercy and pardon under this law or rule of life, and whoever does this will find the blood of this covenant ample to cleanse from all sin, and to preserve the life Jesus has purchased back from the power of death unto life eternal. See John 12 : 25.

If, then, Jesus Christ purchased the race by his death, and included them in *his book of life* from the foundation of the world, and all who are found written there, when Jesus comes, will enjoy the glorious privileges of the holy city (Rev. 21 : 24, 27), it may be asked, How can any be lost, or fail of eternal life?

To this we reply: Two very erroneous views have obtained in our world from a misunderstanding of the covenants, and the enemy has taken advantage of these errors, and driven men to two opposite extremes: the one assumes that, because *Jesus died for all men,* therefore all men must be saved in eternal life; the other assumes that if the names of the finally saved were in *the book of life from the foundation of the world,* and my name is there, then I cannot fail of eternal life, and if not there, then there is no action I can take which will cause it to be entered or written in that book. Therefore this class settle down on the ground of fatality. If I am to be saved I shall be; if I am *not ordained* to be saved, I *cannot be* saved.

The first mentioned of those two classes reject the principle taught throughout the Bible, and referred to so clearly by Jude: "How that the Lord, having saved the people out of the land of Egypt, afterward destroyed them that believed not." Verse 5. The other class have ignored or failed to see that the names of all men were written in *the Lamb's book of life* from the foundation of the world. A few testimonies of Scripture will, we trust, make this subject plain.

The first we will quote from this class is Psa. 69, where David, after giving an account of those who reject and persecute Jesus Christ, who persist in their unbelief, says, "Let them be blotted out of the book of the living, and not be written with the righteous." It should be noticed that this Psalm, from the 20th verse, is a prediction of the treatment and sufferings of Christ in his own person, and in his church in this probationary state, and of the fate of his enemies in the end. It would be strange logic to talk about blotting out their names from a book wherein they were never written.

Again: Jesus says, "He that overcometh, the same shall be clothed in white raiment; and I will not blot out his name out of the book of life, but I will confess his name before my Father, and before his angels." Rev. 3:5.

This statement shows that those whose names are in the book of life, are on trial for victory and eternal life; and if they fail to overcome, their names will be *blotted out of that book*. When the children of Israel sinned a grievous sin, even unto death, Moses pleads with God to pardon them; "and if not, blot me, I pray thee, out of thy book which thou hast written. And the Lord said unto Moses, Whosoever hath sinned against me, him will I blot out of my book." Exod. 32:32, 33.

In the following passage we have the idea forcibly stated, that those who diminish from the words of prophecy of the revelation will have their part taken out of the book of life, and out of the holy city, and out of the promises written in this book. "And if any man shall take away from the words of the book of this prophecy, God shall take away his part out of the book of life, and out of the holy city, and from the things which are written in this book." Rev. 22:19. If one name can be blotted out of the book of life, then many may; and the fact is clearly proved that the wicked do have their names blotted out of the book of life. Therefore the doctrine of fatality, or of Calvinistic election, and also of Universalism, fails of any footing under these considerations, or under any other drawn from scriptural arguments. But another objection to the doctrine that the names of all men were in the book of life, is raised from the latter clause of Rev. 13:8, and 17:8. "And all that dwell upon the earth shall worship him [the beast], whose names are not written in the book of life of the Lamb slain from the foundation of the world." A careful examination of this class of texts will show that in the passages above cited there is an ellipsis or omission of the word *found*, before the word "*written*," which is supplied in other texts on the same subject, as in Dan. 12:1. "At that time thy people shall be delivered, every one that shall be FOUND written in the book." Again: "And whosoever was not FOUND written in the book of life was cast into the lake of fire." Rev. 20:15. It is a common thing in language to omit a statement when it has been given elsewhere, so that the sense is understood.

The obvious reason why the wicked are not FOUND written in the Lamb's book of life when the judgment sits, is because they will have then been blotted out, as shown above. Dear reader, let us strive to be overcomers, that our names may be retained, and not blotted out of the Lamb's book of life.

In Dan. 7:10, 13, we have the scenes of the coming of the Son of man and the judgment of the great day presented, in which the prophet informs us that the books were opened; but what books they are is not stated. In Rev. 20:11-13, we have the same scenes brought to view again: "the books were opened, and another book was opened, which is the book of life." From the language of this text, it is evident that there are two or more books, besides the book of life, opened at the judgment; but the text before us says, "the dead were judged out of those things which were written in the books, according to their works;" hence a record of their works is in the books. One of these books is evidently the book of the law of the Father, which "was ordained unto life," but is found "to be unto death," because it was violated, and a record of the works by which the race perished or died is found in it, as is shown in the words God spoke to Moses concerning the worshippers of the golden calf. Moses pleaded for God to pardon them, and if not, to blot him out of the book which he had written. The Lord replied, "Him that hath sinned will I blot out of the book which I have written." This people were a typical people, and the things which happened unto them were ensamples of what will befall all the race who finally reject God.

God has a book of memorial written of the doings of his people and of his enemies, as also of his dealings with them. See Exod. 17:14. God will bring every work into judgment, with every secret thing, whether it be good or evil.

We are informed by the Scriptures that there is also a book written called the book of remembrance, or of memorial. "Then they that feared the Lord spake often one to another: and the Lord hearkened and heard it, and a book of remembrance was written before him for them that feared the Lord, and that thought upon his name. And they shall be mine, saith the Lord of hosts, in that day when I make up my jewels [or 'special treasure'— *margin*], and I will spare them, as a man spareth his own son that serveth him." Mal. 3:16, 17. This shows a special record of the faithful in the Lord, and agrees with the enrolment or citizenship of God's people, mentioned by Paul: "For our conversation ['our polity'—*Em. Diaglott;* —'our citizenship'— *Am. Bible Union*] is in heaven; from whence also we look for the Saviour, the Lord Jesus Christ; who shall change our vile body, that it may be fashioned like unto his glorious body." Phil. 3:20, 21. In this passage we have the idea of the enrolment of persons who belong to a country or city as citizens. The saints are enrolled in the heavenly city. New "Jerusalem, which is above [and] is free, and is the mother of us [Christians] all." Gal. 4:26. Jesus also taught the same idea to the disciples who returned to him rejoicing in the power he had given them over the devils. Jesus said, "In this rejoice not, that the spirits are subject unto you; but rather rejoice because your names are written in heaven." Luke 10:20.

The above facts show that these records embodied in the old covenant, with the book of memorial written in heaven, and the book of the new covenant, constitute the books which will be opened when the judgment sits, and Jesus shall be revealed from heaven " to execute the judgments written," in flaming fire, " taking vengeance on them that know not God, and obey not the gospel of our Lord Jesus Christ; but to be admired in all them that believe, in that day."

The character of those to whom this gospel covenant, or law of life, is presented, is determined by their acceptance or rejection of it, as stated above: those who obey it have its principles written in their hearts by the Spirit of God, by which God is recognized as their God, and they are sealed as God's people. See 2 Cor. 3 : 3. Heb. 8 : 10.

And thus believers in Christ become real Jews, or "Israelites indeed." "For he is not a Jew which is one outwardly; neither is that circumcision [of the spirit] which is outward in the flesh: but he is a Jew [a disciple of the lawgiver of the tribe of Judah] which is one inwardly: and circumcision is that of the heart, in the spirit, and not in the letter; whose praise is not of men, but of God." Rom. 2 : 28, 29.

Such are in God's book of remembrance. "For [saith God] I will be merciful to their unrighteousness, and their sins and their iniquities will I remember no more." Heb. 8 : 12. These are the ones whose names will not be blotted out of the book of life. "And the Lord thy God will circumcise thine heart to love the Lord thy God with all thine heart, and with all thy soul, that thou mayest live." Deut. 30 : 6.

On the other hand, those who refuse to comply with the terms of this law, and do not have it written in their minds and on their hearts, will have the rights and privileges which they enjoy under the gospel taken away. "For whosoever hath [improved], to him shall be given, and he shall have more abundance; but whosoever hath not [improved], from him shall be taken away even that he hath." Matt. 13 : 12. "God shall take away his part out of the BOOK OF LIFE" (Rev. 22 : 19), for they will have incurred the vengeance to be executed on the wicked, when Jesus comes, and will "be punished with EVERLASTING DESTRUCTION."

O, what a thought! to be blotted out of the book of

life, blotted out from the race of man, blotted out of the universe of God! Dear reader, seek refuge in Jesus's blood, become citizens of the heavenly Jerusalem, and your names will be written in heaven, and not be blotted out of the book of life.

> "Jesus, refuge of my soul,
>   Let me to thy bosom fly,
> While the raging billows roll,
>   While the tempest still is high.
> Hide me, O my Saviour, hide,
>   Till the storm of life is past:
> Safe into the haven guide,
>   O receive me home at last."

CHAPTER XVI.

RESURRECTION OF THE DEAD.

"For the hour is coming, in the which all that are in the graves shall hear his voice, and shall come forth; they that have done good, unto the resurrection of life; and they that have done evil, unto the resurrection of damnation."— *John* 5 : 28, 29.

THERE is no doctrine in the Bible more clearly stated than that of the resurrection of the dead, and none which sceptical minds have made more strenuous efforts to overthrow or to pervert. And although it stands the test of all classes of scepticism and vain philosophy, yet it has been thrown in the background of theological instruction, as though it had served its purpose and been superseded by more important discoveries; consequently, it is seldom mentioned in the religious instructions at the present day: and when it is treated upon, it is too frequently handled as a mystical and undefined doctrine, of little importance.

We will here introduce a remark from Adam Clarke, the commentator: at the close of his notes on 1 Cor. ch. 15, he says, "One remark I cannot help making: the doctrine of the *resurrection* appears to have been thought of much more consequence among the primitive Christians than it is *now!* How is this? The apostles were continually insisting on it, and exciting the followers of God to diligence, obedience, and cheerfulness, through it. And their successors in the present day seldom mention it! So apostles preached, and so primitive Christians believed; so we preach, and so our hearers believe. There is not a doctrine in the gospel on which more stress is laid; and there is not a doctrine in the present system of preaching which is treated with more neglect!"

If the above statement of Dr. Clarke was pertinent in his day, how much more so in ours, when the doctrine has constantly become less and less important in the esteem of the mass of nominal Christians!

The text we have quoted at the head of this chapter is too palpable to be *overcome* without a positive denial of the truthfulness of the passage, and of course of the authority of all Scripture. Some, however, who do not intend to invalidate the Scriptures, have embraced such ideas of man's nature as to blind or greatly bewilder their minds on this all-important subject; for, if their views of man's nature be correct, then the doctrine of atonement and resurrection is of no use, has no place in man's redemption. Consequently, the efforts which are constantly put forth to reconcile this difficulty and harmonize the Bible doctrine of the resurrection with their unscriptural ideas of man's natural immortality, only increase the confusion of views of religious teachers and pupils.

This has led the way for scepticism to introduce its "oppositions of science," — putting forth its mightiest efforts to so construe, gloss, and pervert the passages which teach the resurrection of the dead, as to make them mean something else than their plain testimony declares; and, in doing this, rules of interpretation have been assumed, which, if applied to other points of doctrine, would nullify and destroy the entire system of Bible truth in the minds of men. Ay, this is *being done* to a fearful extent. Scepticism and infidelity have been greatly advanced in their hideous forms, and more especially so in the more insidious and specious form of modern spiritualism.

The result which followed Adam's sin, on him and his race, together with the act of atonement by the death of Christ, and his subsequent resurrection from death, which we have argued and shown in other parts of this work, conclusively prove that there must be a resurrection to life from the grave of Adam's race, or the doctrine of atonement is of no importance, as it effects nothing for man's benefit.

And, notwithstanding Christ's miracles, sufferings, death, resurrection, and ascension to heaven, man will never exist beyond this mortal state: death must be an eternal end of all the race excepting Enoch and Elijah. Such, we claim, would be a logical conclusion from the idea that man will not be brought back from death to life. For, as we have elsewhere shown, there could have been no plan of mercy offered to man, no probation given for future life, no covenant made to give any of the race eternal life on conditions which might be complied with, except through a previous determination to restore man back from death to the life they lost in Adam, by a satisfaction of that law which held them in death; which satisfaction was given by the atonement, in the death of Christ: consequently the race must be restored back to life, or the pledge of the Father is broken, the plan of grace fails, and the promises of Christ will not be fulfilled.

Premises and arguments which lead to such sad conclusions as above stated to result from a denial of the resurrection of the race of man from the grave, we shall reject until we conclude to reject the Bible altogether, and become deists or spiritualists, which we shall not do at present.

The Bible, however, is not to be abandoned: its teachings are authoritative to settle all questions of doctrine touching man's origin, condition, and destiny: we shall therefore believe them, and expect a fulfilment of their promises and propositions according to the rule which has been observed in the fulfilment of all that is past.

The hope which in all past ages and generations has allured the believers in God away from idolatry and vice in all forms, and led them to love and adore their Creator; to love and seek the welfare of their fellow-men; to lead lives of humility, fidelity, and purity, — is not to be bartered away for vain philosophy or necromancy. The hope which has sustained the faithful amid the trials and afflictions of this sorrowing life; which has cheered their hearts, and inspired them with confidence and fortitude, when beset with storms of malice and hatred, and cruel mockings and scoffings, and conflicts of opposition; through sickness and in death; through cruel tortures, imprisonment, and martyrdom, — is built on a foundation not to be undermined nor overturned by unbelief and sophistry. It is based on the resurrection.

The plan of redemption which God in his infinite mercy has revealed, means vastly more than the natural mind comprehends, or than the perverted Christian mind contemplates.

Leave the doctrine of the resurrection out of religious theology, and it ceases to hold the human mind in subjection to Christian discipline and systematic action in life; the mind loses its hold on the prospect of a real tangible *life to come*, and drifts upon the boisterous ocean of time, for some haven of security not on the chart, or rises to float in undefined space, without a guide or compass, driven by every vain imagination, to feed upon the vagaries and fancies which may occupy or entertain an unsettled and wandering mind.

Of this fact we have abundant proof in the examples now existing in this generation among religious classes: we need not specify farther; a little reflection will lead to an acknowledgment of the truthfulness of our statement.

Again: In so far as any religious view is cherished and made prominent, which nullifies or eclipses the doctrine and hope of the resurrection of the dead, so far the tendency is evil, as is manifest in the dogma of purgatory, and the happy condition of the dead saints released therefrom, as held by the Romish church and many Protestants.

We claim that the doctrine of the literal bringing back of the dead from dust to life is the basis of all Christian theology. Christianity stands on this proposition, or falls when this expectation is proved false.

It will be noticed that in all our chapters of this book,

the resurrection of the dead has appeared prominent in our arguments; this is because it stands in the foreground of revelation. We think it proper, however, to devote a little space to it as a special subject.

It has been already argued that Adam's sin brought literal death upon himself and his race, God himself explaining the nature of the penalty to be executed upon him for his transgression. "For dust thou art, and unto dust shalt thou return." Also the recovery of the race by the death of Christ has been shown, as set forth in the doctrine of the atonement, which is the basis of the resurrection.

The doctrine of the resurrection of Adam and his race is involved in the Lord's statement to the serpent concerning the seed of the woman: "it shall bruise [crush] thy head." Gen. 3 : 16.

This is clearly shown in John 3 : 8, and Heb. 2 : 14. It was fully involved in the covenant of mercy which placed man on a second probation, as they could not become party to a covenant until means had been provided to redeem them from the law which held them in death.

It was embraced in the promise made to Abram, Isaac, and Jacob, of the earth for an everlasting possession (Gen. 13 : 15; 15 : 7; 17 : 8; 26 : 3; 28 : 13. Rom. 4 : 13. Heb. 11 : 9, 16. Gal. 3 : 29), for they could not hold such possession in this mortal life, and they understood it.

The most striking evidence given in early time of the resurrection of the dead, was in the birth of Isaac. Abraham had believed the promises God made him of the land for an everlasting possession, and of seed to enjoy it with him; but he makes inquiry how this is to be brought about, when he was in old age, and had no son. Gen. 15 : 1–5. In reply, the Lord says to Abraham, "As for Sarai thy wife, thou shalt not call her name Sarai, but Sarah shall her name be. And I will bless her, and give thee a son also of her. . . . Then Abraham fell on his face and laughed, and said in his heart, Shall a child be born unto him that is an hundred years old? and shall Sarah, that is ninety years old, bear? And God said, Sarah thy wife shall bear thee a son indeed, and thou shalt call his name Isaac, and I will establish my covenant with him for an everlasting covenant, and with his seed after him." Gen. 17 : 15–19.

This Isaac was a child of promise, and was born according to promise, as a type of Christ, which Paul shows in his Epistles to the Romans and to the Galatians.

When Isaac was grown, Abraham is called of God to offer this son as a burnt offering to God, on Mount Moriah, to prove his integrity; he obeys the call, and passes through all the pain and suffering of offering Isaac on the altar of sacrifice, supposing he must actually slay his son, although God's promise was involved in his life. But God did not intend that he should kill Isaac, but offer him. This he did, and God said, It is enough.

We have the comments of an inspired apostle on this child's birth, which shows that Isaac was born to Abraham as a pledge to him (and the family of the faithful of course) of the resurrection of the dead. He says,—

"By faith Abraham, when he was tried, offered up Isaac; and he that had received the promises offered up his only begotten son, of whom it was said, that in Isaac shall thy seed be called, accounting that God was able to raise him up even from the dead, from whence also he received him in a figure." Heb. 11 : 17–19.

In the above we have the fact stated that Abraham believed God was able to raise his son Isaac up from the dead. We also have a second fact stated, which is, that Abraham had received Isaac *from the dead in a figure.* How was this figure of the resurrection presented to Abraham? We reply, Abraham was past age, and Sarah was past age; their powers of generation and conception were dead; yet Isaac is born of them in this condition by a miracle, and thus was a child produced from the dead. Abraham knew it, and received him as such — a figure of the resurrection. See Rom. 4 : 19, 20. Thus Abraham became the father of the faithful by believing God. "Therefore sprang there from one, and him as good as dead, so many as the stars of the sky in multitude, and as the sand which is by the sea-shore innumerable. These all died in faith, not having received the promises [things promised], but having seen them afar off, and were persuaded of them, and embraced them, and confessed that they were strangers and pilgrims on the earth." Heb. 11 : 12, 13.

The Scripture statements of the resurrection are too numerous to be crowded into any one book except the Bible; we can quote but a tithe of them in this chapter. We will notice a few in the Old Testament first. Although some men of high repute as Christian teachers have said the Old Testament furnishes little or no testimony of the resurrection of the dead, we find so much that we must pass over the most of it.

Added to what we have already cited, we hear Job: "If a man die, shall he live again? All the days of my appointed time will I wait, till my change come." "Thou shalt call, and I will answer thee; thou wilt have a desire to the work of thy hands. ... If I wait, the grave is my house. ... For I know that my Redeemer liveth, and that he shall stand at the latter day upon the earth: and though, after my skin, worms destroy this body, yet in my flesh shall I see God, whom mine eyes shall behold, and not another; though my reins be consumed within me." Job 14 : 14 ; 16 : 13 ; 19 : 25-27.

David also treats largely of the resurrection: "But God will redeem my soul from the power of the grave, for he shall receive me." Psa. 49 : 15. "Thou, which hast shown me great and sore troubles, shalt quicken me again, and shalt bring me up from the depths of the earth." Psa. 71 : 20. "Wilt thou show wonders to the dead? Shall the dead arise and praise thee?" Psa. 88 : 10. "I shall be satisfied, when I awake, with thy likeness." Psa. 17 : 15. See Psa. 104 : 29, 30.

Surely the above passages speak out plainly on this subject. Let us hear Isaiah : —

"And he will destroy in this mountain the face of the covering cast over all people, and the veil that is spread over all nations. He will swallow up death in victory. ... Thy dead men shall live; together with my dead body shall they arise. Awake and sing, ye that dwell in dust, for thy dew is as the dew of herbs, and the earth shall cast out the dead."

"For, behold, the Lord cometh out of his place to punish the inhabitants of the earth for their iniquity : the earth also shall disclose her blood, and shall no more cover her slain." Isa. 25 : 7, 8 ; 26 : 19–21.

Ezekiel also is made to testify on this matter: "Therefore prophesy, and say unto them, Thus saith the Lord God : Behold, O my people, I will open your graves, and cause you to come up out of your graves, and bring you into the land of Israel." Ezek. 37 : 12. "And [the] many of them that sleep in the dust of the earth shall awake, some to everlasting life, and some to shame and everlasting contempt." Dan. 12 : 2. "I will ransom them from the power of the grave, I will redeem them from death." Hosea 13 : 14.

We will now notice a few passages from Christ and his apostles touching the resurrection of all the dead. The text we have quoted at the head of this chapter is full on the point, and no one can evade it; all who have attempted it have done violence to all proper rules of language and of its interpretation. We will quote another of the sayings of Christ on this subject : —

"Now that the dead are raised ['that the dead rise'— *Em. Diaglott*], even Moses showed at the bush, when he calleth the Lord the God of Abraham, and the God of Isaac, and the God of Jacob. For he is not a God of the dead, but of the living; for all live unto him." Luke 20 : 37, 38.

The above statement of Christ on the resurrection of the dead, together with a preceding remark which we shall quote in another place, put to silence the Sadducees of that age.

While it is true that "THE resurrection," as the term is several times used in the New Testament, embraces the righteous only, in this passage the language is so used as to attach the definite article *the* to the dead. "Now that *the dead rise,* . . . for to him all are alive." — *Em. Diaglott.*

That Abraham, Isaac, and Jacob were righteous, and that God was their God, is a special point in the passage the Saviour quoted from Exodus; and that his statement about a worthy class to "obtain that world, and THE RESURRECTION *from the dead,*" &c., embraces the righteous only, we claim; but when he says, *the dead* are raised, and that *all live,* or to him *all are alive,* he includes *the dead,* without respect to character. All the race are alive to God because of the covenant of mercy through Christ, by which all were redeemed by Christ's death from the grave, and God recognized them as restored from the death Adam brought upon them: consequently he could, and did, covenant to give Abraham, and Isaac, and Jacob, and all others who would believe and obey him, the earth for an everlasting possession, and to be their God. Paul tells us that "to this end Christ hath died, and rose, and revived, that he might be Lord both of the dead and living." Rom. 14 : 9. Therefore, while the law Adam violated disposed of the race, God is not their God; they are extinct. But as Christ purchases them all back, God recognizes them all as alive from death, and makes them accountable to Christ, and, when speaking of them, "calleth those things that are not [yet come] as though they [already] were." Some have used the above passage from Luke ch. 20 to prove the dead are now alive. Christ quotes it to prove the resurrection of the dead to a class of men who denied the doctrine of a resurrection; they also denied the authority of the Scriptures of the prophets, but claimed the five books of Moses as their standard of faith. Therefore Jesus quotes a promise of God to the fathers from Scripture they acknowledged, and which they knew had not been fulfilled, and which Jesus forces upon their minds out of their own standard of faith — a promise which could never be fulfilled unless Abraham, and Isaac, and Jacob should be raised.

Manasseh Ben Israel, Portuguese rabbi of the sect of the Pharisees, comments on God's promise to the patriarchs thus: "It is plain that Abraham and the rest of the patriarchs did not possess that land; it follows, therefore, that they must be raised in order to enjoy the promised good, as otherwise the promises of God would be vain and false."—*De Resurrec. Mort.*, L. I. c. 1, 4.

While Paul is making his defence before the council at Jerusalem, where he was arraigned for preaching heresy, "he cried out in the council, Men and brethren, I am a Pharisee, the son of a Pharisee: of the hope and resurrection of THE DEAD I am called in question." Acts 23 : 6.

A little after this, while before Felix, the governor at Cæsarea, to answer to the charges of the Jews, Paul said, "But this I confess unto thee, that after the way which they call heresy, so worship I the God of my fathers, believing all things which are written in the law and in the prophets; and have hope toward God, which they themselves also allow, that there shall be a resurrection of THE DEAD, both of the just and unjust."

Acts 24 : 14, 15. As Paul continued his defence, and "reasoned of righteousness, temperance, and judgment to come, Felix trembled:" he feared the resurrection of wicked men, for he was in his sins. But Paul had not finished his testimony; he appealed to Cæsar, appeared before King Agrippa, and said in his defence, "And now I stand and am judged for the hope of the promise made of God unto our fathers: unto which promise our twelve tribes, instantly serving God day and night, hope to come. For which hope's sake, King Agrippa, I am accused of the Jews. Why should it be thought a thing incredible with you that God should raise the dead?" Acts 26 : 6–8. Paul then proceeds with his experience, his conversion, and his commission to preach this hope, and to teach the people the foundation of it, and how it was to be fulfilled: —

"Having, therefore, obtained help of God, I continue unto this day, witnessing both to small and great, saying none other things than those which the prophets and Moses did say should come: that Christ should suffer, and that he should be the first that should rise from the dead, and should show light to the people and to the Gentiles." Acts 26 : 22, 23.

CHRIST THE PATTERN.

Christ is set before us, not only as *the pattern* in obedience, righteousness, faith, love, meekness, patience, and good works, but in the redemption, reconstruction, restitution, resurrection of the church to dwell in the new and glorified earth. This was the reason why Paul preached that he should be *the first that should rise from the dead (to immortality).*

Christ rose from the dead literally; the same material body which hung on the cross. This is too plainly true to need argument by any, for those who reject the testimony of Christ and his apostles on this point are past recovery. We should, however, proclaim continually the truths they taught.

Peter, being called to preach Christ, one day finds himself before an audience who were called to Jerusalem to witness the fulfilment of the promise of the Father and of Christ concerning the pouring out of the Holy Spirit; at least God took that occasion to verify the promise of his Son. They were amazed. Peter lifts up his voice for Christ, charges the Jews with killing him "whom God hath raised up, having loosed the pains of death; because it was not possible that he should be holden of it. For David speaketh concerning him, I foresaw the Lord always before my face, for he is on my right hand, that I should not be moved; therefore did my heart rejoice, and my tongue was glad; moreover, also, my flesh shall rest in hope: because thou wilt not leave my soul in hell [the grave], neither wilt thou suffer thine Holy One to see corruption. Thou hast made known to me the ways of life; thou shalt make me full of joy with thy countenance. Men and brethren, let me freely speak to you of the patriarch David, that he is both dead and buried, and his sepulchre is with us unto this day. Therefore, being a prophet, and knowing that God had sworn with an oath to him, that of the fruit of his loins, according to the flesh, he would raise up Christ to sit on his throne.

"He, seeing this before, spake of the resurrection of Christ, that his soul was not left in hell [the grave], neither did his flesh see corruption. This Jesus hath God raised up, whereof we all are witnesses." Acts 2: 24–32. This was the path of life, the way God has ordained to bring men back to life and his church to eternal life. But Peter puts on the crowning proof that Jesus is raised from the dead. He adds, "Therefore, being at the right hand of God exalted, and having received of the Father the promise of the Holy Ghost, he hath shed forth this, which ye now see and hear." Verse 33.

This application of the miraculous, wonder-working power they saw on that day of Pentecost, to the fulfilment of Christ's promise, and as evidence that he was raised from the dead, and had ascended to the Father, was a hard argument for those who had believed the lie which the priests forged for the soldiers to tell — that the disciples came and stole away Christ out of the grave while they slept.

The fact that the disciples visited the sepulchre "and found not the *body* of the Lord Jesus," and "were much perplexed thereabout," with the testimony of the angels that "he is not here, but is risen" (Luke 24: 3–6); his saying to Mary, "Touch me not;" his language to other disciples, "A spirit hath not flesh and bones, as ye see me have," and, "Behold my hands and my feet, that it is I myself: handle me and see;" his "eating broiled fish and honeycomb," — all prove that the same body, the same material which died on the cross, lay in Joseph's new tomb, rose from the dead, and ascended to heaven, immortalized.

This is the pledge of the resurrection of all the race from death, as is fully shown. Paul predicates the entire hope and prospects of the future life of the church on the resurrection of Christ, as the assurance of their resurrection also by him. "For I delivered unto you first of all that which I also received, how that Christ died for our sins, according to the Scriptures; and that he was buried, and that he rose again the third day, according to the Scriptures; and that he was seen of Cephas, then of the twelve; and after that, he was seen of above five hundred brethren at once; . . . and last of all he was seen of me also, as of one born out of due time. . . . Now, if Christ be preached that he rose from the dead, how say some among you that there is no resurrection of the dead? But if there be no resurrection of the dead, then is Christ not risen; and if Christ be not risen, then is our preaching vain, and your faith is also vain. . . . And if Christ be not raised, your faith is vain; ye are yet in your sins. Then they also which are fallen asleep in Christ are perished. If in this life only we have hope in Christ, we are of all men most miserable. But now is Christ risen from the dead, and become the first fruits of them that slept. For since by man came death, by man came also the resurrection of the dead. For as in Adam all die, even so in Christ shall all be made alive;" or "For since through a Man, there is Death, through a Man, also, there is a Resurrection of the Dead; for as by Adam All die, so by the ANOINTED also will All be restored to life. But each one in his own rank, Christ a first fruit, afterwards those who are Christ's at his appearing. Then the end," &c. 1 Cor. 15: 3–24. — *Em. Diaglott.*

We think language cannot be stated more clearly than Paul has stated it, to teach that the resurrection of the race of man is pledged by that of Christ. Christ is the first fruit — a literal rising from death; the harvest will be a literal rising from death; they that are his at his appearing will not only come up like him literally, but like him immortal also; the harvest from " the good seed sown by the Son of man."

But every man in his own company, rank, or band — TAGMA. Christ the first fruits, afterwards they that are Christ's at his coming. Then the end, — τὸ τέλος, — when he shall have delivered up the kingdom to God, even the Father." TAGMA is the word rendered "*order*," company, rank, band, regiment, division, &c. Consequently, in the resurrection of the dead, they will come in two divisions, or by

TWO RESURRECTIONS.

The passage which stands at the head of this chapter as expressly declares two resurrections, as it divides the race into two classes.

" All that are in the graves shall hear his voice, and shall come forth: (1.) they that have done good unto the resurrection of life, (2.) and they that have done evil unto the resurrection of damnation."

These are the words of Christ, and they embrace the resurrection of one class, band, or troop, *to life* (eternal), and the resurrection of a second class, band, or troop, *to condemnation* (to the second death).

Paul's argument in 1 Cor. 15: 23, 24, gives the same idea, when he says, " But every man in his own order "— TAGMA, rank, band, regiment, or division, like soldiers, who come each under his own standard, and in his own division. It is a military term. "They that are Christ's" disciples belong to his division, have chosen his standard, and will come forth "at the last trump; for the trumpet shall sound, and the dead [in Christ] shall be raised incorruptible." The term "in Christ," which is in brackets, is involved in verse 51, and qualifies the terms "*the dead* shall be raised incorruptible,*" showing what dead are the subjects of this resurrection. It is "the dead in Christ," "Now this I say, brethren, . . . WE shall not ALL sleep, but WE shall ALL be changed, in a moment, in the twinkling of an eye, at the last trump; for the trumpet shall sound, and the dead shall be raised incorruptible, and we shall be changed."

"They that are Christ's at his coming. Then the end," — TO TELOS, the END, the last division or portion of the army of the dead — the wicked dead. Not the end of the world or age, but the *perfection, finishing, completion,* or *consummation* of the work of bringing back the race of man from death. Not the termination of Christ's reign, as some suppose, but the bringing back from a lost, revolted state, to its original state, and restitution, to merge into the eternal reign of Christ, after disposing of the wicked. The word *telos* is not the word generally used to signify the end of the age or world. The learned Dr. Wahl defines *telos* in 1 Cor. 15: 24, "the last part, the last — *the last of the dead.*" Dr. Bretschneider, in his Greek Lexicon, gives the meaning of "Then the end — TELOS — *the last or rest of mankind.*"

The words which express the "end of the age," are "SUNTELEIA TOU AIONOS."*

The last band or company of the dead is expressed in Rev. 20 : 5, " But the rest of the dead," &c.

These facts and considerations show us why the Scriptures contain the following language expressive of priority, and superiority of the resurrection of the righteous : " They that have done good unto the resurrection of life." John 5 : 29. "Thou shalt be recompensed at the resurrection of the just." Luke 14 : 14. "That they might obtain a better resurrection." Heb. 11 : 35. "But they which shall be accounted worthy to obtain that world, and THE RESURRECTION *from* [*among*] *the dead*, neither marry nor are given in marriage ; neither can they die any more ; for they are equal unto the angels, and are the children of God, being the children of the resurrection." Luke 20 : 35, 36.

It will be noticed that these are *worthy of that world* to come, and *worthy of the resurrection* from (among) the dead, not *of the dead*, and that they are the children of THE resurrection, the first one, and the better one, the only one that will bring fruit to the kingdom of God.

Paul gives us the same argument : " That I may know him, and the power of his resurrection, and the fellowship of his sufferings, being made conformable unto his death, if by any means I may attain to the resurrection from the dead."—*American Bible Union Version*. "If possible I may attain to the RESURRECTION from among the DEAD."—*Em. Diaglott* (*Whiting's*), and other versions of Phil. 3 : 11.

---

* See *Retribution*, p. 61, by H. L. Hastings.

As Paul believed all the dead would have a resurrection, he would be sure to attain to a resurrection without striving and suffering for Christ. But his language shows that he had learned of the *first*, the *better*, the one out *from among the dead* who belong in the last division of men, of the army of the dead. Only in this view of the case is there any force in his language; with this view it is forcible indeed.

Also in 1 Thess. 4: 16, Paul gives the same idea: "and *the dead in Christ* shall rise *first*, then we, which are alive and remain, shall be caught up together with them in the clouds, to meet the Lord in the air."

Although the priority of this text relates to those which are alive and remain, who are to be subsequently caught up, yet the apostle is emphatic as to the class which will rise before the living believers are caught up. He says, "*the dead in Christ.*" If all the dead are to rise when "the Lord himself shall descend from heaven with a shout, with the voice of the archangel, and with the trump of God," then the words *in Christ* are superfluous; but these words qualify the sentence.

The above passages, and many others, prove that the passage in Rev. 20: 1–8, is not so wonderfully unlike the current testimony of the Scriptures, and does not therefore need such lengthy essays and so many efforts to show its figurative, symbolic, and metaphoric character, by which "the first resurrection" is made to be a mere myth, or an incomprehensible symbol.

The apostle John saw those who had suffered for and died in the faith of Christ, live; and he tells us "they lived and reigned with Christ a thousand years," prior to something else he saw. "But the rest of the dead lived not again until the thousand years were finished," showing that these living and reigning ones had been dead, but are now alive. He adds concerning them, in distinction from the rest of the dead, "This is the first resurrection. Blessed and holy is he that hath part in the first resurrection; on such the second death hath no power; but they shall be priests of God, and of Christ, and shall reign with him a thousand years."

This thousand years is, then, the space between the two resurrections, during which the Lord's company, band, or troop, reign in life with him, while "the rest of the dead [are yet dead] lived not again until" this time expires. There is no intimation that the saints will reign only a thousand years, but it states that they will reign this length of time before the wicked are raised, or "*live again,*" and before "Satan shall be loosed out of his prison, and shall go out to deceive the nations" of the wicked, who are then raised in their company, band, division, or regiment, with the devil for their captain, who will lead them to the point of final destruction.

After the above scene and order of the two resurrections are witnessed by John, he has another view of the same events, with others, in which to describe the facts more clearly that all the race is embraced in the resurrection and judgment, and rewarded "out of those things which were written in the books, according to their works; and whosoever was not found written in the book of life was cast into the lake of fire."

This is the same class which lived not again for a thousand years; the same class which Satan went out to deceive after he was loosed from his prison; the same which compassed the camp of the saints about, and was devoured by fire. It is only another description of the same events, and a clearer revelation to show that all "the dead, small and great," were not disposed of without *judgment* according to the books of record.

We have not the space in this work to argue the millennium and its order of events; nor is it the object of this book to give a detailed account of much that is interesting and valuable on other points than those already cited; and these subjects are only partially discussed, giving, as we believe, the outlines of them.

There is much more we would like to say on the resurrection of the dead, but this must suffice. There are objections, in some minds, to the views we present, which can be readily met by showing the different classes of descriptive language employed in the Scriptures.

Our views of the millennium between the two resurrections are indicated in what we have said; but we wish to add, we are convinced that it will be a reign of peace and righteousness in immortality, after probation has ceased; when he that is holy will be holy still, and he that is filthy will be filthy still.

The resurrection of the righteous will take place at the personal coming of Christ, which is now nigh at hand; how near we dare not say, for we do not know. The prophecies and their fulfilment, the signs, civil, moral, and religious, admonish us to watch and be ready. Many good and wise men of God have been led to believe this generation will witness the ushering in of those stupendous and all-important events. Some have decided from the prophetic periods, as to the definite time of the event. Such are to be found now in all parts of Christendom. Some of them may be correct: we do not presume to decide. There are many very valuable volumes now published on the prophecies, and signs of the times,* in which all will find benefit in carefully reading. The day of final rewards is close at the door: we should be ready, and watching, and waiting, ourselves, and laboring with our might to induce as many of our fellows to become lovers of Christ as we may, that they, with us, "may know the power of his resurrection, and the fellowship of his sufferings," and obtain a "resurrection out from among the dead," "the resurrection of the just," the "better resurrection," "the first resurrection," or be among those who shall be "alive and remain," ready to be "changed in a moment, in the twinkling of an eye, at the last trump, and caught up with them to meet the Lord in the air."

* See Bible Student's Library, published by H. L. Hastings, Boston; also works by Dr. John Cumming, of London, and many others.

CHAPTER XVII.

THE ETERNAL SALVATION OF GOD'S PEOPLE.

"And being made perfect, he became the author of eternal salvation unto all them that obey him." — *Heb.* 5 : 9.

How sublime and deep are the things of the Spirit of God! None but the eternal mind can fully comprehend them; yet they are given in language which we can understand; they are given *for us* and *to us*, that we may, through the aid of the same Spirit, learn the mind and purposes of God.

The announcement in the passage at the head of this chapter is well calculated to fill the hearts of the humble believers in Christ with sensations of joy and gratitude beyond expression.

> "Salvation! O, the joyful sound!
> What pleasure to our ears!
> A sovereign balm for every wound,
> A cordial for our fears.
>
> "Salvation! O, thou bleeding Lamb!
> To thee the praise belongs:
> Salvation shall inspire our hearts,
> And dwell upon our tongues."

To us, who have been *lost*, who have felt ourselves ruined by sin, wasting by disease, encumbered with infirmities, with the penalty of a violated law hanging over us, ready to bring us down to the dust at any moment, because of mortality entailed upon us by Adam, the news of salvation is sweet indeed.

But to us, who, after having been bought out from under "the law of sin and death," and redeemed from its evils by the sufferings and death of Christ, and placed under the *new covenant*, "under law to Christ," who is set before us "for obedience to the faith among all nations, for his name" (Rom. 1:1–5), and having violated this law ourselves, and wandered from God upon the dark mountains of sin, thus incurring its penalty, — "the second death," — to *such lost sinners*, who have rejected that Saviour which gave himself for us, and placed us in the way of life, the offer of eternal salvation becomes exceedingly important. Let us carefully study this matter.

There are two special points in this subject.

First. The Author of this salvation.

Second. The subjects who are to receive it.

I. The Author of eternal salvation is the Son of God and the Son of man, standing between God the Father and our fallen race. It is he who *took* our nature, who "took on him the seed of Abraham," "was made of the seed of David according to the flesh," born of the Virgin Mary, and of whom Paul says, "God sent forth his Son, made of a woman," "and declared to be the Son of God with power, according to the spirit of holiness, by the resurrection from the dead," of whom we have spoken more fully in our chapters on the atonement, and in other parts of this book.

The idea is clearly involved in our text, that the time was when the Author of this salvation was not perfect.

for it is explicitly stated that "*being made perfect*, he became," &c. This expression has perplexed many inquirers after truth, not because the subject is dark, but because they *assume* that perfection always implies *completeness in degree*, as well as in kind, or that Christ was always perfect in all respects, both of which ideas are untrue.

We have found eminent writers in strange confusion on this subject, because they held erroneous views concerning Christ on other points. In examining this subject we shall find that although the Son of God "had glory with the Father before the world was," and "was rich" before he "took upon him the form of a servant, and was made in the likeness of men," and although he "*thought it not robbery* to be equal with God," he changed this position to become our sacrifice, and to shed blood for the remission of our sins, and thence to become "an high priest which can be touched with the feeling of our infirmities, being in all points tempted like as we are, yet without sin." Heb. 4: 15.

"God manifest in the flesh," is declared by Paul to be "a *great mystery*," and we are ready to admit it; yet we will rejoice that such a manifestation has been made, and seek to learn whatever has been revealed concerning it.

As we have already stated above, our Lord Jesus Christ was a union of God and man, composed of each, with the elements and properties of the Father mysteriously united with man's nature,—*the divine nature* with *flesh and blood*, with its infirmities, but not its sins. As such he was unlike any other being in the world, combining the qualities of divinity and humanity.

Therefore the various singular descriptions of him in the Bible. Isaiah prophesies of him thus: "Behold, a virgin shall conceive and bear a son, and shall call his name Immanuel. Butter and honey shall he eat, that he may know to refuse the evil and choose the good." Isa. 7 : 14, 15. "And Jesus increased in wisdom and stature, and in favor with God and man." Luke 2 : 52. These statements of Scripture are made concerning "Jesus of Nazareth," touching his early days in this mortal world. After he was anointed of the Holy Spirit and entered upon his prophetic office, we hear him saying, "Behold, I cast out devils, and I do cures to-day and to-morrow, and the third day I shall be perfected." Luke 13 : 32.

Paul, the commentator and inspired apostle, in arguing on this point, states it thus: "For it became him, for whom are all things, and by whom are all things, in bringing many sons unto glory, to make the Captain of their salvation perfect through sufferings." Heb. 2 : 10. The great end to be accomplished was the resurrection and change to immortality of obedient believers in Christ, the removal of the curse from their inheritance, the redemption of the earth, and filling it with God's glory, as a fitting abode for his people, and as the place where it was originally designed they should enjoy eternal life.

To accomplish this, Christ must conquer death, which holds all in its grasp and blights all the earth, as is further stated by Paul: "Forasmuch then as the children are partakers of flesh and blood, he also himself likewise took part of the same, that through death he might destroy him that had the power of death, that is, the devil, and deliver them who through fear of death were all their lifetime subject to bondage." Heb. 2: 14, 15.

He must not only conquer death, but must conquer it in humanity, and for humanity, to save MAN, — his form and structure, his *materialism*. This he did, to the praise of his glorious name.

To do this he must suffer; he must feel the tender and multiplying sensations of childhood, the earnest and active passions of youth, the constant desires of manhood for a better state, together with all the weakness, temptations, and infirmities of human nature, the woes and sorrows, the burdens and sadness, of a fallen race. That this was the task to be done to bring back lost man, and to make a sacrifice for the sins of the people, the Scriptures bear the most decided testimony in their teachings, as to the *manner of the work*, as well as the fact that it was done.

Many seem to think that the *spirit of man* is all that is involved in the work of salvation by Christ: though they will admit that the material man is involved someway in sin and in death, yet if the spirit is saved, they conclude it would be a great salvation, and worthy of a God.

If this be so, why did God pay such high regard to materialism? Why was "God manifest in the flesh"? Why did Divinity blend his unfathomable essence with the framework of humanity, and tread the earth in the real form and stature of a man, not as a temporary structure, but as an eternal one, having borne it to the place where he now is interceding for his people? He has entered within the vale, and is seated upon the Father's throne with the very body which hung upon the cross, with the prints of the nails and the mark of the spear which he exhibited to doubting Thomas after his resurrection; and which ate and drank, to convince his disciples that he was not a spirit, bidding them to handle him, and see the *flesh* and the *bones*.

This same materialism and form which groaned and sweat and agonized in the garden, which cried with a loud voice, "*It is finished*," and expired on the cross, which lay in Joseph's new tomb, which arose from the grave, ascended to the Father, and is, one day, to descend to earth in glorified human form, to receive homage from every knee and tongue, is not to be lightly esteemed by the church of Christ.

He was made perfect through suffering — *the suffering of death:* this was the penalty for sin. He was capable of dying, though morally perfect, free from sin, righteous in principle and character; but he had given himself a ransom for all : he entered the dark domain of death, and was raised from this state to life and immortality by the Father. He is now perfect in *degree*, as well as in principle. So Paul states the case, "*knowing that Christ, being raised from the dead, dieth no more; death hath no more dominion over him.*" Rom. 6 : 9. We will hear Christ's testimony to John on this subject after his resurrection. "*I am he that liveth, and was dead; and, behold, I am alive for evermore, Amen, and have the keys of hell and of death.*" Rev. 1 : 18. From the foregoing we learn by what steps our Lord

Jesus Christ became, or was *made*, *perfect*, and became an immortal, conquering Saviour of humanity.

Thus we find him teaching these facts to the multitudes who came to hear him. "As the Father knoweth me, even so know I the Father; and I lay down my life for the sheep. . . . Therefore doth my Father love me, because I lay down my life, that I might take it again. No man taketh it from me, but I lay it down of myself. I have power to lay it down, and I have power to take it again. This commandment ['commission'—*Campbell*] have I received of my Father." John 10 : 15, 18. We will hear him once more: "I am the bread of life: he that cometh to me shall never hunger; and he that believeth on me shall never thirst. . . . And this is the will of him that sent me, that every one which seeth the Son, and believeth on him, may have everlasting life, and I will raise him up at the last day." John 5 : 35–40.

How cheering the prospects set before such poor, frail, dying mortals as we, who, though hungering and thirsting for righteousness, and deliverance from this mortal world of evil, and from the dominion of death, have no power to satisfy the cravings of the soul, nor means of escape from the grasp of death.

We are assured that he who is thus made perfect has become our High Priest, having been practically acquainted with our infirmities, and who sympathizes with us in our yearnings for immortality and eternal life, and under whose discipline we have lived. "Wherefore in all things it behooved him to be made like unto his brethren, that he might be a merciful and faithful High

Priest in things pertaining to God, to make reconciliation for the sins of the people." Heb. 2 : 17.

While, therefore, our Lord and Saviour has come down to our mortal condition to know and share our sorrows, and be "touched with the feeling of our infirmities," suffering death in his own person to perfect our humanity, it becomes us to seek such an acquaintance with him, by faith in his word and the reception of his spirit in our hearts, as will enable us to "know him and the power of his resurrection, and the fellowship of his sufferings, being made conformable unto his death ; if possible we may attain to the resurrection from among the dead." Phil. 3 : 10, 11. — *Em. Diaglott.*

II. THE SUBJECTS OF ETERNAL SALVATION.

The race of man having been reconciled to, justified, and redeemed from the Adamic law by the death of Christ, as we have shown in other chapters of this work, and an atonement having been made by the blood of Christ for the remission of actual sins, led Paul to say, " Much more then, being now justified by his blood, we shall be saved from wrath through him. For if, when we were enemies, we were reconciled to God [in respect to that law Adam violated] by the death of his Son, much more, being reconciled, we shall be saved by his life. And not only so, but we also joy in God through our Lord Jesus Christ, by whom we have now received the atonement." Rom. 5 : 9–11.

The atonement must be received by faith, if we would gain salvation by it; for it is written," If thou shalt confess with thy mouth the Lord Jesus, and shalt believe in thine heart that God raised him from the dead, thou shalt be saved." "For with the heart man believeth unto righteousness, and with the mouth confession is made unto salvation." Rom. 10 : 9, 10.

Jesus himself has declared it in these words : " For God so loved the world that he gave his only begotten Son, that whosoever believeth in him should *not perish*, but have *everlasting life*." John 3 : 16. Again : we hear him saying, " Father, the hour is come ; glorify thy Son, that thy Son also may glorify thee ; as thou hast given him power ['authority'— *Em. Diaglott*] over all flesh, that he should give eternal life to as many as thou hast given him. And this is life eternal, that they might know thee, the only true God, and Jesus Christ, whom thou hast sent. . . . I have manifested thy name unto the men which thou gavest me out of the world : thine they were, and thou gavest them me, and they have kept thy word. Now they have known that all things whatsoever thou hast given me are of thee. For I have given unto them the words which thou gavest me ; and they have received them, and have known surely that I came out from thee, and they have believed that thou didst send me. I pray for them : I pray not for the world, but for them which thou hast given me, for they are thine. . . . Neither pray I for these alone, but for them also which shall believe on me through their word." John 17 : 1–20.

The above testimony conclusively shows the distinguishing characteristics of God's people, and who are given to Christ to receive eternal life. Of them Christ says, again : "And I give unto them eternal life ; and they shall never perish, neither shall any man pluck them out of my hand. My Father, which gave them me, is greater than all, and no man is able to pluck them out of my Father's hand." John 10 : 28, 29.

There can be no failure on the part of God to fulfil his promises, neither on the part of Christ : he has life in himself, and can give it to his followers ; he has a heart to do it ; he has promised it ; and all the children of God will gain *eternal life and salvation.*

Forasmuch, then, as it hath pleased the Father to give the Son all who would believe on him, to be joint heirs with him to eternal life and inheritance, we should joyfully accept the way which leads to it. The apostle Paul gives us another clear statement of God's purpose in the following : —

"Having predestinated us unto the adoption of children by Jesus Christ to himself, according to the good pleasure of his will, to the praise of the glory of his grace, wherein he hath made us accepted in the beloved, in whom we have redemption through his blood, the forgiveness of sins, according to the riches of his grace." Eph. 1 : 5–8.

Although this salvation is bestowed upon *obedient believers,* it is not the reward of works ; it is a gift in Jesus Christ to all who obey him : "Not by works of righteousness which we have done, but according to his mercy, he saved us, by the washing of regeneration and renewing of the Holy Ghost, which he shed on us abundantly through Jesus Christ our Saviour, that, being justified by his grace, we should be made heirs, according to the hope of eternal life." Titus 3 : 5–7.

Again: we hear Paul declaring to the Thessalonians: "But we are bound to give thanks alway to God for you, brethren beloved of the Lord, because God hath from the beginning chosen you to salvation through sanctification of the Spirit and belief of the truth." 2 Thess. 2 : 13.

Peter also presents the same point in the introduction of his First Epistle, addressed to the *strangers* "elect according to the foreknowledge of God the Father, through sanctification of the Spirit, unto obedience and sprinkling of the blood of Jesus Christ." 1 Pet. 1 : 2. A little farther on he tells us that these elected, sanctified, obedient ones "are *kept by the power of God through faith unto salvation, ready to be revealed in the last time.*"

The above testimony clearly reveals the fact that while God has provided a sacrifice for sin, and determined on saving a portion of our race, having elected them to salvation, yet it is as expressly declared to be secured to the individuals on the condition of "THE OBEDIENCE OF FAITH."

Before this eternal salvation is bestowed there must be a position attained to which gives us union with Christ (and a cleansing from sin), which we do not have by nature; and in order to obtain this relation to Christ, there is given us

A TERM OF PROBATION AND SPACE FOR REPENTANCE.

The conditions imposed by which we may become heirs of eternal salvation are clearly stated in the gospel, and should be carefully studied; for while God has *chosen, elected*, and *ordained* that *a class* shall obtain eternal salvation, *we* shall fall short of it unless we *become members* of that *class*.

Christ is God's elect, and all who become associated with him so as to be recognized as his followers are embraced in the covenant between the Father and the Son; they are in Christ, and consequently joint heirs with him. "Behold my servant whom I uphold, mine elect, in whom my soul delighteth; I have put my spirit upon him: he shall bring forth judgment to the Gentiles. . . . He shall not fail, nor be discouraged, till he have set judgment in the earth, and the isles shall wait for his law. . . . I the Lord have called thee in righteousness, and will hold thine hand, and will keep thee, and give thee for a covenant of the people, for a light of the Gentiles, to open the blind eyes, to bring out the prisoners from the prison, and them that sit in darkness out of the prison-house." Isa. 42: 1–7.

This is a declaration of the Father concerning his Son: whosoever believeth in him becomes entitled to the privileges belonging to him, being elected in him, he being the representative head of all believers.

Nearly all the subjects of special importance treated upon in revelation relating to this mortal world are presented in the several stages they pass through from the incipient stage to completion, or perfection in the absolute sense. A few examples will illustrate the point. Adam, although created in the image of God, and *very good*, was undeveloped, and put on probation for immortality, dominion, and eternal life.

The earth, although created with all the elements of

beauty, fruitfulness, and goodness, was put under the care of man to till, dress, subdue, and develop. Since sin entered and the curse followed, God has commenced the work of redeeming and restoring, revealing his purposes by degrees, giving one bud of hope, then another; opening an elementary course of discipline, then instituting a formal civil code of law and government, with its *emblems, types, and shadows of good things to come;* all the while proclaiming the gospel or good news of the coming restitution in various ways, until the "seed of the woman" is manifested, who is to destroy the devil and his works.

Here, again, we find the same plan pursued in relation to our Saviour, the Lord of life.

First, it is the "holy child Jesus," begotten "of the Holy Ghost," born of the Virgin Mary, with the weakness of infancy, not knowing to refuse the evil or to choose the good; then the zeal of youth with the doctors at Jerusalem; the firmness, care, determination, and endurance of manhood in his ministry and temptations; and lastly, the faithfulness and submissive suffering of death on the cross; these were the progressive steps which brought him to that state of perfection he obtained in his resurrection from death.

A similar course of progression is pursued with us to bring us to the enjoyment of eternal life. We are a race of actual sinners; our nature is carnal; we are not willing subjects of the law of God; yet he does not abandon us in our sinful state; though we have incurred the sentence of his law by rejecting Christ, he still seeks to win us to enter his fold. He has explained to us the nature and consequences of sin; he has extended to us the offers of mercy, promising us salvation from sin and death if we will believe in and obey his Son. To us also " is the word of this salvation sent." Jesus is proclaimed constantly in the gospel: "And thou shalt call his name JESUS, for he shall save his people from their sins." Matt. 1 : 21.

After Christ was raised from the dead he commissioned men to " go into all the world and preach the gospel to every creature," and to tell them that " he that believeth and is baptized shall be saved; but he that believeth not shall be damned." Mark 16 : 16.

In pursuance of this commission Paul says, " For I am not ashamed of the gospel of Christ, for it is the power of God unto salvation to every one that believeth, to the Jew first, and also to the Greek. For herein is the righteousness of God revealed from faith to faith, as it is written, The just shall live by faith." " *The righteous by faith shall live*" — *Em. Diaglott.* Rom. 1 : 16, 17.

All this interest and care on the part of God and his Son, in offering mercy, procuring a sacrifice for sin, revealing righteousness, and in publishing the gospel of salvation, is for the benefit of sinners. Formerly, the law gave the knowledge of sin: since Christ ascended to the Father, the *Holy Spirit has been given, to " reprove the world of sin, of righteousness, and of judgment."* The *gospel is given us to explain* the character and offices of Christ as a Saviour of sinners, and to give the promises of salvation and eternal blessedness. When we are convinced of sin, and ready to accept Christ as our sacrifice, our lawgiver, and guide, the Father is ready to *forgive* our sins, and accept us as his sons, through the blood of the new covenant: thus we are given to Christ, as our teacher, to instruct, guide, chasten, and discipline according to the spirit and precepts of the law of faith. Jesus states it on this wise: "All that the Father giveth me, shall come to me, and him that cometh to me I will in no wise cast out. . . . No man can come to me, except the Father, which hath sent me, draw him." John 6: 37, 44. By this it is seen that the Father awakens and convinces the sinner, draws his attention to Christ; if he will choose him as his Saviour, and enter his school of instruction, the Father gives him to the Son, and he becomes a disciple, a scholar, in the school of Christ. This school has a law; it is "the royal law," "the law of faith." It must be obeyed or we must suffer chastisement. Christ "will in no wise cast us out;" he will instruct and love us, and use all the means of mercy to save us.

The terms of discipleship are thus stated by Christ: "Whosoever will come after me, let him deny himself, and take up his cross and follow me." Mark 8: 34. Again: "Whosoever he be of you that forsaketh not all that he hath, cannot be my *disciple*." Luke 14: 33.

All confidence in our own righteousness, wisdom, or ability, or that of any other, must be abandoned for Christ, to learn of him, be saved by him, and kept unto the end of probation. "If we confess our sins, he is faithful and just to forgive us our sins and to cleanse us from all unrighteousness." 1 John 1: 9.

We are saved from our sins by confession through

faith in Christ. We stand by faith. We walk by faith. We run by faith. Therefore we are taught by the Scriptures to "lay aside every weight, and the sin which doth so easily beset us, and let us run with patience the race that is set before us, looking unto Jesus, the author and finisher of our faith." Heb. 12 : 1, 2.

But we must continue in the school of Christ in order to secure our election, maintain the character of disciples, and gain eternal salvation. "If ye continue in my word, then are ye my DISCIPLES INDEED, and ye shall know the truth, and the truth shall make you free." John 8 : 31, 32. "As the branch cannot bear fruit of itself, except it abide in the vine, no more can ye, except ye abide in me. If ye abide in me, and my words abide in you, ye shall ask what ye will, and it shall be done unto you. Herein is my Father glorified, that ye bear much fruit; so shall ye be my DISCIPLES. As the Father hath loved me, so have I loved you : continue in my love. If ye keep my commandments ye shall abide in my love." John 15 : 4–10. These terms need not be misunderstood. The conditions are plain and open for all. If we refuse to comply with them, Jesus does not cast us out; but the Father, who gave us to Christ to train for immortality, takes us away for disregarding and dishonoring him and his Son. "I am the true vine, and my Father is the husbandman. Every branch in me that beareth not fruit he taketh away. . . . If any man abide not in me, he is cast forth as a branch, and is withered." John 15 : 1, 6.

Peter teaches us to add to faith certain graces or fruits of the Spirit, and then remarks, "For if these things be in you, and abound, they make you that ye shall be neither barren nor unfruitful in the knowledge of our Lord Jesus Christ. But he that lacketh these things is blind, and cannot see afar off, and hath forgotten that he was purged from his old sins. Wherefore the rather, brethren, give diligence to make your CALLING and ELECTION SURE: for if ye do these things ye shall never fall: for so an entrance shall be ministered unto you abundantly into the everlasting kingdom of our Lord and Saviour Jesus Christ." 2 Pet. 1: 8–11.

Let us quote again the text at the head of this chapter, and notice the harmony of the Word: "And being made perfect, he became the author of eternal salvation unto all them that obey him." Thus we are taught that eternal salvation is the result of obedience to Christ, and this obedience is the fruit of faith in the Son of God. Unless we have faith enough to lead us to obedience, it is not enough to save us: we must have faith which works, grows, surmounts difficulties, lays hold of the promises of the eternal God, and overcomes the world. This is not a faith which makes us fearful, stupid, indolent, and presumptuous, but gives life, hope, activity, earnestness, and courage to face the devil, declare the truth, live righteousness, reprove sin, and preach Christ with a loving heart, "working out our own salvation with fear and trembling;" not working to buy or produce salvation, but having salvation, and then developing it, as the fountain works out or sends forth the river, or the fruitful tree sends forth its fruit. When we are so saved from sin, controlled by grace through faith, as to be workers with God and for God, there is a living hope of eternal salvation: "For we are saved by hope: but hope that is seen is not hope; for what a man seeth, why doth he yet hope for? But if we hope for that we see not, then do we with patience wait for it." Rom. 8:24, 25.

Though we be saved from our sins by repentance toward God, and faith toward our Lord Jesus Christ, and kept by the faith of obedience, we are yet compassed with many infirmities; we are frail, short-sighted, timid, erring mortals, needing the intercession of Christ, the merits of his shed blood, the admonitions and quickening of the Holy Spirit constantly; for "we walk by faith." We have not yet overcome all; the "fight of faith" ends only when probation closes up.

Our lives here are labor and sorrow, and end in death; our victory here is only a moral one; but if we keep our ground, and hold the victory in Christ over moral enemies, we shall be able to go on to final and everlasting victory *over death*, by the resurrection from the dead to immortality. He who conquered death for us obtained the keys. He has promised us deliverance from death, blessed be his glorious name. "For the Lord himself shall descend from heaven with a shout, with the voice of the archangel and the trump of God, and the dead in Christ shall rise first: then we which are alive and remain shall be caught up together with them in the clouds, to meet the Lord in the air: and so shall we ever be with the Lord." 1 Thess. 4:16, 17.

Again, Paul speaks of the triumph of the church in this wise: "We shall not all sleep, but we shall all be changed, in a moment, in the twinkling of an eye, at the last trump: for the trumpet shall sound, and the dead shall be raised incorruptible, and we shall be changed. . . . So when this corruptible shall have put on incorruption, and this mortal shall have put on immortality, then shall be brought to pass the saying that is written, Death is swallowed up in victory." 1 Cor. 15: 51–54. This will be the final victory of the church of Christ, and they will then be ready to give him the glory for it all. John, while on Patmos, in prophetic vision, heard them saying, "For thou wast slain, and hast redeemed us to God, by thy blood, out of every kindred, and tongue, and nation, and people, and hast made us unto our God kings and priests, and we shall reign on the earth." Rev. 5: 9, 10. John hears another voice also on the same subject: "And I heard a great voice out of heaven, saying, Behold, the tabernacle of God is with men, and he will dwell with them, and be their God; and God shall wipe away all tears from their eyes, and there shall be no more death, neither sorrow nor crying, neither shall there be any more pain, for the former things are passed away." Rev. 21: 3, 4.

What ecstasy of joy arises from a proper contemplation of this theme — ETERNAL SALVATION! Is it for you to enjoy, dear readers? Yes, if you will believe and obey Christ. What a prospect is before the church — God's faithful, humble children! They have been poor and despised by the world; they have been regarded as stupid, mad, foolish, and unworthy the respect of the rich and the proud. They have suffered loss, shame, reproach, scoffing, ridicule, contempt, torture, imprisonment, and death, for their faith in Christ; yet, trusting in a covenant-keeping God, they prayed, and believed, and hoped; they struggled with difficulties; they endured temptations; they suffered hardship; they wept tears of bitterness, and groaned in anxious hope and expectation of the final triumph over sin and its effects. Many are having this experience now. But the victory hasteth; "the Lord is at hand;" the day of redemption cometh; "the year of God's redeemed" is now nigh at hand. "Lift up your heads, and look up, for your redemption draweth nigh." Luke 21 : 28.

Eternal salvation! How sweet the sound! The weakness of mortal nature, the heart tremblings, the alternations between hope and fear, the sadness and weepings over faults and failings, are then to give place to songs of victory. The toils and the cares, the burdens and the sorrows, of the faithful shall all end in eternal rest. The tears and groans, losses, pains, crosses, and yearnings, will be changed for the crown of life and everlasting joy. The sad partings from loved ones in death, endured by stricken and broken-hearted mothers, fathers, and companions, brothers, sisters, and children, who have died in the Lord, will be rewarded by a reunion in the everlasting kingdom of our God, to part no more; and associated with all the faithful, suffering children of God, we shall find unbounded joy and gladness in exchange for the sacrifices, made in this sorrowing world, in the service of God.

> "When time's stormy tempest-roar
>   Is forever closing,
> I shall on the other shore
>   With Him be reposing.

> Loving eyes shall on me shine,
>   Hands shall stretch to meet me,
> Loving arms shall round me twine,
>   Loving voices greet me.
>
> "There my little ones, I know,
>   Round me shall be clinging;
> There the loved of long ago
>   With me shall be singing.
> O, that land I long to see,
>   Where the weary-hearted
> Shall with Christ in glory be,
>   Never to be parted.
>
> "Saviour, come and bring the day,
>   Day of endless gladness;
> Drive our tears and gloom away,
>   Banish all our sadness;
> Let us see the light of home,
>   Hear its music swelling;
> Bring us through the conquered tomb
>   To that heavenly dwelling." — H. L. H.

Come, ye weary, burdened, tempest-tossed children of our heavenly Father, look up, and hope, and trust his grace: in a little while you shall join the glad song of eternal victory. And you, poor, sad, distressed and burdened sinners, come to the banqueting-house. Cast away your garments of sin and self-righteousness, receive Christ as your Saviour, be clothed with the righteousness of faith, confess your sins, accept his terms of discipleship, learn of him, obey his teachings, believe his promises, and obtain eternal salvation in the everlasting kingdom.

CHAPTER XVIII.

GOD'S PEOPLE ISRAEL.

"Then said God. Call his name Lo-ammi: for ye are not my people, and I will not be your God. Yet the number of the children of Israel shall be as the sand of the sea, which cannot be measured nor numbered; and it shall come to pass, that in the place where it was said unto them, Ye are not my people, there it shall be said unto them, Ye are the sons of the living God."— *Hosea* 1: 9, 10.

ALTHOUGH many volumes have been written upon God's relation to, and purposes concerning this remarkable people, the Jewish nation, yet we do not consider the subject exhausted.

A misunderstanding of the Scriptures upon important points has led to many conflicting opinions and false conclusions, which materially affect the expectations of the Christian church.

While the mass of Christians admit the doctrine that the second advent of Christ is yet future, in some form or sense, and that the church is to finally triumph on earth, others, the genuineness of whose faith is more doubtful, claim that the second advent of Christ is in the past, and that the Scriptures relating to that event were fulfilled at the destruction of Jerusalem; yet it is generally admitted that that event sustains some very important relation to the Israelitish nation.

The latter named class claim that it was the overthrow of their polity, or government, and their dispersion among the Gentile nations of the earth; while a portion of the former class claim that the second advent of Christ is spiritual, and accomplishes the restoration of the Jewish nation to the land of Palestine, and the conversion of the nations to the gospel; and yet another portion claim that it is literal, and results in the literal return of the Jews to Jerusalem, and a term of probation for them, together with those nations which they claim have not had the gospel prior to that event.

While we claim that the second advent of Christ is literal, personal, and results in the end of all probation, the resurrection of the righteous dead, the final judgment of the resurrected wicked, the eternal triumph of the true Israel of both Jew and Gentile, and the final establishment of the kingdom of God, and the personal reign of Christ with his people, on the renewed earth.

We shall not attempt to review these various opinions in this chapter, as they have been sufficiently met by the direct Bible argument in this and other works on this subject.

But we shall endeavor to present the direct Bible argument upon the question,

WHO ARE THE TRUE ISRAEL,

And the rightful heirs of the promises made to Abraham, and Isaac, and Jacob, and to their seed, and to David and his seed?

In doing this, we shall endeavor to find and present the Scriptural line of distinction between the Jewish nation as such, and the promises to and concerning THEM, and the TRUE SEED of Abraham, —THE ISRAEL OF GOD, — and the promises which pertain to THEM. Or, in other words, show the difference between "the children of the flesh," and "the children of the promise."

From the earliest history of our race, as given by inspiration, we have the line of difference between God's people and the children of the Devil. This is the line of *faith*, and it is as distinctly drawn, and even more so, through the Jewish nation, than any other nation on the earth.

The apostle John recognizes it as existing in the history of Cain and Abel, the two first sons of Adam.

"Not as Cain, who was of that wicked one, and slew his brother. And wherefore slew he him? Because his own works were evil, and his brother's righteous." 1 John 3 : 12.

Paul shows that line of distinction to be FAITH. He also commences it with Abel, and runs it down through the Jewish nation into the Gentile nations of the earth.

If this line of distinction is kept in view in our investigations, we shall find but little difficulty in determining who are the Israel to be saved, redeemed, restored, at the second advent of the Deliverer who shall come to Zion, and to them that turn from transgressions in Jacob. Isa. 59 : 20.

It is true, there are passages in the prophets that would seem to favor the idea of the restoration of the Jews to Palestine, were it not for the express conditions proposed by the Lord in the beginning, and the inspired expositions of the New Testament, together with the most positive statements in the Old Testament, and by some of the same prophets to the contrary, — such as Jer. 19 : 1, 10, 15. Please read the whole chapter. With such an amount of direct testimony, we consider the question settled.

With these preliminary remarks, we will proceed with the direct argument as to who are God's people, and the Israel of God to whom the promises apply. We remarked that they could be traced from the earliest history of our race, as given by inspiration.

We wish to enter into the investigation of this subject in the spirit of meekness, and with no lower aim than to find and present to the reader the truth of revelation on this great subject; for the glory of God in the advancement of the knowledge of Bible truth, and for the good of our fellow-men, especially those who love truth rather than fables; hoping that we may be found among that class to whom it may be said by our Master, when he comes, "Well done, thou good and faithful servant."

We will now turn to Gen. 4 : 8. "And Cain talked with Abel his brother; and it came to pass, when they were in the field, that Cain rose up against Abel his brother, and slew him."

Here we find the two classes involved in our subject, in the first family on earth, and the first born of Adam and Eve. Here was the first death of a member of the race, and that by violence; — a murder. The earth opens her mouth to receive the blood of Abel, at the hand of his brother. Ver. 11. And why was this? Inspiration answers, Cain " was of that wicked one " —

[the devil]. "His own works were evil [he hated God and his brother also], and his brother's righteous."

At this point we start with the two characters, — the righteous and the wicked. But why this difference? They were the first two born on earth, and of the same parents, nourished and brought up in the same family. They enjoyed the same privileges, they had the same prospects spread out before them, the same right to will and choose. They were both sinners by nature, by the first transgression; both under the sentence of death, which was passed upon their father, and entailed upon them. Gen. 3 : 19; Rom. 5 : 12, 19. They both had the same means of knowing the remedy God had provided for this evil, for he had expressly said, "The seed of the woman shall bruise [crush] the serpent's [devil's] head." And we have good evidence that God elucidated and enforced this great truth by offering sacrifice in Eden, and procuring skins to cover their nakedness.

Thus these two men, the first two born of our race, were placed upon an exact level with the new covenant in its germ placed before them, in the denunciation against the devil, — that the seed of the woman [Christ] should destroy him and his works: as since explained (Heb. 2 : 14, and 1 John 3 : 8), which was a promise to them of future deliverance from death [of which the devil then had the power], and by instituting the symbol of sacrifice, and the shedding of blood [which was imitated by Abel in his offering (Gen. 4 : 4), showing the means by which this deliverance was to be accomplished. Read Heb. 2 : 12, 14.

Thus, eternal life was as really placed within their reach, as it was in Adam's before he sinned. Yet we find one of them is wicked, a child of the devil; the other is righteous, a child of God. One of them striving for eternal life; the other is cursed from the earth, which hath opened her mouth to receive his brother's blood from his hand. Gen. 4 : 11. He is on the road to destruction.

With all these facts touching these two men before us, we repeat the question, Why all this difference in their character and course, and what is the line of demarkation between them? And again we repeat, the Scriptures furnish the answer: It is faith. "By faith Abel offered unto God a more excellent sacrifice than Cain, by which he obtained witness that he was righteous, God testifying of his gifts: and by it he being dead yet speaketh. Heb. 11 : 4.

Thus it is seen that Abel's faith grasped the promises concerning Christ, and his work of atonement; and he expressed this faith in his offering, and God accepted him, and gave him witness that he was righteous, testifying of his gifts; and that testimony has reached us through the long range of six thousand years, to cheer us in our race for the same object which he sought. But his faith cost him his life. Then "marvel not, my brethren, if the world hate you." 1 John 3 : 13.

Cain also brought an offering before the Lord; but in part, at least, of his own works. It represented no faith in Christ, and God did not accept him or his offering. Then his anger and his envy is kindled against his brother, and, prompted by "that wicked one," he slew his brother; thus showing that he hated God and his brother also.

"If a man say, I love God, and hateth his brother, he is a liar: for he that loveth not his brother whom he hath seen, how can he love God whom he hath not seen?" 1 John 4: 20.

With these two well marked and clearly defined monuments, standing at the head of these two grand divisions of our race, — the personifications of faith and of unbelief, of righteousness and wickedness, — with the line of distinction clearly settled, we take our course on the stream of time, to trace the line of distinction between God's chosen people, to whom all his promises of future blessedness in Christ, through Abraham, Isaac, Jacob, and David, belong, on the one hand, and the children of the wicked one, to whom all his threatenings and denunciations of future woe and destruction belong, on the other.

In Gen. 4: 16, we find Cain in the land of Nod, on the east of Eden, and thence we trace the genealogy of the Cain family to the sixth generation, and here we find the same character as in the father. Lamech is another murderer. See Gen. 4: 23.

We next have an account of the birth of Seth, who takes the place [in the genealogy] of Abel whom Cain slew. And Seth begat Enos. And here it is said, "men began to call upon the name of the Lord," or " to call themselves by the name of the Lord," as the margin has it. This marginal rendering looks the more reasonable when we consider, that to call upon the name of the Lord is to ask his favor — to pray; which Abel probably did when he brought his offering and was accepted. But at the time referred to in verse 26, believers had learned that by faith in the promised seed [Christ] they "became the sons of God," as is since declared.

"Ye are all the children of God by faith in Christ Jesus." Gal. 3:26. Or, as in the text at the head of this chapter, "It shall be said unto them, Ye are the sons of the living God." Thus it is shown that unbelief produced enmity towards God and his children, and constituted men the children of the devil.

Christ said to the unbelieving Jews, " Ye are of your father the devil, and the lusts of your father ye will do. He was a murderer from the beginning, and abode not in the truth, because there is no truth in him." John 8:44.

Cain "was of that wicked one" — the devil. Children take the name of their father; therefore the Cain family are called by Christ the children of the devil. For the same reason, Seth, Enos, and other believers of their time, "called themselves by the name of the Lord," by way of distinction from the wicked around them.

With Genesis, 5th chapter, we commence with "the book of the generations of Adam," in which the names of the antediluvian patriarchs, at the head of their families, are given, running down to the time of the flood. It should be noticed, that in this genealogy, Cain and Abel are not found; Abel having been martyred for his faith, and Cain, his murderer, being a child of the devil, and cursed from the earth.

As Adam is recorded as standing at the head of this line of patriarchs, and Seth, his third son, and Enos, the son of Seth, who called themselves by the name of the Lord, it indicates that Adam himself was a believer in the promised seed, who should bruise [crush] the serpent's head. And it is also evident that these patriarchs offered sacrifices, and acted as priests, and endeavored to train up their families in the faith, and did not allow them to intermarry with unbelievers, — the descendants of Cain.

Hence, in Gen. 6 : 2, they are called "the sons of God." And it appears from the first three verses, that when they became numerous, and came in contact with " the daughters of men," — or of the unbelieving families, — they broke over this rule, as the children of Israel did after them, and intermarried with unbelievers, or the children of men, which caused them to forsake the Lord, and to grieve his Spirit; so that at the time of the flood, only Noah and his family were found true to their faith.

Adam, Seth, and Enos were dead, Enoch had been translated, the others of the faithful had fallen asleep, and Noah only was found righteous; and God saved him, and passed him over from the old world to the new one, by water, together with his family (1 Pet. 3, 20) ; while with the same element he swept the wicked from the earth, as with the besom of destruction.

Thus we pass the flood; Noah and his family being the only children of God, by faith, then living on the earth.

And in all this time, 1656 years, not one word do we hear about salvation on any other principle than that of faith. Abel offered his sacrifice by faith, Enoch was translated by faith, and Noah built the ark by faith.

This was their righteousness, and the only righteousness that can please God. See Heb. 11 : 4, 7. And this antediluvian faith was manifested by works, without which faith is dead. Jas. 2 : 17.

Thus God has revealed the genealogical line, or order, of his children from Adam to Noah, through whom the promised seed should come, who was to crush the serpent's head, and upon which their faith fastened, and from which sprang all their hopes of future deliverance, in distinction from the Cain family, or the children of the world. And we should expect to find this line continued after the flood; therefore we will look for it.

We find Noah this side the flood, with his three sons, Shem, Ham, and Japheth, upon whom the Lord pronounces his blessing, and said, "Be fruitful, and multiply, and replenish the earth." Gen. 9 : 1. By these the earth was to be peopled again. In Genesis, 10th chapter, we have their genealogy for several generations, in which no mention is made as to which of the three sons of Noah should be the progenitor of the promised seed. But this matter was not neglected.

In Gen. 11 : 10 to 26 the line is found again, and the question fully settled.

It had been indicated by Noah in this language : " And he said, Blessed be the Lord God of Shem ; and Canaan [son of Ham whom he cursed] shall be his servant. God shall enlarge Japheth, and he shall dwell in the tents of Shem ; and Canaan shall be his servant." Gen. 9 : 26, 27.

But in Gen. 11 : 10 to 26, we have the genealogy from Noah, through Shem, to the birth of Abram, Nahor, and Haran, a period of 292 years from the flood, and 1948 years from Adam, with no intimation of salvation or eternal life on any other principle than that of faith.

At this period we find that Terah had three sons, Abram, Nahor, and Haran, from whom the progenitor of the promised seed is to be chosen, and to whom a more full, clear, and direct promise concerning the aforesaid seed of the woman is to be made; and a more perfect development of God's plan of redemption through that seed, and the eternal salvation of his children by faith, together with the removal of the curse from their inheritance, brought to light.

Yea, more, we are approaching a time when from these three men, God is to choose the founder of the Jewish nation, and the father of the faithful, not in that nation only, but from all the nations of the earth. See Gen. 12 : 1, 3.

Up to this time no record had been kept, so far as we are informed; and, indeed, it would seem that the great longevity of those early fathers would obviate, in a great measure, the necessity for such records. For example, Methusaleh was contemporary with Adam 234 years, and with Noah about 600 years, and with Shem, the son of Noah, 98 years. He could, therefore, have received the facts of the fall, the Lord's subsequent dealings with and instructions to the race, from Adam himself, and related them to Noah and Shem.

And as Noah and Shem were both contemporary with Abram, the father of the Jewish nation, — the former 58 years, and the latter 210 years, — Shem could, and doubtless did, give to Abram the leading facts and incidents of our race for the whole antediluvian period, together with the account of the flood; and thus the faith of Adam, Seth, Enos, and other early fathers [who "called themselves by the name of the Lord" Gen. 4: 26, margin], especially of Abel, Enoch, and Noah, was made known to Abram, as also the basis or promise upon which that faith rested. See Gen. 3: 15.

By such history Abram would be encouraged to follow their example, and obey the voice of the Lord when called to leave his country, his kindred, and his father's house, to become a stranger in a strange country, being cheered by the same blessed hope that sustained the faith of the antediluvian saints.

In Gen. 12: 1, we learn that the Lord makes choice that Abram, of the sons of Terah, shall be the progenitor of the promised seed, and the founder of the nation with which he would deposit the records of the past, and through whom he would transmit to after generations, and finally to all the nations of the earth, his plan of redemption of the race, and the gift of eternal life to all who would obey his voice, and believe on his Son Jesus Christ, the long-looked-for seed of the woman who should bruise the serpent's head. See Rom. 9:4, 6.

These records and purposes are embodied in the five books of Moses, and quoted and enforced by all the prophets, in the Old Testament Scriptures, and lastly, expounded and applied by Christ and his chosen apostles, in the New Testament, who are the rightful and authoritative expounders of those Scriptures thus transmitted "for obedience to the faith among all nations, for his name."

To these sacred oracles, as expounded by Christ and his apostles, we appeal to settle the question,

WHO ARE GOD'S PEOPLE ISRAEL?

If we fail to settle the question by this rule, then time in the future only can do it. With these remarks we return to examine Gen. 12 : 1.

"Now the Lord had said unto Abram, Get thee out of thy country, and from thy kindred, and from thy father's house, unto a land that I will show thee."

It appears from this text, and from Acts 7 : 2, that this command was given before Terah left Ur of the Chaldees with his family and the family of his son Haran, to go into Canaan, but they stopped short of Canaan, and dwelt in Charran (See Gen. 11 : 31), from whence, after the death of his father, Abram removed into the land of Canaan.

In chapter 12 : 3, we have the first intimation of Abram's seed, or his relation to all nations, the Jews not excepted; and it is important that we understand the nature of this promise, with its class, at the outset, in distinction from another class of promises, the first of which we shall notice presently.

We remark, that Abram had three classes of descendants, or children.

I. The seed royal, implied in Gen. 12 : 3, and referred to in Gen. 13 : 15, and in the text at the head of this chapter, as we shall show in its proper place.

II. Ishmael and the Arab tribes, through Hagar, who is a type of the Jewish tribes, according to the flesh, through Isaac. Gal. 4 : 2 to 25.

III. The descendants of Abram, through Isaac, after the flesh, who constitute the Jewish nation, and who in their relation to God as a nation are merely a type of the seed royal through Christ, referred to in the text at the head of this chapter. Gal 3 : 29.

To these three classes, the terms sons, children, and seed, may be, and are applied, especially to the first and third classes. See Gen. 21 : 10, 11, 13, 16 ; 15 : 17, 7 : 17, 22.

Jesus said to some of the Jews, "I know that ye are Abraham's seed, but ye seek to kill me because my word hath no place in you; . . . ye are of your father the devil, and the lusts of your father ye will do." John 8 : 37, 44.

To each of these three classes of Abram's children, God hath made special and specific promises, and we do well, kind reader, to be careful in our interpretation and application of these promises, lest we lose sight of the Scripture rule, and detract from one, and misapply them to the other; for it is quite as absurd, yea, more so, to take the promises to Abraham and his seed, through Christ, and apply them to the Jewish nation as such, than it would be to take the promises to Abraham's seed, or children of the flesh through Isaac, and apply them to Ishmael, or the Arab tribes.

We shall endeavor to show that the promises concerning the second class are unconditional, and are limited to this world, and have been fulfilled to the letter; but to the third class they partake of both the conditional and unconditional, and are also limited to this world, and the unconditional have been fulfilled to the letter, while those that are conditional have been fulfilled, or have been forfeited by a failure to fulfil, the conditions, on the part of the nation to whom they were made.

But the promises to the first class, viz., to Abraham and his seed royal [and who are of all the nations of the earth], are unconditional, and are not to be fulfilled in this world, but in that which is to come. Amen: so let it be.

We come now to examine those promises concerning the second class of Abram's descendants through Ishmael.

"And the angel of the Lord said unto her [Hagar], I will multiply thy seed exceedingly, that it shall not be numbered for multitude." Gen. 16 : 10. "And as for Ishmael, I have heard thee : Behold, I have blessed him, and will make him fruitful, and will multiply him exceedingly : twelve princes shall he beget, and I will make him a great nation." Gen. 17 : 20. See also Gen. 25 : 13 to 16.

That these promises have been fulfilled, may be seen by all who will read the Bible account of Ishmael, beginning at Gen. Ch. 21. But those promises made to the third class require more special care to define and identify, inasmuch as both the first and third classes are blended in the Jewish nation, and the terms Twelve Tribes, Abraham's Seed, Children of Abraham, God's People, Children of Israel, Israel, &c., are sometimes applied to them indiscriminately, so that it would not be surprising if men, unaided by the light of more recent revelation furnished by the New Testament, expounding and applying those promises, together with the fulfilment of prophecy, should fall into the same, or similar errors, which did the Jews themselves; especially when we consider our remote chronological distance from their time, and the general want of acquaintance with their usages and language.

With these considerations, all can see the propriety and importance of our appeal to the New Testament to settle the true application of those promises, and the Jew question, so called.

Let us, then, examine some of the unconditional promises concerning the Jewish nation as such.

"And the Lord appeared unto Abram, and said, Unto thy SEED will I give this land." Gen. 12 : 7. It should be observed that this promise does not include Abram; and that it is distinct from that contained in the first three verses of the chapter, inasmuch as that includes "all families [nations] of the earth." Let us here apply the rule of interpretation indicated by Stephen, Acts 7 : 5. "And he gave him none inheritance in it, no, not so much as to set his foot on; yet he promised that he would give it to him for a possession, and to his seed after him, when as yet he had no child."

Here it is plain that Stephen refers to a promise that includes Abraham, and was made before the birth of Isaac.

This promise, Stephen declares, had never been fulfilled; yet the Jewish nation were then in possession of the land; but this was not the fulfilment of the promise in Gen. 13 : 15, to which Stephen refers, else his argument is of no force.

We conclude, therefore, that the promise in Gen.

12 : 7, " Unto thy seed will I give this land," refers to the Jewish nation as such, and is the first of its class, and being unconditional, we must look for its fulfilment in the past: but before doing so, we will identify it with others of its class.

Thus we read, " In the same day the Lord made a covenant with Abram, saying, Unto thy SEED have I given this land" [this is identical with Gen. 12 : 7]. But what land? " From the river Egypt unto the great river, the River Euphrates; the Kenites, and the Kenizzites, and the Kadmonites, and the Hittites, and the Perizzites, and the Rephaims, and the Amorites, and the Canaanites, and the Girgashites, and the Jebusites." Gen. 15 : 18, 21.

Here we are told what land is meant, so that we cannot mistake. But again, —

" I will set thy bounds from the Red Sea even unto the Sea of the Philistines, and from the desert unto the river." Ex. 23 : 31. See Num. 34 : 3. Once more,—

"And the Lord said unto him [Moses], This is the land which I sware unto Abraham, unto Isaac, and unto Jacob, saying, I will give it unto thy seed: I have caused thee to see it with thine eyes, but thou shalt not go over thither." Deut. 34 : 4.

Has this class of promises been fulfilled? The Scriptures shall answer this question.

" Thou art the Lord the God who didst choose Abram, and broughtest him forth out of Ur of the Chaldees, and gavest him the name of Abraham; and foundest his heart faithful before thee, and madest a covenant with him to give the land of the Canaanites, Hittites, Amorites, Perizzites, and the Jebusites, and the Girgashites, to give it, I say, to his SEED [not to him and his seed], and hast performed thy words; for thou art righteous." Neh. 9: 7, 8.

In the above, it is expressly stated that God's promise to give that land, from the River Nile to the Euphrates, to Abraham's seed, had been fulfilled. See also Joshua 23: 14.

Now, dear reader, if the Scriptures can settle any question, then the question of the fulfilment in the past of all that class of promises made to Abraham, repeated to Isaac and to Jacob, concerning his seed according to the flesh, or to the Jewish nation as such, must be regarded as settled.

But there is another phase of this class of promises, at which we will now look for a moment, as it is involved in the discourse of Nehemiah, to which we have referred. It will be in place here, as it brings out the true relation which the Jewish nation sustains to Abraham and his SEED ROYAL, to whom the first class of unconditional promises belong.

To present this case clearly, let us read — "And the Lord said unto Abram, after that Lot was separated from him, Lift up now thine eyes, and look from the place where thou art, northward, and southward, and eastward, and westward: for all the land which thou seest, to thee will I give it, and to thy seed forever. And I will make thy seed as the dust of the earth: so that if a man can number the dust of the earth, then shall thy seed also be numbered." Gen. 13: 14, 15, 16.

Here we have the first direct promise of land made to Abram and his seed. This promise is repeated, together with a statement of the faith which constituted him righteous, in Gen. 15 : 5, 7. " And he brought him forth abroad, and said, Look now toward heaven, and tell the stars, if thou be able to number them : and he said unto him, so shall thy seed be.

" And he believed in the Lord; and he counted it to him for righteousness. And he said unto him, I am the Lord that brought thee out of Ur of the Chaldees, to give thee this land to inherit it." On hearing this promise, Abram asks, " Lord God, whereby shall I know that I shall inherit it?" Verse 8.

This is a very important question, and should be well considered. Abram must have known, from the nature of this promise, which included himself and an innumerable seed to jointly possess the land, that it could not be fulfilled during his and their probationary life : and realizing that the many generations of his seed which would come after him would want some historical facts or signs to strengthen their faith in the promise, and knowing also that his seed according to the flesh could not be the seed embraced in this promise [for as he must die, so must his seed according to the flesh also die], and that these promises referred to all nations of the earth, for all nations were to be blessed IN HIM ; and therefore, if himself and his seed were to inherit the land promised him forever, he believed it must be by a resurrection from the dead.

We think no careful reader can fail to see this point; especially, when remembering that Stephen said it had not been fulfilled in his day.

But if Abram's seed, according to the flesh, were the

the seed referred to in this promise, it being unconditional to the seed, it must include the whole generation of vipers — Judas Iscariot, and those to whom Jesus said, " Ye are of your father the devil." John 8 : 44. Indeed, some set up this claim : let those who apply this class of promises to the Jewish nation, as such, escape this conclusion if they can. But we shall speak more fully on those points when we take up the promises to Abraham and his seed. We now return to the question, " Lord God, whereby shall I know that I shall inherit it?"

In answering this question, the Lord directs him to prepare a sacrifice to confirm a covenant. Abram prepares the sacrifice as directed, and watches it until the going down of the sun, when " a deep sleep fell upon Abram, and, lo, an horror of great darkness fell upon him."

While in this condition, the Lord gave him a short prophetic history of his seed according to the flesh for four hundred years; informs him that he should go to his fathers in peace, be buried in a good old age, makes a covenant with him to give to his seed [omitting Abram] the land lying between the River Nile and the Euphrates, inhabited by certain heathen tribes. See Gen. 15 : 18–21. But not one word is said in all this transaction and covenant about Abram's inheriting the land; it is only for his seed; he must die and be buried in a good old age, and this is in answer to the question, " Lord God, whereby shall I know that I shall inherit it?"

But what has this to do with the question? We answer, and shall proceed to show that it is a sign whereby Abraham, and all his seed in Christ, may know they shall inherit the land embraced in the former promise, viz., " northward, and southward, and eastward, and westward: for all the land which thou seest, to thee will I give it, and to thy seed forever." · Gen. 13:15. Mark, when Abraham was dead this promise remains unfulfilled (Acts. 7:5); hence the necessity of the sign for the benefit of his posterity.

But we will examine the sign given. After the Lord had made the above promise, Abram asks, " Lord God, what wilt thou give me, seeing I go childless?... to me thou hast given no seed, and, lo, one born in mine house is mine heir."... The Lord said, " This shall not be thine heir, but he that shall come forth out of thine own bowels shall be thine heir." Gen. 15: 2, 3, 4. This settles THAT question: but Sarai is getting old, and bears no children, and Abram is old. How is this to be brought about? They meditate upon it; their faith is tried; they conclude some plan must be devised to bring about a fulfilment of this promise [just as some now think that the Lord cannot fulfil his promise to Israel without getting the Jews back to Jerusalem, of which, the plan we shall examine, brings forth a complete figure. Gal. 4: 21, 26]. Sarai, Abram's wife, bears no children. She devised a plan, and told it to Abram, saying, "Behold now, the Lord hath restrained me from bearing: I pray thee, go in unto my maid; it may be that I may obtain children by her. And Abram hearkened to the voice of Sarai." Gen 16:2. So Hagar became Abram's wife. This was their plan to obtain the promised seed; but it was not the Lord's plan, as the sequel shows. Sarai was brought into trouble, for as soon as Hagar supposed that the promised seed was coming by her, and through her son, then her mistress, Sarai, was despised in her eyes. Gen. 16 : 4. She supposed that all the promises to Abram and his seed centred in her and her son; just as the haughty Jews in Judea supposed that they all belonged to THEM.

This device of Sarai resulted in the birth of Ishmael: and they thought the way open for the fulfilment of the promise; but trouble attended it all the way through; for the haughty and unruly course of Hagar led Abram to reduce her to her former position as a servant — from that of a wife to a bondwoman. Gen. 16 : 6. So also the Lord divorced the Jewish nation, which is the antitype of this act.

"Thus saith the Lord, Where is the bill of your mother's divorcement, whom I have put away?" Isa. 50 : 1. See also Jer. 3 : 8; Hos. 2 : 2. So Hagar fled from her mistress; but the Lord sent her back, with instructions to submit to her. Gen. 16 : 6, 9. And when Abram was eighty-six years old Ishmael was born.

This history of Hagar is a complete prototype of ancient Jerusalem, which is her antitype, as we shall show: but we leave her for the present, to pursue the Jewish people as a sign.

The Lord having, in answer to Abram's question, " Whereby shall I know that I shall inherit it?" given him a prophetic history of his natural seed for four hundred years, and making a covenant with him to give them the land lying between the Nile and Euphrates (Gen. 15 : 9, 21), twenty-four years after he entered the land of Canaan, and thirteen years after the birth of

Ishmael, he appeared unto Abram, and repeated to him the original promise (see Gen. 12: 1, 3; 13: 14; 15; 15: 5-7) to make him a father of many nations, to establish his covenant with him, and his seed after him, for an everlasting covenant, to give HIM and THEM the land wherein he is a stranger for an everlasting possession: then changes his name from Abram to Abraham, and promises to be their God. Gen. 17: 4, 8.

To this covenant, and these promises, which include ABRAM HIMSELF, and make him the father of many [or all] nations, and which is based upon the righteousness of faith, the apostle Paul refers in Gal. 3: 16, 18. "Now to Abraham and his seed were the promises made. He saith not, And to seeds, as of many; but as of one, and to thy seed, which is Christ. And this I say, that the covenant that was confirmed before of God in Christ, the law, which was four hundred and thirty years after, cannot disannul, that it should make the promise of none effect. For if the inheritance be of the law, it is no more of promise: but God gave it to Abraham by promise." Also in Rom. 4: 13, 17, "For the promise that he should be the heir of the world [Kosmos, *habitable*] was not to Abraham, or to his seed, through the law, but through the righteousness of faith. For if they which are of the law be heirs, faith is made void, and the promise made of none effect.... Therefore it is of faith, that it might be by grace; to the end the promise might be sure to all the seed: not to that only which is of the law, but to that also which is of the faith of Abraham, who is the father of us all [believers], as it is written, I have made thee a father of many nations, before him whom he believed, even God, who quickeneth the dead, and calleth those things which be not, as though they were." These comments of the apostle Paul fix, beyond all controversy, the application of the covenant and promises quoted above.

But there is another covenant to which we have referred as a sign, containing another class of promises to Abram's seed, which do not include Abraham, or all nations, only so far as he is required to keep it as a sign whereby he, and his seed in Christ, should inherit the original promise; of which we have before spoken, and will now trace.

This promise and covenant are found first in Gen. 12: 7. "And the Lord appeared unto Abram, and said, Unto thy seed will I give this land; and there builded he an altar unto the Lord, who appeared unto him." It is again recorded in chap. 15: 17, 21. This has been fulfilled, as we have before shown. This covenant, we have said, was given for a sign or token, in answer to the question, "Lord God, whereby shall I know that I shall inherit it" [the land]. This we shall now proceed to show by tracing its history. That the Jewish nation were a typical people, is too generally admitted to need proof here; but they cannot be a type of themselves. Yet as our space is too limited to dwell here, we proceed to examine the covenant. "And God said unto Abraham, Thou shalt keep my covenant therefore, thou, and thy seed after thee, in their generations.

"This is my covenant, which ye shall keep, between me and you, and thy seed after thee; Every man-child among you shall be circumcised. And ye shall circumcise the flesh of your foreskin; and it shall be a token of the covenant betwixt me and you." Gen. 17 : 9, 11.

Of what is this covenant of circumcision a TOKEN? Please remember the question — "Lord God, whereby shall I know that I shall inherit it?" [the land].

We will let Paul tell us what the covenant of circumcision is a *token* of. "For we say that faith was reckoned to Abraham for righteousness. How was it then reckoned? when he was in circumcision, or in uncircumcision? Not in circumcision, but in uncircumcision. And he received the SIGN of circumcision, a SEAL of *the righteousness* of the FAITH which he had, yet being uncircumcised: that he might be the FATHER OF ALL THEM THAT BELIEVE, though they be not circumcised; that righteousness might be imputed unto them also." Rom. 4 : 10, 11.

If these Scriptures do not prove that the Jewish nation, as such, under the covenant of circumcision, in the land of Palestine, are merely a *typical people*, a SIGN to all believers, in all generations, that God will in due time fulfil the original promise to Abraham and his seed in Christ, then we ask, How can anything be proved by the Scriptures.

Remember it was the righteousness of faith that entitled HIM and THEM to the land. But this covenant of circumcision was unconditional with Abram; and without reference to moral character, all must be circumcised, or they broke the covenant. See Gen. 17 : 14.

When, therefore, that covenant ceased to be of force, the end of that theocracy was reached. But as the

Jewish nation was a type of the true seed to whom the original promise was made, and they became the persecutors of the faith; killed the prophets, and stoned God's messengers; persecuted and killed the Messiah, the Prince of life (see Acts 3:15; Matt. 23:31, 39), so they themselves have a prototype, a persecutor of the literal seed of Abram, according to the flesh, and they are his antitype. And from the fate of the prototype we may learn something of the fate of the antitype. Let us examine this figure.

It was said to Hagar, before the birth of Ishmael, "Thou shalt bear a son, and shalt call his name Ishmael. And he will be a wild man; his hand will be against every man, and every man's hand against him: and he shall dwell in the presence of all his brethren." Gen. 16:12.

This was the character of Ishmael and his posterity. Was it not also of the literal seed of Abram through Isaac? Paul says of his brethren in Judea, "which were in Christ Jesus: for ye also have suffered like things of your own countrymen, even as they have of the Jews; who both killed the Lord Jesus, and their own prophets, and have persecuted us; and they please not God, and *are contrary to all men* [the saints]... to fill up their sins alway, for the wrath is come upon them to the uttermost." 1 Thess. 2:14, 15. How striking the analogy between Ishmael and the Jews! Let us remember that this history "was written for our learning." Rom. 15:4. 1 Cor. 10:11. Again we find it written concerning Isaac, the child of promise, "And the child grew and was weaned: and Abraham made a great feast the same day that Isaac was weaned. And Sarah saw [Ishmael] the son of Hagar the Egyptian, which she had borne unto Abraham, MOCKING.

"Wherefore she said unto Abraham, *Cast out this bondwoman and her son, for the son of this bondwoman shall not be heir with my son, even with Isaac.*" . . . "And God said unto Abraham, . . In all that Sarah hath said unto thee, hearken unto her voice: for in Isaac shall thy seed be called." . . . "And Abraham rose up early in the morning, and took bread, and a bottle of water, and gave it unto Hagar, putting it on her shoulder, and the child, and sent her away: and she departed, and wandered in the wilderness of Beersheba." Gen. 21: 8, 14. Here is the final casting out of Hagar, and the rejection of her son. In like manner has the Jewish nation mocked; and God has cast out that nation. And when a re-union takes place between Abraham and the bondwoman and her son, then may we with propriety look for a re-union between God and the Jewish nation, as such, and their restoration to Jerusalem as a peculiar people.

But we will hear Paul's comments, and application of these Scriptures. In his Epistle to the Galatians he says, "If the inheritance be of the law [covenant of circumcision], it is no more of promise: but God gave it to Abraham *by promise*. Wherefore then serveth the law? [or of what service was the law? Answer], It was added [to the promise] because of [to make known the] transgressions. [How long was it to continue, Paul?] Till the seed should come to whom the promise was made." Gal. 3: 18, 19. See Rom. 7: 7, 8, and 5: 20.

How long did the bondwoman, Hagar, and her son remain in the family of Abraham? Until the promised seed, Isaac, came, and was weaned. Reader, please keep your mind on the type and her antitype. This is no cunningly devised fable, but God's own record. Let us pursue it.

"Is the law, then, against the promise of God? God forbid; for if there had been a law given which could have given life, verily righteousness [or justification] should have been by the law. But the Scripture hath concluded all [Jew and Gentile] under sin, that the promise by faith of Jesus Christ might be given to them that believe." Gal. 3: 21, 22. See Rom. 4: 14. "Wherefore the law was our schoolmaster, to bring us to Christ, that we might be justified by faith."

These Scriptures present the law and the gospel in plain contrast, and show clearly that neither the law nor the prophets entitle any man, community, or nation of men to the promises of God made to ABRAHAM AND HIS SEED.

But the promise to Abraham *concerning* his seed, under the covenant or law of circumcision, recorded in Gen. 12: 7; 15: 18; 17: 9, 10, 14, had no reference to their faith or unbelief; it was a covenant in their flesh, not in their heart. Abraham was required to observe the sign, together with all his family, including Ishmael; and Isaac, and all born in his house, or bought with money; all his legal descendants, both Jews and proselytes, bond or free, slaves, priests, or hypocrites, or prophets, kings and people, scribes and Pharisees, children of God and children of the devil, Judas, and the Prince of Life himself, with all his holy apostles, — all must be circumcised.

And here the object of that law or covenant is accomplished; it ended with Christ's crucifixion (Eph. 2 : 15, 16 ; Col. 2 : 14, 16) ; and the theocracy ceased, as we shall further show.

With reference to that law, the apostle inquires, " But now, after that ye have known God, or rather are known of God, how turn ye again to the weak and beggarly elements, whereunto ye desire again to be in bondage?" Then holding up the new covenant in contrast, he proceeds thus : . . . "Tell me, ye that desire to be under the law [covenant of circumcision], do ye not hear the law?" [do ye not read and understand the object of that law?] " For it is written, that Abraham had two sons, the one by a bondmaid, the other by a free woman. But he who was of the bondwoman [Hagar], was born after the flesh [according to natural law] ; but he of the free woman [Sarah], was by [the] promise [of God].

"Which things [these two women and their two sons] are an allegory, for these are [represent] the two covenants ; the one from Mount Sinai [covenant of circumcision in the flesh, which covenant was written on tables of stone, and given to the children of Israel, with its ordinances, Heb. 9 : 1, and], which gendereth to bondage, which is [represented by] Hagar." Every person, therefore, born under, or converted to, that covenant (with all their boasted liberty or enjoyment, John 8 : 33), is in bondage. "For this Hagar is Mount Sinai, in Arabia, and answers to [represents] JERUSALEM which now is, AND IS IN BONDAGE *with her* CHILDREN." Gal. 4 : 9, 25.

The Spirit, by Paul, intends to show, in this comment and argument, that the legal descendants of Abraham, as a nation, and their city, are the antitype of the bondwoman and her son, and have, as such, no more claim to the promise made to Abraham and his seed through Christ, represented by Sarah and Isaac, than Ishmael and the twelve Arab tribes.

Thus he gives the contrast: "But Jerusalem, which is above [represented by the free woman, Sarah, under the covenant confirmed before of God in Christ], is free, and is the mother of us all" [believers]. Verse 26. Consequently, Paul says in another place, "For our citizenship is in heaven." — *Bible Union*, and *Whiting's versions*. Phil. 3: 20. Again he says, "For it is written, Rejoice, thou barren, that bearest not; break forth and cry, thou that travaillest not: for the desolate [Sarah] hath many more children than she [Hagar] which hath an husband." [Abram: for Hagar had become Abram's wife. Gen. 16: 3.]

"Now we, brethren [Christians], as Isaac was, are the children of PROMISE." What promise? See Gen. 15: 5, 6; 22: 16, 17, — that seed which came through faith in Christ, among all nations, who, with Abraham himself, shall inherit the land. Gal 3: 29.

This text has no more reference to the Jewish nation, as such, than it has to the twelve tribes of Ishmael. See Gen. 17: 20; 25: 16.

But as then [in the days of Isaac and Ishmael], he that was born after the flesh [Ishmael the type] persecuted him that was born after the spirit [Isaac the son of promise], even so it is now [the Jews, the antitype of

Ishmael, persecute Christ and the seed royal by faith]. "Nevertheless, what saith the Scripture? CAST OUT *the bondwoman and her son*, for the son of the bondwoman shall not be heir [to the inheritance promised ABRAHAM AND HIS SEED, Christ and all that are his, Gal. 3 : 16, 29], with the son of the free woman. So then, brethren, we are not children of the bondwoman, but of the free." Gal. 4 : 9, 21.

It needs no great critic to understand the force of this language when well considered. The points in the apostle's argument are very clear; but for the benefit of those who do not grasp an idea readily, we will repeat some of them.

Many of the Jewish Christians were very zealous of the law, or covenant of circumcision (see Acts 21 : 20), which God promised Abram he would establish with them; and which he did, at Sinai; and many of them went out from Jerusalem to Antioch, Galatia, and other towns, to persuade the Gentile converts that they must keep the Sinaiac covenant with its ordinances, consequently must be circumcised. Acts 15 : 1. Some of these went to Galatia, and caused distraction among the brethren. This caused grief to Paul, who well knew the nature of that law or covenant; and the Lord leads him to show them, in his epistle, that the observance of that covenant gave them no title to salvation; that it is only a law of bondage; having been broken, it could never justify any man; that it was a shadow or type of something better; that it pointed to Christ, as the true seed of promise, and to his work, as a type points to its antitype, that was fulfilled in, and accomplished by him, and was ended when he suffered on the cross. See Eph. 2. 15. Col. 2 : 14, 18. He then commences his argument, by asking his Galatian brethren a question, and proceeds to show them that Hagar and Ishmael, the bondwoman and her son, are a type, or a figure of the Sinaiac covenant of ten commandments with its ordinances, whose *token — circumcision —* was given to Abram and the Jewish nation, whose capital was Jerusalem; that the promises TO ABRAHAM AND HIS SEED, of an inheritance in the land, or habitable globe (Rom. 4 : 13), was not through the law, but through the righteousness of faith; and therefore they do not belong to the Jewish nation as such, but to the true believers in all nations: that the mocking of Ishmael, when Isaac was weaned, was a representation of the Jews persecuting Christ and his church; and that the final casting out of the bondwoman and her son from Abram's bed and board, and family, was a type of the closing up and fulfilling of the old covenant in the flesh, and the final rejection and fall of the Jewish nation.

We think that when it can be shown by scriptural proof that the bondwoman was ever restored to Abraham's family, then, and not till then, can it be shown that the Jewish nation and theocracy will be restored to Jerusalem as a peculiar people above all nations.

But the promises *concerning* this people, which we have cited, were made to Abram, and were unconditional, without regard to faith, and have been fulfilled, as we have shown. And they being a typical or symbolic nation, under the old covenant of circumcision in the flesh, which token was given to Abram, they have become a sign to him, and all his seed through the Spirit, or in Christ (Rom. 4: 22, 24), in answer to the question, "Lord God, whereby shall I know that I shall inherit it" [the earth]? Gen. 15: 8.

Through this entire history we have not the least intimation of final salvation, or eternal life, to be bestowed on any other principle than that of faith.

This rejection of Israel, after the flesh, is forcibly set forth in the prophet Hosea, in connection with the text at the head of this chapter.

"And God said unto him, Call her name Lo-ruhamah [that is, not having obtained mercy] : for I will no more have mercy upon the house of Israel ; but I will UTTERLY TAKE THEM AWAY. [Has he kept his word?] . . . Then said God, Call his name Lo-ammi [that is, not my people] : *for ye are not my people, and I* WILL NOT BE YOUR GOD." Hos. 1: 6, 9. How fully is this fulfilled! Will God nullify his word? We believe he will not.

Having concluded this part of our subject, we close the chapter, to proceed in another, on The True Israel of God.

CHAPTER XIX.

THE TRUE ISRAEL OF GOD.

'Yet the number of the children of Israel shall be as the sand of the sea, which cannot be measured nor numbered; and it shall come to pass, that in the place where it was said unto them, Ye are not my people, there it shall be said unto them, Ye are the sons of the living God." — *Hos.* 1 : 10

This passage of Scripture, when taken in connection with its context, presents a very clear idea as to what is intended by the Spirit to convey to the Bible reader; but we have an inspired comment on this text, with an application by the Spirit of God, which settles its true meaning.

"And that he might make known the riches of his glory on the vessels of mercy, which he had afore prepared unto glory, *even us, whom he hath called, not of the Jews only*, BUT ALSO OF THE GENTILES. As he saith also in Osee [Hosea], I will call them my people, which were not my people, and her beloved, which was not beloved. And it shall come to pass, that in the place where it was said unto them, Ye are not my people, there shall they be called the children of the living God." Rom. 9 : 23, 26. See also Hos. 2 : 23 ; 1 Pet. 2 : 10.

This can apply to none others than true believers of

all nations, Jews and Gentiles. This we regard as conclusive on this point, and furnishes a key by which we may understand and apply all other promises of this class.

But there is another class of promises, made directly to the Jewish nation as such, which are conditional, and which we will here notice. When the Lord had brought them out of Egypt, and brought them unto himself, at the base of Mount Sinai, he addressed them thus:—

"Now therefore, if ye will obey my voice indeed, and keep my covenant, then ye shall be a peculiar treasure unto me above all people; for all the earth is mine [and therefore open and free to them] : and ye shall be unto me a kingdom of priests, and an holy nation." Exod. 19 : 5, 6. See also Deut. 4 : 2 ; 7 : 6 ; 14 : 2, 20 ; 26 : 18. See also Peter's comment on this. 1 Pet. 2 : 2, 9.

In all this class of texts the conditions must be recognized, although not always expressed ; and a failure to perform the conditions was to forfeit the promises.

But we quote one more text, where the condition is so stated as to furnish a key to the whole subject.

"And at what instant I shall speak concerning a nation, and concerning a kingdom, to build and to plant it ; if it do evil in my sight, that it obey not my voice, then will I repent of the good wherewith I said I would benefit them." Jer. 18 : 9, 10. The nation of Israel having done evil until their national probation ceased, God fulfilled this promise to repent of the good he had promised them, and said, "I will no more have mercy upon the house of Israel, but I will utterly take them away." Hosea 1 : 6.

And when Paul is referring to the "new covenant," he quotes what the Lord says: "Not according to the covenant that I made with their fathers, in the day when I took them by the hand to lead them out of Egypt, because they continued not in my covenant, and I regarded them not [to fulfil it to them], saith the Lord." Heb. 8 : 9.

This passage Paul quotes from Jeremiah, who writes, "Which my covenant they break, although I was an husband unto them, saith the Lord." Jer. 31: 32. They broke that covenant, and disobeyed God's voice, and forfeited the promise.

Thus Moses sang of them in his memorable prophetic song, giving a history of the nation until their final destruction, recorded in Deut. ch. 32 : "They have corrupted themselves, their spot is not the spot [mark] of his children" [or, that they are not his children, that is their blot. *Margin*] : they are a perverse and crooked generation. "Do ye thus requite the Lord, O foolish people, and unwise? Is not he thy father that hath bought thee? Hath he not made thee, and established thee?"

How did they requite him? "They provoked him to jealousy with strange gods, with abominations provoked they him to anger. They sacrificed unto devils, not to God: . . . they are a very froward generation, children in whom is no faith."

Of their final fall as a nation, and the extension of the gospel to the heathen, and the conversion of some of them to the faith of Christ, he says, "They have moved me to jealousy with that which is not God: they have provoked me to anger with their vanities:

and I will move them to jealousy with those which are not a people [Gentiles]; I will provoke them to anger with a foolish nation." Deut. 32: 5, 6, 16, 21.

We will now hear Paul tell us how this is fulfilled. In speaking of, and enforcing the principle of salvation by faith, as taught in the new covenant by Moses, in Deut., Paul says, " But I say, did not Israel know? First, Moses saith, I will provoke you to jealousy by them that are no people, and by a foolish nation [Gentile] will I anger you." Rom. 10: 19. . . . "I say, then, have they stumbled that they should fall?" [or in order to fall. — *Whiting's version.*] Did their stumbling result in their fall or rejection merely? No. " But rather, (1) through their fall salvation [the gospel of eternal life through Christ, at whom they stumbled] is come unto the Gentiles," (2) "for to provoke them to jealousy." [What for?] "If by any means I may provoke to emulation [to equal, or excel the Gentiles in faith in Christ and obedience to God] them which are my flesh, and might SAVE SOME OF THEM." Rom 11: 11, 14.

This is the only hope for Jews, as it is the only hope for Gentiles. It is open for all. It is the boon, and the only boon which God extends to them in the Bible: to preach to them any other, only inflates their pride and unbelief, feeds their self-righteousness, and deters them from embracing the gospel of Jesus. We covet not the responsibility of those who do this.

Having shown that neither the *second class* of Abraham's seed [Ishmael and his family], nor the *third class* [the Jewish nation in the flesh], are God's people

Israel, or Abraham's seed, to whom the promise was made, who constitute the first class, and who with him are to inherit the land, we proceed to the direct argument, viz., to show who they are.

In doing this, we shall try to be very brief, as we have already transcended our designed limits in the first department.

We will here repeat what we have before said, that in all the Scriptures we have examined, we find not one text or word that teaches salvation or eternal life for any adult person only through faith. It is the only righteousness we can plead.

The first promise we find made to Abram is recorded in Gen. 12 : 2, 3. "And I will make of thee a great nation ; and I will bless thee, and make thy name great ; and thou shalt be a blessing : and I will bless them that bless thee, and curse him that curseth thee : and in thee shall all families of the earth be blessed."

In the above, we find that this blessing was to extend to all families [nations] of the earth. Again we learn, in Gen. 13 : 14, 15, "And the Lord said unto Abram, after that Lot was separated from him, Lift up now thine eyes, and look from the place where thou art, northward, and southward, and eastward, and westward : for all the land which thou seest, to thee will I give it, and to thy seed forever."

Here we find the land is promised to ABRAM AND HIS SEED; and in Gen. 15 : 7, after informing Abram that his seed should be as countless as the stars of heaven, and Abram avowed his faith in God, which "was accounted to him for righteousness," God " said unto him, I am the Lord that brought thee out of Ur of the Chaldees, to give thee this land to inherit it."

Here, again, the land is promised directly to Abram. But how extensive is this promise of land and seed? The Lord, in repeating this promise to Jacob, said, "And thy seed shall be as the dust of the earth, and thou shalt spread abroad to the west, and to the east, and to the north, and to the south: and in thee and in thy seed shall all the families of the earth be blessed." Gen. 28 : 14.

Paul explains the boundaries of the land as including the whole world, or habitable globe. Rom. 4 : 13. And Jesus says, "Blessed are the meek, for they shall inherit the earth." Matt. 5 : 5. Peter says, "We, according to his promise, look for new heavens and a new earth, wherein dwelleth righteousness." 2 Pet. 3 : 13.

The above are all the promises made to Abraham [personally] AND HIS SEED OF LAND; but they are quoted and referred to, all through the Scriptures of the Old Testament; quoted, expounded, and applied by the New Testament writers, so that no Bible student need mistake them.

In these promises, three facts, among others, are stated.

I. The blessing in Abraham, and through Abraham, extends to ALL NATIONS *of the earth*.

II. Abraham is to inherit the land, with his seed.

III. That Abraham's seed shall be as innumerable as the stars of heaven, or the sands upon the sea shore.

In connection with these points arises the question, By what law does Abraham and his seed become entitled to this land? Answer, "By the law of faith." These facts involve yet another, which we will notice in its place.

In discussing these points, we shall distinguish the seed included in these promises, by the term — Royal.

I. In relation to the first point, we remark, that the blessing constituted him the father of all the families of the earth, and therefore cannot be limited to the Jewish nation, nor can a Jew claim that blessing by virtue of any legal or national relation he sustains to Abraham, for the promise applies equally to Abraham's seed among all nations; therefore cannot be according to the flesh, else it must apply equally to all that sustain the relation of descendants of Abraham, not excepting Judas. But so far from this, an inspired commentator states, "For if they which are of the law be heirs, faith is made void, and the promise made of none effect." Rom. 4:14.

There is but one sense in which Abraham can be the father of all nations of the earth, and that is by faith.

Paul fully settles the application of this text: "Even as Abraham believed God, and it was accounted to him for righteousness. Know ye, therefore, that they which are of faith, the same are the children of Abraham.

"And the Scripture, foreseeing that God would justify the heathen [Gentiles] through faith, preached before the gospel unto Abraham, saying, In thee shall all nations be blessed. So then they which be of faith are blessed with faithful Abraham." Gal. 3:6, 9.

This Scripture demonstrates the fact that the blessing promised in Gen. 12:3, does not belong to the Jews, or any other nation as such, but is limited to believers in Jesus Christ, among all nations of the earth.

Again we find the same in Romans: "And he [Abraham] received the sign of circumcision, a seal of the righteousness of the faith which he had, yet bein uncircumcised: that he might be the father of all them that believe, though they be not circumcised; that right eousness might be imputed unto them also." Rom. 4:11.

Upon this immovable foundation we stand in the name of the Lord of Hosts, and challenge refutation from Jew or Greek, Papist or Protestant, learned or unlearned. But we will hear Paul further: "Therefore it is of faith, that it might be by grace; to the end the promise might be sure to all the seed: not to that only which is of the law, but to that also which is of the faith of Abraham, who is the father of us all, (as it is written, I have made thee a father of many nations) before him whom he believed, even God, who quickeneth the dead, and calleth those things which be not, as though they were." Rom 4:16, 17. This brings us to the second point stated in the promise, viz.,—

II. That ABRAHAM is to inherit the land with his seed.

It is claimed by some that Abraham inherited the land IN his seed, and Ezek. 33:24 is quoted to support this claim.

We think the advocates of a theory which rests on such a claim, made by such characters, who were so plainly rebuked and denounced by the Lord, as in Ezek 33:24, must be hard pushed for argument, especially when Abraham's whole history in the Scriptures, and the positive declaration of Stephen (Acts 7 : 5), show that he never inherited a foot of it; nor did he ever own a foot of it, excepting a burying-place for his dead, for which he paid in silver four hundred shekels, current money (see Gen. 23 : 16, 20), but the promises say ABRAHAM shall inherit it, AND HIS SEED, not *in* his seed. No amount of sophistry can evade the force of this language.

But Abraham is dead. "Thou shalt go to thy fathers in peace; thou shalt be buried in a good old age." Gen. 15 : 15. The patriarchs, prophets, and apostles are dead; but we leave this point for the present, to notice the third proposition.

III. Abraham's seed, to whom the promise and blessing belong, is to be as innumerable as the stars of heaven, and the sand on the sea shore. Hos. 1 : 10. Rom. 9 : 27 demonstrates that this seed does not apply to the Jewish nation in the flesh, as we have shown, but equally to all nations.

Of this seed Paul says, "Therefore sprang there even of one, and him as good as dead, so many as the stars of the sky in multitude, and as the sand which is by the sea shore innumerable." Heb. 11 : 12.

This is the same seed spoken of in Gen. 15 : 5 and 22 : 7. Of this seed we shall say more presently. But what is the law constituting this relationship? We have before shown that it is not the law of natural descent, else it would include all the Jewish nation, and none others. Hence the law, or legal seed, are not the seed spoken of, for Paul expressly says, "The law is not of faith." Gal. 3 : 12.

This brings us to show who are ABRAHAM'S PROMISED SEED. The Scriptures declare them to be "the children of God by faith," and not by the law. "But now the righteousness of God without the law is manifested, being witnessed by the law and the prophets; even the righteousness of God, which is by faith of Jesus Christ unto all, and upon all them that believe; for there is no difference: for all have sinned, and come short of the glory of God." Rom. 3: 21-23.

Here it will be observed, that the apostle, in discussing this point, has fairly raised the JEW question, and squarely met it in the following language: —

"For not that which is external makes the Jew, nor that which is external in the flesh, circumcision; but the Jew is hidden within, even circumcision of the heart, — Spiritual, not Literal; whose praise comes not from men, but from God." Rom. 2: 28, 29. — *Emp. Diaglott.* See Phil. 3: 3. Col. 2: 11. Rev. 2: 9; 3: 9. And again: "Therefore we conclude that a man is justified by faith without the deeds of the law. Is he the God of the Jews only? and is he not also of the Gentiles? Yes, of the Gentiles also: seeing it is one God, which shall justify the circumcision by faith, and the uncircumcision through faith." Rom. 3: 28-30.

Upon these statements of Paul, we remark, the term JEW sprang from the tribe of Judah; which tribe God retained to the house of David, in Jerusalem [when he rent the kingdom of Israel from Rehoboam, on account of the sin of Solomon his father], because he had promised David "that of the fruit of his loins . . . he would raise up Christ to sit upon his throne." 1 Kings 12. Acts 2: 30.

As, therefore, Christ was to come through the tribe of Judah [hence called the Lion of the tribe of Judah. Rev. 5 : 4], this tribe was a symbol or type of Abraham's seed through Christ. For this reason the Jews claimed that the promises to Abraham belonged to them. This claim Paul opposes and refutes, as above stated, showing that they, as a nation under their law, were only an *outward sign;* that the true Jew was one inwardly, in HEART, circumcised in HEART. IN THE SPIRIT [not outward, in the flesh, by the law], praised of God, not of men.

But Paul anticipates their objection, viz., " What advantage then hath the Jew? or what profit is there of circumcision?" [or what the profit of the circumcision. — *Emp. Diaglott.*] Rom 3 : 1. This objection he meets [not by flattering their pride, and exciting their vain hope of some future exaltation and special favor from God above all other nations, as too many have done since, and are still doing, but] by saying, their advantages are "much every way, chiefly because that unto them were committed the oracles of God" [or because they were intrusted with the oracles of God. — *Emp. Diaglott*].

Thus he shows them that their special advantages above other nations were in the past. They had these oracles, with all the sacred ordinances pointing to Christ and his work ; God had sent the prophets to instruct and admonish them. The Messiah had come to them, first, in strict accordance with the teachings of those oracles, as saith Peter, —

" Unto you first, God, having raised up his Son Jesus,

sent him to bless you, in turning away every one of you from his iniquity" Acts 3 : 26 [or God having raised up his SERVANT, sent him first to you, to bless each one who shall TURN from his EVIL WAYS.—*Emp. Diaglott*].

But with all these advantages they had rejected the light, refused the message, killed the Prince of Life (Acts 3 : 15), and sealed their fate as a nation, yet the promise to David concerning Christ had not thereby failed.

From these texts it is plain that no one can properly claim to be a Jew, in relation to the promised Messiah, except those who believe on him, and are circumcised in heart, in the spirit.

Again, we remark, that as it was Abraham's faith in God's word and promises that was imputed to him for righteousness, and secured to him the promised inheritance, and constituted him the father of many nations, it is the same righteousness which constitutes others his seed, recognized in the promise.

This simple fact leads Paul to say, "But to him that worketh not, but believeth on him that justifieth the ungodly, his faith is counted for righteousness." Rom 4 : 5. And again he says, "that he might be the father of all them that believe, though they be not circumcised; that righteousness might be imputed to them also. And the father of circumcision to them who are not of the circumcision only, but who also walk in the steps of that faith of our father Abraham, which he had, being yet uncircumcised. . . . For if they which are of the law [by virtue of the law] be heirs, faith is made void, and the promise made of none effect" Rom. 4 : 11, 12, 14.

This argument of Paul is sufficient to show that faith only can constitute persons the seed royal of Abraham, to whom the promise is made. But we find him giving still more evidence of this fact. "Know ye, therefore, that they which are of FAITH, the same are the children of Abraham. . . . Now to Abraham and his SEED were the promises made. He saith not, And to seeds, as of many [the Jewish nation]; but as of one, And to thy seed [see Gen. 13: 14, 15], which is Christ. . . . [This is the covenant confirmed of God in Christ before the law was given]. And if ye be Christ's, then are ye Abraham's seed, and HEIRS ACCORDING TO THE PROMISE." Gal. 3: 7, 16, 29.

These Scriptures demonstrate most clearly that faith in Christ, and faith alone, constitutes persons the seed of Abraham, and heirs of the land promised to him and his seed.

The question is often asked, How can Abraham be the father of all them that believe among the Gentiles, when some of them lived and died long before Abraham was born, as Abel, Enoch, and Noah?

We reply, that Christ, and his work of redemption and salvation, is the great object and centre of faith, around which the hope of all believers cluster.

He is the seed of the woman, who shall bruise [crush] the serpent's [Satan's] head. Gen. 3: 15. Rom. 16: 20. He is the seed of promise. Gal. 3: 16. With direct reference to this seed, who was to undo all that the serpent had done by tempting Eve, Abel brought his slain lamb, which expressed his faith in the death of Christ to redeem him from the penalty of the violated law. Thus faith constituted him righteous, and acceptable to God. Heb. 11:4. This constituted Abel a CHILD and MEMBER OF CHRIST. Gal. 3:29. Heb. 2:13. And Christ, being Abraham's seed, makes Abraham the father of all who believe. Thus Abel, Enoch, and Noah are the *seed of Abraham*, according to the LAW OF FAITH.

Having shown who the seed royal are, and by what law the relationship exists, we return to the second point stated in the promise, viz., that ABRAHAM is to inherit the land.

But Abraham is dead, the prophets are dead, apostles and martyrs are dead. How can THEY inherit the land?

Some answer this question thus: Canaan, being a type of the whole earth, and God's children in every generation having inherited the earth and enjoyed its blessings, have gone home to heaven to their final rest, and so we shall pass away, and other generations follow.

This is a very specious delusion, in direct opposition to Scripture; for the Bible declares that God's children "are pilgrims and strangers, as all the fathers [Abraham, Isaac, and Jacob] were." Gen. 47:9. Ex. 6:4. Heb. 11:9, 13, 16. Psa. 39:12. Therefore they are not inheritors, nor citizens of this world; and Stephen declares of Abraham, that God gave him none inheritance in it, no, not so much as to set his foot upon; yet he promised that he would give it *to him for a possession, and to his seed after him.*

But Paul settles this question thus: Of all Abraham's seed, who were then dead, he says, —

"These all died in faith, not having received the

promises, but having seen them afar off, were persuaded of them, and embraced them, and confessed that they were strangers and pilgrims on the earth." Heb. 11: 13. Yet the question returns, How CAN they inherit the land promised?

The Scriptures answer, By the resurrection from the dead. On no other plan can this promise be fulfilled. Of this Abraham was fully apprised. He had been told, before he had any children, that he should "go to his fathers in peace, and be buried in a good old age." Gen. 15 : 15.

And after the birth of Isaac, the Lord told him to cast out Hagar and Ishmael, that he should not be his heir. "But in Isaac shall thy seed be called." Gen. 21 : 12.

This question settled, the way is opened to give us an example of his faith; for this purpose the Lord directs him to offer Isaac for a burnt offering. Gen. 22 : 2.

Now Abraham must have understood that there was no possible way for the promise to be fulfilled if he should slay Isaac, unless God should raise him from the dead; and this was the very point to be settled in his mind. That he went out, and acted without any mental reservation, is most clearly established by the whole history. God was not deceived: he knew Abraham's heart, and sent an angel to save the life of Isaac. He then repeated the original promise, and confirmed it with an oath. Gen. 22 : 15, 16. But had Abraham no previous intimation that God would raise the dead? Yes; he received Isaac, in his birth, from the dead, "in a figure;" and so he reasoned and reflected on his journey to the supposed fatal spot where he was to slay his son Isaac. "Accounting that God was able to raise him up, even from the dead; from whence also he received him in a figure." Heb. 11 : 19.

The fact that Sarah was past age and the circumstances of child-bearing, and he himself about a hundred years old, did not cause him to stagger "at the promise of God, through unbelief, . . . but was fully persuaded that what he had promised he was able also to perform. And therefore it was imputed to him for righteousness." Rom. 4 : 22.

Thus Abraham was enabled to understand that the promise was to be fulfilled by a resurrection from the dead. Therefore Paul says Abraham "is the father of us all, as it has been written, a father of many nations I have constituted thee, in the presence of THAT God whom he believed, who MAKES ALIVE THE DEAD, and calls THINGS not in BEING as though EXISTING." [Rom. 4 : 17. — *Emp. Diaglott*].

Concerning this seed, the Lord, by the apostle, says, —

"Therefore also were born from one who even as to these things had become lifeless [a posterity], like the stars of heaven for multitude, and like THAT SAND on the shore of the sea, innumerable. ALL THESE DIED IN FAITH, NOT HAVING RECEIVED THE PROMISED BLESSINGS, but having seen and saluted them from a distance [BEYOND THE RESURRECTION OF THE DEAD], and having confessed that they were strangers and sojourners on the land." [*Emp. Diaglott*. Heb. 11 : 12 : 13. See also verse 35.]

Paul further says, of those who were persecuted to death, that they "would not accept deliverance [offered], in order that they might obtain a better resurrection."

That is, a resurrection which shall not be succeeded by a second death, — a resurrection UNTO ETERNAL LIFE.

Then, and not till then, will Abraham and his seed inherit the land, and the promise of God be verified.

This is "the immutable counsel" which God "confirmed with an oath, that we might have strong consolation, who have fled for refuge to lay hold upon the hope set before us: which hope we have, as an anchor of the soul, both sure and steadfast."

Dear reader, is *this your* hope? If it is not, then accept the terms on which it is offered, and secure the glorious prize to be gained.

THE TERM "ISRAEL."

Having shown WHAT are the blessings promised to Abraham and his seed, and WHO are the seed, and WHAT is the law which constitutes the relationship, WHEN and HOW they are fulfilled, we proceed to show TO WHOM the term *Israel* originally and primarily belonged.

And in what we may say, we shall endeavor to be guided by the testimony of Scripture.

It has been claimed by some writers that the name *Israel* belongs to the legal descendants of Jacob, and to them alone.

While others think that in its true sense it applies to true believers of that nation only.

But we believe, and shall proceed to show, that in its true and original sense it properly belongs to all true believers of all nations, Jew and Gentile.

We admit, however, that it was applied to the nation, as such, as a family or national proper name, but NOT for the same reason that it was given to the man previously known as Jacob.

We admit, also, that it is properly and especially applied to true believers of the Jewish nation, but NOT of that nation ONLY.

When the Lord would give a significant indication of the character, design, or quality of certain men or things, he gives them names expressive of such character, designs, or qualities, to impress them on the mind.

We have given examples of this principle, in our chapter on "the Necessity of an Atonement," page 97, to which we refer the reader.

As when God would indicate the greatness in multitude, and extensiveness of the locality of Abraham's seed, he does it by changing the name of Abram for Abraham [i. e., "a father of many nations"]. Or, when the Lord would indicate the work of the Messiah, he gives him the name JESUS [i. e., Saviour, for he shall save his people from their sins].

Thus it is clearly seen that these names are given to express the character, work, history, or relation of the persons or things to whom they are given.

With this rule before us, we will examine the name ISRAEL. As the name ABRAHAM expresses the numerical greatness and geographical locality of his seed, so the Lord changed the name of Jacob to ISRAEL, to express his character and relation to God, as one of Abraham's royal seed.

The promises made to Abraham and his seed, were made equally to Isaac and Jacob; and when Jacob wrestled with the angel, and insisted on being blessed of him, he prevailed; and God gave him a name to indicate his character, as, the blessed *of* God, and consequently his relation *to* God. "And he said, Thy name shall be called no more Jacob, but Israel [a prince of God], for as a prince hast thou power with God and with man, and hast prevailed." Gen. 32 : 28. See also ch. 35 : 9, 12.

Here we have the origin of the name ISRAEL, together with its primary meaning and proper application. In this sense Christ uses it when speaking of Nathanael, "Behold an ISRAELITE INDEED, IN WHOM IS NO GUILE."

Every other use and application of the name, therefore, must be secondary and accommodated. Who would claim that in any other sense than secondary it was ever applied by the sacred writers to the Jewish nation? A generation of vipers, and some of whom, Jesus says, were of their father the devil. Are these princes of God? Alas! what next?

The fact that *Israel* was used as a family name no more proves that they were princes, or sons of God, than the name *Jesus*, applied to other men, proves that they are *saviors*. But if it was given to Jacob to express his character and relation to God in its primary sense, then it belongs to all who sustain that character and relation, and to none others.

But what saith the Scripture? In speaking of the nation under the (family) name of Israel, the Lord says he " will cause to *cease the kingdom of the house of Israel*, . . . for I will no more have mercy upon the house of Israel but I WILL UTTERLY TAKE THEM AWAY," as a kingdom and nation. Has he fulfilled his word?

Surely they could not have been princes, or sons of God.

But hear him, when, applying the name in its primary sense, he says, —

"Yet the number of the children of Israel shall be as the sand of the sea, which cannot be measured nor numbered; and it shall come to pass, that in the place where it was said unto them, Ye are not my people, there it shall be said unto them, Ye are the SONS [princes] OF THE LIVING GOD." Hos. 1:4, 6, 10.

Paul applies this text to believers from the Gentiles. Rom. 9:24, 26. See also 2 Pet. 2:10. Let those who Judaize escape this argument if they can.

Again, the Lord says by Isaiah, the prophet, "Though the number of the children of Israel [the nation] be as the sand of the sea, yet a remnant [true Israelites] of them shall return;" or, as Paul applies it, *shall be saved.* Isa. 10:22. Rom. 9:27. Surely the nation could not have been PRINCES OF GOD.

We come now to Paul's great argument upon this point, in his Epistle to the Romans. In speaking of his strong desire for the conversion and salvation of his brethren in the flesh, and of their advantages, he says, —

"Not as though the word of God [in his promises to Israel] hath taken none effect [failed]. For they are not all Israel [princes of God] who are of Israel [Jacob's family]. Neither, because they are the seed of Abraham, are they all children [seed royal]; but in Isaac shall thy seed be called." He then explains and applies this remark, thus: —

"That is, they which are the children of the flesh

these are not the children [princes] of God; but the CHILDREN [seed royal] OF PROMISE ARE COUNTED FOR THE SEED." Rom. 9 : 6, 8.

But, Paul, who are Israel, and children of the promise? Hear him reply, " Now we, brethren [Jew and Gentile], as Isaac was, are the children of promise." Gal. 4 : 28. Can language make anything more plain? Let those who apply these promises to the Jews as a nation consider this argument.

The apostle continues this argument through the ninth, tenth, and eleventh chapters, constantly opposing the claim of the Jew, as such, to God's promises to Abraham, Isaac, and [Jacob] Israel, and their seed [royal] in the primary sense, especially keeping before their minds the law of faith, and its righteousness, as the only basis upon which any one, Jew or Gentile, can claim those promises; contrasting it with the law of circumcision, upon which they laid their claim. Rom. 10 : 4–12.

He declares, "There is no difference between the Jew and the Greek: for the same Lord over all is rich unto all that call upon him." He then goes on to show them that the Scriptures of the prophets, in which they claim to believe, teach this doctrine, and they ought to know it; then quotes from Moses and Isaiah, in proof. Verses 19–21.

Paul then raises another objection for them against his claim. " Hath God cast away his people?" for you, Paul, say God has cast away the nation. To this he replies, "God forbid; for I also am an Israelite, of the seed of Abraham, of the tribe of Benjamin." He then argues that as God had reserved seven thousand, in the days of Elias, who did not worship the image of Baal, "even so then at this present time also there is a remnant according to the election of grace. And if by grace then it is no more of works," or of the law. Rom. 11 : 4, 6.

He then shows them that though the nation were blinded and fallen, yet the election were not; then quotes their prophets, showing their fall, 7–10; then, in 11, 12, he shows them that their fall, as a nation, did not place them beyond the means of grace, but opened the way for salvation to come to the Gentiles by the Gospel, in order to provoke them, the Jews, to jealousy, and thereby to save some of *them.* See verse 14.

Then he reasons thus: "Now if the fall of them [the nation] be the riches of the world, and the diminishing of them [to a level with the Gentiles] the riches of the Gentiles, how much more their fulness?"

If placing Jews on a level with the Gentiles, under the gospel dispensation, brings in a remnant from among the Gentiles (see Acts 15 : 14), how much more shall it enrich the fulness, or remnant, of believers among the Jews, by provoking them to believe, through the influence of the gospel among the Gentiles, and thus the prediction of Moses be fulfilled! as God said, —

"I will provoke you to jealousy by them that are no people; and by a foolish nation will I anger you."

This would be what Paul desired. "If by any means I may provoke to emulation them which are my flesh [Jews], and might save some of them. For if the casting away of them [Jewish nation] be the reconciling of the world [or unbelievers, through the preaching of the gospel], what shall the receiving of them [unbelieving Jews, who have been provoked to jealousy and believed through the influence of the gospel among the Gentiles], be but life from the dead in the resurrection?"

"For if [Christ] the first fruit be holy, the [harvest] lump is also holy; and if [Christ] the root be holy, so are the branches [in him]. And if some of the branches [unbelieving Jews] be broken off [from Christ, because of unbelief], and thou [believing Gentile, being a wild tree while in unbelief] wert [by faith] graffed in among them [believing Jews], and with them partakest of the root [Christ] and fatness of the [family] olive tree, boast not against the [broken off] branches. But if thou boast, [remember] thou bearest not the root, but the root thee.

"Thou wilt say then, The branches were broken off that I might be graffed in. Well; because of unbelief they were broken off, and thou standest by faith. Be not high-minded, but fear. For if God spared not the natural branches, take heed lest he also spare not thee."

Then, in verse 22, he reminds the Gentiles of the goodness of God to them, and his severity towards the Jews; exhorting them to continue in his goodness, lest they also be cut off. Then of the Jews he says, "And they also, IF THEY ABIDE NOT STILL IN UNBELIEF, shall be graffed in: for God is able to graff them in again." The conditions here stated are too plain to be misunderstood by the careful seeker for truth.

Then, continuing his argument, Paul says, "For I would not, brethren, that ye should be ignorant of this mystery, lest ye should be wise in your own conceits;

that blindness in part is happened to Israel"—blindness is happened to a part of Israel. That the blindness here referred to happened to only a part of Israel is clearly proved by the apostle himself; for he says, "Israel [the nation] hath not obtained that [righteousness] which he seeketh for: but the ELECTION [those who believed] HATH OBTAINED IT, and the rest [that part who did not believe] WERE BLINDED. Verse 7. It is supposed by some that this blindness was concerning the Messiahship of Jesus; but the rejection of Christ was only the result of their blindness.

Their blindness was manifest at Sinai, when they received the law and its ordinances; for they were carnal, or "vain in their imaginations, and their foolish heart was darkened." They did not understand the nature and object of the institutions God gave them. See Deut. 29: 4.

Hence the veil on Moses' face indicated the blindness of their heart; "they could not see to the end of that law which is abolished." See 2 Cor. 3: 13.

They entirely mistook their relation to their fathers, Abraham, Isaac, and Jacob, and the promises made to those fathers and their seed.

They did not see that their theocracy was only a typical institution, but supposed it to be a permanent and everlasting arrangement.

They did not comprehend that their temple sacrifices, and table service, and feasts were only shadows or signs of the sufferings of their Redeemer and the blessings which should follow.

The veil was upon their heart; hence Paul **quotes**

largely from their prophets to convince them of their error. But nothing short of the final downfall of the nation would do this; nor has even this convinced them as a people, yet it has convinced and turned to salvation a remnant of them.

In view of the foregoing facts, and many more which might be cited, Paul, in the argument we have been examining, touching their blindness, says, "According as it is written, God hath given them the spirit of slumber, eyes that they should not see, and ears that they should not hear, unto this day. And David saith, Let their table [temple service] be made a snare, and a trap, and a stumbling-block [as was Christ, the antitype of that service], and a recompense unto them; let their eyes be darkened, that they may not see, and bow down their back ALWAY."

A fearful example indeed for those who close their eyes against the light, and persist in unbelief.

But how long is that blindness to continue? We have seen that the gospel aims to remove it by provoking them to jealousy or emulation, and thereby "save them that believe." Verse 14. And this accords with what the apostle says again: "But their minds were blinded, for until this day remaineth the same veil untaken away in the reading of the Old Testament, WHICH VEIL IS DONE AWAY IN CHRIST. But even unto this day, when Moses is read, the veil is upon their HEART. Nevertheless when it [the heart] shall TURN UNTO THE LORD, THE VEIL SHALL BE TAKEN AWAY." 2 Cor. 3: 14, 16.

This is emphatic, and settles the question as to *when* and *how* that blindness may be removed. And unless it is THUS removed they will bow down their back *alway*, even " until the fulness [full number] of the Gentiles be come in," and the gospel has ceased its mission, Christ shall come, and the dead are raised.

"And so all Israel [princes of God, from Jews and Gentiles] shall be saved [ransomed from the grave, Hosea, 13 : 14 ; life from the dead, Paul, verse 14], as it is written (Isa. 59 : 20), There shall come out of Zion the Deliverer, and shall turn away ungodliness from Jacob." Rom. 11 : 26. Is this as Isaiah wrote it? Let us see.

"And the Redeemer shall come to Zion, and unto them that turn from transgression in Jacob, saith the Lord." Isa. 59 : 20.

As this is what the Lord saith, why did not Paul say what the Lord saith?

We think Paul did, because he refers to what was WRITTEN IN ISAIAH; and there can be no conflict between Isaiah and Paul. And therefore we think the text in Romans is a mistranslation of Paul's quotation.

Upon this point Professor Hodge, of Princeton, says, "This version of this passage agrees neither with the Hebrew nor the Septuagint. In the latter part of the verse the departure from the Hebrew is most serious." On the text in Isaiah, he remarks, "We have here a literal translation of the Hebrew."

The most reasonable supposition is, that the error is not in our translators, but in some ancient transcribing of MS.

This being so, all is plain. The passage in Isaiah is in harmony with the whole tenor of the apostle's argument in the 9th, 10th, and 11th chapters of this epistle, and, indeed, with all other Bible descriptions of the work of Christ at his coming.

On the other hand, the version in Romans appears to harmonize in no way with his own argument. And Dr. Clarke, in his comment on the version in Romans, admitting it to be correct, finds himself involved in a perfect mystery, as we think all must be who follow that version instead of Isaiah.

If, then, we follow the version in Isaiah, we can see how all Israel is to be saved when "the Deliverer [Christ] shall come to Zion, and to them that turn from transgression in Jacob." For Jesus is to come "without sin [a sin offering] unto salvation, unto all them that look for him."

The partition wall between Jew and Gentile having been broken down, Jesus having "abolished IN HIS FLESH the enmity, even the law of commandments contained in ordinances: for to make IN HIMSELF OF TWAIN [Jew and Gentile] ONE NEW MAN [true Israel, princes of God], so making peace.

"And that he might reconcile both [Jew and Gentile] unto God in one body by the cross, having slain the enmity thereby [by removing the old covenant of circumcision, engraven on stones]; and came and preached peace to you [Gentiles] which were afar off, and to them [the Jews] that WERE [under the covenant] NIGH." Eph. 2: 15, 17.

Therefore IN CHRIST "there is neither JEW nor GREEK, *there is neither bond nor free, there is neither male nor female; for ye are all* [Jew and Gentile] *one* in CHRIST JESUS.

"And IF YE BE CHRIST'S, THEN ARE YE ABRAHAM'S SEED [true Israelites], AND HEIRS ACCORDING TO THE PROMISE." Gal. 3 : 28, 29.

These Scriptures demonstrate the fact that all distinction between Jew and Gentile, in their relation to Abraham, Isaac, and Israel, and their seed, — Jesus Christ, — is forever abolished. Therefore the apostle says again, —

"For in Christ Jesus neither circumcision availeth anything, nor uncircumcision, BUT [faith which worketh by love, Gal. 5 : 6, and maketh] A NEW CREATURE." This allies believers to the new creation.

"And as many as WALK ACCORDING TO THIS RULE [law], peace be on them [Jew or Gentile] and mercy, and UPON THE ISRAEL OF GOD." Amen.

Dear reader, let us walk according to this rule, that when the Deliverer, Jesus Christ, shall come to Zion, and to them that turn from transgression in Jacob — all true believers which constitute the fulness from the old Jewish stock — when the fulness of the Gentiles is come in, and so all Israel is saved, we with them may enter in through the gates into the city, and enjoy that blessed rest that remains for the people of God.

"For this is my covenant [confirmed before of God in Christ, 430 years before the law — covenant, Gal. 3 : 17] unto them when I shall take away their sins." Rom. 11 : 27.

All true believers receive this covenant in their hearts when their sins are forgiven; and this involves the promise of God to send the DELIVERER. See Jer. 31 : 31. Heb. 8 : 10, 13. Acts 3 : 20.

"As concerning the gospel, they [Jewish nation as such] are enemies [to God and cast away] for your sakes; but as touching the ELECTION [true believers from among them, which is their fulness], THEY [the election] ARE BELOVED FOR THE FATHERS' [Abraham, Isaac, and Jacob] SAKES. FOR THE GIFTS AND CALLING OF GOD ARE WITHOUT REPENTANCE." Rom. 11 : 27, 29.

Thanks be to God, they cannot fail therefore. The Deliverer will come at the time appointed. Amen : even so, come Lord Jesus.

CHAPTER XX.

THE MILLENNIUM.

" To him that overcometh will I grant to sit with me in my throne, even as I also overcame, and am set down with my Father in his throne." — *Rev.* 3 : 21.

" Blessed and holy is he that hath part in the first resurrection; on such the second death hath no power, but they shall be priests of God and of Christ, and shall reign with him a thousand years [THE thousand years — EMP. DIAGLOTT; THOSE thousand years — SYRAIC]." — *Rev.* 20 : 6.

THE above promises and benediction include all the glory, and riches, and blessings which our Lord Jesus Christ has purchased for and promised to his followers, to be enjoyed in the world to come.

Such a position of honor and glory, such a state of blessedness and triumph, has never yet been attained by man; nor can they be in this world of mortality; but such is to be attained and enjoyed by the people of God in the world to come.

This the Scriptures abundantly prove, as we shall proceed to show. The Bible is not simply the record of the works of God, and the acts of men of the past, and the revelation of the duties and responsibilities of the present; but it presents, in no uncertain voice, the work of the Lord, the destinies of man, and the glorious rest of the future.

A careful study of these passages and their contexts, with a proper consideration of the doctrine involved, carefully comparing them with many other Scriptures on the same subject, will demonstrate the fact that they are to have their fulfilment *at, and after* THE SECOND PERSONAL ADVENT OF CHRIST.

The first passage at the head of this chapter embraces the following very important points : —

I. That man is not in a condition, in this world, to reign with Christ : he must first overcome sin, then he will obtain victory over death, in " the first resurrection."

II. That Christ, with our nature, overcame sin and death by his sufferings, death, and resurrection : and by the shedding of his own blood, and entering into heaven as an Advocate, he has prepared the way for us to obtain forgiveness of sin, and to overcome the world, that at his coming again he may give us victory over death, and grant us eternal life.

III. That Christ is now seated on his heavenly Father's throne, *and not on his own throne.*

IV. That Christ is yet to occupy a throne of his own, which he denominates " MY THRONE."

V. That all who will accept Christ as their Lawgiver, Teacher, Sacrifice, Lifegiver, Priest, Judge, and King, in order to obtain remission of sins, and to overcome the world, the flesh, and the devil, shall be raised to immortality, to REIGN WITH CHRIST, when he comes TO REIGN. Many overlook the fact, that while Christ is on his Father's throne as our " Great High Priest," he does not occupy his own throne ; but Christ is yet to ascend his own rightful throne: which event will be attended with honor and glory, surpassing all that which the kings, potentates, and rulers of this world combined, ever received.

Mortal rulers have come to their thrones, generally, and to the honors bestowed upon them, through doubtful claims, by strifes and wars, blood and carnage, at the sacrifice of much human life and happiness; or, by causing heavy burdens and taxations to rest on the multitudes who have not obtained equal rights and joint heirship with their rulers.

But Christ gains his throne by being the only rightful heir, and by the promise of the eternal Father. He gains the worthiness to occupy it, and the glory attending it, by the sacrifice of his own life, the shedding of his own blood, for the redemption of his subjects from death, the cleansing of them from sin, and procuring for them eternal life.

He "had glory with the Father before the world was" (John 17:5), but to redeem that world when it was lost by sin, "he took on him the seed of Abraham," and "for the joy that was set before him, endured the cross, despising the shame, and is set down on the right hand of the throne of God." This he did for us while we were enemies; and then invited us to accept his mercy, believe on him, obey his teachings, overcome sin by faith in his blood, suffer with him for the advancement of his cause, and be raised immortal to share the joint heirship of his eternal reign and glory.

Is not such a Benefactor and Master worthy of our affections and obedience? Should not such goodness lead us to repentance? Ought not all men to acknowledge his right to reign? Such as will not do it, can have no rights in his dominion; and when he ascends the throne of his glory, and executes the reign of judgment, "every knee shall bow before him," confess the righteousness of his claims, and all "his enemies shall lick the dust."

When the angel delivered his message to Mary concerning the birth of Jesus, he said, "He shall be great, and shall be called the Son of the Highest and the Lord God shall give unto him the throne of his father David: and he shall reign over the house of Jacob forever, and of his kingdom there shall be no end." Luke 1: 32, 33.

The reign of Christ must be as literal as was his birth of the Virgin Mary, his baptism, death, and resurrection. When his reign commences, it is shared by his saints, the church of God gathered from all ages and generations, and from all kindreds, and tongues, and peoples, and nations; and marks the fulfilment of the second text at the head of this chapter, and the commencement of the long looked-for

MILLENNIUM.

Mille, a thousand, and *annus* a year, — a thousand years. *Millennium* means "a thousand years; a word used to denote the thousand years mentioned in Rev. xx., during which period Satan will be bound, and holiness become triumphant throughout the world. During this period, as some believe, Christ will reign on earth in person with his saints."— *Webster.*

We do not quote Webster as authority in doctrine, but for the meaning and use of the word. The word *millennium*, as used in religious teachings, is derived from Rev. 20, as above cited.

"Blessed and holy is he that hath part in the first resurrection: on such the second death hath no power, but they shall be priests of God and of Christ, and shall reign with him a thousand years."

The time shall come when Christ will take the throne of David, and reign from henceforth forever: and when it does come, his followers shall also reign with him.

There is, however, a millennium, — a thousand years, as stated in the text, which marks a period between the commencement of that reign, and the final execution of Christ's enemies, — which we denominate the *reign of judgment*.

Many strange views have originated in the Christian church on this subject.

It would seem that every effort has been made that Satanic sagacity or human invention can produce, to either overthrow or prevent the scriptural doctrine of the millennium. The malignant opposition of the Jewish and pagan nations against the doctrine of Christ's personal reign was fully manifested when he was here, in his betrayal and crucifixion. But finding that the doctrine prevailed and spread, the effort was renewed to destroy it, by killing the teachers and followers of Christ. This only increased the number of believers. The next effort was to corrupt the doctrine and pervert the teachings of it, so as to destroy the idea of the *personal* reign during the millennium, or thousand years.

This accomplished, the way is open to successfully oppose the idea that Christ will ever reign *personally*. For the passages which teach such a reign for a thousand years, being spiritualized and perverted, all others which teach his reign *at all* must share the same fate.

To accomplish so important an end, the gospel must be accommodated to the dogmas of paganism. The scriptural rule of interpretation must be abandoned, and rules applied which would allow of any interpretation desired by partisans, or by unsanctified hearts. This point was gained by the enemy while Origen and Augustine became willing instruments to propagate and popularize what is called allegorical and spiritual interpretations of Scripture. A wide door was now opened to misinterpret the nature of man, the penalty of God's law, Christ's atonement, the object of the proclamation of the gospel, the consummation of the plan of grace, the resurrection of the dead, and, lastly, the reign of Christ. For when they obtained a false view of the work of God *preceding* the reign of Christ, it called for a theory *concerning* his reign which should be consonant with that false view of other parts of Scripture doctrine.

In the fourth century the Christian faith had overcome pagan authority, and become the dominant religion; but not in its purity, for in that time when paganism was falling, the papacy was rising to take its place, and to corrupt the church with idolatry, and the Christian faith with pagan superstition.

At that time, as Church history gives abundant evidence, "monks, monasteries, convents, penance, church councils with church control of conscience, excommunication, the smoke of incense, wax tapers in the churches at noonday, prostrate crowds at the altar drunk with fanaticism or wine, imprinting devout kisses on the walls, and supplicating the concealed blood, bones, or ashes of the saints, idolatrously frequenting martyrs' tombs, pictures and images of tutelar saints, veneration of bones and relics, gorgeous robes, tiaras, croises, pomp, splendor, and mysticism, were seen everywhere, and were the order of the day."

And in the words of Mosheim, "The new species of philosophy, imprudently adopted by Origen and many other Christians, was extremely prejudicial to the cause of the gospel, and to the beautiful simplicity of its celestial doctrines."

Coleridge tells us, "The pastors of the church had gradually changed the light and life of the gospel into the very superstitions they were commissioned to disperse, and thus paganized Christianity in order to christen paganism."

"All this," says Dr. Duffield, "was the genuine offspring of the *allegorical system* and *Platonic philosophy of Origen*, who made *the church on earth the mystic kingdom of heaven.*"

"Origen was the most distinguished pupil of a Greek philosopher of great talent, who settled in Alexandria, and though wholly ignorant of divine truth, applied, and was admitted into the church, and became instructor of the Christian youths of Alexandria. His name was Ammonius Saccus. Here Origen received his first impressions in heathen philosophy. He was sent early in life to Chaldea, where he studied, and became initiated in the highest mysteries of the Assyrian apostasy. On returning to Alexandria he became head of the school, and finally bishop. During the reign of Emperor Alexander Severus, who also was a member of the Oriental apostasy, Origen lent the whole weight of his talents and influence to aid the emperor in his design to unite all creeds in one at Rome, and with a view to this end he prevailed upon the emperor to add the name of Christ to the number of the gods. He then immediately changed his own name, originally Admantus, adopting that of Origen.

"From that moment the distinctive doctrines of the gospel ceased to be taught generally. The atonement was no longer spoken of; the second advent of Christ, and his future kingdom, were denied; the resurrection of the body was explained away. The conspiracy triumphed under Pope Damasus (about A. D. 381), who declared the millennium had already commenced, and expelled from the church as heretics all who looked for Christ's second advent and kingdom." — *Church History.*

This prepared the way for the papacy, and the reign of "the man of sin," sustained by the dogma that Christ's kingdom was spiritual, his reign with his saint a moral reign, under the management of the bishops.

The doctrine that the Babe of Bethlehem should rise and rule was hated by Herod. The announcement that Jesus of Nazareth should reign on the throne of David tormented the apostate Jews, and has always been rejected by their antitype. No wonder, then, that the apostate bishops of the Christian church rejected *the personal reign* of Christ, that they might receive *the honor themselves,* and usurp the power to control.

But the doctrine of the personal reign of Christ, and of the thousand years' reign between the two resurrections, was so clearly taught in Revelation, and so tenaciously held to and advocated by the church for the first three centuries, it became necessary to exclude the Apocalypse from the sacred writings, to exclude the doctrine of the millennium.

On this Gibbon remarks, " In the Council of Laodicea, A. D. 360, the Apocalypse was tacitly excluded from the sacred canon by the same churches of Asia to which it was addressed : and we may learn from the complaint of Sulpicius Severus that their sentence had been ratified by the greater number of Christians of his time."

Mr. H. Bonar, in writing on Rev. 20, remarks, " In the first three centuries great stress was laid upon this passage. It was considered the stronghold of chiliasm (the thousand years' personal reign). So strong and decided was its testimony deemed, that the anti-chiliasts believed their only escape from it was the total denial of the Apocalypse. Chiliasm and the Apocalypse were deemed inseparable.

" They could only get rid of the former by rejecting the latter. They never thought it possible to deny that the Apocalypse taught chiliasm. This was not disputed ; and hence those who disliked chiliasm could not tolerate the Apocalypse. It was not until the church had learned to Platonize, or had taken lessons in the school of Origen, that they could condemn chiliasm without disputing the inspiration of the Revelation."

All apostasies in the apostolic church led from the literal to the spiritual, never to the contrary. Have you ever carefully considered this fact, dear reader? The most elaborate and mighty arguments of Paul against the "fool," of Peter against the "scoffers, who were willingly ignorant," and of John against the Gnostics, who "confessed not that Jesus Christ is come in the flesh," and "who seduced" the disciples, were to eradicate these apostate dogmas from the church.

The history of the church furnishes much evidence why such efforts have been made to discredit the book of Revelation. It is because they rejected the PERSONAL REIGN OF CHRIST, and had allegorized the Scriptures on all other doctrines so as to obviate the necessity of such a reign, and were preparing the way for the popes to *reign in his stead*.

Baronius, a Roman Catholic writer of the sixteenth century, in writing of the fifth century, says, "Moreover, the figments of the millenarians being now rejected everywhere, and derided by the learned with hisses and laughter, and being also put under the ban, were entirely extirpated."

Dr. Burnett remarks, "I never yet met with a papish doctor that held the millennium. It never pleased, but always gave offence, to the church of Rome, because it did not suit that scheme of Christianity which they have drawn. The Apocalypse of John supposed the true church under hardships and persecutions, but the church of Rome, supposing Christ reigns already by his vicar the pope, hath been in prosperity and greatness, and the commanding church in Christendom, for a long time. And the millennium being properly a *reward and a triumph* for those that come out of persecution, such as have always lived in pomp and prosperity can pretend to no share in it, nor be benefited by it. This has made the church of Rome always have an ill eye upon this doctrine, because it seemed to have an ill eye upon her; and as she grew in splendor and greatness, she eclipsed and obscured it more and more; so that it would have been lost out of the world, as an obsolete error, if it had not been revived by some at the Reformation."

Apocalyptic Sketches.

Prof. Stuart remarks, " In the end of the fourth century, to guard against chiliasm [the millennium], quite a number doubted the genuineness of the Apocalypse; did not receive it as canonical, and carefully abstained from appealing to it; but after this period we find only here and there a solitary voice raised against it, until at length the reception became all but universal. When the question of chiliasm ceased to excite any special interest in the churches, all opposition to the Apocalypse either ceased, or became quite inactive and indifferent."

Who that examines this history of bitter hatred and persistent opposition to the thousand years' personal reign of Christ, does not see the workings of Satan, and feel convicted that the same evil principles which then infested the church and corrupted her faith still lurks in the church of the ninteenth century, to pervert the same doctrine which it could not destroy in former days, while the Church is not aware of it? Mr. Taylor has well observed,—

"Thus we have seen that through the rejection of the Apocalypse by Caius, Dionysius, and finally the church in general; through the Platonizing and allegorizing of Origen and his numerous followers; through the misrepresentations of Eusebius; through the scoffing of the monk Jerome; through the hate and opposition of a great church of embryotic papists; through the denunciations of church councils; through the comminations and bitterness of popes; through the laughter and hisses of papish doctors; through the influence of an onward-creeping and awful apostasy; through, perhaps, the abuse of millenarian truths by their advocates; and, finally, through the presentation and final reception of a new and erroneous millennial theory more suited to the times, the true Apocalyptic doctrine of the millennium, as held by the primitive church, wasted away, and ultimately well nigh died — died, not at the hands of orthodox Christians, but at the hand of men noted for their unsoundness in the faith — died at the hands of the infant harlot, Rome!

"And, alas, how much truth died with it! how much error lived when it died! But it did not die utterly, for

'Truth crushed to earth, shall rise again;
The eternal years of God are hers.'"

Voice of the Church, p. 116.

From the fourth century, through the dark ages of papal tyranny and superstition, an allegorical interpretation prevailed, teaching what is called the Augustinian view of the reign of Christ and the saints. That scheme was, "that the one thousand years of Satan's binding and the saints' reigning dated from the ministry of Christ, when he beheld Satan fall like lightning from heaven; it being meant to signify the triumph over Satan in the hearts of true believers, and that the subsequent figuration of Gog and Magog indicated the coming of Antichrist at the end of the world — the one thousand years being a figurative numeral, expressive of the whole period intervening. It supposes the resurrection taught, to be that of dead souls from the death of sin to the life of righteousness; the beast conquered by the saints, meant the wicked world; its image, a hypocritical profession; the resurrection being continuous, till the end of time, when the universal resurrection and final judgment would take place."

This view, says Dr. Elliot, "prevailed from Augustine's time down to the Reformation."

But the great Reformation brought about a revolution, and Protestants began to learn by the study of the Bible the same faith which was revealed to John, and which animated the hearts of the primitive saints, leading them to look with anxious interest for the return of Christ from heaven to enter upon his glorious reign. The proclamation of the gospel and the revival of the PRINCIPLE OF THE LITERAL INTERPRETATION OF THE PROPHECIES, turned the current of the Protestant mind to investigate the claims of the papist's millennial reign of Christ, and to compare it with the scriptural doctrine.

This gave the faith of the church a right direction, and opened a thorough investigation of the doctrine, resulting in the revival of the *primitive faith and hope.*

which has continued until the present time. But the doctrine of the personal reign of Christ was not to become a *popular view*, and the elements of a more pleasing theme to human pride culminated in a new form of error to bewilder the church, in the guise of

THE WHITBYAN MILLENNIUM.

Daniel Whitby, D. D., was an English divine and commentator, who died A. D. 1727. He introduced a new system of ideas on the reign of Christ, which he justly denominates "*a new hypothesis;*" which means, a *supposition*, a *conjecture*, an *opinion*, or a system founded upon some principle not proved. He was honest in naming it "a new hypothesis." His hypothesis was that of "a spiritual [and temporal] millennium, consisting of a universal triumph of the gospel, and the conversion of all nations for a thousand years before the coming of Christ." This opinion has since been held and advocated by Hammond, Hopkins, Scott, Dwight, Bougue, and others, says Dr. Henshaw, who well observes, that it "is a novel doctrine, unknown to the church for the space of sixteen hundred years."

Archdeacon Woodhouse, observes, —

"It is remarkable that Dr. Whitby, who had declined to comment on the Apocalypse, assigning as his motive, that he felt himself unqualified for such a work, has ventured to explain this particular prediction of the millennium; which, being, as all agree, a prophecy yet unfulfilled, is, of all others, the most difficult."

Woodhouse on Apoc., p. 470.

It is, indeed, remarkable that a man who admits his

want of qualification to comment on the book of Revelation, should select a single passage from it, and attempt to make it the foundation of "a new hypothesis," based on assumption, contrary to the entire and direct testimony of that book, and the faith and teachings of the church of Christ for sixteen hundred years.

And it is yet more remarkable that so many eminently learned and pious men of modern times should have been ensnared by this insidious opinion of Whitby. But a departure from the true rules of literal interpretation leads to many and great excesses and extravagant errors.

Bishop Russell's remarks on this point are worthy of our careful meditation. He says, "Modern divines have concurred in the use of certain professional terms, which undoubtedly owe their reception to a feeling of convenience rather than to the authority of sound criticism. For example, the phrase 'coming of Christ,' which in former times conveyed the most exalted ideas in regard to the destiny of the world, is conventionally employed in our days to mean the hour of every individual's death. The first resurrection, again, according to Whitby and his followers, implies nothing more solemn than the conversion of the Jews, the reign of the saints with the Redeemer, a thousand years on earth, denotes simply the revival of evangelical doctrine; and by 'the rest of the dead,' we are to understand a generation of bad men, who are to be born about the end of the millennium, and to annoy the congregations of the faithful."

"In short, the main object of the allegorical school is to explain away the proper millennium, by endeavoring to prove that the language of the New Testament has no reference to any personal advent prior to the general judgment, nor to any kingdom except that which is in heaven."

"Every person who reads the book of Revelation without any bias on his mind, and then turns to the far-fetched commentaries of Dr. Whitby and his pupils, will perceive either that undue liberties have been used by them in expounding the original, or that John the divine did not know the meaning of his own words."
Bishop Russell's Disc. on Mill, pp. 113, 115.

Mr. Taylor also well remarks on this subject, —

"It is an occurrence without parallel in the history of theology, that a theory without antiquity, without support from the plain literal sense of Scripture, a theory named by its originator at its birth 'new,' and hypothetical, and which impugns the faith of the church for more than sixteen centuries, has come to be at this time almost universally received and taught among all classes of men as a part of the Christian faith. Reader, is it not passing strange? Did you ever soberly think of this?" *Voice of the Church*, p. 231.

Such are the ravages and inroads upon the doctrine of Christ, caused by following the opinions of a man rather than the testimony of Scripture. By such means the church is infested with the strange notions that Christ has occupied the throne of David in heaven the past eighteen hundred years, and that he has reigned with his church spiritually, and that they have reigned with him, a thousand years on earth; which must be stretched to any length to cover all probationary time;

and in fulfilment of that great promise at the head of this chapter, of a glorious and peaceful reign of the saints with Christ.

Hence the dogmas that "the first resurrection" is a moral resurrection, and that the gospel is destined to convert all the inhabitants of earth, and thus produce the millennium, or "thousand years' reign of the Spirit," in this mortal world, and yet future, where believers are constantly weeping over their dead, and dying themselves.

To overcome this vital objection, the perverted mind has invented the theory that such improvements in temperance, diet, and other habits of life, such discoveries in medical science and physical training will be made, that the people will not die, nor be sick during the "thousand years." Gaunt Death dies of famine.

Can fanaticism produce greater absurdities than these? Added to these strange ideas and philosophical reasonings, is the effort to bring certain passages to speak in harmony with the scheme; which can only be done by an improper application of them, or by so torturing them as to extort a doctrine from them which they do not teach, and which conflicts with the plain teachings of the Word of God. We do not propose to discuss and meet all these erroneous views, though we will give further notice of some of them.

Having adopted false principles of interpretation, they find difficulties arising in the examination of almost every branch of Bible doctrine. Hence the Whitbyan school of teachers found themselves under the necessity of distorting and spiritualizing very much of the Scriptures to make them appear to harmonize with their scheme. Thus in applying Scripture to sustain the idea of the conversion of the world, and temporal reign of Christ a thousand years in this mortal state, they quote, "But as surely as I live, all the earth shall be filled with the glory of the Lord." Num. 14 : 21. And again, " For the earth shall be filled with the knowledge of the glory of the Lord, as the waters cover the sea." Hab. 2 : 14. That such a state of glory and knowledge of the Lord can obtain in this world of mortality is impossible, for it is directly opposed to the current testimony of the Bible, which declares that " the man of sin," " the beast," and " the false prophet," will continue their work *until the judgment.* These symbols represent the papal power, the anti-Christian church, and perhaps the Mohammedan religion. Again, Christ tells us that " the tares are the children of the wicked one," and are to continue with " the children of the kingdom " until " the end of this world " — age. Matt. 13 : 40.

We are also told that when the seventh angel sounds the last trump, " the kingdoms of this world are become the kingdoms of our Lord, and of his Christ. . . . And the nations were angry, and thy wrath is come, and the time of the dead, that they should be judged." Rev. 11 : 15, 18. Christ tells us also, " The son of man shall send forth his angels, and they shall gather out of his kingdom all things that offend, and them which do iniquity : and shall cast them into a furnace of fire, there shall be wailing and gnashing of teeth." Again, Christ tells us that when the Son of Man is revealed, society is to be in the condition it was in the days of Noah and of Lot.

Also that "as a snare shall that day come upon all them that dwell upon the face of the whole earth." Matt. 24 : Luke 21.

Paul also tells us " the time will come " that the people " will not endure sound doctrine, but shall be turned to fables " [novels] ; that "in the latter times some should depart from the faith," &c. " In the last days perilous times shall come," and proceeds to give a list of the flagrant sins of the last days. The whole tenor of Scripture gives the same picture. The difficulty however is not in those Scriptures cited from Num. and Hab. but in the theory that applies them this side the judgment, when the Lord has applied them beyond it.

There are many texts and parts of texts quoted to prove the world's conversion, which relate to the world to come, while others relied upon are not promises of God, but predictions concerning the rise and spread of the delusion which we denominate the Whitbyan millennium. We will notice two passages of the latter class.

"And many people shall go and say, Come ye, and let us go up to the mountain of the Lord, to the house of the God of Jacob ; and he will teach us of his ways, and we will walk in his paths : for out of Zion shall go forth the law, and the word of the Lord from Jerusalem. And he shall judge among the nations, and shall rebuke many people ; and they shall beat their swords into ploughshares, and their spears into pruning-hooks : nation shall not lift up sword against nation, neither shall they learn war any more. O house of Jacob, come ye, and let us walk in the light of the Lord." Isa. 2 : 3, 5. This passage has been used the last hundred years as a sort of key text to prove the universal conversion of mankind by the gospel, and especially the conversion and restoration of the Jews, and the end of all war.

But a careful examination of this text with its context discloses that the Lord's prophet saw that a great delusion would arise in the "last days," which would give great popularity to the mass of the church, so that civil governments would fraternize with and legislate for them. These governments are symbolized by "mountains" and "hills." And "the mountain [government] of the Lord's house shall be established in [united with] the tops of the mountains [heads of civil governments], and exalted above the hills [lesser governments], and all nations shall flow unto it."

Not every person, but "all nations;" "and *many people* shall go and say, Come ye, let us go up to the house of the God of Jacob."

These many people propose to be in union with the popular movements of the church. They turn their attention especially towards the Jews and Jerusalem. They adopt Judaism — the idea that the Lord has a special regard for the Jews, and will yet restore them as a nation to Mount Zion, convert them, and send forth his law and word from old Jerusalem, and thereby convert the heathen nations, and cause them to beat their swords and spears into farming utensils, and enjoy universal peace together with the house of Jacob.

But in the 6th verse, the same prophet declares that the house of Jacob are *forsaken* by the Lord, "because they be *soothsayers* [false teachers], like the Philistines, and they please themselves in the children of strangers." He next speaks of their abounding idolatry and hypocritical worship. "And the mean man boweth down, and the great man humbleth himself: *therefore forgive them not.*" Verse 9. The prophet next introduces the judgment, saying, —

"Enter into the rock, and hide thee in the dust, for fear of the Lord, and for the glory of his majesty, . . . when he ariseth to shake terribly the earth."

The prophet Micah is inspired to write out the same prophetic history of this great apostasy, and to give the word of the Lord concerning it. His language is nearly the same as Isaiah's. It is said to come to pass "in the last days." The same popular condition of the church fraternizing with the governments which make laws for her, and protect her. He declares that, —

"Many nations shall come, and say, Come, and let us go up to the mountain of the Lord, and to the house of the God of Jacob; and he will teach us of his ways, and we will walk in his paths: for the law shall go forth of Zion, and the word of the Lord from Jerusalem. And he shall judge among many people, and rebuke strong nations afar off [the heathen], and they shall beat their swords into ploughshares, and their spears into pruninghooks: nation shall not lift up sword against nation, neither shall they learn war any more." Micah 4 : 1, 3.

Here it is shown that these "*many* nations" teach Judaism; and the conversion of the heathen nations, as nations, and universal peace, and no more war. This is desirable indeed: but it is not what the Lord says; it is contrary to it. These many nations also say of the "nations afar off," "But they shall sit every man under his vine, and under his fig-tree; and none shall make them afraid: for the mouth of the Lord hath spoken it."

This claim which they make, that "the mouth of the Lord hath spoken it," is a false claim. This is the thing the Lord hath not spoken. "They have seen vanity and lying divination, saying, The Lord saith: and the Lord hath not sent them; and they have made others to hope that they would confirm the word. Have ye not seen a vain vision, and have ye not spoken a lying divination, whereas ye say, The Lord saith it, albeit I have not spoken?" Ezek. 13: 6, 7.

Here is a type in Israel of this false proclamation which Isaiah and Micah are shown would be made in "the last days," of universal peace. Paul also warns the church that when the dogma of "peace and safety" is promulgated, "sudden destruction cometh." 1 Thess. 5: 1, 2.

These "many nations" and "many people" tell us the mouth of the Lord hath spoken what they themselves utter. We do not find where the Lord has so spoken; but we *do find* that the Lord's prophets tell us what *many nations* and *many people* will say in the last days, and their claim that the Lord says it. Micah also shows the liberal views, of these false messengers. They declare their views, and say, "For all people will walk every one in the *name of his god*, and *we will walk in the name of the Lord our God*, forever and ever." Micah 4: 1–5.

They do not expect every one to worship the true God, but to be nominally Christian, in subjection to the Christian church, and at peace with it, but each worship his own god.

Here is a prediction of what is called "liberal Christianity" of our own times, which advocates free toleration of all religions : no matter what one believes ; no interference with any one's views ; be at peace with everything ; have universal peace, with purity, or without purity ; with Christ, or without Christ ; peace at the sacrifice of all principles —" UNIVERSAL BROTHERHOOD."

Dear reader, have you ever read the records of the first "World's Christian Alliance," held in London, England, in 1846, and the second, held in Frankfort-on-the-Main, in 1847? If not, please do so, and compare them with the prophecies above quoted.

While there were very many good men present, and many good things said and done, yet one of the leading themes was that specious fable, the Whitbyan "*new hypothesis.*" "Many nations" were represented by "many people" [all Christendom], who declared the world *must be converted*, and they discussed as to the best modes of bringing it about. They preached from Isa. 2 : 2, 4, and declared the Lord had spoken it.

They made free predictions that we were soon to see the world converted, and the dawn of the millennium [the temporal, Whitbyan millennium]. They predicted that we should have *no more wars*, and that the nations would convert their war implements into implements of husbandry and RAILROAD IRON.

How literal and striking a fulfilment of Isa. 2 : and Micah 4 : What mighty wars have occurred since ! What gigantic measures are now adopted for future wars !

We will now notice what the prophet says of the wisdom and knowledge of these "*many nations*" [whose "eyes are upon Zion," and who look for the restoration of the Jewish nation, while they despise THE DAUGHTER of Zion].

"BUT THEY KNOW NOT THE THOUGHTS OF THE LORD, NEITHER UNDERSTAND THEY HIS COUNSEL." Micah 4 : 11, 12.

They do not know the purposes and promises of the gospel, but "*trust in a vain vision.*

>"Some hazy eyes are looking for a time
>Of peace and righteousness in every clime;
>Some ears are listening for a universal chime
>Which shall precede Thy Coming — but the wail
>   Still rises to a gale,
>And Pity weeps, and Purity turns pale, —
>While moans of suffering, songs of revelry,
>Clangor of war, and shouts of ribaldry,
>Alone with their delightsome melody
>Answer these baseless hopes in bitter mockery.
>The darkness deepens : through the tenfold gloom
>Stream on earth's millions to the day of doom :
>While ever and anon the fearful cry
>Of human passion tells the struggle high :
>The last uplifting of the ocean swell ;
>The last proud effort of triumphant hell :
>   The last defiant roar
>Of all thy haters, who the light before
>Of Thine appearing, Lord! with horror sore
>Shall, overwhelmed, sink to rise no more!"
>
>   GUINNESS.

We will now quote a text which contains a millennial promise, and which is always quoted by the Whitbyan school to teach the conversion of the world.

"I will declare the decree : the Lord hath said unto me, Thou art my Son ; this day have I begotten thee. Ask of me, and I shall give thee the heathen for thine inheritance, and the uttermost parts of the earth for thy possession." Psa. 2 : 7, 8.

This text is resorted to as a sure and positive proof that all the heathen will be converted to Christ. But before adopting such an idea we do well to read the whole text : " Thou shalt break them with a rod of iron ; thou shalt dash them in pieces like a potter's vessel."

Who of us would choose such a conversion as this? The latter part of this text is seldom quoted by the class above mentioned ; but when urged upon them, it is claimed that the *rod of iron* is a symbol of the Holy Spirit, and the *dashing in pieces* of the heathen signifies their conversion to Christ.

This is not very ingenious, surely ; but it is in harmony with another from the same school, which explains Dan. 2 : 44 thus : The *stone* which SMOTE the image upon the feet signifies the influence of the gospel which shall convert the world. But the word declares it " shall break them to pieces, and no place shall be found for them."

These few specimens of quotations and interpretations, relied upon as proof for the millennium in this mortal state, give a fair sample of the misapplication which necessity drives them to make of the Scriptures to sustain this " new hypothesis." Let us beware of such necessity.

"According to the plan instituted by Origen," says Dr. A. Clark, " the sacred writings may be obliged to say *anything, everything,* or *nothing,* according to the *fancy,* peculiar *creed,* or *caprice* of the interpreter."

THIS PLAN of interpretation IS MANIFEST in every scheme which locates the millennium in the probationary state, whether future or past. Please observe this.

When put in the past, the "angel which came down from heaven with a key" is made to represent Charlemagne, or some other earthly ruler, "the devil" to mean pagan Rome, "the abyss" is papal mysticism, the "seal set upon" the devil is called papal baptism, the souls [persons] who "lived and reigned with Christ a thousand years" are made to represent those martyred by order of Charlemagne and others during the reign of papacy; or, by another class of this school, they may mean another set of agencies, or anything in general, and nothing in particular.

Was the reign of Christ *during* the reign of papacy? If so, we are thankful that it has ended. We desire no more of it. But as we are not ready to adopt the Augustine and Origen rules of interpretation, and their views of the reign of Christ and his saints during the rise and reign of papal tyranny and martyrdom, we shall look for another — not one in which millions of Christ's followers were slaughtered, and millions more driven to the wilderness and the dens and caves of the earth.

Such a reign was not Christ's reign, nor did *his followers pray for such a one.* In times of peace and prosperity, some of the members of the church, becoming flushed with success, and relieved for a moment from persecution and suffering, have dreamed of reigning with Christ already. Such was the case with some in the Corinthian church. They had begun to apostatize before they had learned "the first principles of the doctrine of Christ." Paul reproves them for it thus, by writing to them as "carnal, even as unto babes in Christ," and saying to them, "Now ye are full, now ye are rich, ye have reigned as kings without us; I would to God ye did reign, that we also might reign with you." 1 Cor. 4 : 8.

Paul desired the return of Christ to reign, when their toils and sufferings would end.

We shall conclude this part of our subject here, and proceed in another chapter to give what we understand to be the scriptural doctrine of the millennium, although it must be in a limited form. It is an extensive subject, involving much Scripture testimony. May the Lord guide us in our studies, instruct us in the truth, and bring us to reign with him forever.

CHAPTER XXI.

SUBJECT OF THE MILLENNIUM CONTINUED.

THE SCRIPTURAL MILLENNIUM.

In our last chapter we treated, at some length, upon the Whitbyan *hypothesis*, the Augustine and Origen rules of interpretation, and Roman Catholic efforts to destroy the scriptural doctrine of the personal reign of Christ, and the consequent evil results which have followed, in perverting the Protestant mind on the subject of the millennium.

We now propose to bring out and argue the main features of evidence the Bible affords concerning the character and chronological relation of the scriptural millennium to the gospel dispensation and the eternal reign of Christ, although in very limited space.

The character, locality, and introduction of Christ's reign with his saints, have been clearly shown in our chapters on "the kingdom of God," and "the resurrection of the dead," to which we refer the reader, as we wish not to reproduce them here.

"Blessed and holy is he that hath part in the first resurrection: on such the second death hath no power; but they shall be priests of God and of Christ, and shall reign with him a thousand years." Rev. 20 : 6.

This Scripture has several specially marked features, which form the chief characteristics of the real object of redemption and its results.

I. The Scripture pronounces a benediction on those who have "part in the first resurrection."

II. This class are exempt from "the second death," and therefore have eternal life.

III. They are made "kings and priests of God and of Christ," and shall reign with him.

IV. They are said to reign with Christ a thousand years.

If this text should be considered apart from its context, and without regard to any other Scripture account of the reign of Christ, it would suggest an end of that reign at the close of the thousand years; but no one who is capable of teaching, or of being taught, will interpret Scripture by such a rule. The Lord tells us by Peter, we should "know this first, that no prophecy of the Scripture is of any private interpretation,"—is not to be interpreted by itself, to teach doctrine independently of other Scriptures.

There is, however, one other text which is supposed by some not "instructed in the things concerning the kingdom of God" to teach that Christ's reign *closes up* at the judgment (1 Cor. 15 : 24), because they do not understand that it refers rather to Christ's closing up his work as Mediator and Redeemer, and transfer of a world once lost but now rescued, brought back, redeemed, to be loyal henceforth to God as a trophy of his sufferings and atonement, while he in turn, having rescued this rebellious world from the usurpations of

Satan, is exalted by the Father to reign over it with his subjects eternally. See page 301.

If any incline to think that Christ's reign ends with the thousand years, we wish them to turn and read carefully the following Scriptures: Psa. 89 : 27, 36. Dan. 2 : 44 ; 7 : 13, 14, 27. Luke 1 : 32, 33. 2 Pet. 1 : 11. Rev. 11 : 15, 18.

The above Scriptures give the united testimony that Christ's reign on earth, conjointly with his saints, once commenced, shall never end. They state that it shall be " as the days of heaven," shall be " an everlasting kingdom," " it shall stand forever," " and of his kingdom there shall be no end," &c.

These statements, with their connections, settle the point with all Bible men that Christ and his saints will enjoy a continued and eternal reign on the new earth.

Why, then, it is asked by some, is a thousand years — a millenary — mentioned in Rev. 20 : 6 as the term of the saints' reign?

We reply, it is not given to show a limit to the reign of the saints, but to show the order and chronological relation of the great and all-important events which are to transpire in closing up the work of redemption, the priority and dignity of the resurrection of the righteous, and their security during the overthrow of the nations of the wicked; the cleansing of the earth of the curse, and of the usurper and his subjects out of the dominion of Christ; and also to give the length of time between the two resurrections.

This thousand years is the JUDGMENT reign, and when the work of judgment closes, the reign continues.

We will now quote the passage in its connection, and examine its parts.

CHRIST'S SECOND ADVENT.

"And I saw an angel come down from heaven, having the key of the bottomless pit [abyss — *Emp. Diaglott, Am. Bible Union and Whiting's Versions*], and a great chain in his hand.

"And he laid hold on the dragon, that old serpent, which is the Devil, and Satan, and bound him a thousand years, and cast him into the bottomless pit [abyss], and shut him up, and set a seal upon him, that he should deceive the nations no more, till the thousand years should be fulfilled: and after that he must be loosed a little season.

"And I saw thrones, and they that sat upon them, and I saw the souls [THE PERSONS — *Emp. Diaglott, Whiting's, Stuart's, and other Versions*] of them that were beheaded for the witness of Jesus, and for the word of God, and which had not worshipped the beast, neither his image, neither had received his mark in their foreheads or in their hands: and they lived and reigned with Christ a thousand years [the thousand years — *Emp. Diaglott;* those thousand years — *Syriac*].

"But the rest of the dead lived not again until the thousand years were finished.

"This is the first resurrection.

"Blessed and holy is he that hath part in the first resurrection: on such the second death hath no power, but they shall be priests of God and of Christ, and shall reign with him a thousand years." Rev. 20:1–6.

This lays the subject fairly before us. The class who are said to LIVE AND REIGN had been DEAD. WHEN THEY LIVE AND REIGN, the *rest of the* DEAD *do not* live for a thousand years.

The apostle expressly states that this class who live and reign embraces those who come up in the first resurrection. For he adds, "this is the first resurrection." And other Scriptures show, beyond all cavil, what class of our race have the promise of the first resurrection. See Dan. 12 : 2 ; John 5 : 28 ; Phil. 3 : 11 ; 1 Thess. 4 : 17 ; and our remarks on the two resurrections, page 300.

The two resurrections have been clearly seen and discoursed upon by most careful Bible students ever since Christ's ministry, as the history of the church shows.

In the Old Testament, the priority and superiority of the resurrection of the righteous is clearly marked, but in the New Testament it is fully developed.

In Christ's instructions on making feasts, he promises that those who make them for "the poor, the maimed, the lame, the blind, . . . shall be recompensed at the resurrection of the just." Luke 14 : 14. If all were to be raised at one time, then his promise would have read "at the resurrection of the" *dead.*

Again, Christ declares, "All that are in the graves shall hear his voice, and shall come forth : (1) they that have done good unto the resurrection of life, (2) they that have done evil unto the resurrection of damnation." John 5 : 29.

Paul says, "I suffered the loss of all things," that, . . "if possible, I may attain to the RESURRECTION from among the DEAD" [*Emp. Diaglott, Whiting's, and other Versions* of Phil. 3 : 11].

In 1 Cor. 15 : 23, 24, and Luke 20 : 35, 36, the same doctrine is fully involved.

Having given the above preliminaries, we will now examine the statement of the apostle of what he saw on this subject. In Rev., 18th chapter, the Lord gives John a symbolical representation of the judgment of the *ecclesiastico-politico Roman harlot*, which is one of the last great events to take place in connection with the coming of the Lord. In chapter 19, another class of events is portrayed before the apostle in symbolic array: such as the glorious advent of the KING OF KINGS, the marriage of the Lamb, the judgment of the nations, and the execution of the beast and of the false prophet in "a lake of fire burning with brimstone." These judgments are national judgments, and judgments upon combined wicked agencies, and presented by symbols appropriate to them.

But there were other classes of events to transpire, and other characteristics to be developed, during the personal judgment of mankind and of the devil, and thus the scenes of chapters 20th, 21st, and 22d are given, to present the various classes of these events.

The angel seen descending from heaven (Rev. 20 : 1) is Christ; for he is the personage whose work it is to bind and also to destroy the devil. It is his prerogative, also, to raise the dead. He is denominated an angel in several Scriptures: In Jude 9, we read of "Michael the archangel." Archangel signifies "chief angel;" Michael means "one like God;" Christ is chief among the angels. The Father saith, "And let all the angels of God worship him."

Again we read, "And at that time shall MICHAEL stand up [reign], the GREAT PRINCE which standeth for the children of thy people. . . . and at that time thy people shall be delivered, every one that shall be found written in the book. And many of them that sleep in the dust of the earth shall awake." Dan. 12 : 1–3.

"For the Lord himself shall descend from heaven with a shout, with the voice of the ARCHANGEL, and with the trump of God, and the dead in Christ shall rise first." 1 Thess. 4 : 16, 18.

"Behold, I show you a mystery. We shall not all sleep, but we shall all be changed, in a moment, in the twinkling of an eye, at the last trump." 1 Cor. 15 : 51.

The above are sufficient to show that Christ is called an angel, and that he raises the dead saints at his coming.

This angel is said to have the key of the abyss, and a great chain in his hand.

A key is a symbol of power, authority, and is so used in various cases. "The keys of the kingdom of heaven"—Matt. 16 : 19—represent power to bind or loose. "Woe unto you, lawyers! ye have taken away the key of knowledge : ye entered not in yourselves, and them that were entering in ye hindered." Luke 11 : 52. This represents power to open and shut. A chain is also used in Scripture to denote confinement. See 2 Pet. 2 : 4. Ezek. 7 : 23.

But it has been suggested that this angel signifies a class of bad agencies, because the term *angel* is so used in Rev. 9, and the language is said to be similar. Let us look at this idea. "I saw a star FALL from heaven unto the earth: and *to him was given the key* of the [abyss] bottomless pit." . . . "And they had a king over them, which is the *angel* of the bottomless pit."

In the above symbols, we have an *angel* and a *star*, used to denote a bad agent. Please notice that he was seen to FALL from heaven to earth, representing *apostasy*. *Also, to him was given* the key — power to open the abyss — and to chastise a class of apostates with greater darkness. In chapter 20, the angel COMES DOWN from heaven, does not *fall*. He has authority in hand to bind the devil, and to open the abyss, and cast him in, and shut him up, and set a seal upon him a thousand years. Rather humane and extensive power for a bad angel! Who would delegate a class of bad agents with power to bind the devil and shut him up? Would not such a class of agents be likely to abuse their power, and do worse than the devil? Ah, He was a dragon.

Read Rev. 1 : 1, 13-18. Here we learn that Christ is represented by AN ANGEL, and as having authority over "death and him that had the power of death, that is, the devil." "I am he that liveth, and was dead; and behold, I am alive forevermore, Amen; and have the keys of [hades] hell and of death." This seems sufficient to settle the question as to who has conquered all his foes, and obtained the power to destroy the devil, and who holds "the key of the abyss."

"These things saith he that is holy, he that is true, he that hath the key of David, he that openeth, and no man shutteth; and shutteth, and no man openeth." Rev. 3 : 7.

"THE ABYSS." This is now admitted to be the most proper version. What does it represent?

It is defined thus: "A bottomless gulf, used also for a deep mass of waters, also for an immense cavern in the earth; that which is immeasurable, that in which any thing is lost."— *Webster.*

Let us remember that it is recorded of Christ (Matt. 28 : 18), "All power is given unto me in heaven and in earth." Also, that when the seventh angel sounds, thanks are given to Christ, " because thou hast taken to thee thy great power, and hast reigned." Rev. 11 : 17. When the time arrives for Christ to exercise his great power, all his enemies will be at his disposal, and the unfathomable abyss and unlimited time under his control.

THE DEVIL BOUND.

"And he laid hold on the dragon, that old serpent, which is the Devil, and Satan, and bound him a thousand years, and cast him into the abyss, and shut him up, and set a seal upon him, that he should deceive the nations no more, till the thousand years should be fulfilled; and after that he must be loosed for a little season." Verse 3.

The dragon of this text is a symbol of the devil. The inspired penman so explains it, or rather he emphatically states that he "is the DEVIL, AND SATAN." He who attempts to give any other explanation than the Holy Spirit has given must bear the responsibility, and answer for it. But since some pious persons have been misguided by the false rules of interpretation of Origen and Augustine, by which symbols may be interpreted to represent anything which agrees with one's opinions in theology, we will be more specific.

It has been taught that because the dragon of Rev. 12:9 represents pagan Rome [which was named after its father, the devil], it must represent the same in Rev. 20th.

But this does not prove it. One might as correctly claim that because the lion once symbolized the Chaldean empire, and the eagle once symbolized the church, therefore they do wherever mentioned in the Scriptures. But both these are used to symbolize other agencies.

Let the Lord explain his own symbols.

When he would impress upon the minds of the people that a terrible government, cruel and destructive to the church, would arise, he symbolizes it by one of the most cruel and destructive of beasts — "a great red dragon." Then, in giving an account of the work and history of that government, he says, "And the great dragon was cast out, that old serpent, *called the devil, and Satan*, that deceiveth the whole world."

Please notice, it is specifically stated to be "the great dragon," and then added, "*called* the devil, and Satan." And why thus called, or named? We reply, because the government symbolized by the "dragon" was a combination of robbers, thieves, liars, pirates, murderers, and other base criminals, concentrated at Rome, escaped from the executioners of law, from all parts of the world where they had committed their former evil deeds, and had now organized, conquered, the world, and become the idolatrous Roman empire — a true child of the devil. He was and is a *murderer* and *a liar from the beginning*. There is great propriety in calling a child by his father's name. None will deny this. It is added in Rev. 12:12,

"Woe to the inhabiters of the earth and of the sea, for the devil is come down unto you, having great wrath," &c. This, of course, represents the woe and trouble which came upon the world by the devil, through pagan Rome, his namesake.

The terms, the serpent, Satan, dragon, and the devil, are used interchangeably in Revelation, as applying to the devil, the real actor, or to the agents by which he does his work. He works through his agents, and they take his name, so also he is called by their names.

When the Lord would reveal to his church the imprisonment and finally the destruction of the devil, the father of Rome and of all evil, he uses the same symbol — the dragon — to impress upon us the terrible and murderous character of the devil, because a full development of his attributes had been seen in the history of that child — pagan Rome.

Then, lest we misunderstand, he explains, that old serpent, WHICH IS THE DEVIL, AND SATAN. Yes, the devil is to be confined in the abyss, the great deep, the unfathomable pit, and Christ is to execute the work by his almighty power. The nature and locality of the abyss, and the manner of the confinement, are not revealed, therefore not for us to speculate upon. They are incomprehensible subjects. We are thankful for the *facts which are revealed.*

When a person is deprived of all the members of his family, of all his associates, and all means of action in or upon society, he finds himself confined to very narrow limits. His privileges and fortunes are gone; his course of action ceased; but add to this, consignment to the abyss, and confinement is complete.

This is to be the condition of the devil in person and influence. He is a person, as clearly described such as any being mentioned in the Bible.

Those who reject God's record of him must meet the consequences of so doing.

When Christ comes the second time, all the race of man will be removed from the associations and conflicts of the devil,— the righteous eternally, and the wicked for a thousand years.

For, at the advent of Christ, all the righteous will be made immortal, and no longer be subjected to the annoyances and temptations of the devil.

At that time Christ leaves the mediatorial office and throne, ceases to offer his blood for the remission of sins, removes his people from among the wicked, withdraws the influence of the Holy Spirit from this world.

This will leave the wicked to act out, unrestrained, all the fruits of their depravity upon each other in the war of universal slaughter, as predicted in Jer. 25: 15–37; Joel 3: 9, 15; Dan. 12: 1, 2; Rev. 16: 14, 16; 19: 15, 19. This will be "the battle of the great day of God Almighty." The calamities of war, the rain of hail, fire, and brimstone; the pestilence, famine, lamentation, and anguish, will produce the death of all the wicked then on the earth. [For all the wicked must die the Adamic death under sentence of that law Adam violated, before they can be executed for their own sins by dying the second death.] This will produce the desolation predicted.

"Behold, the Lord maketh the earth empty, and maketh it waste, and turneth it upside down, and scattereth abroad the inhabitants thereof." Isa 24 : 1. "I beheld the earth, and lo, it was without form and void: and the heavens, and they had no light. I beheld the mountains, and lo, they trembled, and all the hills moved lightly. I beheld, and lo, there was no man, and all the birds of the heavens were fled," &c. Jer. 4 : 23–28.

"I will consume man and beast; I will consume the fowls of the heaven, and the fishes of the sea, and the stumbling-blocks with the wicked." Zeph. 1 : 3.

"Thus saith the Lord, My determination is to gather the nations, that I may assemble the kingdoms, to pour upon them mine indignation, even all my fierce anger: for all the earth shall be devoured with the fire of my jealousy." Zeph. 3 : 8. It should be noticed that the above Scriptures treat of *national* and *not personal* judgment. They therefore involve the first and not "the second death" of the wicked.

But in connection with these passages just quoted, we find expressions which show that some will escape the general doom, such as, "and few men left," "yet will I not make a full end," &c. A careful examination of their contexts will show that those who escape, and are left of the nations, are the redeemed of the Lord. For it is said of them, "They shall lift up their voice, they shall sing for the majesty of the Lord." Isa 24 : 14.

"For then will I turn to the people a pure language, that they may all call upon the name of the Lord, to serve him with one consent." Zeph. 3 : 9.

These who are left, and sing, and speak a pure language, serving the Lord with one consent, must be the resurrected and changed saints, who have made Christ their Rock, and Shield, and sure Hiding-place. The Revelator sees them, having gained the victory over death, exalted to reign with Christ.

THRONES OF JUDGMENT.

"And I saw thrones, and they sat upon them, and judgment was given unto them." These are the thrones of judgment, upon which the apostles of the Lamb shall sit.

There were thrones of judgment in the temple service at Old Jerusalem, and there will be in New Jerusalem also.

"Jerusalem is builded as a city that is compact together, whither the tribes go up, the tribes of the Lord, unto the testimony of Israel, to give thanks unto the name of the Lord. For there are set thrones of judgment, the thrones of the house of David." Psa. 122 : 3, 5.

"And Jesus said unto them [his apostles], Verily, I say unto you, That ye which have followed me in the regeneration [the renovation — *Campbell*, *Emp. Diaglott*, *and others*], when the Son of Man shall sit on the throne of his glory, ye also shall sit upon twelve thrones, judging the twelve tribes of Israel." Matt. 19 : 28.

"Ye are they which have continued with me in my temptation; and I appoint unto you a kingdom, as my Father hath appointed unto me; that ye may eat and drink at my table in my kingdom, and sit on twelve thrones judging the twelve tribes of Israel." Luke 22 : 28, 30.

And Paul teaches that they shall judge angels. "Know ye not that we shall judge angels? how much more things that pertain to this life?" 1 Cor. 6:3. This last, of course, relates to the fallen angels, "reserved unto judgment." 2 Pet. 2:4.

THE FIRST RESURRECTION.

"And I saw the souls [persons] of them that were beheaded for the witness of Jesus, and for the word of God, and which had not worshipped the beast, neither his image, neither had received his mark upon their foreheads, or in their hands; and they lived and reigned with Christ a thousand years."

That the term PERSONS, instead of "souls," in the above text, is the proper rendering, seems now settled by most modern scholars and versions. In the translations of WHITING, STUART, and others, they render it PERSONS. In the EMPHATIC DIAGLOTT, it is rendered persons.

On this point, Professor Stuart remarks, —

"There would seem to remain, therefore, only one meaning which can consistently be given to "THEY LIVED," viz., that they [the martyrs who renounced the beast] are now restored to life, viz., such life as implies the revivification of the body. Not to a union of the soul with a gross, material body, indeed, but with such a one as the saints in general will have at the final resurrection — a spiritual body. 1 Cor. 15:44. In no other way can this resurrection be ranked as *correlate* with the second resurrection named in the sequel." Once more he remarks: "I do not see how, on the ground of exegesis, we can fairly avoid the conclusion that John has taught in the passage before us that there will be a resurrection of the martyr-saints at the commencement of the period after Satan shall have been shut up in the dungeon of the great abyss."

No other just conclusion can be arrived at; and when the martyred saints rise, all the saints rise with them. It is "Christ the first fruits; afterward THEY THAT ARE CHRIST'S at his coming." When he comes, it is "with the voice of the archangel, and with the trump of God; and THE DEAD in Christ shall rise first."

This passage must include all the church of God, who have the promise of the resurrection to eternal life. When Christ was seen by the apostle to come down and bind the devil, and dispossess the earth of its inhabitants, it must be his second advent, and "his reward is with him, and his work before him;" "when the Son of Man shall come in his glory, and all the holy angels with him, then shall he sit upon the throne of his glory. . . . Then shall the King say unto them on his right hand, Come, ye blessed of my Father, inherit the kingdom prepared for you from the foundation of the world." Matt. 25: 31, 34.

The Scriptures are full in descriptions of the events which then occur. As we have already quoted, Christ first raises his dead saints, changes his living ones, and takes them up from the earth into what the prophet Isaiah calls "thy chambers, for a little moment, until the indignation be overpast." Isa. 26: 20. Also described in Rev. 15: 2, as "a sea of glass mingled with fire, and them that had gotten the victory over the beast, and over his image, and over his mark, and over the number of his name, stand on the sea of glass, having the harps of God, and they sing the song of Moses the servant of God, and the song of the Lamb, saying, Great and marvellous are thy works, Lord God Almighty; just and true are thy ways, thou King of saints. Who shall not fear thee, O Lord, and glorify thy name? for thou only art holy: for all nations shall come and worship before thee; for thy judgments are made manifest."

Thus the saints stand above and behold the judgments of God, declaring that all nations shall come and worship before the Lord, submit to his judgments, and acknowledge his right to reign, while they shall perish; as many passages declare they must do when he comes whose right it is to reign.

"Fear, and the pit, and the snare, are upon thee, O inhabitant of the earth. And it shall come to pass that he who fleeth from the noise of the fear shall fall into the pit; and he that cometh up out of the midst of the pit shall be taken in the snare; for the windows from on high are open, and the foundations of the earth do shake.

"The earth is utterly broken down, the earth is clean dissolved, the earth is moved exceedingly. The earth shall reel to and fro like a drunkard, and shall be removed like a cottage, and the transgression thereof shall be heavy upon it, and it shall fall and not rise again."

"And it shall come to pass in that day that the Lord shall punish the host of the high ones that are on high, and the kings of the earth upon the earth, and they shall be gathered together, as prisoners are gathered in the pit, and shall be shut up in the prison, and after many days shall they be visited."

"Then the moon shall be confounded, and the sun ashamed, when the Lord of Hosts shall reign in Mount Zion, and in Jerusalem, and before his ancients gloriously." Isa. 24 : 17–23.

How perfectly the above accords with our subject in Rev. 20 : 1–6! "And they lived and reigned with Christ a thousand years. But the rest of the dead lived not again until the thousand years were finished. This is the first resurrection."

How clear is the light of truth! "And after many days shall they be visited." "There shall be weeping and gnashing of teeth when ye shall see Abraham, and Isaac, and Jacob, and all the prophets, in the kingdom of God, and you yourselves thrust out." Luke 13 : 28.

"Like sheep they [the wicked] are laid in the grave: death shall feed on them; and the upright shall have dominion over them in the morning; and their beauty shall consume in the grave from their dwelling. But God will redeem my soul from the power of the grave: for he shall receive me." Psa. 49 : 14, 15.

And again, the Psalmist speaks of the condition of the wicked at the beginning and closing of the millennium. "Consume them in wrath, consume them, that they may not be [in the thousand years rest day] : and let them know that God ruleth in Jacob unto the ends of the earth. And at evening let them return, and let them make a noise like a dog, and go round about the city. Let them wander up and down for meat, and grudge if they be not satisfied. But I will sing of thy power; yea, I will sing aloud of thy mercy in the morning." Psa. 59 : 13–16.

Let us now compare the millennium with the subject called "the rest that remains for the people of God," and we shall find it in harmony

"THERE REMAINETH A REST."

"And on the seventh day God ended his work which he had made: and he rested on the seventh day from all his work which he had made. And God blessed the seventh day, and sanctified it; because that in it he had rested from all his work which God had created and made." Gen. 2 : 2, 3.

The above passage has been generally understood by the church, both in the Jewish and Christian dispensations, to give a record of God's rest day as a type of the seventh millenary, and that each day of the creation week was a type of a thousand years; that it signified the world was to continue six thousand years in its mortal probation state, and the seventh thousand be a rest in an immortal state, which they denominated "the Sabbatical Millennium of Rest."

This view is well sustained by Scripture testimony. Paul refers to this rest thus: —

"To whom sware he that they should not enter into his rest, but to them that believed not?... Let us therefore fear, lest a promise being left us of entering into his rest, any of you should seem to come short of it.... For he spake in a certain place of the seventh day on this wise, And God did rest the seventh day from all his works. And in this place again: If they shall enter into my rest. . . . For if Jesus [Joshua] had given them rest, then would he not afterward have spoken of another day. There remaineth therefore a rest [keeping of a Sabbath, *margin*] to the people of God." Heb. 4 : 1, 4, 5, 8, 9.

The prophet Isaiah tells us whose rest this is. "And in that day there shall be a root of Jesse, which shall stand for an ensign of the people; to it shall the Gentiles seek: and his rest shall be glorious." [Heb., *glory*.] Isa. 11 : 10. This evidently refers to the thousand years' reign, and end of the work of mediation. Again, we learn by another prophecy relating to the closing up of probationary time: "For so the Lord said unto me, I will take my rest, and I will consider in my dwelling-place like a clear heat upon herbs, and like a cloud of dew in the heat of harvest." Isa. 18 : 4. Yes. The Lord will rest, and give rest to his people. A rest remains to them — a thousand years' Sabbath. It will be glorious!

"Let us labor, therefore, to enter into that rest. Paul speaks to his persecuted Thessalonian brethren, and says, "And to you, who are troubled, rest with us, when the Lord Jesus shall be revealed from heaven with his mighty angels, in flaming fire taking vengeance on them that know not God," &c. 2 Thess. 1 : 7.

JEWISH AND CHRISTIAN COMMENTS.

"I think that after six thousand years the world shall be destroyed, upon one certain day, or one hour; that the arches of heaven shall make a stand as immovable; that there will be no more generation or corruption; and that all things by the resurrection shall be renovated, and return to a better state." — *R. Menasse, a Jewish rabbi.*

The opinion of the ancient Jews may be gathered from the statement of one of their rabbins, who said, "The world endures six thousand years, and in the thousand or millennium that follows, the enemies of God would be destroyed."— *Bishop Russell, Professor Ecclesiastical History.*

"The divine institution of a sabbatical or seventh year's solemnity among the Jews has a plain typical reference to the seventh chiliad, or millenary of the world, according to the well-known tradition among the Jewish doctors, adopted by many in every age of the Christian church, that this world will attain to its limit at the end of six thousand years." — *Mede.*

"Let philosophers know, who number thousands of years, ages since the beginning of the world, that the sixth thousand years is not yet concluded or ended. But that number being fulfilled, of necessity there must be an end, and the state of human things must be transformed into that which is better."— *Lactantius, Book of Divine Inst., A. D.* 310.

Among the thousands of testimonies of faith and hope of this glorious millennial rest, we quote a few lines from the poetic musings of Charles Wesley, which have been sung by the pious, hoping ones for more than a hundred years. Why not yet?

> "Come, then, our heavenly Friend,
> Sorrow and death to end;
> Pure millennium joy to give.
> Now appear on earth again,
> Now thy people saved receive,
> Now begin thy glorious reign."
>
> *Wesley's Hymns,* p. 362

"Resolved to toil and suffer on,
Till thou the second time appear,
Ascend thy bright millennial throne,
And reign the king of glory here." —*Ib.* p. 418.

"Mightier joys ordained to know,
When thou com'st to reign below,
We shall at thy side sit down,
Partners of thy great white throne,
Kings a thousand years with thee,
Kings through all eternity." —*Ib.* p. 425.

"Blessed and holy is he that hath part in the first resurrection: on such the second death hath no power, but they shall be priests of God and of Christ, and shall reign with him a thousand years."

What a privilege is here promised the faithful servants of the Lord! What a benediction pronounced upon the redeemed of our God, in contrast with the calamity of the wicked who have lived out their day of probation, in disregard of the offers of mercy, and in neglect of the claims of God; boasting in their own wisdom and righteousness, and refusing to submit themselves unto the righteousness of God!

The bride of Christ has been long waiting, she has passed through many severe conflicts, and encountered many storms of malice, envy, and bitter hatred from the enemy. She has "waited for the Lord more than they that watch for the morning." The Lord's people have been in great derision among the wicked; but they have studied and believed the promises of the return of their king. They have labored in sadness and care, in sickness and affliction, and gone down to the dark chambers of death, with anxious looking and waiting for the day of rest.

The omens of the return of their glorious Lord cheers the heart with solemn awe and gladness, seeming like the majestic tread of the King of kings upon the golden pavement of the New Jerusalem, in eager haste to come down to earth for the emancipation of his bride, the vindication of his cause, and the taking possession of his rightful throne, to "rule in the midst of his enemies."

In preparing the earth for the abode of the immortal saints, and the rest that remains, great changes are to take place. As we have before stated and proved, the righteous are to be raised, and with those changed, caught up to meet the Lord in the air, and enter upon the sea of glass, probably into the New Jerusalem; while the wicked all die the Adamic death, though under national judgment.

How long the battle of Armageddon will continue (Rev. 16: 14, 16), and the last generation of the wicked live, we are not informed.

Those who apply Ezekiel, 39th and 40th chapters, and Zechariah 14th to this time, think they get a clew to it, but we make no such application of those prophecies to the day of the Lord. That there will be no generation of the human species after the second advent of Christ and change of his people is fully evident from the nature of the case and the scope of Scripture doctrine relating to the events to transpire then and subsequently.

The earth and the firmament are to be changed and brought back to their Edenic state, or to that state of perfect development to which it would have arrived at the close of the six thousand years' culture of Adam and his race, had he not sinned.

This change is to be wrought by the action of fire, as the Scriptures fully show. There are many Scriptures in which we are taught that the Lord will use fire to refashion the heavens and the earth, and to cleanse it of the curse, and the works of man: also to consume the wicked after their resurrection from death.

Some of these passages, where we do not doubt literal fire is the agent mentioned, are not so explicit as to the time and order, to be easily located, although there is clear evidence as to the work revealed by them. Many of the details of events during and subsequent to the millennium are not revealed.

ATTENDED BY FIRE.

"Our God shall come, and shall not keep silence: a fire shall devour before him, and it shall be very tempestuous round about him. He shall call to the heavens from above, and to the earth that he may judge his people." Psa. 50: 3, 4.

"A fire goeth before him, and burneth up his enemies round about. His lightnings enlightened the world: the earth saw and trembled. The hills melted like wax at the presence of the Lord, at the presence of the Lord of the whole earth." Psa. 97: 3, 5.

"His throne was like the fiery flame, and his wheels as burning fire. A fiery stream issued and came forth from before him." Dan. 7: 9, 10.

"Before him went the pestilence, and burning coals

went forth at his feet. He stood, and measured the earth: he beheld, and drove asunder the nations." Hab. 3: 5, 6.

"But the heavens and the earth which are now, ... are kept in store, reserved unto fire against the day of judgment and perdition of ungodly men.... But the day of the Lord will come as a thief in the night; in the which the heavens shall pass away with a great noise, and the elements shall melt with fervent heat, the earth also, and the works that are therein shall be burned up. Nevertheless we, according to his promise, look for new heavens and a new earth, wherein dwelleth righteousness." 2 Pet. 3: 7, 10, 13.

The above passages relate to the second advent of Christ, and to events to occur during the day of the Lord — the day of judgment. They speak of the element of fire as an agent of destruction and of purification: there are many other statements relating to the events of the day of the Lord, in passages where fire is stated to be in use for the purpose of cleansing the earth, and consuming the wicked.

In many of these passages, as in prophecies relating to other parts of the work of the Lord, there is an announcement made, that in or at the coming of Christ, such and such events will occur, while the time occupied, and the order of the events, are not mentioned. There is much prophecy given in this manner relating to the gospel dispensation, which would appear to bring the events of the whole dispensation into a year or a day; and to bring the judgment and reign of Christ, and destruction of the wicked, at, or immediately after, his first advent; as in Isa. 9 : 5, 7 ; 11 : 1–7 ; 61 : 2. These prophecies span at least eighteen hundred years.

In other prophecies the order and the time of these events are stated ; showing us that we need to compare Scripture with Scripture to get the mind of the Spirit. The same principle is seen in those passages which relate to the events of the day of the Lord. In Matt. 3 : 12, John refers to Christ, and his work of redemption, thus : " Whose fan is in his hand, and he will thoroughly purge his floor, and gather his wheat into the garner ; but he will burn up the chaff with unquenchable fire."

In the above text no one would get the idea that there was to be eighteen hundred years' probation before the harvest or burning.

In Matt., 13th chapter, we have Christ's explanation of his parable of " the wheat and the tares," in which he says, " So shall it be in the end of this world. The Son of man shall send forth his angels, and they shall gather out of his kingdom all things that offend, and them which do iniquity, and shall cast them into a furnace of fire : there shall be wailing and gnashing of teeth. Then shall the righteous shine forth as the sun, in the kingdom of their Father."

But in Matt. 25 : 31, 41, where the judgment scene is again described, it is first stated that " the king shall say unto them on his right hand, Come, ye blessed of my Father, inherit the kingdom prepared for you from the foundation of the world." . . . "Then shall he say also unto them on his left hand, Depart from me, ye cursed, into everlasting fire, prepared for the devil and his angels."

All intelligent readers can see that no attention is given

to state the time occupied, or order of the events in these passages, for the events are put in *one* order in one text and in an entire *opposite* order in another.

But there are other Scriptures which *do* give *both time and order*, though they do not explain all the items.

THE WICKED RAISED — SATAN LOOSED.

The Spirit carefully states, by John, that those who lived and reigned with Christ a thousand years were embraced in the first resurrection, adding, "This is the first resurrection."

In regard to the fifth verse, it is said, by eminent scholars who have translated the Scriptures, that the first part of the verse is not in the Vatican MS.; they therefore call it an interpolation. MURDOCK omits it in his SYRIAC VERSION. WILSON inserts it in his EMPHATIC DIAGLOTT, considering it an oversight of the transcriber of the Vatican MS.

"But the rest of the dead lived not again until the thousand years were finished," is the disputed clause. Whether this be genuine or an interpolation, it does not change the sense of the subject involved; for the statements concerning the class who *do* live and reign, that they are "blessed and holy," are exempt from "the second death," are "priests of God and of Christ," with the distinct declaration that "this is the first resurrection," fully involves the idea that all others of mankind must be included in the second resurrection and in "the second death."

It is objected that in Rev. 20 no mention is made of the resurrection of the wicked. True, the term is not applied, yet it is as fully involved as though it were stated. They are become an inferior class by dying in their sins. They are not worthy of "THE RESURRECTION," therefore they are not to come forth as liberated captives to the enjoyment of "the glorious liberty of the children of God," but as prisoners released from the fetters of the prison, to be brought forth to final execution, justified, indeed, from Adamic law, to live again to receive the wages of their own sin. There is no shout of victory, no song of redemption, no acclamation of triumph for this class; they come forth, but under condemnation, under sentence. They have been "reserved to the day of destruction; they shall be brought forth to the day of wrath." Job 21:30.

"The Lord knoweth how to deliver the godly out of temptation, and to reserve the unjust unto the day of judgment, to be punished." 2 Pet. 2:9.

There is no cause for wonder why John makes no mention in this scene of the *act* of resurrection, when the wicked come forth, for there is no sounding of a jubal trump, no shaking of earth and rending of tombs, no throes of nature to deliver up her sacred trust, as in the case of the righteous. But they come forth from earth at the order of the Judge, to receive the reward of unrighteousness.

"And when the thousand years are expired, Satan shall be loosed out of his prison, and shall go out to deceive the nations which are in the four quarters of the earth, Gog and Magog, to gather them together to battle: the number of whom is as the sand of the sea."

"To deceive the *nations*," — this term, in the original,

ις εθνη, and does not necessarily imply organized political bodies under civil rulers, as in this world; it is defined by Robinson to be "a multitude, people, race, belonging and living together." Such will be the wicked when raised: they form one common mass of rebels, belonging to one family.

Satan, being loosed from his prison, finds himself surrounded by his old associates and dupes — his children, whom he had deceived and led in all their evil ways, and through whom he had battled against Christ and his church for six thousand years: though having but one generation at a time, he has done much to establish his claim of owning "all the kingdoms of the world."

He has "ruled in the hearts of the children of disobedience," and by them he has slain millions of God's people, routed and driven multitudes of them from their homes, to take refuge "in deserts, and in mountains, and in dens and caves of the earth:" and now he finds all the generations of his family alive again. They have "returned," and a fitting metaphor is used by the apostle to represent them.

"GOG AND MAGOG."

These names are used in Scripture, metaphorically, to represent the chief nations of the earth, as in Ezek. 38. On examination, they are found to be the chief of the descendants of Noah, through Ham and Japheth, while God's people descended through Shem.

These chiefs — descendants of Gog and Magog — took the control of affairs among men, "and by these were the nations divided in the earth after the flood."

Examine Gen. 10th chapter. Xenophon, Pliny, Cicero, Strabo, Josephus, Wolf, Bochart, and the maps of Bagster's Polyglott Bible, furnish much valuable information on the history and geographical localities and character of Gog and Magog's descendants. It is proper, therefore, that the names of these chiefs should stand by metaphor as representing the nations which sprang from them, and which followed their examples, seeking to control the world. Having loved this evil world, they have combined their forces under Satan, constructed and managed governments after their own evil principles, which in Scripture are symbolized by "the wild beast," "the dragon," "the serpent;" and "vine of the earth," "clusters of the vine of the earth," &c., &c.

They have always claimed the earth, and the right to rule it, but were obliged to die; they are all alive again, the earth has greatly changed — been renewed; there, too, appears the holy city, New Jerusalem, the metropolis of the whole earth. Will they covet the new earth, redeemed and beautiful? Will they envy the saints who possess this renewed and fair abode, and seek to dislodge them, to get the control of it for themselves?

This was the course pursued by Satan with Adam and Eve in Eden; and this, the record shows, he and his children will seek to do in the new earth.

He now has every generation "returned" for a time to his association, and with whom to make his last attack upon the church of God, that their overthrow may be the more signal, and the final victory more distinguished. "The number of them is as the sand of the sea." Satan's plan is, to institute a reorganization of his army, declare war against the citizens of the new world, overcome their leader, whose heel he had once bruised, and become master of the new earth by conquest, as he did of the first by flattery.

And how well fitted are the resurrected wicked to be again deceived by their old master — the devil ! As men individually, as clans, as associated in mobs, as trained armies and navies, as nations of depraved, self-willed, unrestrained men, they had fought to carry out their selfish and wicked designs with and without weapons of warfare, to maintain their own wills and please the devil, who had led them captive at his will.

They had died in the same spirit of war, ill will, selfishness, hating God and his people; they come up from the grave in the same spirit — in moral darkness and pollution. They are still deceived. Satan rallies them in a grand army, such in numbers as no general ever led on in war. It is not an *armed* force, however; they have no weapons: it is a mob, and such a mob! Think of it, dear reader. Will you be with them, and share their fate? The design seems to culminate in the plot to besiege the holy city. It is a last and desperate attempt of the devil and his followers: it proves a fatal one to them. There is no battle fought. Christ had fought the decisive battle on the cross, and bore off the plan of victory from "Joseph's new tomb."

They had often rallied, and skirmished, and brutally slain the followers of Christ, and the time of battles had passed; it closed up with the contest of nations among themselves, under the management of demons, a thousand years before, called " the battle of that great day of

God Almighty." Rev. 16 : 14, 16. This was at the beginning of that great day of God : they destroyed each other then ; they *are destroyed* now before -the battle begins.

He who saith, "I am God, and there is none like me ; declaring the end from the beginning, and from ancient times the things that are not yet done, saying, My counsel shall stand, and I will do all my pleasure " (Isa. 46 : 9, 10), never slumbers nor sleeps. The time has come to purge out sin, and remove forever its agents.

"And they went up on the breadth of the earth, and compassed the camp of the saints about, and the beloved city : and fire came down from God out of heaven, and devoured them."

The Lord breathes upon this mighty host of ruined, condemned rebels a storm of fire and brimstone, which envelopes them : they sink, and seethe, and " wail, and gnash their teeth," and melt away. "Our God is a consuming fire," " and with the breath of his lips shall he slay the wicked." Isa. 11 : 4.

"For tophet is ordained of old ; yea, for the king it is prepared ; he hath made it deep and large : the pile thereof is fire and much wood ; the breath of the Lord, like a stream of brimstone, doth kindle it." Isa. 30 : 33.

"For the king it is PREPARED ; " and Christ declares, in Matt. 25 : 41, that the subjects must perish in the place prepared for their king. "Depart from me, ye cursed, into everlasting fire, PREPARED for the devil and his angels."

Thus will the Lord of hosts bring to nought every

evil purpose, work, and agent, when he utterly consumes all the workers of iniquity. "They shall consume; into smoke shall they consume away." Psa. 37 : 20.

"For behold the day cometh, that shall burn as an oven; and all the proud, yea, and all that do wickedly, shall be stubble: and the day that cometh shall burn them up, saith the Lord of hosts, that it shall leave them neither root nor branch." Mal. 4 : 1.

Yes, He shall reign, "whose fan is in his hand, and he will thoroughly purge his floor, and gather his wheat into the garner, but he will burn up the chaff with unquenchable fire." Matt. 3 : 12.

This "fire," "breath of the Lord," "burning as an oven," "everlasting fire," "unquenchable fire," &c., is also called "the lake of fire burning with brimstone," in which all the wicked shall have their part, as stated in Rev. 21 : 8.

When the wicked are raised from their graves to meet their final doom, Christ will be revealed to all his enemies: the most of them have never seen him before.

When he comes to take possession of his kingdom and dominion, only the generation then living will see him; but it is said, "and every eye shall see him, . . . and all kindreds of the earth shall wail because of him." Rev. 1 : 7.

Paul also comforts the persecuted with the prospect of resting "when the Lord Jesus shall be revealed from heaven with his mighty angels, in flaming fire taking vengeance on them that know not God, and obey not the gospel of our Lord Jesus Christ; who shall be punished with everlasting destruction from the presence of the

Lord, and from the glory of his power." 2 Thess. 1: 7, 9.

This is said to be " when he shall come to be glorified in his saints, and to be admired by all them that believe in that day." Yes, it is in the time when the Lord exercises his great power, and is revealed to all his enemies to destroy them, which must be at the end of the thousand years, and is the closing act towards the children of the wicked one. It is in the day of the Lord.

But it is objected by some that if the day of the Lord is a thousand years, during which the world is to be renewed, and each class of mankind rewarded, it should be all accomplished *in* the one thousand years: whereas we show that the wicked are raised and executed at the close of the one thousand years. To this we reply, that in the declarations of events and measurements of time in the Scriptures, there is seen an incipient stage, then a fulness, and at the close another stage of warning to a final end. In the colors of the rainbow, the hue or tint is pale at the margin, and deepens to a full brilliant color. If you measure from any shade of it, yet it is from that color or stripe. So in the epochs of the flood, the giving of the law at Sinai, the introduction of the gospel dispensation, the same principle is seen; and so it will be in the reign of judgment; the one thousand years, as applied to each event, in its beginning and ending, will have its appropriate commencement and terminus.

THE DEVIL TORMENTED.

" And the devil that deceived them was cast into the lake of fire and brimstone, where the beast and false prophet are [were cast, *Emp. Diaglott*], and shall be tormented day and night forever and ever." Verse 10.

This is the final execution of the devil, the long desired period on the part of the Lord's faithful ones; an event for which they will give glory to God and the Lamb. Not in the torment of the devil; we do not believe the redeemed of the Lord will take delight in the pain of any being, even the devil; but they will be glad and rejoice in his final and eternal doom and destruction.

The term of "torment," stated in the passage, will be measured by the length of time the devil will *live* in fire and brimstone. We are not informed as to his physical nature and power of endurance. The terms "day and night," "forever and ever," are commonly used in the Scriptures to express continual, without intermission, so long as the things or beings to which they are attached shall exist. It will therefore be dependent on the constitutional ability of the devil against fire and brimstone.

But there are several considerations which lead us to conclude that the fire and brimstone will consume the devil.

I. The expression used by the Lord in Eden to the serpent: "I will put enmity between thee and the woman, and between thy seed and her seed; it shall bruise [Heb., CRUSH] thy head," — is expressive of destruction, extinction of life.

II. Paul declares that Christ took flesh and blood, "that through death he might DESTROY him that had the power of death, that is, THE DEVIL, and deliver them who, through fear of death, were all their lifetime subject to bondage." Heb. 2:14.

III. Fire is an agent of destruction, and consumes all combustible bodies; and as we have no evidence, or cause to believe, he is immortal, the fire must devour him.

IV. There is a time to come when every creature in heaven, and earth, and sea are to give praise to God, as we shall show.

V. We cannot, in the absence of all evidence, believe the Lord will allow his great antagonist — the devil — to live eternally in his dominion to curse him, nor that the devil will ever be so converted as to honor and praise God. For the use of the term "forever and ever," examine the Scriptures, and you will find "forever" used near two hundred times in a limited sense. As, therefore, the terms "forever," "day and night," are so generally used in Scripture to express constant, continual, without intermission, so long as the things or beings to which they are applied shall exist; and as we find the devil and wicked men constantly represented as combustible, perishable, and destructible; and as they are expressly threatened with destruction in fire, and by fire, we conclude that the fire which comes down from God out of heaven constitutes the lake of fire and brimstone which submerges the resurrected wicked, and their leader, — the devil, — where they will be utterly consumed, and the devil tormented continually until consumed.

The lake of fire will be no longer needed, as there will be no more combustible matter to be consumed, and will therefore cease to exist.

The thousand years' reign of judgment will then have passed. The marriage supper of the Lamb partaken. The day of rest will have been enjoyed (Heb. 4 : 7), "the keeping of a Sabbath," the wicked raised, Satan loosed to deceive them once more, and each to meet their final end in the lake of fire; which, having been reached, the earth is eternally freed from evil, while the redeemed reign with Christ in the kingdom which shall have no end. Listen to their song.

THE UNIVERSAL SONG OF TRIUMPH.

"And they sung a new song, saying, Thou art worthy to take the book, and to open the seals thereof: for thou wast slain, and hast redeemed us to God by thy blood out of every kindred, and tongue, and people, and nation; and hast made us unto our God kings and priests: and we shall reign on the earth.

"And I beheld, and I heard the voice of many angels round about the throne, and the beasts [living ones, *Emp. Diaglott*], and the elders: and the number of them was ten thousand times ten thousand, and thousands of thousands; saying with a loud voice, Worthy is the Lamb that was slain to receive power, and riches, and wisdom, and strength, and honor, and glory, and blessing. And every creature which is in heaven, and on the earth, and under the earth, and such as are in the sea, and all that are in them, heard I saying, Blessing, and honor, and glory, and power be unto him that sitteth upon the throne, and unto the Lamb forever and ever." Rev. 5: 9, 13. What a song! It comprehends everything that can be desired by us, and ascribes all the riches, and power, and honor, and glory to Christ.

The class who commence to sing it, is distinguished from the masses of mankind and from the angels.

Their song shows that they fully realize the great change in their condition, and appreciate the love, sufferings, power, and blessings of their benefactor, 'for thou wast slain, and hast redeemed us to God by thy blood."

Thus they confess they had been aliens from God, and in bondage to sin and death. It declares that those who sing it had been gathered "out of every kindred, and tongue, and people, and nation." Consequently there were others of these kindreds, tongues, peoples, and nations who were not thus redeemed by the blood of Christ.

These redeemed ones confess to their Redeemer, not only that they had been redeemed from sin and death, but they sing, "and hast made us unto our God kings and priests: and we shall reign on the earth."

This song is descriptive of the acclamations of praise, and honor, and glory, which the children of God will extend to Christ after their resurrection to immortality.

MADE KINGS AND PRIESTS.

The Lord once made a conditional promise to the children of Israel, by Moses, thus: "Now, therefore, if ye will obey my voice indeed, and keep my covenant, then ye shall be a peculiar treasure unto me above all people: for all the earth is mine.

"And ye shall be unto me a kingdom of priests, and an holy nation. These are the words which thou shalt speak unto the children of Israel." Exod. 19: 5, 6.

This promise rested on the condition of "obedience to God's voice and covenant." The nation of Israel, as such, never complied with this condition, therefore can never obtain the benefits of the promise. Yet there were some of that nation who did comply with the condition, and such became heirs of this promise. There have been some in all other nations who have obeyed the voice of the Lord, and kept his covenant, and have therefore become fellow-heirs of the same promise. Consequently in this new song all nations are represented, and are heard confessing that the promise has been fulfilled to them in the immortal state.

Peter gives us an inspired, and therefore an important comment on this subject. He is addressing converts to Christ from Jewish and Gentile nations, and states the condition on which they were chosen. "Wherefore also it is contained in the Scripture, Behold, I lay in Sion a chief corner-stone, elect, precious: and he that believeth on him shall not be confounded.

"Unto you therefore which believe, he is precious: but unto them which be disobedient, the stone which the builders disallowed, the same is made the head of the corner, and a stone of stumbling, and a rock of offence, even to them which stumble at the word, being disobedient; whereunto also they were appointed. But ye are a chosen generation, a royal priesthood, a peculiar people; that ye should show forth the praises of him who hath called you out of darkness into his marvellous light: which in time past were [Gentiles] not a people, but are now the people of God; which had not obtained mercy, but now have obtained mercy." 1 Pet. 2: 6–10.

In the above comment of the apostle, we have the facts shown, that while God has chosen Christ as the chief corner-stone, or foundation of his church, and the founder of his "holy nation," he has also chosen them who believe on him from among all nations, to be "fellow-heirs;" and such are to be brought together under one Lord, to constitute the members of the kingdom of God, and being "a royal priesthood," they will become the "kingdom of priests" which God promises those who would obey his voice and keep his covenant.

This holy nation, royal priesthood, and peculiar people, when brought back from death in the first resurrection, and changed at the last trump, will sing the song cited above, confessing that Jesus has made them "kings and priests," while they exclaim, "and we shall reign on the earth."

Dear reader, will you strive to be among them? Are you interested in the crown of life; the kingdom of God; the immortal state; the day of redemption; the rest that remaineth? Who that loves the Son of God, that has shared in his sufferings, enjoyed his fellowship, and seen the vanity, the sinfulness, and the sufferings of this mortal world, does not long and pray for the returning of our glorified, immortal, eternal King, to bestow everlasting blessedness upon his waiting church?

In that glad hour, when Christ shall say, "Come, ye blessed of my Father," the united response will rise,—

> "From every voice, with one accord,
> It is the Lord! it is the Lord!
> And full, in every raptured eye,
> His image shines resplendently!
> O, long-believed in, seen at length,
> Outshining in thy sun-like strength,
> Thy glory mingling with thy grace,
> We see thee, Jesus, face to face!
> With all the armies of the sky
> We shout thy glad epiphany!

> Thrice welcome, earth-rejected King!
> From every lip thy praises ring!
> Thrice welcome to thy rightful throne;
> For thou art worthy, Lord, alone!
> For thou art He who once was slain,
> And we are now to share thy reign;
> For thou hast washed us in thy blood,
> And made us kings and priests to God!
> O, silver angel-trumpets clear,
> Uplift the joy from sphere to sphere!
> O, saintly voices, sweet and strong,
> Roll through eternity along
> The thunder of redemption-song!"
>
> *H. G. Guinness.*

OBJECTIONS CONSIDERED.

It is objected to by some, that the one thousand years embrace the resurrected state of the church and the day of judgment, because the apostle proceeds to give an account of the judgment, from the 11th to the 15th verses. To this we reply, the same objection is as good against admitting this last account to describe the judgment scene; for in chapter 21: 1–8, we have the subject again described, and the reward of each class stated. But the principle on which these several descriptions are given is this: —

The apostle proceeds to unfold these events in separate classes, as other Scriptures do other events, all through the Apocalypse especially. In chapter 19, we have an account of the advent of the King of kings; the statement of the saints being arrayed in fine linen; an announcement that the marriage of the Lamb had come. Then the call for the fowls to the supper of the great God. All these events are to transpire in *the day of the Lord,* but they are only one class. Next we have another class, in chapter 20 : 1–10, in which the binding of Satan, judgment-thrones, rising of the saints, reign of judgment, loosing of Satan, living again of the wicked, their last effort, and final destruction, is stated. This class represents Christ's authority over Satan and over death under the symbol of an angel with the key and chain; also the exaltation of his church to reign with him, and enjoy the great Sabbath of rest; then his authority over all the race of the wicked, to bring them "forth to the day of wrath," and final execution. But in this description of events there is no rule of judgment stated, and no cause shown for these events so glorious and terrible.

In the next class of events described, the apostle gives scenery covering the same space of time, because they could not be given in the same statement with the preceding; in which he mentions " a *great white throne*," representing "*justice* and *judgment*;" then " *the books were opened*," representing *law* and *righteousness* in the great transactions which are seen : then the dead, all the dead, in earth, and sea, and hades, come before God. In this is demonstrated the claim that "Christ is Lord both of the dead and of the living," and has the RIGHT to reward them, "every man according to their works." In each scene the events with the wicked terminate in the lake of fire. But *these descriptions* do not bring out all the important features, and the apostle proceeds in the next chapter to give other scenes which passed before him in prophetic vision; and thus we have a description of the new heaven and the new earth, the holy city, the tearless, deathless, sorrowless state described; with the announcements that "the tabernacle of God is with men," and all things are made new; then the lake of fire into which the wicked were cast, to receive their part, which is the "second death."

This is the third time in this description that we reach "the lake of fire" (20:10, 15; 21:8), showing that the various classes of scenery cover the same space of time, and each are parts of the work of the day of judgment, which is one thousand years — the seventh millenary.

But it is objected, that the devil and the wicked would defile the new earth if they should come upon it, and claimed that nothing shall enter into it that defileth, &c. We do not learn that Satan or the fallen angels defiled heaven before they were cast out. It is moral defilement, not physical, that these characters produce, but there is to be nothing for them to thus pollute in the new earth. It is the holy city from which the *defiled* are excluded. Rev. 21:27. And it is "the highway cast up" which leads into it, that "the unclean shall not pass over." Isa. 35:8.

A criminal might be brought into a palace for judgment and not defile it, unless *physically* polluted. The dust of which the wicked will be composed will be as pure as that of which Adam was made; but they will come forth to execution with a defiled moral character: this cannot pollute the earth, nor immortal saints. But it is asked, How can the wicked be raised out of the new earth?

Why not ask, "How are the dead raised up" at all? Paul said, some man *would*. It may be as easy for the Lord to raise men out of the new earth as to raise the millions of martyrs and others who have been burned to ashes, out of the old earth. Ay, as easy as to raise any one. Is anything too hard for the Lord? Cannot he who promised, perform it? God has declared what HE WILL do. He has shown what HE CAN do; we have no fears that he will fail to accomplish ALL HE HAS STATED HE WILL DO.

"His word is settled in heaven," it "cannot be broken." All things in this world bespeak that the great Sabbatic year is about to commence. The millennial morn is about to dawn: what mighty events it will bring with it! Are we ready, dear reader, to meet them with joy and gratitude? Let us study the Word of the Lord; believe him with all the heart, and labor on in his vineyard to build up each other in the Lord, and to gather sinners from the highways and hedges to the fold of Christ, the little time that remains for us to work.

It is known to some of you who read, that we are upon the very eve of that time, to which very many of the most devout, candid, learned, and pious of the church, for the last three hundred years, have looked for the commencement of the day of the Lord and the millennium. It is known to you, and to us, that there are thousands of ministers and teachers in all branches of the Christian church now eagerly searching the prophetic Scriptures, watching the signs of this time, and teaching their fellows that the Lord is soon to return, to bring about the stupendous events upon which we have been discoursing. Let us watch, and be ready to obtain the rest that remains for the people of God. AMEN AND AMEN.

www.ingramcontent.com/pod-product-compliance
Lightning Source LLC
Chambersburg PA
CBHW022132300426
44115CB00006B/154